15.95

A Parts of speech **B** The sentence—use and structure | **A/B**

C Syntax | **C**

D Punctuation **E** Division of words **F** Abbreviations **G** Numbers | **D/E/F/G**

H Capitals | **H**

I Spelling | **I**

J Diagraming | **J**

K The sentence—rhetoric | **K**

L The paragraph | **L**

M The theme | **M**

N Exposition | **N**

O Description **P** Narration **Q** Argument | **O/P/Q**

R Interest and force | **R**

FOR WRITING ENGLISH

for writing

A *handbook, a reference book,*

CHARLES W. MULLIGAN, S.J.

MICHAEL P. KAMMER, S.J.

English

for college students, teachers, writers, editors, secretaries—as well

as for all those who cherish accuracy in English

LOYOLA UNIVERSITY PRESS

Chicago, Illinois

PE
1408
M74

FOR WRITING ENGLISH is a handbook, a reference book, for college students, teachers, writers, and editors—and secretaries as well.

It contains a summary of English grammar and syntax; a method of sentence diagraming, which is ever a help to understanding the grammar and syntax of a sentence; rules for such mechanics as punctuation, capitalization (particularly of seldom-treated religious terminology), and writing numbers and abbreviations; and a summary of the rhetoric of sentences, paragraphs, and longer compositions.

Some of the sections may seem overly long, but they attempt to be as complete as the limitations of a handbook will allow. Syntax, a large and complicated subject, is of the first importance for thought, both for understanding another's and expressing one's own. Punctuation and capitals often present difficult problems of usage, and a handbook that does not supply many detailed rules is almost worthless. Without these detailed rules, moreover, a writer or editor is in danger of being inconsistent, following two or more different styles at the same time. The rules of mechanics given in FOR WRITING ENGLISH are not the only rules; rules change from generation to generation, and the rules in America differ from those in Britain; still, the rules in this book represent good contemporary usage in the United States.

FOR WRITING ENGLISH is a revision of *Writing Handbook* that, several years ago, Michael P. Kammer, S.J., and I wrote as part of the "Writing" series of high-school English books. I want to thank Father Kammer, who is now teaching English at Loyola University, New Orleans, for the gracious and generous permission he gave me to use his material as I wished. The section on exposition is the only one that I have made extensive changes in. That section I expanded to meet the needs of college students, who, in their writing, must do a good deal of library reference work, notetaking, and footnoting, and must have models and norms for their work.

Much of FOR WRITING ENGLISH was composed at Canisius House in Evanston, Illinois, a house that was given to the Jesuits by Mr. Carl E. Koch as a residence for Jesuit authors and the permanent directors of Loyola University Press.

Charles Wise Mulligan, S.J.

Fusz Memorial,
College of Philosophy and Letters
of Saint Louis University

CONTENTS

This table of contents lists matters by pages;

but the index found at the back of the book

lists them by rule, with letter and number.

A | Parts of speech

Parts of speech, continued

B | **The sentence — use and structure**

C | **Syntax**

Syntax, continued

D | Punctuation

E | Division of words

F | Abbreviations

G | Numbers

H | Capitals

Capitals, continued

I | Spelling

J | Diagraming

K | The sentence — rhetoric

Contents, continued

L | The paragraph

M | The theme

N | Exposition

Contents, continued

R | Interest and force

In general

A1 Words are classified as parts of speech chiefly according to the way in which they are used in sentences, though they can be classified to some extent according to what they mean outside sentences.

A2 There are eight parts of speech: nouns,[1] pronouns, verbs, adjectives, adverbs, prepositions, conjunctions, and exclamatory words (interjections). Other elements of speech are the expletives (*it* and *there*) and the verbals (gerunds, participles, and infinitives).

A3 The same word, spelled the same way, can sometimes be several parts of speech in turn.

The *little* man was peering at me again.   *Little* is an adjective.

The cymbal player cared *little* for music of any kind.   *Little* is an adverb.

Let me have a *little*, please.   *Little* is a pronoun.

The noun

A4 A noun is the name for something.

Straighten the *calendar*.

KINDS OF NOUNS

A5 A common noun is the name shared by all persons or things of the same kind. It can be applied to every member of a group or class of things.

man   knife
house   dog

---

[1] Nouns are called substantives; so are other words or groups of words that function as nouns.

1

A6 A proper noun is the particular name of a particular person, place, or thing.

Daniel Boone   Chicago   Buick

A7 A concrete noun is the name of something that exists by itself. Often, not always, such a thing is perceived by the senses.

mountain   soul
violin   angel
flame   air

A8 An abstract noun is the name of a quality or an attribute apart from any object. It sometimes names the general as opposed to the particular.

whiteness   courage
humanity   sport
man (in general, as opposed to a particular man like George Washington)

A9 A collective noun is the name of a group of persons or a group of things.

team   herd
army   school (of fish)

GENDER OF NOUNS

A10 Nouns are of masculine gender when they carry with them the notion of the male sex.

The *boy* looked searchingly at me.
The *waiter* seemed to sneer without sneering.
My *uncle* really did intend to pay the rent.
The *stallion* reared his fine head.

A11 Nouns are of feminine gender when they carry with them the notion of the female sex.

The *girl* says she heard no call.
The *waitress* sniffed and disappeared.
My *aunt* hopes to attend the classes for adults.
The *mare* was altogether proud of the colt and showed it.

2

A12 Nouns are of common (masculine-or-feminine) gender when they do not distinguish between the sexes. (Such nouns are usually treated as masculine.)

People are funny.

Parents often have no way of letting a child know how completely they understand the problems of young social life.

It is dangerous to take a bone from a *dog*.

Ask any *musician* for *his* opinion.

A13 Nouns are of neuter gender when they name things that have no sex.

A great *rock* lay some yards to the left.
The *idea* was new to me.

A14 Some sexless things are always given masculine or feminine gender by tradition or necessity.

God has *His* plan for you.

My guardian *angel* has had *his* disappointments—if an *angel* can be disappointed.

A15 Some sexless things are sometimes given a gender in lively or poetic writing.

When you feed the body, you should remember to let the *soul* also have *her* food.

She was a graceful *ship*, much in love with speed.

Russia has made no move that would lead us to trust *her*.

The *moon* hid *herself* for a moment.

That ol' *man river, he* don't say nuthin'.

A16 The vegetable kingdom is ordinarily treated as neuter.

The *tree* lay in ruins, *its* upended roots high in the air.

Now here is a *blossom* that certainly has not wasted *its* sweetness on the desert air.

A17 Collective nouns naming groups as groups (not as individuals) are treated as neuter.

The *crowd* had *its* attention diverted by the frantically waving man on the fire escape.

As usual, the *army* overextended *its* supply lines.

3

A18   The common-noun names of very young children are often treated as neuter in passages where the sex of the child has no bearing on the thought.

A *child* [an *infant*, a *baby*] has *its* rights no less than an adult.

A19   The common-noun names of animals are often treated as neuter regardless of the thought of the passage.

A *hen* is perfectly happy trying to hatch a darning egg along with *its* own real eggs.

PERSON OF NOUNS

A20   A noun that designates the speaker is in the first person.

This revolver belongs to me, *James Horder.*

A21   A noun that designates the person or thing spoken to is in the second person.

I mean you, *Bill.*
For you, my *country,* I will gladly die; but I had rather live.

A22   A noun that designates the person or thing spoken of is in the third person.

St. Barbara is the *patron* of *gunners* and *miners.*

NUMBER OF NOUNS

A23   A singular noun names one person or thing; a plural noun names more than one person or thing.

Singular	*Plural*
boy	boys
tree	trees

A24   Some nouns are plural in form but singular in meaning; other nouns are singular in form and either singular or plural in meaning.

The *news is* all good.
Measles is catching.
Physics is my most difficult subject.
Politics is not my field.

4

The *sheep is* lost.
The *scissors is* in the drawer.
The *sheep have been* slaughtered.
Moose are to be found in Canada and the northern United States.

The pronoun

A25 A pronoun is a word that is used in place of a noun or other substantive.

Helen said *she* would make ham sandwiches.

She is used in place of *Helen*.

Tom made this bow. *He* is clever with tools but so hasty that *he* cut *himself* a number of times.

The two *hes* and *himself* take the place of *Tom*.

My uncle has an unconventional spaniel *that* does not sit up and beg.

That takes the place of *spaniel*.

A26 The antecedent of the pronoun is the noun whose place the pronoun takes.

Helen said she would make ham sandwiches.

Helen is the antecedent of *she*.

Tom made this bow. He is clever with tools but so hasty that he cut himself a number of times.

Tom is the antecedent of the two *hes* and *himself*.

A27 Some words may be thought of as nouns, pronouns, or adjectives. They differ from ordinary pronouns in this, that they can modify an implied but unexpressed noun.

The *good* enjoy two worlds.

As an adjective, *good* modifies the absent noun *people*.

They enjoy two worlds.

They is a pronoun. It cannot modify *people*. *Good people* makes sense, but *they people* does not.

PERSONAL AND POSSESSIVE PRONOUNS

A28 The personal pronouns indicate the speaker (first person), the person or thing spoken to (second person), or the person or thing spoken of (third person).

The personal pronouns are—

	First person	
	Singular	*Plural*
Nominative	I	we
Possessive	my	our
Objective	me	us

	Second person	
	Singular	*Plural*
Nominative	you (thou)	you (ye)
Possessive	your (thy)	your
Objective	you (thee)	you (ye)

	Third person	
	Singular	*Plural*
Nominative	he, she, it	they
Possessive	his, her, its	their
Objective	him, her, it	them

Personal pronouns in the possessive case are always used as adjectives: "This is *my* hat." (They are sometimes called possessive adjectives. See A79.)

A29 The possessive pronouns denote either ownership or origin or source.

The possessive pronouns are—

	First person	
Singular		*Plural*
mine		ours

	Second person	
Singular		*Plural*
yours (thine)		yours

	Third person	
Singular		*Plural*
his, hers, its		theirs

6

The possessive pronouns are always used as nouns, or substantives, and are always in either the nominative or the objective case: "This hat is *mine;* give him *his.*"[2]

A30 *He, his,* and *him* are used when the antecedent is masculine or common; *she, hers,* and *her,* when the antecedent is feminine; *it* and *its,* when the antecedent is neuter; the rest of the personal-pronoun forms are used no matter what the gender of the antecedent.

On the witness stand the policeman testified that *he* had fired in self-defense.

Grace decided to buy the orange hat, even though *she* thought *it* was rather expensive.

DEMONSTRATIVE PRONOUNS

A31 The demonstrative pronouns are—

Singular	*Plural*
this	these
that	those

A32 The demonstrative pronouns are used to specify, to point out, to call attention to their antecedents with special emphasis.

This is my choice.
I did not say *that.*
This is fine; *that* simply will not do.
Deliver *those* to my home; *these* I'll take with me.

A33 The demonstrative pronouns take the place of their antecedents; they do not accompany and modify nouns as the demonstrative adjectives do.

This is my home.

This—demonstrative pronoun —takes the place of *house* or *home* as subject of the predicate verb *is.*

---

[2] In many cases, perhaps most, *his* and *its* can be taken either as a personal pronoun in the possessive case (that is, an adjective) or as a possessive pronoun (that is, a substantive).

7

| *This* home is mine. | *This*—demonstrative adjective —is not the subject or object but accompanies and modifies the noun *home*. |

A34 The demonstrative pronouns have the same forms for all persons, genders, and cases.

A35 *This* and *these* ordinarily refer to what is present, near, just referred to, or about to be referred to; *that* and *those*, to what is more remote in time or place.

Look at *this* [referring to something near the speaker].
Look at *that* [referring to something across the room].

People call me stupid. *This* would anger me if I did not reflect that they would call me something worse if they knew me better.

And now *this* is what I am going to say to you.

A36 Demonstrative *that* and *those* are used to refer to the thing or idea indicated or understood from the situation or context.

The writing is *that* of Claiborne, but the sentiments are not his.

[The first word spoken to a man who has just entered a room:] *That* is why I like you—you are always prompt.

Self-PRONOUNS

A37 The *self*-pronouns (compound personal pronouns) are—

	First person	
	Singular	*Plural*
Nominative and objective	myself	ourselves
	Second person	
	Singular	*Plural*
Nominative and objective	yourself	yourselves
	Third person	
	Singular	*Plural*
Nominative and objective	oneself	
	himself	themselves
	herself	
	itself	

A38 *Himself* is used when the antecedent is masculine or common; *herself,* when the antecedent is feminine; *itself,* when the antecedent is neuter; but all the rest of the *self*-pronouns are used no matter what the gender of the antecedent may be.

It has been said of Abe Lincoln that *he* pulled *himself* up by his own bootstraps.

My *sister* climbed the tree *herself* and rescued her kitten before the firemen arrived.

A large *boulder* detached *itself* from the mass atop the hill, and began to roll down toward us with increasing momentum.

I found *myself* wishing that we had not involved *ourselves* with such a reckless group.

A39 When a *self*-pronoun is used to show that the action is reflected upon the doer of the action, it is called a reflexive pronoun.

Fleavy hurt *himself.*

He wrote *himself* a note.

He wrote a note to *himself.*

They are sitting by *themselves.*

A40 As reflexives the *self*-pronouns can be used only in the objective case as direct objects, indirect objects, or the objects of prepositions.

Turner has betrayed *himself* [direct object].
That week Rossiter gave *himself* [indirect object] no peace.
Of *ourselves* [object of a preposition] we can do nothing.

A41 When a *self*-pronoun is not used as described in A39 but merely in apposition as reinforcement for another word in the sentence, it is called an intensive pronoun.[3]

He *himself* trained the seals.
He trained the seals *himself.*

---

[3] Some grammarians call intensive pronouns adjectives.

9

A42 As intensives, the *self*-pronouns may be used in apposition with a word in the nominative or objective case.

He himself voted against the proposal twice.
We met none other than our *neighbors themselves* downtown.
Here is a picture of *John himself* when he was two.
I myself have no objections to the plan.
It was necessary that the *captain himself* set the course.

RELATIVE PRONOUNS[4]

A43 The relative pronouns are—

		Singular or plural	
Nominative	who	that	which
Possessive	whose[5]		
Objective	whom	that	which

A44 The relative pronouns take the place of nouns and join or relate a dependent (adjective) clause to an antecedent in another clause.

I know the girl *whom* you mean.

The moon, *which* was rising, looked huge and yellow.

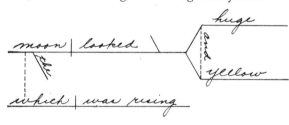

---

[4] Relative pronouns are sometimes used as indefinites: "*Whom* I marry is my business."

[5] *Whose* is often used as the possessive of *that* and *which:* "I was blinded by the sun, *whose* light was intense."

10

I want the one *that* I saw first.

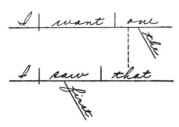

A45 In general, use relative *who* and *that*[6] when the antecedent is a person or a personification, and *which* and *that* when the antecedent is not a person.[7]

That *boy whom* I considered so worthless turned out to be the most reliable back on the team.

That *boy that* I considered so worthless turned out to be the most reliable back on the team.

The *wheel, which* fell off, rolled into the canal and sank.
The *wheel that* fell off rolled into the canal and sank.

A46 Relative *which* is often preferred to *who* when the antecedent is a collective noun naming a group of persons as a group and not as individuals.

The committee, *which* met regularly, deserved its pay.
I consulted the family, *which* didn't like the idea at all.
The crowd, *which* had been quiet, broke into a roar.
The audience, *which* was larger than expected, filled the hall.

A47 Where the antecedent nouns are both persons and things, use relative *that* when you can; use *which* when you cannot use *that*, or else get around the difficulty by rewording the sentence.

Where are the men and the money *that* will save our school?
Johnny Kerr and his dogs, of *which* I have spoken so often, have gone to Hollywood.
Johnny Kerr, of *whom* I have spoken so often, has gone to Hollywood with his dogs.

---

[6] There is an increasing tendency to use *that* only when the antecedent is a thing.

[7] In restrictive clauses, *that* is preferred to *which*.

A48   The relative pronouns have the same form for all persons and numbers.

A49   A relative pronoun refers to an antecedent in another clause. This fact makes a relative pronoun and its adjective clause easy to distinguish from *(a)* an interrogative or indefinite pronoun or adjective and its noun clause, *(b)* the demonstrative-pronoun and demonstrative-adjective *that,* and *(c)* the conjunction *that.*

I know the *girl whom* you refer to.	*Whom* is a relative pronoun because it has an antecedent, *girl,* in the independent clause of the sentence.
Tell me, *whom* do you mean?	*Whom* does not have an antecedent in the independent clause. It is, therefore, an interrogative pronoun.
I know *whom* you mean.	*Whom* does not have an antecedent in this sentence. It is, therefore, an indefinite pronoun.
I know *what* man you mean.	*What* is an indefinite adjective.
Here are the *blueprints that* you were looking for.	*That* is a relative pronoun because it has an antecedent, *blueprints,* in the independent clause.
I was looking for the blueprints when I found *that* on the floor.	*That* has no antecedent in the independent clause. Demonstrative pronoun.
I was looking for something else when I found *that* blueprint on the floor.	*That* has no antecedent in the independent clause. Demonstrative adjective.
I knew *that* you were looking for the blueprints.	Once again, *that* has no antecedent in the independent clause. This time, however, it is a conjunction.

12

INTERROGATIVE PRONOUNS

A50 The interrogative pronouns are—

		Singular or plural	
Nominative	who	which	what
Possessive	whose	whose	
Objective	whom	which	what

A51 The interrogative pronouns are so called because they ask questions. .

Whom do you want?
No one asked me, *What* did I want?
No one asked me *what* I wanted.
Who wrote *Moby Dick?*
Whose is that beautiful dog?
Which is the one you like?

A52 Use interrogative *who* in any kind of question when the antecedent is a person. Use interrogative *what* when the antecedent is not a person.

Whom do you want?
Whose is this pastrami sandwich?

What are you carrying?
What do you think of these?

A53 Use interrogative pronoun *which* whether or not the antecedent is a person, but only in questions involving a choice.[8]

Which did you choose (Myron or Clark)?
Which did you choose (the trip to Miami or the scholarship)?

A54 The interrogative pronouns are all third person.

Who of us *is* brave enough to take the man's dare?
Who of us *are* brave enough to take *their* places?
Which of us *are* going?
Whose are these rubbers?

---

[8] Many good writers will not use the interrogative pronoun *which* when the antecedent is a person, unless the pronoun is followed by an *of* phrase.

13

INDEFINITE PRONOUNS[9]

A55 Some common indefinite pronouns are—

Singular		Plural	Singular or plural
another	much	both	all
anybody	neither	few	any
anything	nobody	many	more
each	nothing	others	none
either	one	several	some
everybody	other		
everyone	somebody		
everything	someone		
little	something		

A56 The indefinite pronouns are so called because they often take the place of antecedents that are not named and that cannot be pinned down to any particular persons or places or things.

Anybody coming through the door would trip.
One of these has onions on it.
I found *nobody* with *whom* to play cricket.

A57 *All, any, more, none,* and *some* are singular pronouns if they indicate how much; they are plural if they indicate how many.[10]

All of the cake *was* burned.
All of the cakes *were* burned.

Was any of the cake burned?
Were any of the cakes burned?

Some of the cake *was* burned.
Some of the cakes *were* burned.

---

[9] Relative pronouns are sometimes used as indefinites: "*Whom* I marry is my business."

[10] *None* can indicate how many and yet be singular if there is good reason for stressing the notion of "not a single one." For example, "I went to the dog pound today and looked at every dog there, but *none* of them *was* mine." The same is true of *any* when there is reason to stress the notion of "a single one": "*Any* at all—the red, the maroon, or the vermilion—*is* good enough."

We looked for crepe paper, but there *is none*.
None of the people you expected *have* come.

A58 If the antecedent is masculine, or masculine and feminine, treat the indefinite pronoun as masculine; if the antecedent is exclusively feminine, treat the indefinite pronoun as feminine.

Everybody at the stag party made *his* contribution to the welfare fund.	Exclusively masculine.
Everyone of us has *his* own cross to bear.	Masculine and feminine.
Has *anybody* lost *her* purse?	Exclusively feminine.

A59 Singular indefinites are all third person. Plural indefinites get their person from their indefinite antecedents.

Each of you has a funny look on *his* face.
All of you have funny looks on *your* faces.
All of us have funny looks on *our* faces.

RECIPROCAL PRONOUNS

A60 The reciprocal pronouns are *each other* and *one another*. They are called reciprocal because they are used in pairs to show an interaction.

The twins helped *each other*.
Each helped the *other*.

The soldiers slaughtered *one another* mercilessly.
One slaughtered *another*.

A61 Use *each other* to refer to only two, *one another* to refer to more than two.

The verb

A62 A verb is a word that expresses the actuality of its subject. Either it shows the subject as acting or as being acted upon; or it shows the subject as possessing an attribute, or character, or a relation; or it shows the subject as having actuality.

Tim *ran* forward and *was shot.*
You *have* good looks and good manners; you *have* good clothes.
God *exists.*

CONJUGATION OF VERBS

A63 Model conjugation of the verb *praise*:

ACTIVE VOICE

INDICATIVE MOOD

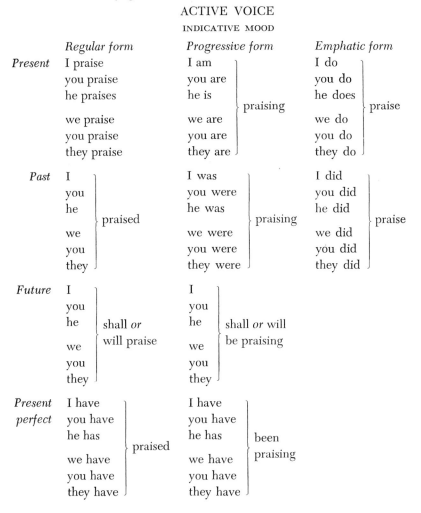

	Regular form	*Progressive form*	*Emphatic form*
Present	I praise you praise he praises we praise you praise they praise	I am you are he is ⎫ praising we are you are they are ⎭	I do you do he does ⎫ praise we do you do they do ⎭
Past	I you he ⎫ praised we you they ⎭	I was you were he was ⎫ praising we were you were they were ⎭	I did you did he did ⎫ praise we did you did they did ⎭
Future	I you he ⎱ shall *or* we ⎰ will praise you they	I you he ⎱ shall *or* will we ⎰ be praising you they	
Present perfect	I have you have he has ⎫ praised we have you have they have ⎭	I have you have he has ⎫ been we have ⎰ praising you have they have	

16

	Regular form	Progressive form
Past perfect	I you he we you they } had praised	I you he we you they } had been praising
Future perfect	I you he we you they } shall *or* will have praised	I you he we you they } shall *or* will have been praising

SUBJUNCTIVE MOOD[11]

	Regular form	Progressive form	Emphatic form
Present	I you he we you they } praise	I you he we you they } be praising	I you he we you they } do praise
Past	I you he we you they } praised	I you he we you they } were praising	I you he we you they } did praise
Present perfect	I you he we you they } have praised	I you he we you they } have been praising	

---

[11] Some word like *although, if, in order that, lest, that, though, till,* or *unless* is regularly used with the subjunctive mood.

17

	Regular form	*Progressive form*
Past perfect	I you he we you they } had praised	I you he we you they } had been praising

IMPERATIVE MOOD

	Regular form	*Progressive form*	*Emphatic form*
Present and future	(you) praise	(you) be praising	do (you) praise

PARTICIPLES[12]

	Regular form	*Progressive form*
Present	praising	
Present perfect	having praised	having been praising

INFINITIVES

	Regular form	*Progressive form*
Present	(to) praise	(to) be praising
Present perfect	(to) have praised	(to) have been praising

GERUNDS

	Regular form	*Progressive form*
Present	praising	
Present perfect	having praised	having been praising

---

[12] Some grammars maintain that there is an active past participle, as, for instance, *returned* in the following sentence, "Recently returned from Denver, Mr. Alton had some interesting things to say about the Western dispute over water rights." FOR WRITING ENGLISH takes the traditional view that such a participle is the present perfect, with *having* implied but not expressed in the sentence.

The participles are verbals, half adjective and half verb. They are used in conjugating verbs, however, primarily in their verb sense, which stresses actuality, rather than in their adjective sense, which stresses modification—changing the meaning—of nouns.

18

PASSIVE VOICE
INDICATIVE MOOD

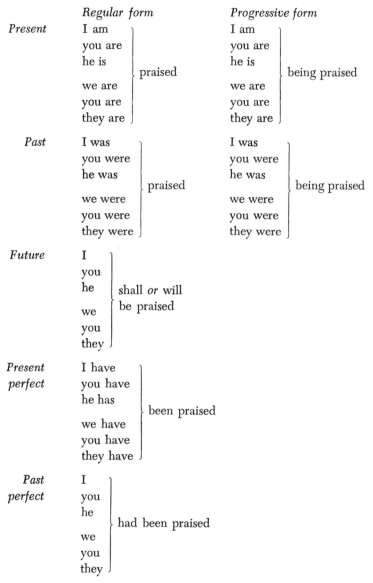

	Regular form	Progressive form
Present	I am you are he is we are you are they are } praised	I am you are he is we are you are they are } being praised
Past	I was you were he was we were you were they were } praised	I was you were he was we were you were they were } being praised
Future	I you he we you they } shall *or* will be praised	
Present perfect	I have you have he has we have you have they have } been praised	
Past perfect	I you he we you they } had been praised	

19

Regular form

Future perfect	I, you, he, we, you, they } shall *or* will have been praised

SUBJUNCTIVE MOOD[13]

Regular form   *Progressive form*

Present	I, you, he, we, you, they } be praised

Past	I, you, he, we, you, they } were praised	I, you, he, we, you, they } were being praised

Present perfect	I, you, he, we, you, they } have been praised

Past perfect	I, you, he, we, you, they } had been praised

[13] Some word like *although, if, in order that, lest, that, though, till,* or *unless* is regularly used with the subjunctive mood.

IMPERATIVE MOOD

Regular form

Present	(you) be praised
and	
future	

PARTICIPLES

Present	being praised
Past	praised
Present perfect	having been praised

INFINITIVES

Present	(to) be praised
Present perfect	(to) have been praised

GERUNDS

Present	being praised
Present perfect	having been praised

A64 Conjugation of the verb *be:*

INDICATIVE MOOD

Present		*Past*	
	I am		I was
	you are		you were
	he is		he was
	we are		we were
	you are		you were
	they are		they were
Future	I shall be	*Present perfect*	I have been
	you will be		you have been
	he will be		he has been
	we shall be		we have been
	you will be		you have been
	they will be		they have been

21

Past perfect	I you he	} had been	*Future perfect*	I shall have been you will have been he will have been
	we you they			we shall have been you will have been they will have been

SUBJUNCTIVE MOOD[14]

Present	I you he we you they	} be	*Past*	I you he we you they	} were

Present perfect	I you he we you they	} have been	*Past perfect*	I you he we you they	} had been

IMPERATIVE MOOD		PARTICIPLES	
Present and future	(you) be	*Present*	being
		Past	been
		Present perfect	having been

INFINITIVES		GERUNDS	
Present	(to) be	*Present*	being
Present perfect	(to) have been	*Present perfect*	having been

A65 A progressive form of the verb *be* (usually followed by a predicate adjective) exists, but as a general rule only in the following moods and tenses:

---

[14] Some word like *although, if, in order that, lest, that, though, till,* or *unless* is regularly used with the subjunctive mood. See the section on verbs of the subjunctive mood, C108-15.

Present indicative		Past indicative		Past subjunctive	
I am		I was		I	
you are		you were		you	
he is		he was		he	
	being		being		were being
we are		we were		we	
you are		you were		you	
they are		they were		they	

THE PRINCIPAL PARTS OF VERBS

A66 The principal parts of a verb are those forms from which all the voices, moods, and tenses of the verb can be formed. They are the present infinitive; the past indicative, first person singular; and the past participle.

Present infinitive	Past indicative first person singular	Past participle
be	was	been
praise	praised	praised
begin	began	begun

A67 The greater number of verbs regularly form their past indicative and past participle by adding *d, ed,* or *t* to the present infinitive.

Present	Past	Past participle
praise	praised	praised
guide	guided	guided
rip	ripped	ripped
bless	blessed	blessed
bend	bent	bent
kneel	kneeled *or* knelt	kneeled *or* knelt

A68 The principal parts of the following verbs sometimes cause difficulty.

	Present	Past	Past participle
1	arise	arose	arisen
2	attack	attacked	attacked
3	awake	awaked *or* awoke	awaked
4	awaken	awakened	awakened

23

Present	*Past*	*Past participle*
5 be	was	been
6 bear[15]	bore	borne *or* born[16]
7 beat	beat	beaten
8 become	became	become
9 begin	began	begun
10 bend	bent	bent[17]
11 beseech	besought	besought
12 bid	bade *or* bid[18]	bidden *or* bid[18]
13 bind	bound	bound
14 bite	bit	bitten
15 bleed	bled	bled
16 blow	blew	blown
17 break	broke	broken
18 bring	brought	brought
19 broadcast	broadcast *or* broadcasted[19]	broadcast *or* broadcasted[19]
20 build	built	built
21 burn	burned *or* burnt	burned *or* burnt
22 burst	burst	burst
23 buy	bought	bought
24 carry	carried	carried
25 catch	caught	caught
26 choose	chose	chosen
27 climb	climbed	climbed
28 cling	clung	clung
29 come	came	come
30 deal	dealt	dealt
31 dig	dug *or* digged	dug *or* digged
32 dive	dived	dived
33 do	did	done

[15] Carry, suffer, tolerate, give birth to.

[16] When applied to pregnancy or birth, *borne* can be used as part of verbs in the passive only when they are followed by *by*, expressed or implied. *Born* means only brought into life, is always passive, and is never followed by *by*.

[17] The archaic *bended* is used in expressions like "on bended knee."

[18] Use *bid, bade, bidden* only in some sense of command or order; use *bid, bid, bid* in all senses—command, offer a price for something, name a number and a suit in cardplaying.

[19] Use either *broadcast* or *broadcasted* when speaking of television and radio; use only *broadcast* in all other senses.

24

	Present	Past	Past participle
34	drag	dragged	dragged
35	draw	drew	drawn
36	drink	drank	drunk
37	drive	drove	driven
38	drown	drowned	drowned
39	eat	ate	eaten
40	fall	fell	fallen
41	feed	fed	fed
42	fight	fought	fought
43	find	found	found
44	flee	fled	fled
45	fling	flung	flung
46	flow	flowed	flowed
47	fly	flew	flown
48	forbid	forbade *or* forbad	forbidden
49	forget	forgot	forgotten *or* forgot
50	forsake	forsook	forsaken
51	freeze	froze	frozen
52	get	got	got *or* gotten
53	give	gave	given
54	go	went	gone
55	grind	ground	ground
56	grow	grew	grown
57	hang	hanged	hanged[20]
58	hang	hung	hung
59	hold	held	held
60	kill	killed	killed
61	kneel	knelt *or* kneeled	knelt *or* kneeled
62	know	knew	known
63	lay[21]	laid	laid
64	lead	led	led
65	lean	leaned *or* leant	leaned *or* leant
66	leap	leaped *or* leapt	leaped *or* leapt
67	learn	learned	learned

[20] *Hanged* is preferred to *hung* for putting to death by suspending.
[21] Transitive; to set or put something down.

25

Present	*Past*	*Past participle*
68 leave	left	left
69 lend	lent	lent
70 let	let	let
71 lie[22]	lay	lain
72 lie[23]	lied	lied
73 light	lighted *or* lit	lighted *or* lit
74 loose	loosed	loosed
75 lose	lost	lost
76 mean	meant	meant
77 meet	met	met
78 pay	paid	paid
79 prove	proved	proved *or* proven
80 raise[24]	raised	raised
81 read	read	read
82 ride	rode	ridden
83 ring	rang	rung
84 rise	rose	risen
85 run	ran	run
86 say	said	said
87 seal	sealed	sealed
88 see	saw	seen
89 seek	sought	sought
90 sell	sold	sold
91 set[25]	set	set
92 sew[26]	sewed	sewed *or* sewn
93 shake	shook	shaken
94 shoot	shot	shot
95 show	showed	shown *or* showed
96 shrink	shrank	shrunk
97 sing	sang	sung
98 sink	sank *or* sunk	sunk
99 sit	sat	sat
100 slay	slew	slain

---

[22] Intransitive; to recline.
[23] To tell an untruth.
[24] Do not confuse with *arise* or *rise*. (See Nos. 1 and 84 of this list.)
[25] Do not confuse with *sit*. (See No. 99 of this list.)
[26] As with thread.

	Present	*Past*	*Past participle*
101	sleep	slept	slept
102	slide	slid	slid *or* slidden
103	slink	slunk	slunk
104	smite	smote	smitten
105	sow[27]	sowed	sowed *or* sown
106	speak	spoke	spoken
107	split	split	split
108	spring	sprang *or* sprung	sprung
109	steal	stole	stolen
110	stick	stuck	stuck
111	sting	stung	stung
112	stink	stank *or* stunk	stunk
113	stride	strode	stridden
114	string	strung	strung
115	strive	strove *or* strived	striven *or* strived
116	swear	swore	sworn
117	sweat	sweat *or* sweated	sweat *or* sweated
118	swim	swam	swum
119	swing	swung	swung
120	take	took	taken
121	teach	taught	taught
122	tear	tore	torn
123	tell	told	told
124	thrive	throve *or* thrived	thrived *or* thriven
125	throw	threw	thrown
126	tread	trod	trodden *or* trod
127	wake	waked *or* woke	waked
128	wear	wore	worn
129	weave	wove	woven
130	win	won	won
131	work	worked *or* wrought[28]	worked *or* wrought[28]
132	wring	wrung	wrung
133	write	wrote	written

[27] As, for example, seed or, figuratively, discord.

[28] The past verb-form *wrought,* always transitive, is nowadays heard only in such an expression as "The hurricane wrought great havoc," which is a cliché, or "The chain was wrought in gold throughout." The ordinary, though not frequent, use of *wrought* is as an adjective: *wrought* iron which refers to iron which has been fashioned or worked into shape.

A69 Do not use the past participle for the past indicative.

drank
He ~~drunk~~ the poison.

saw
I ~~seen~~ it myself.

Came
The cold drinks ~~come~~ earlier than we expected.

A70 Do not use the past indicative but the past participle with helping verbs.

run
The ink had ~~ran~~ down the length of the paper.

fallen
Snow had ~~fell~~ all night.

A71 Do not invent parts for verbs.

brought
Rodney ~~brung~~ the beer.

thrown
The test papers were ~~throwed~~ out during the summer.

broke
The blast ~~busted~~ the window.

HELPING VERBS[29]

A72 Helping verbs are verbs that are used together with other verbs to express changes of thought such as voice, mood, and tense, and other shades of meaning. The principal helping verbs are—

be	must
can *and* could	ought
do	shall *and* will
have	should *and* would[30]
may *and* might	

---

[29] Helping verbs are treated in general in C36-39. Particular helping verbs are treated in C40-93.

[30] *Should* and *would* are sometimes called past-tense forms of *shall* and *will*. But they are very frequently used to express a great deal more than mere past time. The same is true of *might* and *could*, which are considered past-tense forms of *may* and *can*. See C70-93.

The adjective

A73 An adjective is a word that modifies a noun or some other substantive.[31]

That is *dangerous* fun.
Do you want to see something *strange?*
Who is *this wonderful* "she" you're talking about?

A74 An adjective can be distinguished from an adverb by this, that an adjective always modifies a noun or a pronoun, never a verb, an adjective, or an adverb.

DESCRIPTIVE AND LIMITING ADJECTIVES

A75 A descriptive adjective gives a word picture of (describes) the appearance or character or condition of the noun or pronoun it modifies.

    green apples   *young* thief   *sick* boy

A76 A limiting adjective modifies a noun or pronoun by narrowing down (limiting) or enlarging or multiplying the person or thing without describing it.

this street	*five* boys
his shirt	*triple* play
some games	*second* trial
any trick	*no* chance

A77 The limiting adjectives are these: possessive, demonstrative, relative, interrogative, indefinite, and numeral (cardinal and ordinal); the articles *a, an, the.*

A78 The possessive, demonstrative, relative, interrogative, indefinite, and numeral adjectives are called pronominal adjectives because they are part pronoun: they modify nouns and pronouns or are used as substantives.

---

[31] In sentences like "The *good* die young," words ordinarily adjectives are sometimes said to be used as nouns or pronouns. They may be considered as nouns or pronouns or else as adjectives modifying an implied word like *people.*

29

POSSESSIVE ADJECTIVES

A79 The possessive adjectives are in fact the personal pronouns in the possessive case (see A28).[32]

First person		Second person		Third person	
Singular	*Plural*	*Singular*	*Plural*	*Singular*	*Plural*
my	our	your (thy)	your	his	
				her	their
				its	

Here is *my* contribution.
Here is *our* contribution.
Your make-up is too heavy.
Its name is Shep.
Their name is well known.

A80 The possessive adjectives (since they are pronouns) show person, number, and gender to agree with their antecedents as far as they can.

My plan is to train myself little by little to do without sleep altogether.	The first person is used because the antecedent is the speaker.
As for Grace and me, *our* plan is to see Europe while there is something left of it.	*Our* is plural because the compound antecedent, *Grace and me*, is plural.
This stone has *its* story to tell to a man who can read it.	*Its* is neuter gender because the antecedent, *stone*, is neuter gender.

A81 Do not use the apostrophe with the possessive adjectives.

his
He spends ~~his~~ holidays collecting and blowing eggs.

its
It's a friendly little beast. What's ~~it's~~ name?

your
Is that ~~you're~~ chignon?

---

[32] Any substantive in the possessive case functions as an adjective.

A82 Do not use *there* or *they're* for *their.*

Isn't that ~~there~~ *their* swimming pool?

~~They're~~ *Their* trouble is pride.

A83 The demonstrative adjectives are—

Singular	Plural
this	these
that	those

The is considered a weak demonstrative adjective.

A84 The demonstrative adjectives specify the nouns (or, rarely, the pronouns) they modify, point them out, or call attention to them.

These people around us, I feel, are not friendly.
No, *those* permits; not the ones in your hand.

A85 *This* and *these* ordinarily refer to what is present, near, just referred to, or about to be referred to; demonstrative *that* and *those* ordinarily refer to what is more remote in time or place.

Look at *that* new Chrysler [referring to an automobile passing in the street].

And now *this* proverb may interest you: God's help is nearer than the door.

Centuries ago someone first said, "An argument cannot batter down a fact." *That* statement is still true.

A86 Do not use *them* as a demonstrative adjective.

Give me ~~them~~ *those* pliers that you borrowed from me.

A87 Do not say *this here* and *that there, these here* and *those there.*

This ~~here~~ bed is not nearly so comfortable as that ~~there~~ one.

A88 Use *this* and *that* with singular nouns, *these* and *those* with plural nouns.

That   makes
~~These~~ sort of people ~~make~~ me ill.

This   is an
~~These~~ kind of words ~~are~~ adjective~~s~~.

This   burns
~~These~~ make of automobile~~s~~ ~~burn~~ alcohol.

Those sorts of candy—peppermints and chocolates—make me ill.
These kinds of words are called adjectives and pronouns.
These makes of automobile—Daimler and Isotta—are foreign.

RELATIVE ADJECTIVES

A89 The relative adjectives are—

which   whose

A90 Relative adjectives modify a noun (or, rarely, a pronoun) and also connect the dependent clause in which they stand with an antecedent in another clause.

The man *whose* window we broke just went into the police station.

We spent more than seven years in Juárez, in *which* city, by the way, we met Tracy.

A91 The relative adjective *which* seldom makes for pleasant reading. It is usually best to avoid it when you do not have to use it.

[Unpleasant:] I met a stranger in Miami, *which stranger* turned out to be a man with an indifferent attitude toward money.
[Better:] I met a stranger in Miami who turned out to be a man with an indifferent attitude toward money.

INTERROGATIVE ADJECTIVES

A92 The interrogative adjectives are—

whose   which   what

32

A93 The interrogative adjectives modify a noun (or, rarely, a pronoun) and also ask a question.

Whose picture is that?

Vickie asked *which* show we intended to see.

What sort of technician is your friend?

INDEFINITE ADJECTIVES

A94 Some common indefinite adjectives are—

Singular	Singular or plural	Plural
a, an[33]	all	both
another	any	few
each	no	many[34]
either	other	several
every	such	
neither	what	
	whatever	
	whatsoever	
	which	
	whichever	

A95 The indefinite adjectives modify nouns (or, rarely, pronouns) by limiting the nouns somewhat vaguely, saying indefinitely which one, how many, or how much.

Let me have *another* chance.

Any kind of yacht will do.

Both eyes are blue, of course.

No one has ever seen the *other* sisters.

Someone should have told the general *what* password was being used that night.

Slice it in any way *whatsoever*, it's still cold pheasant.

Whichever road you take, you will have a lonely journey.

---

[33] *A, an* are indefinite adjectives; but they may also be called indefinite articles.
[34] In the expression *many a* ("Many a boy has been a hero"), *many* may most conveniently be considered an adverb modifying *a*.

NUMERAL ADJECTIVES

A96 A numeral adjective limits a noun by stating its number.

A97 The cardinal numeral adjectives give the amount, tell how many. They are *one, two, three,* and so on.

I have *six* dollars.

A98 The ordinal numeral adjectives give the rank or place in an order or line-up.

Franklin, by carefully concealing his brilliance, managed to rank *twenty-ninth* in a class of thirty.

By the *sixth* day we were getting a little weary of pork chops.

If you sail from New York on the *fifth,* you should dock at Southampton on the *eleventh.*

ARTICLES

A99 The articles are limiting adjectives. *The,* the weak demonstrative akin to *this* and *that,* might be called a definite adjective; *a* and *an,* indefinite.

A100 *A* is used before a word beginning with a consonant sound, *an* before a word beginning with a vowel sound.

a drugstore	a one [sound of *w*]
a hawk	an apple
a historian	an hour [sound of *o (ou)*]
a union [sound of *y*]	

The adverb

A101 An adverb is a word that modifies a verb, an adjective, or another adverb.

Ferdinand growls *fiercely.*

A *very* high wall surrounded the place.

Jeanne was *not* entirely surprised.

A102 Whether a word is an adverb or not depends upon the work it does. Thus not every word that ends in *ly* is an adverb, nor must every adverb end in *ly; lovely* is an adjective, for instance, and *slow* may be an adverb. Again, a word ordinarily used as an adverb may sometimes be used as an adjective or a noun.

Here [adverb] is the man who rules baseball.
The cloister runs to *here* [noun].

A103 An adverb adds affirmation, negation, degree, manner, time, place, doubt, conclusion, and so on, to the word that it modifies.

[Affirmation:] yes, surely, certainly, indeed

[Negation:] no, not, hardly, scarcely, never

[Degree:] almost, barely, hardly, scarcely, completely, entirely, merely, only, partially, mainly, little, much, more, less, very

[Manner:] well, fast, slowly, lazily, busily, badly

[Time:] now, yesterday, immediately, always, recently, daily

[Place:] here, there, within, behind, everywhere

[Doubt:] maybe, perhaps, possibly, probably

[Conclusion:] consequently, therefore, hence, wherefore [but these words are usually conjunctive adverbs][35]

A104 Some adverbs have two forms, one like the adjective and the other in *ly;* for example, *slow, slowly; sharp, sharply; cheap, cheaply.* You may use the briefer form where it does not sound awkward, usually in imperative sentences.

Drive *slow.*
Look *sharp!*

Slowly the marquis mounted the guillotine.
Scrooge looked *sharply* at Marley's ghost.

A105 An adverbial noun is a noun in the objective case that modifies a verb, an adjective, or an adverb.

Ronald went *home.*
The *Cyprus* sank ninety *feet* deep.

---

[35] See A116-17.

A106 A conjunctive adverb is an adverb that has a connective function (see A116).

The habit is a bad one; *consequently,* it must be broken.
Mullins is a lunatic; he is, *moreover,* a dangerous lunatic.

The preposition

A107 A preposition is a word that always has a noun or other substantive as its object and along with that object forms a single unit, which is used as a modifier or, infrequently, a substantive.

The vertical lines *in* newspapers are column rules.	*In* has an object, *newspapers,* and together with *newspapers* makes one adjective phrase modifying *lines.*
He left *with* me.	*With* has an object, *me,* and together with *me* makes one adverb phrase modifying *left.*
Over the fence is out.	*Over* and its object, *fence,* form a substantive (a noun phrase) that is the subject of *is.*

A108 Some of the more common prepositions are—

about	besides	notwithstanding	through
above	between	of	throughout
across	beyond	off	till
after	but [except]	on	to
against	by	out	touching
along	concerning	outside	toward
among	considering	over	towards
around	despite	past	under
at	down	pending	underneath
barring	during	regarding	until
before	except	respecting	up
behind	in	round	upon
below	inside	save	with
beneath	into	saving	within
beside	like	since	without

36

A109 Some words are called participial prepositions because they are participles given a prepositional use but keeping the *ing* form. Some common participial prepositions are *concerning, including, notwithstanding, pending.*

I should like to talk to you *concerning* your passport.

Everyone, *including* the captain, thought the ship had sailed.

We shall have to proceed *notwithstanding* your objections.

Why don't you write your memoirs, *pending* your release from the penitentiary?

To determine whether you are dealing with a participial preposition or a verbal, substitute *about* for *concerning; with* for *including; in spite of* for *notwithstanding;* and *until* for *pending.* If the sentence makes sense after the substitution, the chances are good that you have a participial preposition.

We shall have to proceed *notwithstanding* your objections.	Substitute *in spite of* for *notwithstanding* and the sentence makes sense. *Notwithstanding* is, consequently, a participial preposition here.
I am afraid, sir, that we shall have to proceed, your objections *notwithstanding.*	Substitute *in spite of.* The substitution makes nonsense of the end of the sentence. *Notwithstanding* is not a participial preposition here.

A110 A compound preposition is a preposition that is made up of more than one word; for example, *because of, on account of, along with, together with, in spite of, in order to, with a view to.*[36]

The conjunction

A111 A conjunction is a word or group of words whose function is to connect words with words, phrases with phrases,

---

[36] It is equally common, however, to treat *on account, in spite, in order,* and *with a view* as preposition and object followed by another phrase.

clauses with clauses, sentences with sentences, and paragraphs with paragraphs.

Joseph *and* I are the pleasantest people!

It is impossible for him to talk to you *or* for me to give you the least information.

I hope that you have a good trip *and* that you enjoy your vacation.

The rest, I'm afraid, is up to you. *For* you will be alone, quite alone, with no one to turn to.

At length it was decided to strike for Kotuk afoot. ¶ *But* that decision turned out to be a mistake and a bad one.

A112 A co-ordinating conjunction connects words, phrases, and clauses that are of the same order or rank: two subject nouns, two predicate verbs, two adjective modifiers, two independent clauses, two dependent clauses, and so on.

A113 The common simple co-ordinating conjunctions are—

and	but not	neither	or
but	for	nor	

Raphael *and* Michael were originally Jewish names.	*And* connects the two subjects.
It should rain, *for* the wind has shifted to the south.	*For* connects the two independent clauses.
They do not toil, *neither* do they spin.	*Neither* connects the two independent clauses.
The explanation was not that Austin was cold *but* that he was bashful.	*But* connects the two dependent clauses.

Since *for* very often introduces dependent clauses of cause or reason, it is not recognized as a co-ordinating conjunction by all grammarians.

A114 The correlative co-ordinating conjunctions are so called because they are used in split pairs.

The common correlatives are—

both . . . and	if [in the sense of *whether*]
either . . . or	. . . or

neither . . . nor   whether . . . or

not only . . . but (also)

Both the children *and* the adults of the tribe are adept in the use of the blowgun.

Not only did we lose the supplies, *but* our guide came down with cholera just beyond Mamba.

Either Carmichael is telling the truth, *or* we have been cruelly unjust to Williams.

It is difficult to decide *whether* to abandon the prisoners *or* to send them back with an inadequate guard.

A115 Use *neither . . . nor*, not *neither . . . or*.

Gilbert was neither strong ~~or~~ *nor* intelligent.

A116 Conjunctive adverbs—and a few phrases that serve as conjunctive adverbs—are those that have only a connective function. They have no grammatical connection with the sentence; they are used independently (or absolutely) and connect independent clauses logically, in thought. The common ones are—

accordingly	furthermore	notwithstanding
again	hence	now
also	however	so
as a matter of fact	in brief	still
at any rate	in fact	then
besides	indeed	therefore
consequently	likewise	thereupon
finally	moreover	thus
first (second, etc.)	nevertheless	too
further	nonetheless	yet

The job had to be done; *consequently,* the Marines did it.

Whirligig beetles can skitter fast across the surface of the water; *furthermore,* they can dive.

Verano likes flattery; *indeed,* he thrives on it.

I haven't a dollar; *as a matter of fact,* I haven't any money at all.

A117 Do not confuse conjunctive adverbs with subordinating conjunctions or relative adverbs. Conjunctive adverbs are never used in dependent clauses unless some subordinating connective is also expressed or implied.[37]

Now you contradict yourself; *before*, you said that you could not possibly have overheard the accused.	Conjunctive adverb. Independent clause.
The experiment took place on the day *before* Mr. Kenna and his son disappeared.	Relative adverb. Dependent adjective clause.
We had left *before* you and Aleck arrived.	Subordinating conjunction. Dependent adverb clause.

A118 Subordinating conjunctions are those that connect sentence parts that are not of the same order or rank. Most importantly, they connect noun and adverb clauses with independent clauses or subordinate them to other dependent clauses.

A119 The following subordinating conjunctions are commonly used to connect noun clauses with independent clauses or with other dependent clauses.

how	where
that	whether
when	why

I don't know *whether* Alfred has the popcorn concession.

Tell me *where* we can vote.

A strutting, apoplectic little man in a rusty black suit asked *why* the doors had been locked and *how* he was supposed to get home in time for dinner.

A120 The following subordinating conjunctions are commonly used to connect adverb clauses with independent clauses or with other dependent clauses.

after	as . . . as	because
although	as if	before
as	as though	even if

[37] *So* is an exception. In informal speech, *so* is sometimes used in place of the subordinating conjunction *so that;* avoid the usage especially in writing.

40

even though	so as (so . . . as)	when
if	so that (so . . . that)	whence
in order that	that	whenever
lest	though	where
now that	till	wherever
provided (that)	unless	while
since	until	whither

No one looked up *when* I tripped on the kneeler.

I feel a kinship with Achilles *because* he also had difficulty with a heel.

Everything was fine *until* the dog, excited by the jarring start of the train, barked once and attracted the attention of the conductor.

A121 Some subordinating conjunctions usually introducing adverb clauses are also used to introduce adjective clauses. These conjunctions are called relative adverbs.

| after | since | whence | whither |
| before | when | where | why |

This is the place *where* I always hide the bodies.

Holt told us the reason *why* the fan belt had broken.

This is the hour *when* witches brew.

The exclamatory word

A122 Exclamatory words are words or groups of words that express feeling, usually strong feeling, but have no grammatical connection with the rest of the sentence.

Oh, someone will take care of it.

Ah! There's the sniveling little ape.

Great heaven, what was that?

A123 Some common exclamatory words are—

| ah | for heaven's sake | oh | oh my |

A124 *O,* without *h,* is nowadays capitalized and used almost exclusively with nouns in direct address in rather formal and poetic contexts.

O Diana, these are your forests!

41

The expletive

A125   The expletives are the words *it*[38] and *there* standing before the verb in place of the real subject, which usually follows the verb.

It is evident that your rifle needs cleaning.	*That your rifle needs cleaning* is the subject noun clause.
There will be a field Mass next Sunday morning.	*Mass* is the subject noun.
How many cats *there* are in Farrell's cabin!	*Cats* is the subject noun.
Was *it* very difficult to scrape the paint off?	*To scrape the paint off* is the subject noun phrase.

The gerund

A126   A gerund is a verbal that is part noun and part verb. It is always used as a noun.

Smoking is not permitted here.
My husband has never really enjoyed *hiking*.
The fun of *waiting* is yours.
Their occupation is *mining*.
The Nazis depended on careful *planning*.

A127   Since a gerund is part noun, it can do what any substantive does in a sentence: be a subject, an object, or a complement; and it can have an adjective modifier.

Smoking is not permitted here.	*Smoking* is the subject.
My husband has never really enjoyed *hiking*.	*Hiking* is the object.
The fun of *waiting* is yours.	*Waiting* is the object of *of*.
Their occupation is *mining*.	*Mining* is the predicate complement after *is*.

---

[38] Similar to *it* as an anticipatory subject is the *it* that serves as an anticipatory object: "I take *it* that you are happy?" "Bruno found *it* easy to agree."

The Nazis depended on careful *planning*.	*Planning* is modified by *careful*.

Since a gerund is part verb, it has voice and tenses; it can take a direct or indirect object or a complement; and it can be modified by an adverb.

Having been praised once made Alex conceited.	*Having been praised* is passive voice, present perfect tense.
There is no question of his *having given* me help.	*Me* is the indirect object and *help* the direct object of *having given*.
His *being* a butler does not disturb Catherine.	*Butler* is a complement after *being*.
God gave Fritzl the equipment for *talking* loudly.	*Talking* is modified by the adverb *loudly*.

The participle

A128 A participle is a verbal that is part adjective and part verb. It is always used as an adjective.

A *roaring* wind swept through the valley.
Returning, she bolted the door.
The principal looks *pleased*.
The others, highly *dissatisfied* with the result, stalked off.

A129 Since a participle is part adjective, it can modify a noun or pronoun, be a complement, or take an adverb modifier.

A *roaring* wind swept through the valley.	*Roaring* modifies *wind*.
Returning, she bolted the door.	*Returning* modifies *she*.
The principal looks *pleased*.	*Pleased* is the predicate complement after *looks*.
The others, highly *dissatisfied* with the result, stalked off.	*Dissatisfied* is modified by the adverb *highly* and the adverb phrase *with the result*.

Since a participle is part verb, it has voice and tenses; it

can take a direct or indirect object or a complement; and
it can be modified by an adverb.

Having buried his last victim and *feeling* tired, Rip curled up for a nap.	*Having buried* is present perfect tense and *feeling* present tense; both are active voice.
There sat Siegel *selling* Itzy a broken penknife.	*Selling* has *Itzy* as an indirect object and *penknife* as a direct object.
Fleetwood, *feeling* angry, stiffened and frowned.	*Feeling* has *angry* as a complement.
Rising slowly, the old man put out a hand for the paper.	*Rising* is modified by the adverb *slowly*.

The infinitive

A130   An infinitive is a verbal that is used as a noun, or substantive, as an adjective, or as an adverb. (Sometimes *to*, the sign of the infinitive, is omitted, especially after verbs like *make, see,* and *hear.* See infinitive phrases, C374.)

A131   When used as a noun, an infinitive can do what any substantive does in a sentence: be a subject, an object, or a complement; and it can have a predicate adjective.

To lie avails you nothing.	*To lie* is the subject of the verb *avails*.
Gerald wanted *to leave.*	*To leave* is the object of the verb *wanted*.
Our best plan now is *to hide.*	*To hide* is the complement after *is.*
To err is human.	*To err* has the predicate complement *human.*

When used as an adjective, an infinitive can modify a noun
or other substantive.

The will *to conquer* can be highly important.	*To conquer* modifies *will*.

To eat *to live* is what matters.	*To live* modifies the substantive *to eat*.

When used as an adverb, an infinitive can modify a verb, an adjective, or another adverb.

We hurried *to be seated.*	*To be seated* modifies *hurried.*
Are you ready *to return?*	*To return* modifies *ready.*
Max did not wait long enough *to hear.*	*To hear* modifies *enough.*

Since an infinitive is part verb, it has voice and tenses; it can have a subject (which is always in the objective case) and take a direct or indirect object or a complement; and it can be modified by an adverb.

It started *to rain.*	*To rain* is active voice, present tense.
We considered him *to be* almost negligible.	*To be* has the subject *him.*
If you want *to give* yourself a fright, look down.	*To give* has *yourself* as the indirect object and *fright* as the direct object.
Once again the bull began *to struggle* violently.	*To struggle* is modified by the adverb *violently.*

B The sentence—use and structure

Definition

B1 A sentence is a judgment that is expressed in words and stands as an independent statement. It makes an affirmation or a denial, asks a question, or gives a command.

Lights were burning in the house.
We are not amused.
Did Plato learn nothing in Syracuse?
Stand right there.

B2 An elliptical sentence is a sentence from which words have been omitted that can be *easily and naturally* supplied by the reader or listener.

Meeting tonight at eight-fifteen.
A smart boy!
Anybody home?
Happy birthday!
[In answer to a question:] Three o'clock.
[In answer to a question:] No.
O to be in England, now that April's there!

Sentence sense

B3 A half-sentence is not a complete judgment and cannot stand as an independent statement.[1]

You mean that you have not read the famous Father Brown detective stories? Father Brown, a jovial, keen-witted little priest, being one of the great fictional detectives, much beloved not only by readers but by writers of mysteries.

A nominative absolute poses as a complete sentence.

From boyhood Howard Pyle was captivated by the daredevil spirit of pirates. Being able, moreover, to express his dreams with the pen.

A participial phrase poses as a complete sentence.

Although he was born in the humblest surroundings and reared almost without schooling, Mark Twain lived to achieve world-wide fame. To be honored by generations of men, many of whom never noted his pessimism.

An infinitive phrase poses as a complete sentence.

---

[1] The half-sentence is also known as the incomplete sentence, the sentence fragment, the no-sentence, and the period-fault sentence.

Damon Runyon made himself a national reputation as a newspaperman. Before writing the now-famous stories of the bandits of Broadway and adding many a word to the American language.

A prepositional phrase poses as a complete sentence.

I found Mr. Canterbury at work in his place at the very end of Fordham Road. A peculiar establishment, uncluttered by anything but Mr. Canterbury, an oriental rug, and a telephone.

An appositive poses as a complete sentence.

Treason and loyalty, mystery and adventure, tragedy and comedy—all play their part in making *Ivanhoe* a romantic book. Which should be read by everyone.

An adjective clause poses as a complete sentence.

The Nigger of the Narcissus is one of the greatest sea stories ever written. Because Conrad, the author, put into this novel all his love and understanding of ships, seamen, the winds, and the great sea.

An adverbial clause poses as a complete sentence.

He claims that there are dramatic stories behind the invention of the streamlined train, the radio, the typewriter. That an interesting story lies behind every invention in the world.

A noun clause poses as a complete sentence.

B4 A runover is a sentence that runs over into the next sentence, being stopped only by a comma or by no punctuation at all.

He enjoyed reading *Captain Blood,* it is a book of adventure.

B5 Correct runovers by (*a*) putting a period and a capital between the sentences, (*b*) inserting a semicolon, if there is sufficient unity in the thought, (*c*) inserting *and, or, nor, but,* or *for,* or (*d*) subordinating the less important idea.

He enjoyed reading *Captain Blood. It* is a book of adventure.

He enjoyed reading *Captain Blood;* it is a book of adventure.

He enjoyed reading *Captain Blood, for* it is a book of adventure.

He enjoyed reading *Captain Blood, which* is a book of adventure.

Sentences according to use

B6 According to use, sentences are declarative, interrogative, imperative, and exclamatory.

B7 A declarative sentence makes a statement.

The noises began at midnight.

Charles asked when the noises began.

"When did the noises begin?" asked Charles.

"The man is dangerous!" cried Evanston with what seemed to be genuine alarm; and, I must admit, I was inclined to agree.

"Go at once," said Emily, quietly but with unmistakable determination; so Charles went—at once.

B8 An interrogative sentence asks a direct question.[2]

When did the noises begin?

Now that I come to think of it, why would anyone wish to fish the snapper banks at a season when the snappers will not bite?

B9 An imperative sentence in general gives a command. The command may be an entreaty, a warning, a prohibition, and so on.

Stop.

Come.

Save me!

---

[2] A direct question is a question expressed in the words of the speaker; for example: "Where is the wampum?" An indirect question gives the sense of the speaker's question without quoting him; for example: "He asked where the wampum was." An indirect question does not make an interrogative sentence, since it involves rather a statement about a question than the mere question itself.

Please come!
Proceed at your own risk.
Thou shalt not kill.
You shall not pass.

B10 An exclamatory sentence expresses a sudden or strong emotion.

Mother!
Patriots, arise!
Must I see this!
Yes! Essex still rebels!

Sentences according to structure

B11 According to structure, sentences are classified as simple, compound, complex, and compound-complex.

B12 A simple sentence is a sentence that has only one subject and one predicate.

Witchmen howled.

Herman Melville published *Moby Dick*, his greatest and best-known novel, in 1851.

Starvation affects a man's mind as well as his body.

It was a peculiar place of business, uncluttered by furniture, files, secretaries, or anything but Mr. Canterbury and a telephone.

B13 The subject of a simple sentence can be a noun or any other substantive except a clause.[3]

Frogs [noun] croak.
They [pronoun] croak.
To croak dismally [noun phrase] is natural to frogs.

B14 The subject of a simple sentence may be simple or compound. The predicate of a simple sentence may be simple or compound.[4]

Chieftains pranced.
Witchmen and chieftains howled.

---

[3] A substantive is a noun or any other word or group of words that is used as a noun.
[4] See C4 and C6.

Witchmen pranced and howled.
Witchmen and chieftains pranced and howled.

B15 A compound sentence is a sentence made up of two or more independent clauses properly connected.[5]

The cougar looked down, and I shot him.	Independent clause: *The cougar looked down.* Independent clause: *and I shot him.*
The cougar looked down; I shot him.	Independent clause: *The cougar looked down.* Independent clause: *I shot him.*

B16 A complex sentence is a sentence made up of one independent clause and one or more dependent clauses.[6] (See B17.)

When the cougar looked down, I shot him.	Independent clause: *I shot him.* Dependent clause: *when the cougar looked down.*
I shot the cougar as he looked down and before he was aware of the child.	Independent clause: *I shot the cougar.* First dependent clause: *as he looked down.* Second dependent clause: *and before he was aware of the child.*

B17 The definition of a complex sentence in B16 is true in only a general sense, for a complex sentence with a noun clause as the subject or complement or object of the verb does not contain an independent clause at all. In such sentences there is no independent clause distinct from the dependent clause. (See C383 and C387.)

Where Terry is going concerns only him.	The noun clause, *where Terry is going*, is the subject of *concerns*; and *concerns only him*, the predicate, passes for the independent clause.

---

[5] For independent clauses see C378-79. For proper connection of the clauses of compound sentences, see D42-44.
[6] For independent and dependent clauses, see C378-82.

Candy is what I like.

The noun clause, *what I like,* is the predicate complement after *is;* and *candy is* must pass as the independent clause.

You get what you pay for.

The noun clause, *what you pay for,* is the object of *get;* and *you get* must pass for the independent clause.

B18 A compound-complex sentence is a sentence that contains two or more independent clauses and one or more dependent clauses.

Magellan was killed in the Philippines; nevertheless, his companions, eager to prove that the world is round, continued their westward journey until their ships at length cast anchor off the coast of Spain.

Independent 1: *Magellan was killed in the Philippines.* Independent 2: *nevertheless, his companions, eager to prove . . . continued their westward journey.*
Dependent 1: *that the world is round.* Dependent 2: *until their ships at length cast anchor off the coast of Spain.*

C Syntax

Subjects and predicates

C1 The subject is the part of a clause or sentence that is talked about. The predicate is the part of a clause or sentence that talks about the subject.[1]

Jim prays.

Subject | Predicate
Jim | prays.

---

[1] Many grammars call subject and predicate in this general sense *complete subject* and *complete predicate.* This book distinguishes between *subject* and *subject noun* or *substantive* and between *predicate* and *predicate verb.* In one-word subjects and predicates, of course, *subject* and *subject substantive* will coincide, as will *predicate* and *predicate verb.*

	Subject	*Predicate*
Were you waiting for me?	You	were waiting for me?
The man in the bowler hat was leaning against the lamp-post, waiting for me.	The man in the bowler hat waiting for me.	was leaning against the lamppost . . .
Go!	[You]	go!
There is something strange about you tonight, Count Dracula.	Something strange	is about you tonight, Count Dracula.
Squatting on the sandy ground, his eyes looking off beyond us to the hills, the wrinkled old Indian took the drum between his knees and began to beat a hypnotic rhythm.	Squatting on the sandy ground, his eyes looking off beyond us to the hills, the wrinkled old Indian	took the drum between his knees and began to beat a hypnotic rhythm.

C2 The subject noun or other substantive is the word in the subject that governs the predicate verb.

	Subject noun	*Predicate*
Jim prays.	*Jim*	prays.
Marcia sneered.	*Marcia*	sneered.
Is the train waiting for me?	*train*	is waiting for me?
The man in the bowler hat was leaning against the lamp-post, waiting for me.	*man*	was leaning against the lamppost . . .
Squatting on the sandy ground, his eyes looking off beyond us to the hills, the wrinkled old Indian took the drum between his knees.	*Indian*	took the drum between his knees.

52

C3 Do not insert immediately after a subject noun a subject pronoun meaning exactly the same thing.[2]

Jules ~~he~~ wants to be a chemical engineer.
Willa Cather and Edna Ferber ~~they~~ are American novelists.

C4 A compound subject is a subject that is made up of two or more subject nouns or other substantives. (See C6.)

Johnson and *Powers* disappeared.
He and *you* and *I* are the winners.
To play records and *to go to shows* are all Jack cares about.

C5 The predicate verb is the verb in the predicate that is governed by the subject noun(s) or other substantive(s).

	Subject noun	*Predicate verb*
Jim prays.	Jim	*prays*
Marcia sneered.	Marcia	*sneered*
Were you waiting for me?	you	*were waiting*
The man in the bowler hat was leaning against the lamppost, waiting for me.	man	*was leaning*
Squatting on the sandy ground, his eyes looking off beyond us to the hills, the wrinkled old Indian took the drum between his knees.	Indian	*took*

C6 A compound predicate is a predicate that is made up of two or more predicate verbs. Note that some sentences have a compound subject and a compound predicate.

Johnson *bowed* and *disappeared*.
The ship *sank* at the bow, then *heeled* a little to port, and finally *plunged* beneath the surface.
John and Mary *sang* and *danced*.

---

[2] This does not affect those constructions in which a speaker is represented as mulling over names; for example, "Willa Cather and Edna Ferber—they were American novelists, weren't they?"

VERB AGREEMENT IN GENERAL

C7 Make a predicate verb agree with its subject noun(s) or other substantive(s) in person and number.

John *sings* like an excited bullfrog.
This machine *crushes* rock.
Paul and Jim *have* a live platypus.
Everybody is to be inoculated, *say* the authorities.
An excellent athlete and a good student *is* Jonathan.

C8 Make the predicate verb agree with the real subject substantive after the expletive *there*.[3] (But see C34.)

There is only one glass.

       are
There ~~is~~ others besides you.

C9 Make the predicate verb agree with the subject substantive and not with words in apposition.

                order
I, your commanding officer, ~~orders~~ this retreat.

                        has
The doubles team, Ogden and McCarthy, ~~have~~ not won a set.

C10 Make the predicate verb agree with the subject substantive and not with words introduced by *with, along with, including, as well as, no less than, of,* and so on.

              have
I, together with my dog, ~~has~~ hunted these woods for five years.

         has
Joe, as well as I, ~~have~~ stayed up, getting the annual ready for the printer's deadline.

                   has
Bad health, along with many years, ~~have~~ weakened poor Featherstonhaugh.

                   has
The light on the new Raleigh bicycles ~~have~~ a generator.

---

[3] For sentences like "There *is* more than one way to skin a cat" and "There *are* more than two ways to skin a cat," see C18.

C11 The number and person of a relative pronoun depend upon its antecedent. Make sure you have the right antecedent, according to sentence sense, before you make the predicate verb agree with a relative-pronoun subject.

Pasteur was one of those men who *are* not easily discouraged.

Pasteur was the only one of those men who *was* not easily discouraged.

The only one of his stories that *was* amusing was a tale of three men locked in an elevator.

One of the people who *were* present was a Don Q

The number of members *who were* absent was truly deplorable.

C12 Always use a third-person singular predicate verb after *it,* whether expletive or pronoun.

It *is* fun swimming and sailing.
It *was* they; it *was* not I.
It *was* two hours before he returned.

C13 When a collective noun names a group acting as a unit, use a singular predicate verb with it.[4]

The committee ~~are~~ *is* angry.

The jury ~~have~~ *has* been out an hour and a half.

The congregation ~~sing~~ *sings* badly.

C14 When a collective noun names a group acting as individuals, use a plural predicate verb with it.[5]

The jury ~~has~~ *have* disagreed among themselves.

The crew ~~is~~ *are* not yet all in their places.

The senior class ~~was guest~~ *were guests* of the Stoneleighs.

---

[4] At times, deciding whether a collective noun names a group acting as a unit is difficult. Use a singular or plural verb depending on what you want to say.

[5] See the footnote above. Often, changing the sentence is better than using such awkward expressions as this: "The class are each sitting in a different seat." Say rather: "Each member of the class is sitting in a different seat."

C15 Use a singular predicate verb with the singular indefinite pronouns and adjectives.

Each of the thieves ~~were~~ *was* caught.

Everyone ~~are~~ *is* asked to be there.

Neither plan is worth anything.

Each wave and ripple ~~sparkle~~ *sparkles*.

C16 Use a plural predicate verb with expressions like *the rest, a part, half, two thirds, all, any, none,* and *some* when they indicate how many, and a singular predicate verb when they indicate how much.

Half of the exercises *were burned* by the janitor.
Half of the exercise *was burned* by the janitor.

The rest of the books *are* trash.
The rest of the book *is* trash.

Part of the horses *were shipped* to Miami.
Part of the horse *was shipped* to the glue factory.

C17 Use a plural predicate verb with *a number* (meaning several, quite a few), but a singular predicate verb with *the number.*

A number of people ~~has~~ *have* asked us for the recipe.

The number of people ~~have~~ *has* increased greatly.

C18 If a noun or pronoun following *more than* is singular, use a singular predicate verb. If it is plural, use a singular predicate verb if it indicates how much, a plural predicate verb if it indicates how many.

There *is* more than one way to skin a cat.
There *are* more than two ways to skin a cat.
There *is* more than two gallons in the tank.
There *is* more than ten dollars in the billfold.
There *are* more than ten one-dollar bills on the counter.

C19 Use a plural predicate verb when adjectives connected by *and* so modify a subject noun or other substantive as to show that it means more than one thing.

are
Both good and bad butter ~~is~~ sold here.

have
The chocolate and the pound cake ~~has~~ been won.

C20 Use a singular predicate verb with words that are plural in form but singular in meaning.[6]

was
The gallows ~~were~~ erected beside the road.

is
Measles ~~are~~ catching.

was
The news ~~were~~ good.

was
Physics ~~were~~ my easiest subject.

C21 Ordinarily use a singular predicate verb with the names of sciences like *mathematics, physics,* and *economics.*

Mathematics *is* my downfall.
Physics *is* the study of matter and motion.
Economics *is required* in third year.

C22 Ordinarily use a plural predicate verb with the names of practical affairs like *politics* and *athletics.*

Athletics *are* much *fostered* at North High.
Politics *play* havoc with a policy based on principle.
Gymnastics *have been* highly *developed* by some nations.
Foreign affairs *are* much *debated* in the Senate.

C23 In sentences where the notion of one thing is emphasized, use a singular predicate verb even with words like *politics* and *athletics.*

Politics *has become* a complicated study.
Athletics *wastes* too much of a student's time.
Foreign affairs *offers* real opportunity for a fascinating career.

---

[6] See C21-23.

C24 Use a singular predicate verb with plural nouns that are felt to express a single unit.

isn't
Four gallons ~~aren't~~ much gas.

is
Ten miles ~~are~~ too far on worn-out tires.

was
There ~~were~~ five hundred dollars in his pocket.

C25 Use a singular predicate verb with a word that is discussed as a word.

They is a pronoun.
Lilacs has a very pleasant sound.

C26 Use a singular predicate verb with plural titles and plural proper names used to designate one person or one thing.

has
The United States ~~have~~ great responsibilities.

is
The Fishermen ~~are~~ an interesting book.

has
The *Times* ~~have~~ a full sports coverage.

has
Shelley, Shark, and Shumack [one business firm] ~~have~~ gone into bankruptcy.

Twin Oaks *is* a ramshackle house at the bend of the river.

VERB AGREEMENT WITH COMPOUND SUBJECTS

C27 Use a plural predicate verb with a compound subject whenever *and* is used or implied between the words.[7]

have
Johnson and Powers ~~has~~ disappeared.

were
The water polo and the diving contest ~~was~~ called off.
Three sandwiches and a quart of milk *are* waiting for you.
Knapp, Wallace, Berger *are* the leaders.
Cal and Haas, Wills and Smith *are* our tennis teams.

---

[7] See C35 for an exception.

C28 When a compound subject has both affirmative and negative parts, make the predicate verb agree in person and in number with the affirmative rather than with the negative part.

am
I, not you, ~~are~~ deciding.

are
You, not I, ~~am~~ deciding.

are
Terry and Bill, hardly Kenneth, ~~is~~ to be relied on.

C29 When awkwardness results from carrying out this rule, however, rewrite the sentence.

I am deciding, not you.
You are deciding, not I.
Terry and Bill are to be relied on. Kenneth seems less trustworthy.

C30 When the parts of a compound subject are of different person or number and are connected by *or, either . . . or, not only . . . but also, neither . . . nor,* and other disjunctives,[8] make the predicate verb agree in person and number with the nearer part.

Either they or I *am* to go.
Not only Jean but also Jane and Paul *are* invited.
Not only you but also Jim *was* mistaken.
Neither the mother nor the daughters *were* invited.
Neither the daughters nor the mother *was* invited.

C31 When awkwardness arises from carrying out C30, rewrite the sentence.

If they don't go, then I must.
Jean, Jane, and Paul are invited.
You were not the only one who was mistaken; Jim was too.
The mother was not invited; but neither were the daughters.
The daughters were not invited; but neither was the mother.

---

[8] Disjunctives are co-ordinating conjunctions that separate, or offer a choice between, the words that they connect. Grammatically, they connect; in thought, they separate. They connect because they show that words go together as subject nouns or objects and so on; but they also separate, offer a choice between, or break into units, the meanings of those same words.

C32   When the parts of a compound subject represent one person or thing, or are felt to make up one collective idea, use a singular predicate verb.

My friend and neighbor, Kittredge, ~~play~~ *plays* the flute.

A coach and four ~~were~~ *was* rattling down the King's Road.

The hop, skip, and jump ~~are~~ *is* no longer a common event at track meets.

Rioting and violence often leads [*or* lead] to tyranny.

He was of the old school, and maintained that a blackboard and a switch was [*or* were] all that any teacher needed to turn dullards into scholars.

[Singular verb would be incorrect:] A destroyer and a cruiser were standing by.

C33   When each of the singular parts of a compound subject is considered separately, make the predicate verb agree with the nearest. (To decide whether or not you have such a case, mentally insert *or* before the last part. If *or* makes sense in the sentence, each part of the subject is being considered separately. If it does not, then they are being taken together.)

A shred of a tune, a face vaguely familiar, the *odor* of a hallway, *unleashes* a flood of memory to sicken or delight us.

A shred of a tune, a face vaguely familiar, *or* the odor of a hallway *unleashes* a flood of memory to sicken or delight us.	*Or* makes good sense here.
A pitcher, a catcher, a batter, *or* a fielder-baseman *is* all one needs to play a simple form of baseball.	*Or* makes nonsense of this sentence. Change *is* to *are*.

C34   When several words (at least four) separate the subject nouns or pronouns of a compound subject, the predicate verb after dummy subject *there* may agree with the nearer subject noun or pronoun.

There *was* a plain, unpainted wooden *table* in a corner of the kitchen under the window and, near the stove, two ancient and scabrous wicker *chairs* of doubtful comfort and uncertain strength.	A good many words intervene between *table* and *chairs*.

C35 When a whole compound subject is modified by *each, every, many a, such a,* and *no,* use a singular predicate verb.

Each man, woman, and child *has* received some sort of souvenir to take home with *him.*

Every officer and member *was* there to answer to *his* name at the roll call.

Each back, *each* lineman, and *each* coach *was* quizzed before the ruling was changed.

Many a man and woman *is* allergic to ragweed.

Such an idea and attitude *is* unworthy of you.

No hat and *no* purse *was* to be found.

Verb use

HELPING VERBS IN GENERAL

C36 Helping verbs are verbs that are used together with other verbs to express changes of thought such as voice, mood, tense, and other shades of meaning. The principal helping verbs are—

be	must
can *and* could	ought
do	shall *and* will
have	should *and* would[9]
may *and* might	

---

[9] *Should* and *would* are sometimes called past-tense forms of *shall* and *will.* But they are used to express a great deal more than mere past time. The same is true of *might* and *could,* called past-tense forms of *may* and *can.*

C37 Helping verbs together with the verb they help, form one predicate verb—even when the helpers are separated from the rest of the verb. The one predicate verb in each of the following examples is italicized.

Poison *was mentioned.*
The three tethered horses *must have been frightened.*
Did he *call?*
Are you *coming?*
Isn't all this mournful talk *depressing* you?
Copperheads *have* often *been seen* in this swamp.
May I—excuse this interruption—*make* a remark?
This code *has* twice *been* completely *lost.*
Should not Del *have been* more quickly *alerted?*

C38 Do not separate parts of the predicate verb when awkwardness results.

[Awkward:] They referred to the speech which the president *had* late this past summer *delivered.*

[Better:] They referred to the speech which the president *had delivered* late this past summer.

C39 Do not use the past indicative active but the past participle with helping verbs.

The ink had ~~ran~~ *run* down the length of the paper.

Snow had ~~fell~~ *fallen* all night.

I had never before *swum* so far.

HELPING VERB *be*

C40 Helping verb *be* is used to make up its own progressive form and the progressive form of other verbs.

C41 The progressive form of a verb presents the action not merely as something that happens but as something that continues to happen or that progresses.

[Regular form:] She *sews.*
[Progressive form:] She *is sewing.*

C42 The progressive form of the present tense of verbs is commonly used as a substitute for the future tense.

[Future:] I *will return* tomorrow.
[Progressive present:] I *am returning* tomorrow.

C43 The progressive present of the verb *go* is commonly used as a substitute for the future tense.

[Future:] You *will regret* this.
[Progressive present of *go:*] You *are going* to regret this.

[Future:] I *will go.*
[Progressive present of *go:*] I *am going* to go.

C44 The progressive form of the present tense active is used to avoid awkwardness or archaic formality in asking direct questions.

[Regular form, to be avoided:] *Swim* you with us today?
[Progressive form:] *Are* you *swimming* with us today?

C45 The progressive form of the past tense active of *go* is sometimes used to express supposition, expectation, intention, or purpose.

Hilton *was going* with us, but at the last moment he found that he could not go.

I thought Reinke *was going* to scream.

C46 Helping verb *be* is used to form the passive voice.

C47 Helping verb *be,* followed by an infinitive with *to,* is used to express futurity, obligation, expectation, supposition, or an indirect command.

[Futurity:] I *am to be* queen of the May.

[Obligation:] We *are to obey* God in all things.

[Expectation:] A department store *is to be built* on the site of the finest old theater that this section of the country possessed.

[Supposition:] You are basing your investment on the guess that there *is to be* a new market for automobile cranks.

[Indirect command:] You *are* all *to be* up and dressed by four-thirty tomorrow morning.

63

HELPING VERB *do*

C48 Helping verb *do* is used to make up its own emphatic form and the emphatic form of other verbs.

C49 The emphatic form of a verb lends insistence or emphasis to what the verb asserts.[10]

[Regular form:] I *finished* my homework.
[Emphatic form:] I *did finish* my homework.

C50 Helping verb *do* is used with the present and past active to avoid awkwardness or archaic formality when *not* is used with regular forms of *do*.

[Regular form, to be avoided:] I *did* not what I was told.
[With helping verb:] I *did* not *do* what I was told.

[Regular form, to be avoided:] Did she complain about the extra charge? No, she *complained* not.

[With helping verb:] Did she complain about the extra charge? No, she *didn't*.

C51 Helping verb *do* is used with the present and past active to avoid awkwardness or archaic formality when asking direct questions.

[Regular form, to be avoided:] *Play* you the saxophone?
[With helping verb:] *Do* you *play* the saxophone?

[Regular form, to be avoided:] *Heard* you Buster calling?
[With helping verb:] *Did* you *hear* Buster calling?

C52 Helping verb *do* is used in the imperative to express polite insistence.

Do sit down, Mr. Topeavy.

Do tell us, Father Smithers, whether we will have to associate with, well, all sorts of people in heaven.

Do have a fifth helping of the turkey, Alfred; we weren't really planning on serving it cold for supper 'this evening.

---

[10] In old verse and in some modern verse, helping verb *do* is often used simply for rhythm or sound, with no note of emphasis.

HELPING VERB *have*

C53 Helping verb *have* is used to form the perfect tenses.

C54 Helping verb *have*, followed by an infinitive with *to*, is used to express obligation or necessity.

We *have to leave* everything just as we found it.

Ray, please try to understand that Eric *had to do* what he did.

If you *had had to earn* your money as a boy, you might now have more respect for other people's property.

C55 Do not use *of* for *have* or *'ve*, and do not insert an *of* after *had*.

You should ~~of~~ *have* seen the crowd at Dinny's last night.

They ought to ~~of~~ *have* gone to a vocational school.

If Duke had ~~of~~ let go, the rest of us ~~would of~~ *would've* fallen.

HELPING VERB *must*

C56 Helping verb *must* has only one form for all tenses, persons, and numbers.

C57 Helping verb *must* is most commonly used to express obligation or necessity.

Someone *must stay* with Phineas until the doctor comes.

When you increase the pressure to that point, then something *must give* somewhere.

To win the jackpot you *must answer* four of the five questions.

C58 Since helping verb *must* has only one form, it is often wise to substitute another verb for it in order to avoid ambiguity or awkwardness.

[Ambiguous and awkward:] Ray, please try to understand that Eric *must have done* what he did.

[Better:] Ray, please try to understand that Eric *had to do* what he did.

C59 Helping verb *must* is used with other verbs to express supposition or speculation.

> Someone *must have broken* the news to my father before I finally arrived home.
>
> The window *must have been broken* by the storm.
>
> Whoever it was *must have worn* gloves.
>
> It *must have been* about three before the mailman finally brought it to the house.

HELPING VERB *ought*

C60 Helping verb *ought* has only one form for all tenses, persons, and numbers.

C61 Use the infinitive with *to* after *ought*, without *to* after *ought not*.

C62 Do not use *had ought*.

> *ought to have seen*
> You ~~had ought to see~~ the people at the festival.
>
> *ought not*
> You ~~hadn't ought to~~ be disrespectful.

C63 Helping verb *ought* expresses obligation, supposition, expectation, speculation, or fitness.

> [Obligation:] You *ought to set* an example to your children if you expect good conduct from them.
>
> [Supposition, expectation, speculation:] There *ought to be* another train in ten minutes.
>
> [Fitness:] I *ought to have been told* of the family's plans even if I am the black sheep.

HELPING VERBS *shall* AND *will*

C64 Helping verbs *shall* and *will* have only one form for all tenses, persons, and numbers.

C65 Helping verbs *shall* and *will* are used to form the future and the future-perfect tenses.

C66 Use *shall* with the first person and *will* with the second and third to express simple futurity or expectation, a mere statement of fact.[11]

At this rate *I shall graduate* in three years.

If things happen as they usually do, *you will* someday *regret* your silly threat.

Tchaikovsky, the copyright owner, *will give* no trouble.

C67 Use *will* with the first person and *shall* with the second and third to express intention, purpose, or determination on the part of the speaker.

I will cut right through all this red tape.	Clearly determination, intention, or purpose.
You shall go where you're told!	Spoken in reprimand.
They shall not *pass.*	Spoken by a general rallying his troops against an enemy.
What kind of dinner *shall they give* us?	This indicates that we have control over the dinner.
What kind of dinner *will they give* us?	This indicates that we do not have control over the dinner but are merely asking what the menu will be.

C68 In questions, use *shall* with the first person; use *shall* with the second and third person if *shall* is expected in the answer, but use *will* if *will* is expected in the answer.

Shall I or *shall I* not *eat* another peanut?
Shall we dance, or are you tired?

Will you be quiet?	Answer expected: *I will* or *I will not*—for this is a matter of intention or willingness.
Shall good old *Joe be made* to eat crow?	Answer expected: *he shall* or *he shall not*—for this is a matter of determination.

---

[11] In the United States even the best writers tend to make *will* do *shall*'s work as well as its own, especially in informal usage.

Shall you graduate this June? Answer expected: *I shall* or *I shall not* (C66)—for this is a matter of mere futurity or of expectation.

C69 In conditions that carry no notion of "contrary to fact," but are simple, straightforward conditions, use *shall* with the first person and *will* with the second and third in the *if* clause. (Use *shall* or *will* in the independent clause according to C66-67.)

If *I shall get* home in time, I shall have first chance at the paper.
If *you will* come, we shall be delighted.

HELPING VERBS *should* AND *would*

C70 Helping verbs *should* and *would* have only one form for all moods, tenses, persons, and numbers.

C71 Use *should* after *if* in all persons to express a supposition or imagined conditions or a condition contrary to fact.[12]

C72 If *if . . . should* has been used in a condition, then in the conclusion use *should* with the first person and *would* with the second and third to express a simple future result.[13]

If Barbara should sing, *I should be* sure to have another sleepless night afterwards.
If Tom should not return, then *you would be* one of the six to share the pie.
If Rome should fall, *would* the *pope* still *be* bishop of Rome?

C73 If *if . . . should* has been used in a condition, then in the conclusion use *would* with all three persons to express intention or willingness.

If Barbara should sing, *I would make* for that exit.
If I should ask you, I'm sure *you would oblige* me.
If Bill should hit Stein, *Stein would hit* him.

---

[12] This rule holds, of course, in conditions where *if* is implied but not expressed; for example, "*Should* he come, we should be delighted."

[13] In the United States even the best writers tend to make *would* do *should's* work as well as its own, especially in informal usage.

C74 Use *would* after *if* in all persons to express imagined or supposed willingness or a condition of willingness that is contrary to the facts.

If *I would* [usually expressed today by *if I wanted to*], I could take the day off.

If *you would try*, you could become a very effective speaker.

If *Evans would* only *talk* to me, I think I could persuade him to buy an advertisement in the *Post*.

C75 Use *should* with the first person and *would* with the second and third to express a modest opinion.

I should say that this oyster is asserting itself.
You would hardly *say*, would you, that I look like a criminal?
One would imagine that O'Leary dislikes talking in public.

C76 Use *should* with the first person, *would* with the second and third with *prefer, care, like, be glad, be inclined.*

I should prefer, of course, to breathe.

You would be inclined, I think, to consider mayhem good fun.

The *Millers would* not *care* to have their goldfish pond used as a wading pool.

C77 Use *should* with all persons to express duty, obligation, desirability, expectation, doubtful necessity.

[Duty or obligation:] If you are going to join us, *you should be* here before ten o'clock.

[Desirability:] I think it better that *someone* known to the family *should attend* the funeral.

[Expectation:] There *should be* another *car* in ten minutes.

[Doubtful necessity:] Ordinarily, a *rock* of that size *should fall* with terrific force.

C78 Use *would* with all persons to express habit or inclination (except in the case considered in C76).

I would put my foot in the bucket every time at bat.

Even as a baby, *you would take* Homer down from the shelf and gaze at the beautiful Greek words.

But an *American would think* that there is nothing more delicious than steak and potatoes.

C79 Use *would* with all persons in a polite expression of a desire.

> I *would make* a final remark.
> *Would* you *come* this way, please?
> Mr. and Mrs. Bright *would have* you join them at their table.

C80 Questions with *should* and *would* are governed by C71-79.

C81 Use *should* as a past of *shall* and *would* as a past of *will*.

> At that time I was sure that *I should be* a lawyer some day.
> At that time you were sure that *you would be* a lawyer some day.
> At that time he was sure that *he would be* a lawyer some day.

HELPING VERBS *may* AND *might*

C82 Helping verbs *may* and *might* have only one form for all tenses, persons, and numbers.

C83 Use *may* to express permission.[14]

> Please, Ma, *may* I *keep* the puppy?
> You *may stay* in swimming until the car comes back.

C84 Use *might* as a past of *may*.

> Mother said that I *might keep* the puppy; but when I returned to look for it, it was gone.
>
> The coach had told us that we *might stay* in swimming until the car came back.

C85 When no *if* clause is involved, use *may* to express a near possibility, *might* to express a remote one.

> It *may rain.* [The sky is cloudy.]
> It *might rain.* [The climate is treacherous.]
>
> They *may go;* in fact, I should not be surprised if they did.
> They *might go;* but, judging by the way that Steve was talking at lunch, I don't think they will.

C86 When an *if* clause expresses a supposition, an imagined condition, or a condition that is contrary to fact, use *might*

---

[14] In the United States even the best writers tend to make *can* do *may's* work as well as its own, especially in informal usage.

in the independent clause even to express a near possibility. Do not use *may*.

If you were more careful, you *might be allowed* to use the drill press.

If Creon would control his temper, we *might be* able to use him as the father in the play.

If someone could invent a way of putting two colors, red and black, on paper typewriter-tapes, he *might make* a fortune.

C87 When an *if* clause does not fall under C86, use either *may* or *might* in the independent clause.

If someone invents a way of putting two colors, red and black, on paper typewriter-tapes, he *may* [or *might*] *make* a fortune.

C88 Use *may* and *might* (*might* for the past) to express purpose or intention.

I'm working in order that I *may encourage* the others.
I worked in order that I *might encourage* the others.

HELPING VERBS *can* AND *could*

C89 Helping verbs *can* and *could* have only one form for all tenses, persons, and numbers.

C90 Use *can* or *could* to express power, ability, skill: *can* suggesting a near possibility and *could* a more remote one.[15]

I don't know whether I *can sail* so large a boat by myself.
I don't know whether I *could sail* so large a boat by myself.

C91 Use *could* as a past of *can*.

I didn't know whether I *could sail* so large a boat by myself.

C92 When an *if* clause expresses a supposition, an imagined condition, or a condition that is contrary to fact, use *could* in the independent clause.

If there were less talk, we *could finish* the cracker-eating contest.

He really believes that he *could sing* the title role [if he should be asked to do so].

---

[15] In the United States even the best writers use *can* and *could* to express permission. See C83.

If we had had a third, we *could have played* three-man territory, a game invented by a madman.

If nobody would object, we *could leave.*

C93 Use *could* as a softer, more polite, more indirect form of *can.*

Could you *get* me another table, please?

ACTIVE AND PASSIVE VOICE

C94 Voice is that form which a verb takes to show whether the subject is acting or being acted upon. The active voice is the form of the verb that shows that the subject is acting. The passive voice is the form of the verb that shows that the subject is being acted upon.

[Active:] Herbert *teased* the lion.
[Passive:] The lion *was teased* by Herbert.

C95 Do not confuse passive voice with past time (tense).

C96 Avoid awkward passives.

[Awkward:] The streets *are being walked* by restless crowds.
[Use the active:] Restless crowds *are walking* the streets.

C97 A verb used in an intransitive sense cannot usually be changed into the passive voice. But sometimes a preposition and an intransitive verb are so closely associated that together they become a compound transitive verb and can be put into the passive.[16]

[Active:] The truck *ran into* the bus.
[Passive:] The bus *was run into* by the truck.

[Active:] Tim's friends *thought* well *of* him.
[Passive:] Tim *was* well *thought of* by his friends.

C98 A verb in the passive may have a predicate complement; that is, a predicate noun or predicate adjective.

---

[16] When such constructions are used, it is sensible to think of the word that was a preposition in the active as part of a compound verb in the passive and to analyze it and diagram it accordingly. However, it may justly be considered a preposition retained from the active and diagramed to one side.

Mervin was elected *treasurer.*
Ursula is considered *clever.*

C99 A predicate complement results in the passive when the verb in the active has an objective complement.

The committee elected Mervin *treasurer* [objective complement in the active].

Mervin was elected *treasurer* [predicate noun in the passive].

Everyone considers Ursula *clever* [objective complement in the active].

Ursula is considered *clever* [predicate adjective in the passive].

C100 Although a verb cannot have an ordinary direct object when it is in the passive, it can yet have an object held over from the active and called a "retained object."[17]

We were asked the *price.*

We were given *directions* by a policeman.

Someone must have been given a *warning,* for the enemy artillery was waiting for us.

C101 A retained object results in the passive when the verb in the active has two direct objects, one of which is made the subject noun or pronoun of the active.

[Active:] The customer immediately asked *us* the *price.*	*Us* and *price* are the double object of *asked.* (Do not confuse with compound object.)
[Passive:] *We* were immediately asked the *price.*	*Us* has been made the subject pronoun *(we),* and *price* is the retained object, held over from the active.

C102 A retained object results in the passive when the indirect object of the active (or the object of *to* or *for* acting as an indirect object) is made the subject noun or pronoun

----

[17] Ordinarily retained objects are not pronouns; but, if one were, it should of course be put in the objective case. Since retained objects are so seldom pronouns, and hence case is not involved, the retained object is of no consequence in English and, along with a good number of other fine points of grammar, is treated in this book only because it may give difficulty from time to time in the analysis of a sentence.

in the passive. For then the direct object is retained in the passive.

[Active:] A policeman gave us *directions*.

[Passive:] We were given *directions* by a policeman.	Indirect object *us* has been made the subject pronoun *(we)*, and *directions* is the retained object, the direct object held over from the active.

[Passive:] Just outside the library, I was handed a *summons*.

THE THREE MOODS

C103 The mood of a verb is the grammatical form that shows how the verb expresses the actuality of its subject— whether as a fact, as a possibility, as a doubt, as a wish, and so on.

C104 In English there are three moods: the indicative, the imperative, and the subjunctive.[18]

C105 Use the indicative mood to state something as a fact, to deny that something is a fact, or to ask questions about it as a fact.

Robert W. Service *was born* in England in 1874.
The sun *is* not *shining*.
Will the dog *bite?*
I wonder whether there *is* any use in waiting.

C106 Use the imperative mood to give commands. (*Command* is here taken to include direct second-person orders, pleas, warnings, instructions, and so on.)

Honor thy father and thy mother.
Save me!
Proceed at your own risk.
Let's go.[19]

---

[18] Many grammars list also an optative mood, a potential mood, and so on. This book acts on the principle that all the manners of expression of a verb are well accounted for by the three moods given here and by the helping verbs.

[19] Many grammars treat this as a hortatory (exhorting) subjunctive. Calling it an imperative seems more realistic and accurate.

C107 The present and future indicative are frequently used as substitutes for the imperative mood.

This is my command: Malcolm Guerny *dies*.	Substitute for *execute Malcolm Guerny*.
Thou *shalt* not *kill*.	Substitute for *do not kill*.
You *shall be* here tomorrow at eight.	Substitute for *be here at eight*.

C108 In general, use the subjunctive mood to show that conditions, concessions, and wishes are contrary to the facts. The subjunctive mood indicates that what is said is in some way not actual or certain but is imagined or wished or desired or conceived as possible. However, since some subjunctive forms have fallen into rather general disuse, keep the following particular rules.

C109 Use the present subjunctive after verbs of ordering, willing, resolving, and proposing, and after expressions of necessity when these are followed by the conjunction *that*. Other forms of the verb may take the place of the formal construction of *that* followed by the present subjunctive. (It is better, however, to keep the formal construction in sentences beginning *Resolved*.)

The dean *has ordered that* Fleming *take* another examination on Friday.

God *wills that* all men *be saved*.

We *are determined that* no one *be admitted* who cannot speak persuasively.

The rule *requires that* a person *reach* his twenty-first year before he may apply for admission.

It *is necessary that* Igor *play* loud enough to cover the noise of shifting the set.

Mrs. Reingold *asks that* a guest not only *enjoy* her parties but also *work* hard at doing so.

I *move* that Mr. Hall *represent* us in Washington.

Resolved, That the secretary *take* our complaint to the president.

God wills *that* all men *should be saved*.

God wills all men *to be saved*.

The principal has ordered *that* Fleming *should take* (or *shall take*) another examination on Friday.

The principal has ordered Fleming *to take* another examination on Friday.

C110 Use *were* (past subjunctive) to indicate that what you are saying is contrary to present or future fact.

If only I *were* class president. [I'm not.]

Even if he *were* to beg me, I wouldn't drive my car to the beach. [And he hardly will.]

If I *were* you, I would apologize. [But I'm not.]

C111 Use *had* plus the past participle, either the regular or progressive form (past-perfect subjunctive), to indicate that what you are saying is contrary to past facts.

If only I *had been* at home! [But I was not.]

Even if he *had begged* me, I wouldn't have driven my car to the beach. [But he didn't.]

If I *had been listening* to the radio, I'd have won a prize. [But I was not.]

C112 Do not use *would have* (for *had* plus the past participle) to express a wish, a concession, or a condition that is contrary to past facts.

                    had
If the apartment ~~would have~~ been on the first floor, we would have taken it.

C113 When using the subjunctive after *as if* and *as though*, use *were* to express an action or state that is simultaneous with that of the main verb; use *had* plus the past participle to express an action or state that is prior to that of the main verb.

Simultaneous

Douglas
⎧ acts
⎪ acted
⎨ will act
⎪ has acted
⎩ had acted
⎫ as if he *were* owner of the place.

76

Prior

Douglas $\begin{cases} \text{acts} \\ \text{acted} \\ \text{will act} \\ \text{has acted} \\ \text{had acted} \end{cases}$ as if he *had been* owner of the place.

C114 Nowadays the present and present-perfect subjunctives are scarcely used. The indicative, the past and the past-perfect subjunctive, and helping verbs are used instead.

Instead of—	*Ordinarily use—*
If Karl *be* here, he will answer for me.	If Karl *is* here, he will answer for me. [Indicative.]
If Karl *have been* here, he will have left a note for us.	If Karl *has been* here, he will have left a note for us. [Indicative.]
	If Karl *had been* here, he would have left a note. [Past-perfect subjunctive.]

C115 When they carry the sense and do not sound awkward, helping verbs may be substituted for the subjunctive forms of C109-11 and C113.

Instead of—	*You may find—*
Even if you *were* to pay me, I would tell the truth.	Even if you *should pay* me, I would tell the truth.
If Tooky *were* here, he would prove that I caught that fish.	If Tooky *could be* here, he would prove that I caught that fish.
We are determined that no one *be admitted* who cannot speak persuasively on many subjects.	We are determined that no one *shall be admitted* who cannot speak persuasively on many subjects.
If you *played* [past subjunctive] your cards right, you might get Mr. Acton to equip the darkroom.	If you *should* [or *would*, depending on the meaning] *play* your cards right, you might get Mr. Acton to equip the darkroom.

C116 The tenses are the different forms that a verb takes to indicate the time of an action or state.

C117 In general, the present tense indicates that something is happening now.

I *eat* now.
I *am eating* now.
I *do eat* now.

C118 The present (indicative, chiefly) is used to express facts and truths that are independent of time.

Man's soul *is* immortal.
He said that blue and yellow *make* green.

C119 The present (indicative) is used to indicate habitual action that still continues.

He *takes* a nap in the afternoon.
Alison *is* always here by four o'clock.

C120 The present (indicative) is sometimes used for vividness in narratives about the past. Once introduced into a narrative, this present-for-past device must be kept until there is a reason within the narrative for changing to a past tense.

Booth *shoots* Lincoln and *leaps* to the stage.

C121 The present tense of all moods, and of the participle, gerund, and infinitive is frequently used with a future meaning.

When *does* this morning's mail *get* in?
Max's ship *sails* at midnight.
We *may*—we're not sure—*have* a meeting next Monday.
Someone said that we *might be asked* to repeat the performance.
I suggest that he *see* Mr. Carroll, who handles all such complaints.

C122 In general, the past tense (indicative) is used to indicate that something happened in the past and is no longer happening now.

I *came;* I *saw;* I *conquered.*

I *was hoping* to find a small sailboat for my youngest son.

The wailing *began* yesterday at sunset and *stopped* just a moment or two ago.

C123 The past (indicative), usually the progressive form, may indicate an action or state that was the background of another action or state in the past.

I *was swimming* alone when the shark attacked me.

C124 The past (indicative) may indicate past habitual action.

Moreland *ate* twice a day.

Moreland *used* to eat twice a day.

C125 The past subjunctive is used to express present and future time.

If you *were* interested, I would show you a quicker method of factoring.

If you *sang* the song with the same naturalness during the performance tomorrow, we should have a hit. But I'm afraid you will be a little tense.

C126 The future tense indicates that something will take place later.

The rest *will be sent* out later.

I *will phone* for a taxi this minute.

C127 The present perfect (indicative) indicates that something has taken place in the past but continues into the present or has consequences that continue into the present. Use the present perfect when you wish to stress a link between the present time and what happened in the past.

No one *has heard* from Bud since he went away.

The examinations *have begun.*

I *have been* ill for two months.

There *has been* a riot.

Obviously the war *has been* a sorry failure.	The war is definitely over, but the writer wishes to stress that it was recent and that its consequences are still present.

79

C128 The past perfect (indicative) indicates that an action or state took place prior to some other past action or state.

Father De Smet learned that the tribe *had retreated* farther west.

The fire *had been burning* briskly for an hour or more when we began to see some change in the glowing metal.

Mr. Kane *had* already *bought* his ticket before he went to the station.

C129 The past perfect (indicative) is used with *before* to indicate that an action or state that was begun in the past and that might, could, should, or would have been completed in the past was not completed.

He was interrupted before he *had finished* the story.

We were ready an hour before anyone *had arrived*.	The past perfect implies that people might, could, or should have arrived. If a mere statement of fact is wanted, the past should be used: *before anyone arrived*.

C130 The past may properly be used for the past perfect when it is not important to show that one action has preceded another.

Weeks was discharged because he washed the dishes too hastily.	Although the dishwashing preceded the discharging, the statement is clear without using the past perfect.
We changed our plans after we *got* the message.	Although receiving the message preceded the changing of plans, the statement is clear without the past perfect.

C131 The past should be used for the past perfect when the latter would detract from the thought of the sentence.

Men *heard* the news and leaped into the air for joy.	"Men *had heard* the news" would be distracting here. The writer wants to stress the sudden impact of the news and the men's almost simultaneous reaction to it.

80

C132 The future perfect is used to indicate that something will already have happened before something else will happen.

I *shall have finished* this typing before night [falls].
They *will have left* before you arrive.

C133 Sometimes the future perfect is used in a sentence to go with a future thought that is not expressed but merely implied.

If Tom has been here, he *will have left* a note.	Implied thought: as we *shall discover* later.
By now Grandmother Webster *will have arrived* at the farm.	Implied thought: as we *shall find* out later. (Here the future perfect also carries a connotation of *should* or *ought to have arrived.*)

C134 The future perfect is not much used in the United States today. For it are substituted the present, the future, or the present perfect.

Instead of—	*You may find—*
I *shall have finished* the typing before night.	I *shall finish* the typing before night.
Please telephone me as soon as you *will have heard.*	Please telephone me as soon as you *hear.*
	Please telephone me as soon as you *have heard.*

SEQUENCE OF TENSES

C135 The tense of verbals and subordinate predicate verbs frequently depends on the tense of the main verb.

C136 If the main verb is present, the subordinate verbs are usually present, present perfect, or future.

Jane *says* that tea *is* ready.	Both the saying and the being ready occur at the same time.
Buddy *will* not *talk* now, because he *is* afraid.	The talking and the being afraid occur at the same time. *Will* not *talk* is present here.

81

The examination *seems* easy because we *have studied* hard.	The studying preceded the examination; so the present perfect is used.
We *have* some fine indoor games ready, so that the rain *will* not *spoil* the children's fun.	The rain is a future possibility; so the future is used here.
[Exception:] The examination *seems* easy because we *studied* hard.	The rule is not ironclad. Here the past is used rather than the present perfect because the writer does not wish to present the studying as something recent or not yet over.
[Exception:] I *believe* that Columbus *discovered* America in 1492.	The rule is not ironclad. Here the sense simply demands the past rather than the present-perfect tense.

C137 If the main verb is past or past perfect, make the subordinate verbs past or past perfect if you can do so and still express your meaning fully and accurately.

Margate *said* that he *was* too busy to come and hear what you *might propose* at the meeting. So don't expect him.	*Was* indicates the same time as the main verb, *said.* And the past, *might propose,* is better than the present, *may propose,* after the past.
Margate *said* that he *would be* out of town and hence *could* not *attend* tomorrow's meeting. So don't expect him.	*Would* and *could* are better than *will* and *can* to express the proper time relation.
Whenever he *heard* the owl hoot, he *shuddered.*	*Hears* would be quite incorrect, as it would give no hint of the time relation of one act to the other.
Josue *could conquer* the city only after God *had come* to his aid.	At the time Josue was able to conquer the city, God's help had already been given.

82

[Exception:] Tavitt *ordered* that I *report* for KP.

The present, *report*, is called for, according to C109, after verbs of ordering, and so on. *Should report,* however, could also be used.

C138 Do not keep the sequence of tenses asked for in C137 if the dependent clause is intended to present something as usual, characteristic, or always true.

Did you *ask* when the eastbound train *comes* in?

I *have told* you that Nigel *studies* hard, *plays* hard, and *is making* good grades in school.

Junior *had* never *heard* that the earth *is* round.

C139 In a single sentence or in a series of sentences or paragraphs connected by one line of thought, do not change the verb time unless you have to.

[Wrong:] When first we meet him, he is lying on the cropped grass in front of the grandstand watching with an idle eye the afternoon scrimmage of the football team. His pose is altogether graceful and seems to imply relaxed power rather than lethargy or weakness. He *had* a good head, strong, with features cleanly but not sharply chiseled.

[Right:] When first we meet him, he is lying on the cropped grass in front of the grandstand watching with an idle eye the afternoon scrimmage of the football team. His pose is altogether graceful and seems to imply relaxed power rather than lethargy or weakness. He *has* a good head, strong, with features cleanly but not sharply chiseled.

[Right:] When first we met him, he was lying on the cropped grass in front of the grandstand watching with an idle eye the afternoon scrimmage of the football team. His pose was altogether graceful and seemed to imply relaxed power rather than lethargy or weakness. He *had* a good head, strong, with features cleanly but not sharply chiseled.

C140 Use the present participle if the action of the participle takes place at the same time as that of the predicate verb.

Working for thirty-six hours hand running, that single shift cleared the ways of three oil tankers.

Being a little uncomfortable even in my sleep, I was not able to get the rest I needed.

Leaving the parking lot, you will hand your ticket to the attendant.

I am without a care in the world, *sailing* along between the islands that wall off the sound.

C141   Use the present-perfect participle if the action of the participle is prior to the action of the predicate verb.

Having scuttled the clipper, Johannsen sat in the dory planning his next move.

Having been refused by every publisher in the city, Schmidt may buy his own printing press.

Having paced sixty feet from the shore, we came to the mound and began to dig feverishly.

C142   Use the past participle regardless of the time of the predicate verb.

Delighted with my job, I see no reason to change.

Wearied with waiting, the dog had curled up on a seat of the ferris wheel and gone to sleep.

Given half a chance, he will win the TV contest hands down.

Frightened by the deafening crash, she jumped from her chair and ran to the window.

C143   Use the present-perfect infinitive if the action of the infinitive is prior to that of the predicate verb. Use the present infinitive in all other cases.

He is said to *have died* of apoplexy while delivering a frenzied television commercial.

The doctor was reported to *have come* to Tranquillity Beach to study the effects on the human body of sand in picnic lunches.

I want to *leave* now.

I wanted to *leave* yesterday.

I had expected to *leave* tomorrow.

C144   Use the present or present-perfect gerund if the action of the gerund is prior to that of the predicate verb. Use the present gerund in all other cases.

Noble was accused of *having written* a ditty lampooning the dean.

84

Noble was accused of *writing* a ditty lampooning the dean.
"I have no intention of *budging*," said the immovable object.

TRANSITIVE VERBS AND OBJECTS

C145 A transitive verb is one that requires an object to complete its meaning.

The Ford▷—hit—▷Jimmy.   *Hit* is transitive; *Jimmy* is the object needed to complete the meaning of *hit*.

We▷— enjoy —▷music.   *Enjoy* is transitive; *music* is the object needed to complete the meaning of *enjoy*.

C146 The same verb may be transitive in one sentence and intransitive in another.

Jack▷— is dancing—▷ the minuet.
Jack▷— is dancing—↖ .

C147 A direct object is the noun or other substantive that completes the meaning of the verb and is directly governed by it.

The Ford hit *Jimmy*.   The Ford hit whom? Jimmy.

We enjoy *music*.   We enjoy what? Music.

I hate *lying*.   I hate what? Lying (gerund).

I like *to loaf*.   I like what? To loaf (infinitive).

I prefer *that you remain*.   I prefer what? That you remain (noun clause).

C148 A direct object may be compound.

We bought *caramels* and *liverwurst*.

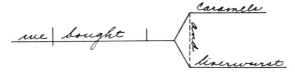

C149 In some sentences, some verbs—like *ask, teach, lead,* and *hear*—take two direct objects. (Do not confuse two direct objects with a compound object.)

You led *us* a merry *dance.*

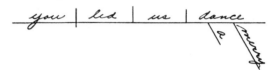

Ask *me* my *name.*

Hear *me* my *lessons.*

You can teach *yourself to swim.*

You made *me* go.

C150 In some sentences, some verbs—like *name, choose, elect, deem,* and *find*—take both a direct object and an objective complement.

C151 An objective complement is a noun, pronoun, or adjective (in the objective case) referring to the direct object and filling out the meaning of the verb.

We elected Dorothy *captain.*

86

My parents named me *Bottomley*.

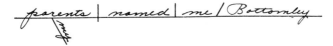

I find this paint *sticky*.

C152 Put a pronoun which is being used as a direct object in the objective case.

I rather like *him*.

Did I miss anyone? Yes, h̶e̶ and s̶h̶e̶. *him* *her*

I don't know w̶h̶o̶ I invited. *whom*

C153 Expressions like *I believe* and *do you suppose* complicate the use of the proper case of *who* or *whom*. Whenever in doubt, diagram the sentence and see where *who* or *whom* falls in the diagram.

This is the gentleman whom, I believe, you distrust.

Whom is the direct object of the verb *distrust*.

Who do you suppose ate the icing?

Who is the subject pronoun of the verb *ate*.

| I must find someone whom I can believe. | *Whom* is the direct object of the verb *can believe*. |

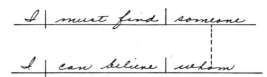

C154 The indirect object of a transitive verb names the person or thing that receives the direct object. In other words, the indirect object names the person or thing to, for, or toward whom an action is done.

Professor Trinkle gave *me* a retort.

I only told *Roddy* and *Allen* the time.

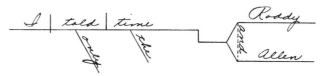

They handed *Jim* and *me* a bowl of watery soup.

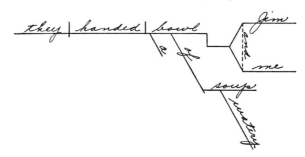

C155 Insert the preposition *to* or *for* before a likely object. If the insertion makes good sense, the chance is excellent that you have an indirect object.

| Father Burns brought Mother Holy Communion. | Insert *to* before *Mother*, and you make sense. *Mother* is the indirect object. |

A taxi brought Mother home.

Insert *to* before *Mother,* and you do not make good sense. *Mother* is not the indirect object in this sentence.

C156 Put a pronoun that is the indirect object in the objective case.

[Answering the question, "Did Ralph give anybody a bite?":] Not *me.*

INTRANSITIVE VERBS AND COMPLEMENTS

C157 An intransitive verb is a verb that does not have a direct object.

Who *is singing?*
The plot *thickens.*
My blood *boiled* when he told me to bring him his slippers.
The wind *is blowing.*

C158 Some verbs—like *be* and *seem*—cannot be used transitively; other verbs may be transitive in one sentence and intransitive in another.

[Transitive:] Jack▷—is dancing—▷the minuet.

[Intransitive:] Jack▷—is dancing—⌐.

C159 A linking verb is an intransitive verb that only connects its subject with another substantive or an adjective, which is in the nominative case.

Pete *is* president.

Is connects *Pete* with *president,* a noun in the nominative case.

89

You *seem* strange.   *Seem* connects *you* with
                                             strange, an adjective in the
                                             nominative case.

C160 A predicate complement is a substantive or an adjective
in the nominative case (*a*) that is used with a linking verb
or a verb in the passive voice and (*b*) that represents,
describes, or refers to the subject noun.

They are *brothers.*	Predicate noun.
That is *what I asked.*	Predicate noun clause.
The artist was really *she,* Charlotte Burns.	Predicate pronoun.
The iron is becoming *red.*	Predicate adjective.
Kurt was appointed *waterboy.*	Predicate noun after a passive predicate verb.

C161 Although pronouns that are used as predicate complements should be in the nominative case, an exception is
made for "It is *me,*" where *me* is accepted as correct.

C162 Say *feel bad, ill, well, good, right* (adjectives after linking
verb). Do not say *feel badly, rightly* (adverbs).

I don't feel ~~badly~~ *bad* about voting the Republican ticket.

After working all afternoon laying pipes, I had a swim that felt very
good indeed.

C163 Say *do well, badly* (adverbs), since *do* in the sense of *succeed* is not a linking verb. Do not say *do good, bad, nice.*

I did pretty ~~good~~ *well* in my examination.

This will do [succeed, fill the bill] very ~~nice.~~ *nicely*

C164 The following verbs are frequently used as linking verbs.

act [*in the sense of* pretend   bang (shut)
   to be] (stupid)   be (sure)
appear (strange)   become (wise)

90

break (free)
burn (blue)
burst [out] (singing)
continue (agreeable)
fall (dead *or* sick)
feel (bad)
flame (red)
get (sick)
go (mad)
go [on] (studying)
grow (ridiculous)
hold (true)
keep (honest)
lie [*in the sense of* remain] (quiet)
look (funny)
loom (large)

prove (worth while)
rank (fifth)
remain (puzzled)
rest (assured)
ring (true)
rise (triumphant)
run (true [to form])
seem (odd)
shine (golden)
show (cowardly [*adjective*])
smell (sweet)
sound (harsh)
stand (corrected)
stay (united)
take (sick)
taste (strong)
turn (white)

VERBS CONFUSED

C165 Do not confuse—

Lie—meaning to recline. (Intransitive.)

Present	Past	Past participle
lie	lay	lain

lie
People ~~lay~~ down when they're tired.

lay
The bicycle ~~laid~~ in the weeds for three days.

lain
I had scarcely ~~laid~~ down on my bed when the alarm rang.

Lay—meaning to put *something* down. (Transitive.)

Present	Past	Past participle
lay	laid	laid

lay
Now I ~~lie~~ me down to sleep.

laid
Hollings ~~lay~~ his big hand on my rifle.

laid
Christ has ~~lain~~ down His life for His friends.

91

C166 Do not confuse—

Sit—meaning to rest upon the haunches. (Intransitive.)

Present	*Past*	*Past participle*
sit	sat	sat

sit

Don't ~~set~~ in that chair; that's the cat's.

sat

Imperturbable Jones has ~~set~~ so long in front of Cornby's Drugstore that people think that he and the wooden Indian are related.

sat

Kings have ~~set~~ on that bench you are polishing your boots on, soldier.

sat

[Exceptional, transitive use:] Ichabod ~~set~~ his horse like a loose-jointed scarecrow athwart a great beer barrel.

sat

[Exceptional, transitive use:] Mr. Northrup ~~set~~ himself down and chatted for an hour.

Set—meaning to put, place, or fix *something*. (Transitive.)

Present	*Past*	*Past participle*
set	set	set

Gubbins had *set* a pail of water on the lowest step to catch a thief but caught his own astonished father.

Set the coffeepot on the stove, Sam.

Set your watches to agree with mine; we attack in exactly six minutes.

Set—meaning chiefly to sit on eggs as does a fowl. (Intransitive.)

Present	*Past*	*Past participle*
set	set	set

set

Hens will ~~sit~~ on darning eggs or light bulbs.

C167 Do not confuse—

Hang—meaning to suspend or be suspended (but preferably not used of putting to death by suspending).

Present	*Past*	*Past participle*
hang	hung	hung

Hang your clothes on a hickory limb; the water's fine.

hung
We ~~hanged~~ our clothes on a hickory limb but found crocodiles in the water.

hung
You should have ~~hanged~~ your clothes on a higher limb where the goat couldn't have reached them.

hung
That suit ~~hanged~~ on Longjohn like a slack tepee around a tent pole.

Hang—meaning to put to death by suspending.

Present	Past	Past participle
hang	hanged	hanged

Hang your friend from a hickory limb; he used up all the hot water.

hanged
Tommers was ~~hung~~ from a hickory limb for confusing other ranchers' brands with his own.

hanged
Before they ~~hung~~ him, they put Edmund Campion through a mock trial whose verdict was set before its date.

C168 Do not confuse—

Rise—meaning to ascend, to get up, or to emerge. (Intransitive.)

Present	Past	Past participle
rise	rose	risen

rose
The sun ~~raised~~ at about four-thirty that morning.

rise
Come on, marine; ~~raise~~ and shine!

rising
There we saw peak ~~raising~~ above peak sharply, till the last seemed a pinnacle upon which a man could never stand—though an angel might dance there.

risen
We had ~~raised~~ early, for fish greet the dawn hungry.
You could almost see the dough *rising* in the pan.

Raise—meaning to make something rise. (Transitive.)

Present	Past	Past participle
raise	raised	raised

93

The sun had ~~risen~~ *raised* itself for a look over the rim of the world.

Our Lord ~~rose~~ *raised* Lazarus from the tomb.

Here's a story that may ~~rise~~ *raise* a laugh.

C169 Do not confuse—

Lose—meaning to fail to keep, to suffer defeat.

Present	Past	Past participle
lose	lost	lost

I am afraid you are going to ~~loose~~ *lose* a hubcap.

Leoville should ~~loose~~ *lose* to Damien by six points.

Loose and *loosen*—meaning to free, to untie, to relax.

Present	Past	Past participle
loose	loosed	loosed
loosen	loosened	loosened

~~Lose~~ *Loose* the prisoners and let them go.

~~Losen~~ *Loosen* the girth on the black stallion.

C170 Do not confuse—

Teach—meaning to attempt to cause someone to learn.

Miss McBride ~~learned~~ *taught* us how to square dance.

Christ had a difficult time ~~learning~~ *teaching* the apostles.

Learn—meaning to acquire knowledge or skill.

We *learn* that Richelieu had some good points.
Why should a boy *learn* to cook?

C171 Do not confuse—

Effect—meaning to bring about or cause something.

Present	Past	Past participle
effect	effected	effected

94

effected
My white mouse, Squeaky, has ~~affected~~ his escape.

effect
If McCoy will keep his temper, we can ~~affect~~ a compromise.

Affect—meaning to influence, to move the emotions; to pretend or feign something.

Present	Past	Past participle
affect	affected	affected

affected
Too much sun has ~~effected~~ poor Maddern's brain.

affected
All the coarse louts in the crowd were visibly ~~effected~~ by the sentimental movie.

affect
Mr. Pringle tried to ~~effect~~ surprise; but he was a poor actor, and so he deceived nobody.

C172 These are the principal parts of *let* and *leave*:

Present	Past	Past participle
let	let	let
leave	left	left

C173 Use *let*, not *leave*, with *be*.

Let
~~Leave~~ me be.

C174 Use *let*, not *leave*, in the sense of *permit*.

Let
~~Leave~~ me tell you.

Let
~~Leave~~ them enter.

Let
~~Leave~~ us know if there are any changes.

C175 Use *let*, not *leave*, to give a sense of exhortation to a verb.

Let
~~Leave~~ us go to the matinee.

Let
~~Leave~~ us answer tyranny with a smile.

95

C176 Use *leave,* not *let,* in the sense of *abandon, forget.*

left
I must have ~~let~~ the keys in the car.

left
Who ~~let~~ his ice cream on top of the stove?

C177 Ordinarily use either *let* or *leave* with *alone.*

> *Let* me *alone.*
> *Leave* me *alone.*

[Exception:] Two men, *let alone* one, would be unable to budge him if he fell down.

Only *let alone* may be used in this peculiar, idiomatic sense of *not to mention.*

Case

C178 Case is the form of a substantive that indicates its sense relation to other words in a sentence. The nominative shows that the substantive is the subject or predicate complement of a verb; the objective, that it is the object of some other word; and so on.

C179 There are three cases in English, the nominative, the possessive, and the objective.

C180 Nouns in English have a distinctive form only for the possessive case. Sense and position indicate the nominative and objective relationships.

C181 Some pronouns have distinctive forms for all three cases.

Nominative	I	we
Possessive	my	our
Objective	me	us

Possessive of nouns and pronouns

THE POSSESSIVE CASE

C182 If a noun or pronoun denotes ownership, origin, source, right, responsibility, and so on, put it in the possessive case.

Mr. Witherspoon's car is here.	The possessive here denotes ownership.
Michael's jokes are dull.	Michael does not strictly own the jokes, but he tells them or originates them.
Hilda's father delights in doing the unexpected.	In the strict sense Hilda does not own her father, and yet he does belong to her.
This is all *Hillman's* fault.	In the strict sense Hillman does not possess the fault; and yet it does belong to him, for he is responsible for it.

C183 The possessive case is an adjective case, and any substantive in the possessive case is ordinarily used as an adjective.

This is all *Hillman's* fault.

THE *of* POSSESSIVE[20]

C184 *Of* followed by a noun or pronoun is frequently used to show ownership.

The clamor *of the alarm* finally awakened them.	The alarm's clamor.
The Mohicans tortured the brother *of Andaiuga*.	Andaiuga's brother.
That old Model T *of Henry's* should be laid to rest in a junk yard.	Henry's old Model T.

---

[20] This is commonly called the possessive genitive.

C185 When the owner is a living thing, the *of* possessive is used where it sounds better or is clearer than the ordinary possessive.

For the life *of me*, I could not think of the answer [rather than *for my life*].

C186 A combination of the *of* possessive and the ordinary possessive is very common, especially when the object possessed is modified by a demonstrative. This combination is known as the double possessive. Notice that in this instance a noun that is possessive in form does not function as an adjective but as a substantive.

That old hat *of Father's* might fit you.	*Father's*, though possessive in form, is a substantive, the object of *of*.

He is a friend *of mine.*
Those remarks *of Colby's* have cost us a holiday.
A cousin *of the Joneses'* painted that—er—picture.

C187 The *of* possessive is the more common form when the owner is not a living thing.

[Common:] the back *of the chair*
[Less common:] the *chair's* back

[Common:] the pleasure *of reading*
[Unusual, because awkward and ambiguous:] *reading's* pleasure

[Common:] the call *of the sea*
[Unusual, because awkward:] the *sea's* call

[Common:] the end *of the line*
[Unusual, because awkward:] the *line's* end

C188 Inanimate objects that are personified use the possessive case and the *of* possessive with equal ease.

the *wind's* murmur
the murmur *of the wind*

death's cold fingers
the cold fingers *of death*

the *rose's* breath
the breath *of the rose*

C189 The possessive case is more common than the *of* possessive with the following expressions and some others.

the law's delay	a three-days' drive
for pity's sake	the year's events
two-hours' walk	six-months' interest
a stone's throw	the world's work
a day's work	fifty-cents' worth
a month's notice	a dollar's worth

Some of the expressions above consist of a numeral plus a measure of time, like *a two-hours' walk.* These expressions may be written in three ways:

a two-hours' walk   a two-hour's walk   a two-hours walk

Many authors and editors prefer *a two-hour* walk, which is classical English.

When the numeral in these expressions is *one* or less than one, they are written thus: *a one-hour's walk, a half-hour's walk.* (Here *'s* is not required, but it is recommended.)

Nominative absolutes

C190 A nominative absolute is a peculiar kind of phrase related to the rest of the sentence in sense but not in grammar and made up of a noun or pronoun plus a participle or a participial phrase.

Classes having been dismissed, we found time heavy on our hands.

C191 Elliptical nominative absolutes, with the participle omitted but understood, are rather common.

(kneeling)
An acolyte ʌ at his feet, the priest was saying Mass.

(being)
The game ʌ over, Marty collapsed in the locker room.

C192 Put the "subject" pronoun of a nominative absolute in the nominative case.

He
~~Him~~ absent, there was no one to play the piccolo.

Direct address

C193 A noun in direct address is a noun used to address someone or something, or to attract his attention. A noun in direct address is related to the rest of the sentence in sense but not in grammar; that is, it is not subject noun, object, modifier, and so on.

Drop that, *brother!*
Pulasko, where's your story?
Remember, *sister dear,* the times I've done the dishes for you.
Sorry, *friend,* you'll just have to look for the gold by yourself.

C194 Words that are usually adjectives may be used as nouns in direct address.

Turn on the ignition, *stupid.*
Where, my *sweet,* did you hide my pipe?
Those are my feet you're stepping on, *graceful.*
Well, *speedy,* what took you so long?

Appositives

C195 An appositive is a word, phrase, or clause used only to explain another substantive and meaning practically the same thing.

Our neighbors, the *Tuttles,* raise vultures.	The head word[21] is *neighbors;* the appositive noun, explaining *neighbors,* is *Tuttles.*
Bwana has gone with my brother, the witch *doctor.*	The head word is *brother;* the appositive noun, explaining *brother,* is *doctor.*

---

[21] For convenience, the noun that is explained by an appositive noun is called "head word."

Whom did you forget—*me?*	The head word is *whom;* the appositive pronoun, explaining *whom,* is *me.*
His favorite sport, *hunting,* cost him his life.	The head word is *sport;* the appositive gerund, explaining *sport,* is *hunting.*
My job, *to sing two songs a night,* is pleasant.	The head word is *job;* the appositive infinitive phrase, explaining *job,* is *to sing two songs a night.*
The fact *that you are here* proves your innocence.	The head word is *fact;* the appositive clause, explaining *fact,* is *that you are here.*

C196 Except for the cases in C197, put appositive substantives into the same case as the head word.[22]

This is Stoat's [possessive], the catcher's [possessive], expensive new chest protector.

Whose [possessive] is this—yours [possessive]?

Whom [objective] did you forget—me [objective]?

C197 Do not use the possessive case for both head word and appositive when (*a*) agreement would sound awkward or (*b*) head word and appositive are treated as a unit.

The next two meetings will be held at *Smith's,* the best *host* among us.	*Host's* would sound awkward.
I bought this pith helmet at *Carlton* the *Hatter's.*	*Carlton the Hatter's* is the trade name used by the company; therefore it is considered a unit.
Have you seen *Brando* the *Great's* new trick—the one in which he pulls a hat out of a rabbit?	*Brando the Great's* is a unit.

---

[22] For convenience, the noun that is explained by an appositive noun is called "head word."

C198 Some appositives are introduced by *or, namely,* and similar expressions.

A pirogue, or *dugout,* is the main means of transportation on some bayous.

Dugout is used to explain *pirogue* and means practically the same thing; therefore it is clearly an appositive.

A pirogue or a *raft* was what we needed.

Raft does not explain *pirogue* or mean the same thing; therefore it is clearly not an appositive.

There is only one person for whom I would vote; namely, my *uncle.*

Uncle explains *person* and in this sentence means the same thing; therefore it is clearly an appositive.

C199 An appositive may be accompanied by objects, modifiers, and other words closely associated with it.

His favorite sport, *hunting lost documents,* nearly cost him his life.

The whole noun phrase, *hunting lost documents,* is the appositive.

RESTRICTIVE AND NONRESTRICTIVE APPOSITIVES

C200 Appositives are restrictive when the writer uses them as necessary to the sense or identity of the head word.

The very fact *that you are here* proves that you did not telephone me from Washington just now.

Suppose that you have not told the reader previously what fact you are talking about; *that you are here* is necessary to the sense. Therefore you want *that you are here* joined very closely to the head word. The noun clause is restrictive.

At that moment, someone at the back of the hall raised the cry *"Down with Carrigan!"*

Suppose that you have not previously told the reader what the cry was; the sense would be incomplete without *down with Carrigan.* So you want *down with Carrigan* joined very closely to the head word. The noun phrase, therefore, is restrictive.

My cousin *John Keating* is brighter than all the rest of my cousins put together.

Suppose that you have several cousins and you want the reader to know that none of the others is meant but only John Keating. Then you must join *John Keating* very closely to the head word *cousin.* In other words, the noun *John Keating* is restrictive.

C201 Appositives are nonrestrictive when the writer joins them loosely to the head word merely as added information, as a point worth bringing in but not very necessary to the thought.

Let me tell you how lucky is your presence here at this moment. This fact, *that you are here,* proves that you did not telephone me from Washington just now.

Suppose that you have already told the reader what fact you mean and only add *that you are here* for emphasis and unmistakable clearness or even just for better rhythm. Then you want *that you are here* joined only loosely to the head word. In this case the noun clause is nonrestrictive.

This cry, *"Down with Carrigan!"* was taken up first by one throat, then by another, until it swelled into a hoarse, frightening chant.

Suppose that you have told what the cry was in an earlier sentence (not given here). Here you mention it only to remind the reader what it was and to emphasize it. So you do not want *down with Carrigan* joined very closely to the head word. The noun phrase is just added information and hence nonrestrictive.

A young cousin of mine, *John Keating*, stumbled upon the hide-out quite by accident.

Suppose that you add the information that your cousin is named John Keating simply because the addition might please a reader who knows him or might brighten the sentence by adding a bit of identification. Then you do not want *John Keating* joined very closely to the head word *cousin*. The noun *John Keating* is nonrestrictive.

C202 Often context or circumstances force a writer to use an appositive restrictively.

[If there has been no previous mention of the word *garrison*, then it must be restrictive in this sentence:] The word *garrison* does not sound Anglo-Saxon to me.

[If *novelist* and *statesman* were nonrestrictive in this sentence, the result would be nonsense:] I believe you are talking about Churchill the *novelist* rather than Churchill the *statesman*.

C203 Use this test: Read the sentence without the appositive. If the sentence still says essentially what you want it to, the appositive is nonrestrictive. If the sentence does not say what you want it to but something else, the appositive is restrictive.

The butcher, Abell Miller, won't give us any credit.

[Without the appositive:] The butcher won't give us any credit.

Suppose that you are chiefly interested in saying that the butcher cut off your credit. You add *Abell Miller* not from need but as an extra. The sense does not change. The appositive is nonrestrictive.

Dominic was very fond of the expression "on the nose."

[Without the appositive:] Dominic was very fond of the expression.

Suppose that you chiefly intend to tell which expression Dominic was fond of. The omission changes the sense entirely. The appositive *on the nose* is clearly restrictive.

104

I dropped the rescue note from the window on the chance that someone might be passing below.

[Without the appositive:] I dropped the rescue note from the window on the chance.

Suppose that you chiefly wish to state what it was that made you drop the rescue note from the window. The omission changes the sense entirely and leaves the sentence puzzling and incomplete. The appositive noun clause *that someone might be passing below* is clearly restrictive.

Pronoun use

PRONOUNS IN GENERAL

C204 A pronoun is a word that is used in place of a noun or other substantive.

Crabtree was expected to object, but *he* didn't.

C205 Do not use *same* as a pronoun unless you wish to stress identity or similarity.

I have received your letter and thank you for ~~same~~ *it*.

Here there is no reason to stress identity. *It* carries the full meaning perfectly.

Water seeks its own level. The *same*, I think, may be said of mean characters.

Here there is reason to stress identity or similarity.

C206 Do not insert immediately after a subject noun a subject pronoun meaning exactly the same thing.[23]

Jules ~~he~~ wants to be a chemical engineer.
Willa Cather and Edna Ferber ~~they~~ are American novelists.

C207 Do not say *let's us*, which is the same as saying *let us us*.

~~Let's us~~ *Let us* be very careful in using contractions.

---

[23] Not affected by this rule are those rare constructions in dialogue in which a person is represented as thinking over names and then breaking off into a statement about them. Such a construction requires a dash; for example, "Willa Cather and Edna Ferber—they were American novelists, weren't they?"

C208 Politeness usually requires that the personal pronouns *I* and *we* be placed last in a compound subject.

Mary and I [*not* I and Mary] have a suggestion.

PRONOUN SUBJECTS, OBJECTS, AND COMPLEMENTS

C209 Put the subject pronoun of a predicate verb in the nominative case.

He   she
~~Him~~ and ~~her~~ will come at eight.

                                                                      they
Would Charles or his brother take a catfish off a hook? Not ~~them~~.

C210 Put the "subject" pronoun of a nominative absolute in the nominative case.

He
~~Him~~ absent, there was no one to play the piccolo.

They being what they are, I'm afraid that you will simply have to make allowances for them.

C211 Put the subject pronoun of an infinitive in the objective case.

The judges expected *him* to be nervous.

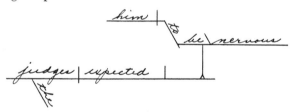

For *her* to object is unusual.

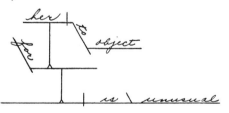

C212 When a word in the possessive form accompanies a gerund, treat that word as a simple adjective. In cases where the possessive form cannot be used, put the word in the objective case and treat it as the subject of the gerund. (See C369.)

Hal's coming home was a surprise.

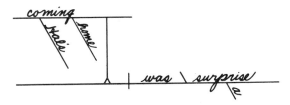

There is no doubt about *his* being elected.

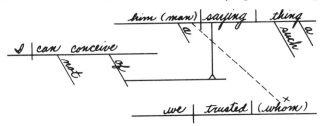

I can't conceive of *him,* a man we trusted, saying such a thing.

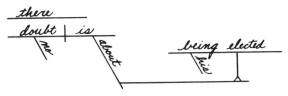

C213 Put the predicate pronoun of a predicate verb in the nominative case.

It is *I.*[24]

This should be *he.*

this | should be \ he

---

[24] The expression "It is *me*" is now accepted as correct usage. "It is *I*" is better suited to a formal context.

C214 Put the predicate pronoun of an infinitive in the nominative case if a nominative precedes the infinitive; put it in the objective case if an objective precedes the infinitive.

It [nominative] seemed to be *he* [nominative].

The assistant principal took him [objective, subject of the infinitive] to be *me* [objective].

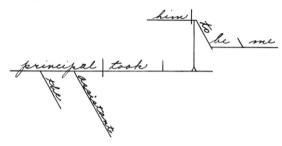

C215 Put a pronoun used as direct object of a predicate verb or of a verbal in the objective case.

Did I miss anyone? Yes, ~~he~~ *him* and ~~she~~ *her*.

Whom
~~Who~~ did you invite?

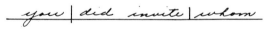

C216 Expressions like *I believe* and *do you suppose* complicate sentences containing *who* or *whom* and make it difficult to apply C215. Whenever you are in doubt, mentally diagram the sentence and see where *who* or *whom* falls in the diagram.

This is the gentleman *whom,* I believe, you distrust.

Whom is the direct object of the verb *distrust.*

Who do you suppose ate the icing?

Who is the subject pronoun of the verb *ate.*

I must find someone *whom* I can believe.

Whom is the direct object of the verb *can believe.*

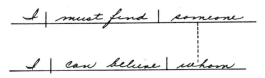

C217 Put a pronoun that is the indirect object in the objective case.

Generous though he usually is, Ralph did not give *me* a bite of the olive.

[Answering the question, "Did Ralph give anybody a bite?":] Not *me.*

C218 Put the object pronoun of a preposition in the objective case.

me
Between you and ~~I~~, I think Marty's personality is his new Lincoln.

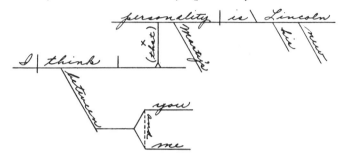

whom
I'm sure I gave the carbolic acid to someone. Now to ~~who~~?

C219 In order to use the right case of a personal pronoun after *than* or *as*, mentally complete the elliptical sentence.

Tush! You are much stronger than *he* [is strong].
I'd trust Marcus sooner than [I'd trust] *her*.
I'd trust Marcus sooner than *she* [would trust Marcus].
There is no other so strong as *he* [is].

PRONOUNS AND ANTECEDENTS

C220 The noun whose place a pronoun takes is called the antecedent of the pronoun.

Helen said she would make   *Helen* is the antecedent of *she*.
ham sandwiches.

C221 Sometimes a pronoun takes the place of another pronoun. The latter is then called the intermediate antecedent.

Each of the boys has his own   *Each* is the intermediate an-
way of making a bed.   tecedent of *his*.

C222 Except for the instances discussed in C223, make sure that every pronoun and possessive adjective has an antecedent.

Lack of antecedents

I want to tell you about a little experience I had while driving from Albuquerque to Santa Fe last week. They don't have culverts to carry off rain under the road. They just dip, and rain rushes down from the hills and over the road, usually leaving a lot of sand and gravel on them. We were driving too fast, I'll admit, when he shouted, "Look out! There's a dip." Well, the other didn't see the dip in time; and so it plowed right into the sand, skidded off the road, and stopped on the brink of a ravine some twenty feet deep. It is certainly dangerous, and I'll tell you it taught us a lesson.

Proper use of antecedents

I want to tell you about a little experience I had while driving from Albuquerque to Santa Fe last week. There are no culverts to carry off rain under the road. The highway just dips, and rain rushes down from the hills and over the road, usually leaving a lot of sand and gravel in the depressions. My companions and I were driving too fast, I'll admit, when one of them— not the driver—shouted, "Look out! There's a dip." Well, the driver didn't see the dip in time; and so the car plowed right into the sand, skidded off the road, and stopped on the brink of a ravine some twenty feet deep. Driving fast, especially over such treacherous roads, is certainly dangerous; and I'll tell you it taught us a lesson.

C223 In some expressions it is impossible and undesirable to give a definite antecedent for a pronoun. This, for instance, is true with the interrogative pronouns, the indefinite pronouns, and with *they* or *we* when the pronoun means "people in general," or *one* when it means "a man" or "a person."

I say, *somebody* knocked.

The antecedent must be kept indefinite until it is disclosed who did knock.

Who is behind you?

It is impossible to give the antecedent of *who*—at least until the person being questioned answers.

[Right:] *It* is raining.	This is impersonal *it,* an idiomatic use. No antecedent can be named.
[Wrong:] *It* explains radar in this book.	*It* lacks an antecedent, and there is no reason for the construction. Say "This book explains radar."
[Wrong:] *It* says in the paper that the game was rained out.	Say "The paper says."
[Right:] *We* are all inclined to like people who like us.	*We* needs no antecedent here, because it means "people in general."
[Right:] *One* does not notice the rapid calculations the eye makes when one is guiding a bulky automobile through close-packed traffic.	*One* means "a man" or "a person" here; hence no antecedent is needed.
[Wrong:] A pronoun is *one* that takes the place of a noun.	*One* should have a clear antecedent here, or it should be replaced by *a word.*
[Right:] *He* who prays is [*They* who pray are] certainly blessed.	*He* and *they* need no antecedent here, for the pronouns are the equivalent of "any person" or "people in general."
[Wrong:] I went down to the newspaper, and *he* gave me my name on a slug of type.	*He* should have an antecedent in an earlier sentence.

C224 *You* is quite commonly used in the sense of "people in general," but it is so frequently confusing that it should be avoided in this sense as far as it can be without considerable awkwardness.

Vague reference

"That old pinchbeak, Mrs. Snoop, and the other two neighborhood busybodies,

Clear reference

"That old pinchbeak, Mrs. Snoop, and the other two neighborhood busybodies,

112

Miss Small and Miss Prim, caught us just as we were about to leave."

"I'll bet she told you off about teasing her old cat."

"Yes. Well, you know what I told her? I told her if she didn't stop scratching my dog when she's asleep and harming nobody, I'd take her to the quarry pond and drown her in a sack."

"The old cat!"

"She is. She's an old cat."

Miss Small and Miss Prim, caught Johnny and me just as we were about to leave."

"I'll bet Mrs. Snoop told you two off about teasing her old cat."

"Yes. Well, you know what I told her? I told her that if her cat didn't stop scratching my dog when the dog is asleep and harming nobody, I'd take the cat to the quarry pond and drown her in a sack."

"Mrs. Snoop is an old cat herself."

"She is. She's an old cat."

C225 If a pronoun might cause confusion, do one of these things:

A Put the pronoun so close to its antecedent that the reader must see without any trouble that the two go together.

B Repeat the antecedent or use another noun.

C Avoid the antecedent-pronoun arrangement altogether.

[Wrong:] On my last visit to Seaux, before it was bombed off the map, I saw a thing that moved me very much. *It* was a little town in the South of France, hardly more than a village. *It* moved me so deeply because *it* was unexpected and at the same time thoroughly American.

It is not immediately clear whether *it* refers to Seaux or to the thing that moved the writer so much.

[Correction by moving antecedents and pronouns closer together:] I remember my last visit to *Seaux* before it was bombed off the map. *It* was a little town in the South of France, hardly more than a village. My recollection is vivid because while I was there I saw a *thing* that moved me very much. *It* moved me so deeply because it was unexpected and at the same time thoroughly American.

113

[Correction by repeating the antecedent or using another noun:] On my last visit to Seaux, before it was bombed off the map, I saw a thing that moved me very much. *Seaux* was a little town in the South of France, hardly more than a village. The *incident* moved me so deeply because it was unexpected and at the same time thoroughly American.

[Correction by rewriting so as to avoid the antecedent-pronoun arrangement:] On my last visit to Seaux (until it was bombed off the map, Seaux was a little town in the South of France, hardly more than a village), I saw a thing that moved me very much. *I was moved* so deeply because what happened was unexpected and at the same time thoroughly American.

C226　The case of a pronoun depends on how the pronoun is used in its own clause or sentence.

We met an Eskimo ~~whom~~ *who* had been converted by Father Buliard.

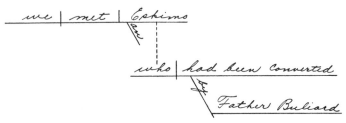

The Eskimo *whom* we met had been converted by Father Buliard.

C227　Make a pronoun agree with its antecedent in person, number, and gender.

Jim [second-person antecedent], you [second person] put those books behind you [second person].

My fellow *officers* and *I* [plural antecedents (*I* is an intermediate antecedent)] promise that we [plural] will give safe-conduct to any messenger sent to us [plural].

The *tree* [neuter antecedent], strong as it [neuter] looked, splintered as it [neuter] fell.

C228　When the antecedent is the context or situation, make the pronoun third person, singular number, neuter gender.

It's Anna coming up the stairs, isn't *it?*

It was another magazine salesman at the door.

114

C229 Use a singular pronoun with a singular collective noun, unless the group is clearly acting as separate individuals.

its
The *team* lost ~~their~~ second game through sheer nervousness.

their
The *team* were either standing, kneeling, or lying at ~~its~~ ease in the end zone.

C230 Use a singular pronoun when the antecedent is two or more singular nouns or pronouns joined by *or, nor, either . . . or, neither . . . nor,* or other disjunctives.

his
Have you no pen? *Joe or Ted* will lend you ~~theirs~~.

hers
Whose hat is this? *Neither Lou nor Meg* left ~~theirs~~.

C231 Use a plural pronoun when the antecedent is made up of a plural and a singular word.

My *brothers* and *I* have *our* quarrels, but *we* get along.

If *Mary* and her *friends* come in after school to make fudge, tell *them* not to use all the sugar.

C232 When an antecedent is made up of words in the first and the second or third persons, put the pronoun in the first person.

You, your *sister,* and *I* are to wait for *our* group captain on the corner of Washington and Beloit.

You and *I* are to wait for *our* group captain on the corner of Washington and Beloit.

My *teammates* and *I* met *our* match at bowling last night; *we* lost.

C233 When an antecedent is made up of words in the second and third persons, put the pronoun in the second person.

You and *Clifford* ought to wait for *your* group captain on the corner of Washington and Beloit.

You and your *teammates* certainly met *your* match at bowling last night; *you* lost.

C234 When agreement is complicated by an *of* expression (*the number of, best of, one of,* and so on), make sure that you

115

select the right antecedent according to the meaning you wish to convey.

The only one of his stories that *was* amusing was a tale of three men locked in an elevator.	*One* is the antecedent, not *stories,* since all of the stories but one were dull.
One of the people who *were* present was a Don Q.	*People* is the antecedent, not *one.*
This was the best of the stories that *were* told.	*Stories* is the antecedent, not *best* or *this.*
The number of members, *which runs* [or *who run*] into the thousands, surprises me.	Either *number* or *members* may be the antecedent.
The number of members who *were* absent was truly deplorable.	*Members* is the antecedent, not *number.*

C235 Except for the cases in C236, make a pronoun agree in person, number, and gender with an indefinite pronoun that is the (intermediate) antecedent.

As for schedule cards, *all* of us lost *ours.*
I remembered my lines, but *several* forgot *theirs.*
Does *anyone* want to buy *his* ticket now?
Someone left *her* earrings at our house.

C236 *Everybody* and *everyone,* though taking a singular verb, are usually referred to by *they.*

When I came up out of the dark cellar, everybody was laughing at me; but even so I was glad to see *them.*

The candidate made an excellent impression on everyone, and *they* cheered him wildly.

C237 When the indefinite pronoun *one* is the (intermediate) antecedent, put the pronoun in the third person, singular number.

[Wrong:] One does *their* [or *your*] best in life by serving God.
[Right:] One does *one's* best in life by serving God.
[Right:] One does *his* best in life by serving God.

C238 Put a pronoun in the third person singular when its antecedent is modified by a singular indefinite adjective. *Each* and *every*, however, are referred to by *their* (see C236).

Neither one looks like *his* father.

If *another* man throws *his* hat into the ring, the campaign should be a lively one.

A gentleman, according to Cardinal Newman, strives to put *every* person at *their* ease.

Each truck and *each* automobile and trailer must have *their* license.

PERSONAL-PRONOUN USE

C239 Do not write *theres* or *there's* for *theirs*.

The money is *theirs*, belongs to them.

There's [there is] food enough for everybody. Please take your time.

These must be friends of ~~theres~~ *theirs*.

C240 Do not write *it's* or *its'* for *its*.

What a pretty kitten! What's ~~it's~~ *its* name?

DEMONSTRATIVE-PRONOUN USE

C241 Do not use *them* where you should use a demonstrative.

[Housewife, pointing to the cheapest grapefruit on the counter:]

"I'll take a dozen of ~~them~~ *those*."

~~Them~~ *Those* are just the words I expected to hear, Clarence.

C242 Do not say *this here*, *that there*, *these here*, and *those there*.

These ~~here~~ will fit, but those ~~there~~ will not.

C243 If you insert words between the demonstrative and *here* or *there*, the expression can stand in good writing but

117

should not be used unless the rhythm or some other quality of the sentence will be helped.

"Now *these melons here,*" said Mr. Grover, leading me down the row of exhibits, "are about the size of a healthy California grape."

Self-PRONOUN USE

C244 Do not use a *self*-pronoun where a personal pronoun can carry the full meaning without sounding awkward.

[Wrong:] John and *myself* were here at seven-thirty.
[Right:] John and *I* were here at seven-thirty.

[Wrong:] Robert gave the old bicycle to my brother and *myself.*
[Right:] Robert gave the old bicycle to my brother and *me.*

[Wrong:] *Ourselves* and the others made twenty people.
[Right:] *We* and the others made twenty people.

[Right:] There goes Careless Smith hurting *himself* again.	If you used the personal pronoun here, you would change the meaning of the sentence to something else.
[Right:] Finally the guard left us to *ourselves.*	*Left us to us* would sound strange indeed.
[Right:] They are quite able to get along by *themselves.*	*By them* would sound strange and mean nothing.

C245 Do not write *ourselfs* for *ourselves, hisself* for *himself,* or *theirselves* for *themselves.*

We are proud of *ourselfs.* ~~*ourselfs*~~ *ourselves*

I think he hurt ~~hisself~~ badly. *himself*

I say let them take care of ~~theirselves~~. *themselves*

RELATIVE-PRONOUN USE

C246 The relative pronouns are used only to introduce (dependent) adjective clauses.

118

I know the girl *whom* you mean.

Whom you mean is a dependent adjective clause modifying the noun *girl* in the independent clause.

We found the weapon *that* he probably used.

That he probably used is an adjective clause modifying *weapon.*

The newspaper account, *which* I read last night, didn't give his name.

Which I read last night is an adjective clause modifying *account.*

C247 A relative pronoun refers to an antecedent in another clause. This fact makes a relative pronoun and its adjective clause easy to distinguish from (*a*) an interrogative or indefinite pronoun or adjective and its noun clause, (*b*) the demonstrative-pronoun and demonstrative-adjective *that,* and (*c*) the conjunction *that.*[25]

I know the *girl whom* you mean.

Whom is a relative pronoun. It has an antecedent, the noun *girl,* in the independent clause of the sentence.

I know *whom* you mean.

Whom is not a relative pronoun. It does not have an antecedent in the independent clause.

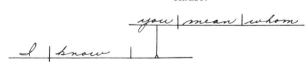

---

[25] A relative pronoun sometimes has as its antecedent the whole idea expressed in the independent clause; for example, "She sang badly, which made the maestro wince." But it is difficult to use this construction without awkwardness and confusion. Avoid it until you are a professional writer.

Here are the *blueprints that* you were looking for.

That is a relative pronoun. It has an antecedent in the independent clause: *blueprints.* So the dependent clause is an adjective clause.

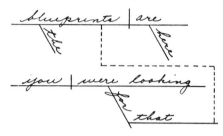

I was looking for the blueprints when I found *that* on the floor.

That is not a relative pronoun. It has no antecedent in the independent clause.

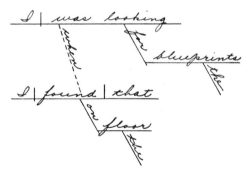

I was looking for something else when I found *that* blueprint on the floor.

That is not a relative pronoun. It has no antecedent in the independent clause.

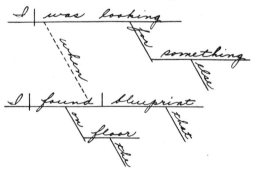

I knew *that* you were looking for the blueprints.

That is not a relative pronoun. It has no antecedent in the other clause (the independent clause).

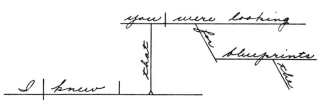

C248 For the sake of clarity, *that* is usually preferred to *which* in restrictive adjective clauses; *which* is preferred to *that* in nonrestrictive adjective clauses. (If, however, awkwardness results, simply ignore this rule and use whichever word seems best.)

[Restrictive:] The gun *that* I sold is very different from the gun *that* you sold.

[Nonrestrictive:] The gun, *which,* by the way, I sold the other day, had become an object of police investigation.

C249 The case of the relative pronoun does not depend on the case of the antecedent but is determined by the way the relative is used in its own clause.

We met an Eskimo ~~whom~~ *who* had been converted by Father Buliard.

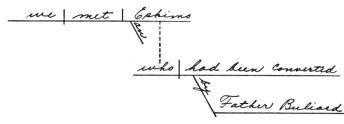

C250 Parenthetical clauses that intervene between the relative pronoun and the rest of its own clause do not affect the case of the relative.

who
Tim is a man ~~whom~~ we know will fight for us.

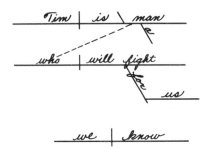

C251 To determine whether a clause is parenthetical or not, read the sentence omitting the clause in question. If the sentence continues to say what you want it to, the clause is parenthetical.

Tim is a man who ~~we know~~ will fight for us.

Cancel the clause *we know* and the sentence still makes easy, good sense, and the meaning is largely unchanged. It is clear, therefore, that *we know* is parenthetical.

INTERROGATIVE-PRONOUN USE

C252 Do not use an apostrophe with *whose* when it is used as an interrogative pronoun, and do not confuse *whose* (of whom) with the contraction *who's* (who is).

Whose
~~Who's~~ are you wearing?

INDEFINITE-PRONOUN USE

C253 Use *less* to indicate how much, *fewer* to indicate how many.

Fewer   *are*
~~Less~~ than five instructions ~~is~~ insufficient.
Less than a bushel is insufficient.
There is *less* time and *fewer* workers than we had expected.

Adjective and adverb use

ADJECTIVE USE

C254 A predicate adjective is one that follows a linking verb, whose subject it modifies.

The iron is becoming *red*.
You are called *lucky*.

C255 An attributive adjective is one that modifies its substantive directly, without the intervention of any sort of a linking verb.

Don't eat *green* apples.
There is a *sick* boy.

C256 Attributive adjectives are often used as objective complements, directly modifying the object of a verb or preposition.

I find this paint *sticky*.
Simpson dropped his chin like a man *shot*.

C257 An appositive adjective is an attributive adjective that is used in an appositive way; that is, it is loosely attached to its substantive as a kind of afterthought, an extra description, an added detail. Ordinarily an appositive adjective follows the substantive it modifies, though it may sometimes precede.

The wind, *mournful* and *desolate*, howled all night through the branches of the empty trees.
Long, gleaming, two-edged, a knife stuck in the wall.

C258 Clarity often requires that the article be used with each substantive or adjective to show that more than one person or thing is meant.

The secretary and *the* treasurer were arrested. [Two men.]
The secretary and treasurer *was* arrested. [One man.]

A black and *a* white purse *were* lost. [Two purses.]
A black and white purse *was* lost. [One purse.]

123

ADVERB USE

C259 Do not use *most* (to the maximum degree) for *almost* (not quite).

almost
The milk is ~~most~~ gone.

C260 Do not use two negatives.

anything
I didn't do ~~nothing~~ wrong!

C261 In connection with C260 remember that words like *scarcely, hardly, barely, nothing, nobody,* and *never* are negative.

was
There ~~wasn't~~ scarcely any recoil.

barely recognized
His face was so battered I ~~didn't barely recognize~~ him.

any
There was hardly ~~no~~ water in the radiator.

anybody
No, sir, I didn't see ~~nobody~~.

anything
In his whole life he never did ~~nothing~~ worth while.

C262 Do not use *never* when you mean simply *not*.

didn't take
I ~~never took~~ those letters for you this afternoon.

C263 Do not add an *s* to *somewhere, anywhere, nowhere,* or *anyway*.

somewhere
Let's go ~~somewheres~~ else.

C264 Do not use *kind of* or *sort of* as an adverb; use *somewhat, rather, fairly,* and so on.

a little
I'm ~~kind of~~ tired.

C265 Do not use *real* for *really* or for *very* or *extremely*.

very
The coffee is ~~real~~ hot.

124

C266 Do not use *some* for *somewhat* or *a little*.

He reads ~~some~~ *somewhat* faster than he used to.

I'm *a little* perplexed by your argument.

C267 Do not use *sure* but *surely* to mean undoubtedly, indeed, yes indeed.

You ~~sure~~ *surely* told him.

Will I work for a dollar an hour? ~~Sure~~ *Surely*!

C268 Do not place *too* or *very* immediately before a past participle that usage has not as yet established as an adjective. Between *very* or *too* and the past participle insert an appropriate adverb, like *deeply, genuinely, greatly, much*.

Questionable	*Preferable*
Yes, indeed, we were *very* impressed.	Yes, indeed, we were *very much* impressed.
But, sir, I am *too* indebted to you already.	But, sir, I am *too deeply* indebted to you already.

[Correct:] You could hardly expect him to admit that he is a *very* distinguished man.

C269 It is preferable, ordinarily, not to use *up* after such verbs as *ascend, connect, cripple, divide, end, finish, open, rest,* and *settle*.

Our Lord ascended ~~up~~ into heaven.
Please connect me ~~up~~ with the superintendent.
Poor Mother is all crippled ~~up~~ with rheumatism.
Let's divide ~~up~~ the candy now!
Where does this highway end ~~up~~?
At last Angus has finished ~~up~~ drying the dishes.
Don't open ~~up~~ this package until Christmas.
It will take me a long time to rest ~~up~~ completely.
Why don't these people settle ~~up~~ their bills?

[Not affected by this rule, because *up* is necessary:] On the seventh day we broke *up* several packing cases for fuel.

CONFUSION OF ADJECTIVE AND ADVERB

C270 Do not use adjectives to modify verbs, adjectives, or adverbs.[26]

well
I didn't do very ~~good~~ in the physics test.

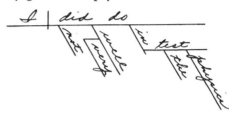

well-
This is a ~~good~~-built house.

nicely
She played a bit of Chopin very ~~nice~~.

heavily
Don't walk about so ~~heavy~~.

---

[26] For "I feel bad" and the use of adjectives with linking verbs, see C162-64.

badly
Robert behaved very ~~bad~~ at Mrs. Snifton's tea.

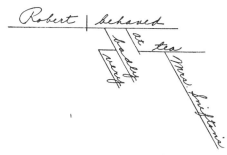

C271 Do not use *this* or *that* for the adverbs *so* or *very*.

so
He was ~~that~~ happy he could only cry.

so   *as this*.
I have never seen the lake ~~this~~ blue ∧

Comparison of adjectives and adverbs

THE THREE DEGREES OF COMPARISON

C272 Comparison is the change made in the form of adjectives and adverbs to show that the word they modify is greater or less in quantity or quality than something else.

C273 The positive degree indicates that the substantive modified is not being compared with anything else. The comparative and superlative degrees indicate that the substantive modified is being compared with something else. (The comparative involves only two things; the superlative, at lease three.)[27]

[Positive degree:] A hamburger is a *beautiful* thing.

[Comparative degree:] A hamburger is *more beautiful* than anything else I know.

[Superlative degree:] A hamburger is the *most beautiful* thing in the world.

---

[27] The superlative degree of an adjective or adverb (usually with *most*) may be used without any suggestion of comparison to express a high degree of perfection, imperfection, and the like (C297).

127

[Positive degree:] What a *large* onion that is.

[Comparative degree:] Bermuda onions are a great deal *larger* than chives.

[Superlative degree:] This is the *largest* onion of the three.

[Positive degree:] Mr. Marble closed the store *early*.

[Comparative degree:] Mr. Marble closed the store *earlier* than Mr. Kemp closed his.

[Superlative degree:] Of all the merchants on Clay Avenue, Mr. Marble closed his store *earliest*.

FORMING THE COMPARATIVE AND SUPERLATIVE

C274 Many adjectives and adverbs of one and two syllables form the comparative by adding *er,* and the superlative by adding *est,* to the positive.

Positive	*Comparative*	*Superlative*
dull	dull*er*	dull*est*
small	small*er*	small*est*
large	larg*er*	larg*est*
few	few*er*	few*est*
humble	humbl*er*	humbl*est*
flighty	flight*ier*	flight*iest*
high	high*er*	high*est*
near	near*er*	near*est*
early	earli*er*	earli*est*

C275 If the adjective or adverb ends in *e,* drop that *e* before *er* and *est.* If the adjective ends in *y* preceded by a consonant, change the *y* to *i.*

humble	humbler	humblest
flighty	flightier	flightiest

C276 If the adjective or adverb is of one syllable, double a final consonant after a vowel that is short in sound.

fat	fa*tt*er	fa*tt*est
wet	we*tt*er	we*tt*est
thin	thi*nn*er	thi*nn*est
hot	ho*tt*er	ho*tt*est

C277 Many adjectives and adverbs of one and two syllables and all adjectives and adverbs of more than two form the comparative by placing *more* or *less,* and the superlative by placing *most* or *least,* before the positive.

Positive	Comparative	Superlative
dull	*more* dull	*most* dull
dull	*less* dull	*least* dull
humble	*more* humble	*most* humble
humble	*less* humble	*least* humble
softly	*more* softly	*most* softly
softly	*less* softly	*least* softly
absurdly	*more* absurdly	*most* absurdly
absurdly	*less* absurdly	*least* absurdly
delightfully	*more* delightfully	*most* delightfully
delightfully	*less* delightfully	*least* delightfully
elaborate	*more* elaborate	*most* elaborate
elaborate	*less* elaborate	*least* elaborate
joyously	*more* joyously	*most* joyously
joyously	*less* joyously	*least* joyously
admirable	*more* admirable	*most* admirable
admirable	*less* admirable	*least* admirable
near	*less* near	*least* near
close	*less* close	*least* close

C278 The following adjectives and adverbs form the comparative and superlative irregularly as shown.

ADJECTIVES

Positive	Comparative	Superlative
good	better	best
well	better	best
bad	worse	worst
ill	worse	worst
little	smaller [size] less [quantity]	smallest [size] least [quantity]
much	more	most

ADJECTIVES

Positive	Comparative	Superlative
many	more	most
	further	furthest
far	farther	farthest
	[distance only]	[distance only]

ADVERBS

well	better	best
ill	worse	worst
badly	worse	worst
much	more	most
little	less	least
	further	furthest
far	farther	farthest
	[distance only]	[distance only]

C279 Note that the comparison of *few* is *fewer* and *fewest,* not *less* and *least.* Do not say "Less people came than were expected." Say "Fewer people came than were expected."

C280 Of their very nature some adjectives and adverbs have, strictly speaking, no comparative or superlative. Such are *unique, dead, circular, triangular.* Some of them, however, are used in loose or figurative comparisons; for example, *deader than a doornail.* But it is considered a blunder to attribute any degree whatever to *unique* or *peerless,* since *unique* means the only one of its kind and *peerless* means without equal. So do not say "very unique" or "more peerless."

USING THE COMPARATIVE

C281 Use the comparative with *than.*

Horrowitz is a *better* quarterback *than* Flugel.
Chetwood was hurt *less severely than* Tracy or Cameron.
Schmidt proved *more obstreperous than* we expected.

C282 Do not use the comparative if you are comparing more than two persons or things or more than two groups of persons or things.

Geraldine is clearly the *most* bashful of the three Hollingsworth girls.

If you are talking about the Sneeds, the Clarks, and the Lapierres, the Clarks are to my mind the *most* charitable couple of the three.

C283 Finish a comparison involving *than* before beginning one involving *as* or *so*, and vice versa.

[Wrong:] She is prettier but not so entertaining as her sister.
[Right:] She is prettier *than* her sister but not so entertaining.

C284 Keep balance in a comparison.

[Wrong:] The freshmen's awards are far, far handsomer than the sophomores.	Awards are compared with sophomores.
[Right:] The freshmen's awards are far, far handsomer than the sophomores'.	Freshmen's awards are compared with sophomores' awards.

C285 Do not use double comparatives.

Wait! I know a ~~more~~ better way.

C286 When using the comparative with things of the same group, use *other*, *else*, or an equivalent word.

[Wrong:] Dr. Black has more elaborate gadgets than any dentist in his town.	This compares Dr. Black with himself and says that he has more elaborate gadgets than he himself has.
[Right:] Dr. Black has more elaborate gadgets than any *other* dentist in his town.	This compares Dr. Black with the rest of his group—the dentists in his town. *Other* keeps the doctor from being compared with himself.

[Wrong:] I have made smaller contributions to the poor-fund drive than anybody in my class.
[Right:] I have made smaller contributions to the poor-fund drive than anybody *else* in my class.

[Wrong:] I like tutti-frutti better than any flavor.
[Right:] I like tutti-frutti better than any *other* flavor.

131

C287 When using the comparative with things of different groups, do not use the words *other, else,* or some other equivalent expression.

[Wrong:] This steam engine develops as much power as any *other* diesel.

This statement implies that a steam engine is a diesel engine. The word *other* illogically puts the two engines in the same group or class.

[Right:] This steam engine develops as much power as any diesel.

[Wrong:] Without training, Stani sings as well as somebody *else* with years of music school behind him.

This statement implies that the untrained Stani has had years of music school. *Else* puts Stani in the group of those who have had training.

[Right:] Without training, Stani sings as well as somebody with years of music school behind him.

[Wrong:] This plane is as big and as comfortable as any *other* moderate-sized ocean liner.

[Right:] This plane is as big and as comfortable as any moderate-sized ocean liner.

C288 In order to use the right case of a personal pronoun after *than* or *as*, mentally complete the elliptical sentence.

Tush! You are much stronger than *he* [is strong].
I'd trust Marcus sooner than [I'd trust] *her*.
I'd trust Marcus sooner than *she* [would trust Marcus].
There is no other so strong as *he* [is].

C289 Do not substitute *all the farther, all the further, all the faster, all the longer, all the quicker,* and similar expressions for *as far as, as fast as, as long as, as quick as,* and similar expressions of comparison.

This is ~~all the longer~~ *as long as* I can wait.

Four knots an hour is ~~all the faster~~ *the fastest* that the Q will sail.

[Right, since it is not a substitute for *as soon as*:] If you leave now, you will get to Covington all the sooner.

USING THE SUPERLATIVE

C290 Use the superlative degree when *than* is not used and more than two persons or things or groups of persons or things are compared.

There are faith, hope, and charity, of which the ~~greater~~ *greatest* is charity.

Which was the ~~fatter~~ *fattest*—Cassius, Casca, or Caesar?

C291 When an *of* phrase limits an adjective or adverb in the superlative degree, do not use *other, else,* or an equivalent word.

[Wrong:] That suggestion is the most cowardly of all the *others.*
[Right:] That suggestion is the most cowardly of all.

[Wrong:] I am the least known of all the *other* poets in my class.
[Right:] I am the least known of all the poets in my class.

C292 When an *of* phrase limits an adjective or adverb in the superlative degree, make the object of *of* a plural noun or a collective noun.

[Wrong:] Paul has the sincerest friends of any *boy* in our class.
[Right:] Paul has the sincerest friends of all the *boys* in our class.

[Wrong:] You are the least responsible person of *anybody* I know.
[Right:] You are the least responsible of all the people I know.

C293 When an *of* phrase limits an adjective or adverb in the superlative degree, make sure that the object of *of* includes the person or thing to be compared.

[Wrong:] Nolan Kane is the most talented of his brothers, Kerry and "Sugar" Kane.   This sentence says that Nolan is one of his two brothers, which is absurd.

[Right:] Of the three Kane brothers—Nolan, Kerry, and "Sugar"—Nolan is the most talented.

[Wrong:] Of all the *cities* along the Mississippi, the *people* of Natchez seem to me the most charming.   This sentence compares cities with people, instead of people with other people.

[Right:] Of all the *dwellers* in the cities along the Mississippi, the *people* of Natchez seem to me the most charming.

[Wrong:] You are the least responsible of all the *others* I know.
[Right:] You are the least responsible of all the boys I know.

C294 Do not use a superlative where the comparative is called for and is sufficient.

less

Of the two plans, this is the ~~least~~ effective.

C295 Do not use double superlatives.

You do the ~~most~~ oddest things!

C296 Make all comparisons grammatical and complete.

[Wrong:] She maintained that Rudolph Valentino was one of the handsomest actors, if not the handsomest, of modern times.

[Right:] She maintained that Rudolph Valentino was one of the handsomest actors, if not the handsomest *actor,* of modern times.

[Wrong:] Salmon is one of the greatest, if not the greatest, export articles of Alaska.

[Right:] Salmon is probably the greatest export article of Alaska.

[Wrong:] One of, if not the oldest, priests of the diocese is Father James Hardy.

[Right:] Father James Hardy is either the oldest priest of the diocese or one of the oldest.

C297 The superlative degree of an adjective or adverb (usually with *most*) may be used without any suggestion of comparison to express a high degree of perfection, imperfection, and the like.

This cowardly remark is *most unworthy* of you.
I must say he was a *most unruly* little boy.
And, of course, all of your teachers have treated you *most kindly?*

Restrictive and nonrestrictive modifiers

C298 Modifiers are classified as restrictive and nonrestrictive. By modifiers are meant adjectives (including participles used adjectivally) and adjective phrases and clauses, adverbs and adverb phrases and clauses.

C299 Modifiers are called restrictive when the writer wants them joined very closely in sense to the words that they modify.

The girl *that I marry* will have to support me in the manner to which I am accustomed.

C300 Modifiers are called nonrestrictive when the writer wants them joined loosely to the words that they modify—as added information, as a by-the-way thought, as a point worth bringing in but not necessary to the chief notions of the sentence.

A comb—*which, by the way, costs very little*—is equipment that you should have and even use.

C301 Use this test: Read the sentence without the modifier. If the sentence still says essentially what you want it to, the modifier is nonrestrictive. If the sentence is changed—if it does not say what you want it to but something else—the modifier is restrictive.

I prefer freshmen, enthusiastic and willing.

[Without the modifier:] I prefer freshmen.

Suppose that you wish mainly to say that you had rather teach freshmen than other classes. Suppose you add *enthusiastic and willing* as extra and secondary information explaining why you prefer freshmen. The adjectives, then, are nonrestrictive.

I prefer freshmen enthusiastic and willing.

[Without the modifier:] I prefer freshmen.

Suppose you wish to say that you like freshmen better when they are enthusiastic and willing than when they are lazy. The omission of *enthusiastic and willing* would change this sense. Here the adjectives are restrictive.

135

Johnson, blubbering, was a sight to behold.

[Without the modifier:] Johnson was a sight to behold.

Suppose your chief thought is that Johnson was a sight to behold. You add *blubbering* as an interesting detail, unnecessary to the main idea. In this sentence the participial adjective is nonrestrictive.

Johnson blubbering was a sight to behold.

[Without the modifier:] Johnson was a sight to behold.

Suppose that you wish to say that it was an astonishing thing to see an ordinarily brave man like Johnson mumbling tearfully. Omit *blubbering* and the sentence no longer expresses your meaning. In this sentence the participial adjective is restrictive.

Joan Drew was, probably, the only person at the table who had ever tasted enchiladas.

[Without the modifier:] Joan Drew was the only person at the table who had ever tasted enchiladas.

Suppose that your main point is that Joan was the only one who had tasted enchiladas. You add *probably* as an afterthought, just to be accurate. Omit *probably* and your chief thought is unchanged. The adverb is nonrestrictive.

Joan Drew was probably the only person at the table who had ever tasted enchiladas.

[Without the modifier:] Joan Drew was the only person at the table who had ever tasted enchiladas.

Suppose that you want it part of your chief thought that you are not certain but nearly so that only Joan had tasted enchiladas. Omit *probably*. The sentence is not what you intend. The adverb is restrictive.

That column of Allen's, about fast driving, made Oliver Hornsby angry.

[Without the modifier:] That column of Allen's made Oliver Hornsby angry.

Suppose your chief thought is that Allen's column made Hornsby angry. Your reader knows the column you refer to. You add *about fast driving* only to be sure he remembers. The phrase is nonrestrictive.

136

That column of Allen's about fast driving made Oliver Hornsby angry.

[Without the modifier:] That column of Allen's made Oliver Hornsby angry.

Suppose you are sure that your reader will not know which column you are talking about unless you name it. *About fast driving* is necessary to your chief thought. The adjective phrase is restrictive.

I did take the car back, right after the dance.

[Without the modifier:] I did take the car back.

Suppose your chief thought is that you took the car back. You add *right after the dance* only as some extra information that might impress your reader. In this sentence the adverb phrase is nonrestrictive.

I took the car back right after the dance.

[Without the modifier:] I took the car back.

Suppose your chief purpose is to tell *when* you took the car back. In this sentence the adverb phrase is restrictive.

Mr. Ruhlman, who was here less than an hour ago, has just died.

[Without the modifier:] Mr. Ruhlman has just died.

Suppose your chief thought is that Mr. Ruhlman just died. *Who was here less than an hour ago* is an interesting, but extra, detail. The adjective clause is nonrestrictive.

The Mr. Ruhlman who was here less than an hour ago just died.

[Without the modifier:] The Mr. Ruhlman just died.

Suppose that you are using the dependent clause to distinguish the dead Mr. Ruhlman from another Mr. Ruhlman. It is necessary to your thought. In this sentence the adjective clause is restrictive.

No one will be in the office on the Fourth, because that's a holiday.

[Without the modifier:] No one will be in the office on the Fourth.

Suppose that you add *because that's a holiday* only to emphasize what has already been made clear. The adverbial clause is nonrestrictive.

137

No one would commit murder just because he did not like a hat.

[Without the modifier:] No one would commit murder.

Suppose that you are discussing motives for murder. The motive is then part of the chief thought. Omit *just because he did not like a hat* and you say something you do not intend—something silly, in fact. The adverbial clause is restrictive.

C302 Adjectives that precede their nouns must, in most cases, be restrictive if they are to make any sense at all. But there are exceptions.

[Restrictive:] The *perfect* friend is a hard one to find.
[Restrictive:] Someone played a *cracked* and *asthmatic* record.

[Nonrestrictive:] *Unafraid,* he faced the crowd.

[Nonrestrictive:] The last balloon popped and, *dismayed,* he burst into tears.

[Nonrestrictive:] The ice cream, *melted,* and the sandwiches, *hard* and *stale,* proved unappetizing fare.

C303 Articles are always restrictive.

The solution did not appeal to Blackbeard.
A bat and *an* eagle should not be kept in *the* same cage.

C304 Almost all adverbs that precede and modify adjectives or adverbs must be restrictive if they are to make sense at all.

The fumes were *quite* strong.
I have never seen you behave *more* disagreeably.

C305 *Possibly, probably, certainly, perhaps, therefore, consequently, doubtless,* and some other adverbs expressing certainty, doubt, or conclusion almost always modify verbs and hence may be used restrictively or nonrestrictively.

[Restrictive:] The boy was tall and *probably* strong.
[Nonrestrictive:] The boy was tall and, *probably,* strong.

C306 Introductory phrases have their own rules of punctuation (D58, D65), regardless of whether they are restrictive or nonrestrictive.

C307 Adverb clauses that precede their independent clause have their own rule of punctuation (D56), regardless of whether they are restrictive or nonrestrictive.

Misplaced (dangling) and squinting modifiers

MISPLACED (DANGLING) MODIFIERS

C308 Misplaced (dangling) modifiers are those that modify the wrong word or no word at all. (When participles are misplaced, they are generally called dangling participles.) Place modifying words, phrases, and clauses as near as you reasonably can to the words that they modify, making sure that every modifier modifies a definite word that is expressed in the sentence.

[Misplaced adjective:] *Restless,* the forbidden door seemed to taunt the two little children.

[Right:] The forbidden door seemed to taunt the two restless little children.

[Misplaced adjectives:] *Orange and crimson,* the poet gazed long at the sunset.

[Right:] The poet gazed long at the orange and crimson sunset.

[Dangling participle:] *Exhausted,* the bench looked inviting.
[Right:] Since I was exhausted, the bench looked inviting.

[Dangling participial phrase:] *Peeling onions,* our eyes watered.
[Right:] Peeling onions, we found that our eyes watered.

[Dangling participial phrase:] An hour later, *strolling the beach and climbing the sand dunes,* an outrigger canoe emerged from behind Starvation Point.

[Right:] An hour later, while Mary and Ronald were strolling the beach and climbing the sand dunes, an outrigger canoe emerged from behind Starvation Point.

[Misplaced phrase with gerund:] *Before rising,* a flavorful cup of coffee is comfortable indeed.

[Right:] It is comfortable indeed to have a flavorful cup of coffee before rising.

139

[Misplaced phrase with gerund:] *After having been in the sun for two hours,* the punch tasted cool and refreshing.

[Right:] After having been in the sun for two hours, Tom and Janet found the punch tasted cool and refreshing.

[Misplaced infinitive phrase:] Water wings are silly *to swim.*

[Right:] It is silly to use water wings to swim.

[Misplaced infinitive phrase:] *To sing well,* the diaphragm should be expanded.

[Right:] To sing well, expand your diaphragm.

[Misplaced prepositional phrase:] *With the face of a dinosaur,* the hunter killed the prehistoric monster.

[Right:] The hunter killed a prehistoric monster with the face of a dinosaur.

[Misplaced elliptical dependent clause:] *When two days old,* my father died.

[Right:] When I was two days old, my father died.

[Misplaced adjective clause:] He hid the jewel in a fragile cigar box, *which was worth many fortunes.*

[Right:] He hid the jewel, which was worth many fortunes, in a fragile cigar box.

C309 Do not use a misplaced elliptical dependent clause. The omitted subject noun or pronoun of an introductory elliptical dependent clause must be the same as the subject noun or pronoun of the independent clause.

I was
When ˄ two days old, my father died.

C310 An introductory infinitive used as an adverb expressing purpose must logically refer to the subject noun or pronoun even though grammatically the infinitive modifies the predicate verb.

one must read books
To be educated, ~~books must be read~~.

C311 A few participial and infinitive phrases are said to be used in the absolute construction when they have no grammatical connection with the rest of the sentence. But do not make use of such a construction unless you are certain that it is common in good writers.

Talking of football, who won the Army game?

Coming to the point, the answer is no.

He may be wrong—*granting,* of course, his truthfulness.

Granted that he is a persuasive speaker, will he make a steady worker?

Allowing for minor errors, the experiment can be called a success.

To judge from her looks, she's about forty years old.

To think you'd be so unmannerly!

SQUINTING MODIFIERS[28]

C312 Squinting modifiers—often adverbs, adverb phrases, or adverb clauses—are modifiers so placed that they seem to modify either of two expressions.

frequently I was⌃ advised ~~frequently~~ to review Latin.	Without the correction it is difficult to tell whether *frequently* modifies *advised* or *to review*.
On the following day ⌃Frank was told ~~on the following day~~ to enlist.	Without the correction it is difficult to tell whether *on the following day* modifies *was told* or *to enlist*.
When I was too tired to think, ⌃ I agreed ~~when I was too tired to think~~ to work on Saturdays.	Without the correction it is difficult to tell whether *when I was too tired to think* modifies *agreed* or *to work on Saturdays*.

C313 Place a modifier so that it unmistakably modifies only the word or expression that you want it to.

---

[28] Squinting modifiers are simply one special kind of misplaced modifier. A modifier is said to squint when one cannot tell whether it is looking toward the expression that precedes it or toward the expression that follows. It is corrected by a change of position.

Preposition use

CORRECT PREPOSITION USE

C314 You may end a sentence with a preposition, unless such use is awkward or lacking in euphony.

I can tell you what the shouting is *about*.
Craig has nobody to eat lunch *with*.

C315 Do not make a preposition do its own work and that of a different preposition as well.

He is willing to listen~*to*~ but not to argue with you.

C316 Do not omit a preposition when the omission dulls the parallel between the sentence elements or makes the sentence a little difficult to understand at first reading.

Seven of us will be back by nine if not~*by*~ eight.

C317 Do not use *of* for *have* or *'ve*, and do not insert an *of* after *had*.

You should ~of~ *have* seen the crowd at Dinny's last night.

They ought to ~of~ *have* gone to a vocational school.

If Duke had ~of~ let go, the rest of us ~would of~ *would've* fallen.

C318 *Upon* and *on* may be used interchangeably, except where one or the other sounds unpleasant.

C319 Use *into* for entrance, not *in*.

Boris *dropped* the corpse's clothing ~in~ *into* the well.
That Crosley has been *parked in* the same place all day.

142

C320 *Onto* (one word) may be used whenever it functions as a preposition. (Very often *to* alone is sufficient—and preferred.)

Wales climbed *onto* the top of the shed.
Invite His Excellency *onto* the platform.
All the climbing equipment fell *onto* the ledge below.

C321 Use *on to* (two words) whenever *on* is an adverb, *to* being a preposition.

We must walk *on to* the next town.
Play *on to* the end of the song.
The sailors were lured *on to* destruction.

C322 Use *beside* when you mean at the side of or next to; use *besides* when you mean in addition to.

Beside
~~Besides~~ the ice cream there stood a mountain of cookies.
Besides
~~Beside~~ ice cream there were mountains of cookies.

C323 Use *different from* before a noun or pronoun.

Oh, she is entirely *different from* other girls.
You are *different from* him in many ways.

(In these cases *different than* is sometimes used and cannot be censured; but *different from* is more widely established in current American usage. *Different to* is British usage.)

Use *different than* before a clause, whether complete or elliptical.

Vincent uses the word in a *different* sense *than* it was used a generation ago.
At night the world appears *different than* in the day.

C324 When *differ* means to be different, use *from* after it.

You differ a great deal *from* your studious brother.

C325 When *differ* means to disagree, use *with* for persons and *on, about,* and so on, for things.

I differ *with* you *about* the oddest things!

143

C326 Use *part from* to mean leave or bid farewell to; use *part with* to mean give up.

> He parted *from* his parents.
> He parted *with* his last cent.

C327 Use *agree with* with persons; use *agree on, to,* and so on, with things.

> I don't agree *with* you.
> Let us all agree *to* his nomination.
> I cannot agree *on* that plan of action.

C328 Do not use *at* or *to* after *where.*

> Now where on earth can he have gone t̶o̶?
> I don't know exactly where I am a̶t̶.

C329 Do not use *off* where *from* will make sense.

> *from*
> Jerry bought the motorcycle o̶f̶f̶ a friend.

C330 Do not use *of* after *remember, recollect,* or *recall.*

> I don't remember o̶f̶ hearing him say that.
>
> Do you recollect o̶f̶ the days when we used to gig frogs in this same pool?
>
> I don't recall o̶f̶ that incident.

C331 Use *between* in reference to two; use *among* in reference to more than two.

> *between* *among*
> The disagreement was a̶m̶o̶n̶g̶ Tom and James, not b̶e̶t̶w̶e̶e̶n̶ the entire club membership.
>
> *among*
> The old man divided his wealth b̶e̶t̶w̶e̶e̶n̶ his four sons.

C332 Do not use the expression *want in* (*out, off, through, up, down,* and so on), or one like *want next the window.*

> *to get*
> This man wants∧off at the next stop.
>
> *to sit*
> Does little Herbie want∧near the window?

144

POLISHED PREPOSITION USE[29]

C333 Use *like* as a preposition, not as a conjunction. (In other words, always use *like* with an object.)

You have a jacket like *mine* ~~I have~~.

Put a little alcohol into the tank *as* ~~like~~ he told you.

C334 Do not use *inside' of* for *within* in reference to time, or *outside of* for *aside from*.

We should finish *within* ~~inside of~~ a day.

Aside from ~~Outside of~~ a month of zero weather, the winter has been mild.

C335 Do not use *around* when you actually wish to mean *nearly* or *about*.

The baby weighs *about* ~~around~~ eight pounds.

We had to paddle *nearly* ~~around~~ seven miles for food.

C336 Do not use *on* after *continue* unless you need it to make sense.

Then we continued ~~on~~ walking for another day.
Paul continued *on* the road to Damascus.

C337 Say *forbid to* and *prohibit from*.

The constitution forbids a man *to hold* ~~from holding~~ two offices at once.

People are prohibited *from parking* ~~to park~~ their cars in the schoolyard except during the eleven-o'clock Mass.

C338 Do not use *of* after *off*.

The maid knocked the picture off ~~of~~ the table.
They took his name off ~~of~~ the roster of candidates.

---

[29] These rules are sometimes ignored, even by writers and speakers of note. If, however, you keep them, your writing will gain in simplicity, clarity, and elegance.

C339 Do not use *of* after *inside* and *outside.*

Dent was trapped inside ~~of~~ the burning hotel.
We had locked ourselves outside ~~of~~ the house.

C340 Omit the prepositions in such expressions as these: *cover over, over with,* and *start in.*

Cover ~~over~~ the stew.
Thank the Lord the war is over ~~with~~.
John had better start ~~in~~ to read his book.

C341 Use *at* or *about* but not *at about.*

[Poor:] This snapshot was taken at about ten o'clock.
[Better:] This snapshot was taken at ten o'clock.
[Better:] This snapshot was taken about ten o'clock.

C342 In expressions like *angry with* and *angry at* use *with* for persons, *at* for things.

The block leader was angry *with* me *at* my carelessness.

C343 Since *due* is an adjective, use it only as a predicate complement or the modifier of a noun; do not use it as a preposition.

Because of
~~Due to~~ Cardinal Schmidt's visit, there will be no school tomorrow.
[Predicate complement:] The applause was *due* to him.
[Adjective:] I am waiting for the discount *due* to me.

C344 Do not say *back behind;* and use *behind* rather than *back of* or *in back of.*

Behind
~~Back behind~~ me sat the Martins.
Behind
~~Back of~~ me sat the Martins.
Behind
~~In back of~~ me sat the Martins.

Conjunction use

C345 Use *neither . . . nor,* not *neither . . . or.*

nor
Gilbert was neither strong ~~or~~ intelligent.

C346 Do not use *because* to introduce a noun clause that is the subject of a sentence. Use *that* or *the fact that*.

That

~~Because~~ you are sleepy does not exempt you from the examination.

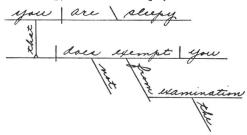

The fact that

~~Because~~ you are sleepy does not exempt you from the examination.

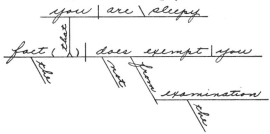

C347 Do not use *because* to introduce a noun clause that is the predicate complement after *the reason is*. Use *that* or *the fact that*.

that

The reason for his broad smile is ~~because~~ he won the essay contest.

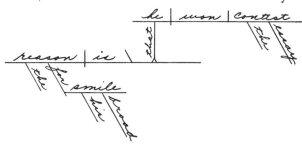

the fact that
The reason for his broad smile is ~~because~~ he won the essay contest.

The reason why I've changed my mind is *that* this horse is absolutely uncontrollable.

The reason why I've changed my mind is *the fact that* this horse is absolutely uncontrollable.

C348   Do not use *when* or *where* to introduce a predicate complement in definitions or explanations.

the senior dance
The big event of the year is ~~when the seniors have their dance~~.

the refraction and reflection of the sun's rays
A rainbow is ~~when the sun's rays are refracted and reflected~~ by raindrops.

The jackknife is *a dive in which you bend from the waist and touch your ankles while keeping your knees unflexed.*

Most people will agree that one of the loveliest times of the year is *the coming of spring.*

C349   Do not use *where* for *that* in object clauses.

that
I saw in the bulletin ~~where~~ Jones was appointed.

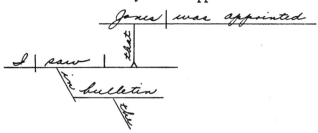

Did you hear *that* Mrs. Wipperman keeps more than fifty cats in her house?

C350 Do not use *as, as if,* or *as though* to introduce an object or predicate noun clause after verbs of thinking, saying, or feeling. Use *that.*

It seems to me [same as *I*
think] ~~as if~~ *that* that's a great deal of automobile for so small a boy.

That that's a great . . . a boy is the predicate noun of *seems.*

Well, he didn't say ~~as~~ *that* he agreed with me.

That he agreed with me is the object of *say.*

Mother doesn't feel ~~as though~~ *that* she should go without a particular invitation.

That she should go without a particular invitation is the object of *doesn't feel.*

C351 Do not use *being as* or *being that* when you should use *since* or *because.*

~~Being as~~ *Since* you are my brother, you should lend me the tie.

~~Being that~~ *Because* I have no ticket, I shall have to watch from the doorway.

C352 Do not use *except* for *unless.*

You will get nowhere ~~except~~ *unless* you talk to a powerful man like Rooney.

C353 Do not use *without* as a conjunction.

[Wrong:] Don't leave without you pay your dues.
[Right:] Don't leave *before* you pay your dues.
[Wrong:] There's no hope without they find another halfback.
[Right:] There's no hope *unless* they find another halfback.
[Wrong:] I seldom eat peanuts without I think of the circus.
[Right:] I seldom eat peanuts *that I do not think* of the circus.

C354 Do not omit the second *as* when expressing a comparison.

[Wrong:] Cleve's average is as good if not better than mine.
[Right:] Cleve's average is as good *as,* if not better than, mine.
[Right:] Cleve's average is as good *as* mine if not better.

C355   Do not omit *than* when it is needed to complete a comparison.

[Wrong:] Your explanation is more convincing but altogether different from his.

[Right:] Your explanation is more convincing *than*, but altogether different from, his.

C356   Do not use *as* ambiguously, so that it could indicate either time or cause or reason or circumstance.

[Ambiguous:] *As* Blackie was   Time or cause.
being pommeled, Mary was
smiling coldly.

[Clearly time:] *When* Blackie was being pommeled, Mary was smiling coldly.

[Clearly cause:] *Because* Blackie was being pommeled, Mary was smiling coldly.

[Ambiguous:] *As* I was talk-   Time or cause.
ing, my wife left the room.

[Clearly time:] *While* I was talking, my wife left the room.

[Clearly cause:] *Because* I was talking, my wife left the room.

[Ambiguous:] *As* you are go-   Reason or circumstance.
ing downtown, please leave this
prescription at the hospital.

[Clearly reason:] *Since* you are going downtown, please leave this prescription at the hospital.

[Clearly circumstance:] *As* you go downtown, please leave this prescription at the hospital.

[Clearly time:] *As* I lay on the beach, someone stole my watch and class ring.

[Clearly cause:] *As* I was very late, I took a short cut through Forest Park.

C357   Do not use *on account of* or *on account of because* as a conjunction.

I play the oboe ~~on account of~~ *because* I like to play the oboe.

Olive fell ~~on account of because~~ *because* the stairs were slippery.

C358 Do not use *while* in place of *although* unless the meaning is perfectly clear.

although

~~While~~ John was only two months old, his aunt read him the Bible.

C359 Do not use *directly* or *immediately* in place of the conjunction *as soon as*.

As soon as

~~Immediately~~ volunteers were called for, Jud stepped forward.

As soon as

~~Directly~~ the painters left, little Maury, with a gleam in his eye, raised his dirty hands to the wall.

C360 *So that* is preferred to *so* in expressing purpose.

[Doubtful:] Chris built a shelter up in the tree *so* he could have a place to himself.

[Better:] Chris built a shelter up in the tree *so that* he could have a place to himself.

C361 *When* is preferred to *than* after *scarcely, hardly, barely.*

when

The Greshams had *scarcely* met her ~~than~~ she began to rearrange their lives for them.

C362 *And* is clearer and is considered better usage than *while* for expressing addition.

and

A book lay open on his knees, ~~while~~ a blanket was wrapped about his feet.

C363 Use *different from* before a noun or pronoun. See also C323.

Oh, she is entirely *different from* other girls.

Phrases

IN GENERAL

C364 A phrase is a group of words not containing a predicate verb and used as a noun, an adjective, or an adverb.

C365 According to their form phrases are divided into prepositional, gerund, participial, and infinitive phrases.

151

PREPOSITIONAL PHRASES

C366 A prepositional phrase consists of a preposition plus its object and whatever modifiers there may be.

Caesar was certainly a master *of men.*

C367 A prepositional phrase can be used (uncommonly) as a noun,[30] as an adjective modifying a noun or pronoun, or as an adverb modifying a verb, an adjective, or an adverb.

[Adjective phrase:] The girl *in blue* is Sid's cousin.

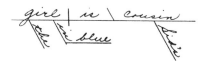

[Adjective phrase:] The house *to the left* is going to be the parish youth center.

[Adverb phrase:] Mr. Clark lost his billfold *in the rain barrel.*

[Adverb phrase:] This is very good *of you.*

---

[30] Prepositional phrases are sometimes nouns rather than modifiers. In "Over the fence is out," *over the fence* is a substantive, the subject of the predicate verb. This, however, is not a common use of a prepositional phrase.

[Adverb phrase:] Where *in the world* are they?

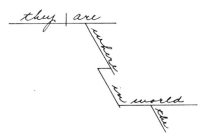

GERUND PHRASES

C368 A gerund phrase is a gerund plus an object or a predicate substantive or adjective or an adverb modifier. A gerund phrase is always used as a noun. (Whenever a gerund is accompanied only by an adjective, treat it simply as a noun.)

[Subject of predicate verb:] *Fighting sharks* is unpleasant.

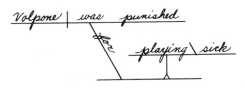

[Object of preposition:] Volpone was punished for *playing sick*.

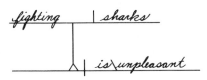

[Object of a verb:] She resents his *having been a butler*.

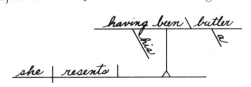

[Predicate noun:] One witch's occupation was *killing swine*.

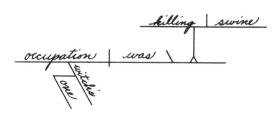

C369   Ordinarily use a possessive form of an adjective modifier with the gerund.[31] Often, however, a possessive form cannot be used with a gerund. In some instances there is no possessive form of the word; in other instances the word is modified by a phrase or clause. In all these instances use another form and treat the word as the subject of the gerund. (See C212.)

None were moved by *John's* pleading.

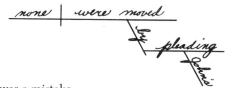

Her singing was a mistake.

I have no hope of *these* being sold.

---

[31] Grammarians speak of this possessive as the subject of the gerund. It appears more convenient and practical, however, to treat it as it is treated here.

I understand *young and old* falling under her spell.

On the *permission to go* being repeated, she gathered together her things and left the room.

Have you heard of Lynch, *who used to be on the faculty here,* publishing his memoirs?

C370 Sometimes it is hard to tell the difference between a gerund phrase and a participial phrase. In such instances the writer's thought must be sought out. (In your own writing rearrange the sentence so as to leave no room for ambiguity.)

[Clearly a gerund phrase:] There is no question of *our leaving today.*	Evidently the question is not about us but about leaving today.
[Clearly a participial phrase:] Can't you see Gus *running for a bus!*	Evidently Gus is not the kind of person who would or could attempt to catch a bus by running for it.
[Uncertain:] Martin was surprised at *her talking so sharply.*	Martin could be surprised at her or at her sharp words. What the writer means can be determined only by considering the sentence in its context in the paragraph.

PARTICIPIAL PHRASES

C371 A participial phrase is a participle plus the words that accompany it as object, predicate substantive or adjective, or adverb modifier.[32]

A man *fighting an octopus* gets wrapped up in his work.

---

[32] See C370.

Fargrave, *looking rather pale,* stepped back from the balcony.

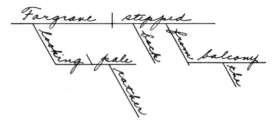

C372 Participial phrases are used only as adjectives.

A man *fighting an octopus* gets wrapped up in his work.

INFINITIVE PHRASES

C373 An infinitive phrase is an infinitive—with or without *to*—plus the words that accompany it as subject substantive, object, predicate complement, or adverb modifier.[33]

The other choice is *to fight manfully.*

---

[33] Put the subject of an infinitive in the objective case (C211). Note that the subject of an infinitive is quite often preceded by the preposition *for,* as, for example: *"For* her to lose courage now would be fatal." Put the predicate pronoun of an infinitive in the nominative case if a nominative precedes the infinitive; put it in the objective case if an objective precedes the infinitive (C214).

Adam Boyd planned *to betray John Ogilvie.*

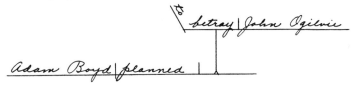

I never manage *to look neat.*

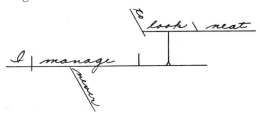

I heard *the motor roar.*

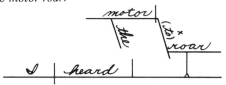

It is absurd for you to like *only funeral* marches.

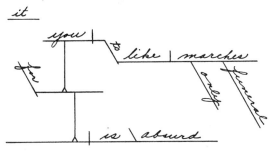

C374 Infinitive phrases are used as nouns, as adjectives, and as adverbs.

[Noun:] *To return now* would be impossible.

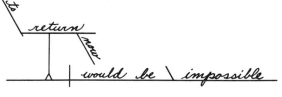

[Noun:] The other choice is *to fight manfully*.

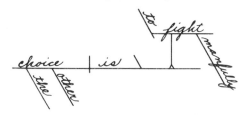

[Noun:] My new glasses make *me feel uncertain about steps and curbings*.

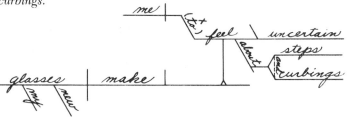

[Noun:] Adam Boyd planned *to betray John Ogilvie*.

[Adjective:] A desire *to run far away* took hold of me.

[Adjective:] I don't doubt your ability *to thrash me*.

[Adverb:] The filly seemed ready *to obey promptly*.

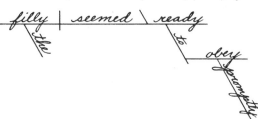

[Adverb:] The little fellow slipped from his horse *to retrieve the gun.*

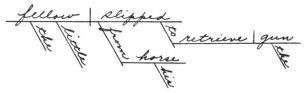

Clauses

IN GENERAL

C375 A clause is a judgment that either can stand alone as an independent statement (an independent clause) or cannot stand alone as an independent statement but is part of a sentence (a dependent clause).

Three men left last night,	and three will leave today.
Clause 1	*Clause 2*

My hope has sickened,	but it has not died.
Clause 1	*Clause 2*

C376 The predicate of a clause must contain a predicate verb, not merely a verbal.

Three men left last night, *and three will leave today.*

And three will leave today is a clause. *Will leave* is the predicate verb.

Three men left last night, *slipping away in the dark.*

Slipping away in the dark is not a clause. There is no predicate verb, merely the participle *slipping.*

Three men left last night *to destroy the main span.*

To destroy the main span is not a clause. There is no predicate verb, merely the infinitive *to destroy.*

C377 The subject substantive and the predicate verb of a clause may either or both be compound.

Three men and a child left last night, and another man will leave today.

Three men and a child left last night is one clause. It has only one (compound) subject: *three men and a child.*

Three men and a child packed and left last night, and another man will leave today.	*Three men and a child packed and left last night* is one clause. It has only one (compound) subject and one (compound) predicate.

INDEPENDENT CLAUSES

C378 An independent clause is a judgment that is expressed in words and can stand alone as an independent statement (a simple sentence). (See B17 and C387.)

Three men left last night, | and three will leave today.
Independent clause | *Independent clause*

[*Three men left last night* could make a simple sentence by itself. *And three will leave today* could make a simple sentence by itself.]

While we were sleeping, | three of the men left.
| *Independent clause*

[*Three of the men left* could make a simple sentence by itself: independent clause. *While we were sleeping* could not make a simple sentence by itself. It is a clause, but not an independent clause.]

C379 A second independent clause may be connected to the first by punctuation alone or by punctuation and co-ordinating conjunctions or conjunctive adverbs.

DEPENDENT CLAUSES

C380 A dependent clause is a judgment that is expressed in words but cannot stand alone as an independent statement. It is used in a sentence as a substantive, adjective, or adverb.

While we were sleeping, | three of the men left.
Dependent clause | *Independent clause*

[*While we were sleeping* is a clause. But were it standing alone, it would make only a half-sentence; so it is a dependent clause.]

C381 An essential part of every dependent clause is either a subordinating conjunction; a relative or interrogative pronoun, adjective, or adverb; or indefinite *who, which, what,* or *whose.* Be sure never to leave them out when you are reading a clause to determine whether it is a dependent or independent clause.

Elias didn't say *that* he would return.
Elias didn't say *when* he would return.
This is *what* I want.
Ask him *what* he is doing here.
We paid five dollars, *which* price was not exorbitant.
There is the car *that* I want.

C382 Since the connective is often omitted from an elliptical sentence, be sure to insert it mentally before deciding whether a clause is independent or dependent.

    that
I say ⋏you're not going.

      that
That little box ⋏you hold contains death.

The other box, he said, would   *He said* is independent. No
not hold so much.   connective can be inserted.

NOUN CLAUSES

C383 A noun clause is a dependent clause that is being used as a noun.

[Noun clause, subject:] *What you are saying* does not interest me.

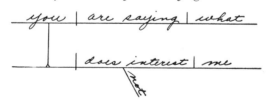

[Noun clause, direct object:] I see *that you are determined.*

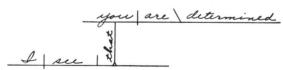

[Noun clause, object of a preposition:] Nothing is clear except *that Flau has escaped.*

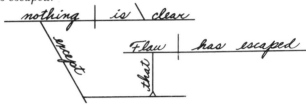

C384 The following subordinating conjunctions are commonly used to connect noun clauses with independent clauses or with other dependent clauses.

how	when
if [in the sense	where
of *whether*]	whether
that	why

I don't know *whether* Alfred has the popcorn concession.
Tell me *where* we can vote.
It is certain *that* ground-controlled approach was inadequate.
Where he could have hidden is the question.

C385 The interrogative and indefinite relative pronouns and adjectives *who, whose, whom, which,* and *what* introduce noun clauses.

What you mean is not clear.

The question is, *who* has the chipmunk?

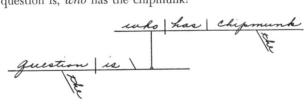

Russ would not say to *whom* he had given his ring.

We had an argument about *whose* snapshot should be submitted.

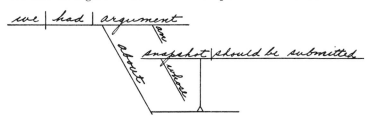

Mr. Ebbetts couldn't decide *which* was the worst.

Mr. Ebbetts couldn't decide *which* trombonist was the worst.

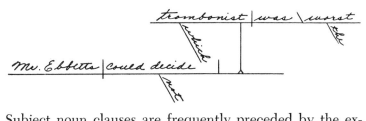

C386 Subject noun clauses are frequently preceded by the expletive *it*.

It is clear *that a crowbar was used.*

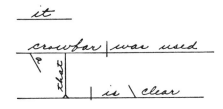

C387 It is a peculiarity of some sentences that the independent clause cannot be stated without the inclusion of the noun clause. (See B17.)

What you have said to me is frightening.

Noun clause: *what you have said to me.*

Independent clause: *what you have said to me is frightening.*

ADJECTIVE CLAUSES

C388 An adjective clause is a dependent clause that modifies a substantive.

The one *that sneezed* is a penguin.

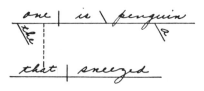

C389 Adjective clauses are relative clauses; that is, they are introduced by relative adverbs, relative pronouns, and relative adjectives.

[Relative adverb:] I have been quite busy in the time *since* I committed my last murder.

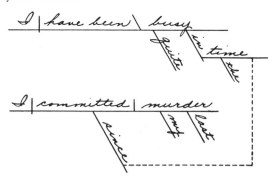

[Relative pronoun:] I know the girl *whom* you mean.

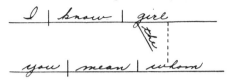

[Relative adjective:] We spent seven years in Juarez, in *which* city, by the way, we met Mark Tracy.

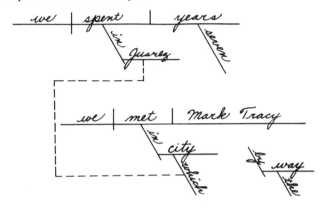

C390 A relative pronoun refers to an antecedent in another clause. (See A49 and C247.)

I know the *girl whom* you mean.	*Whom* is a relative pronoun. It has an antecedent in the other clause (the independent clause): *girl*. So the dependent clause is an adjective clause.

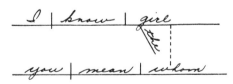

I know *whom* you mean.	*Whom* is not a relative pronoun. It does not have an antecedent in the independent clause.

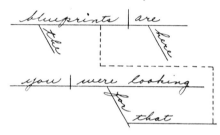

Here are the *blueprints that* you were looking for.	*That* is a relative pronoun. It has an antecedent in the independent clause: *blueprints.* So the dependent clause is an adjective clause.

C391 A relative adverb refers to an antecedent in another clause.

I can remember the *period* *when* no one took the telephone seriously.	*When* is a relative adverb. It refers to the noun *period* in the independent clause. The dependent clause is an adjective clause.
There was a great deal of talk *when* you left.	*When* is not a relative adverb. It does not refer to a noun in the independent clause; so the dependent clause is not an adjective clause.
I don't know *why* you should worry.	*Why* is not a relative adverb here. It does not refer to a noun in the independent clause; so the dependent clause is not an adjective clause.

C392 The case of the relative pronoun has nothing to do with the antecedent but depends on how the relative is used in its own clause.

We met an Eskimo ~~whom~~ *who* had been converted by Father Buliard.

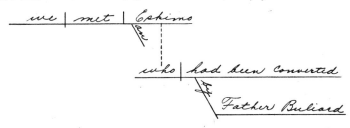

C393 The relative adjective *which* seldom makes for pleasant reading. It is usually best to avoid it when you do not have to use it.

> I met a stranger in Miami, who [*not* "which stranger"] turned out to be a man with an easygoing attitude toward money.

> [All right, because it somehow increases the humor:] Demarre made a bombastic speech about Demarre; and then Horner proclaimed him the modern Aeolus, *which* term Demarre did not understand and so took for a compliment.

ADVERB CLAUSES

C394 An adverb clause is a dependent clause that modifies a verb, an adjective, or an adverb.

> [Modifying a verb:] *When he had revived,* he said a strange thing.

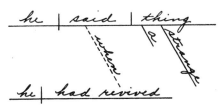

[Modifying an adjective:] Television long remained unsatisfactory *because it could be transmitted only some fifty miles.*

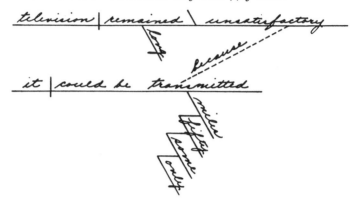

[Modifying an adverb:] Charles behaved so badly *that we had to put him into a strait jacket.*

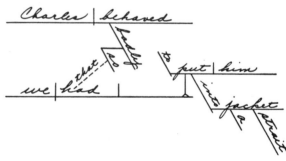

C395 Adverb clauses are introduced by subordinating conjunctions.

Because Fonder had the only automobile, we elected him president of our motor club.

After the death of their leader in 1521, Magellan's men continued their westward journey *until* their ships at length cast anchor off the coast of Spain.

C396 Do not confuse subordinating conjunctions with conjunctive adverbs, which cannot be used in dependent clauses unless a subordinating connective is present; or with relative adverbs, which must have an antecedent in some other clause of the sentence.

168

C397 If an elliptical adverb clause dangles—modifies or seems to modify nothing or the wrong thing—simply fill in the missing words.

the pot is   *it*
When ‸simmering, carefully remove ‸from the stove.

C398 *If* is sometimes omitted from conditional clauses, and the subject noun or pronoun is put after the predicate verb.

Had Father the means, he most certainly would give us children an education.

Same as *if Father had the means.*

Should you ever come West, be sure to visit us.

Same as *if you should ever come West.*

D Punctuation

End punctuation

D1 Every sentence must end with a period, a question mark, or an exclamation point.[1]

D2 Put a period at the end of a declarative sentence.

The sun is shining.

D3 Put a period at the end of an imperative sentence if the feeling expressed is mild. (See D16.)

Do what I tell you.
Close the door when you leave.
Don't forget to remind me.

D4 Put a period at the end of a request, order, or command that—for the sake of courtesy—is phrased as a question.

Will you please see me before you go home.
Would you type this letter before any of the others.
May I have a reply by tonight.
Will the witness take the stand, please.

---

[1] For punctuation of sentences that are interrupted or that trail off, see D20 and D23.

D5 Put a period at the end of an indirect question.[2]

A man asked me where I was going.

D6 Use a period after a sentence that is interrogative in form but ends with a declarative quotation.

Was it merely coincidence that John, seeing the book lying on my bed, declared, "Browning is my favorite author, too."

D7 Put a question mark at the end of a direct question.[2]

Where are you going?

Who wrote "To a Skylark"?

"Where are you going?" a man asked me.

He asked, "What do you think you're doing?" in a threatening tone of voice.

D8 Use a question mark after a sentence that is interrogative in meaning though declarative in form.

The executioner is ready?

Paris calls *that* a hat?

D9 Words or phrases or clauses in a series may each be followed by a question mark if each is equivalent to a fully expressed question.

Where did you come from? why? how?

Where did you find this dog? at what time of day?

Shall I tell Mother you called? that you will return again?

D10 When an emphatic question that is not a quotation occurs within a sentence or at the end of a sentence, use a question mark after it. Often, however, when the question is not felt as emphatic, only a comma is used after it.

He had no answer to the question, Where are you going?

To the question, Where are you going? he had no answer.

Have we enough fuel for the trip? is always the first question.

---

[2] A direct question is a question expressed in the words of the speaker; for example: "Where is the wampum?" An indirect question gives the sense of the speaker's question without quoting him; for example: "He asked where the wampum was." Indirect questions are frequently introduced by *whether* and by *if* in the sense of *whether*.

The first thing you will be asked is: What are you qualified to do?
How can I arrange my schedule, is what I must think of next.

D11 Use a question mark at the end of a question within parentheses or dashes.

His first name was just plain C (can you imagine it?), the third letter of the alphabet.

Truffles—have you ever eaten any?—are a subterranean fungus.

D12 If a question mark belongs to both the parenthesis and the rest of the sentence, or only to the rest of the sentence, place the mark outside the parenthesis at the end of the sentence.

Would you care to join us (in other words, will you take the dare)?

Can you tell me where Ribbon Parkway is (it's the road to the Tallons')?

D13 Do not use a question mark if an exclamation point or another question mark would precede it.

Where is the fool who cried, "Fire! Fire!"
Who asked, "What is truth?"

D14 For the use of a question mark with quotation marks, see D124.

D15 Put an exclamation point after a word, a phrase, a statement or command or question (exclamatory elements) to indicate strong feeling.

What! You wouldn't dare!
Jump!
How splendid!
The safe was empty!
The ghost was gone!

D16 Put an exclamation point at the end of an imperative sentence if the feeling expressed is strong. (See D3.)

Do what I tell you!
Help!
Call the police!
Drop it!

D17 Use an exclamation point at the end of an exclamation within parentheses or dashes.

His first name (imagine!) was just plain C, the third letter of the alphabet.

D18 For the use of exclamation points with quotation marks see D124.

D19 Do not use exclamation points often.

D20 Use a dash (—) to show that a sentence is interrupted before its close.

Besides, I see no reason for thinking that we must have the Merkels over just because—You are not listening to me, George Lindquist!

D21 Use three ellipsis periods to indicate an omission of words or sentences from a quotation.

A *Ellipsis periods at the beginning of a sentence.*

. . . there was not the slightest trace of fear; indeed, he was smiling a slight, amused smile.

B *Ellipsis periods within a sentence.*

On the brown face . . . there was not the slightest trace of fear; indeed, he was smiling a slight, amused smile.

C *Ellipsis periods at the end of a sentence.*

On the brown face of the fellow there was not the slightest trace of fear . . .

D *Ellipsis periods between sentences.*

1. The first sentence not finished.

Within an hour it was apparent that he was meeting the full resistance . . . No one was creating a diversion at the eastern end of the little town.

2. The first sentence finished (place the ellipsis periods after the end punctuation of the sentence, whatever that punctuation may be—period, question mark, exclamation point), the following sentence (or sentences) omitted.

172

Within an hour it was apparent that he was meeting the full resistance of Templi. . . . Hard pressed for a decision, he fanned his men out in a quarter circle in the southwest.

3. The first sentence finished (place the ellipsis periods after the end punctuation of the sentence, whatever that punctuation may be—period, question mark, exclamation point), the next sentence (or sentences) omitted, the third sentence beginning after its opening.

Within an hour it was apparent that he was meeting the full resistance of Templi. . . . he fanned his men out in a quarter circle in the southwest.

4. The first sentence unfinished, the next one (or ones) omitted, the third beginning after its opening.

Within an hour it was apparent that he was meeting the full resistance . . . he fanned his men out in a quarter circle to the southwest.

D22 Use a full line of ellipsis periods to indicate the omission of a paragraph from prose or a line from poetry.

I have tried to show you how you may enrich your life by giving yourself seriously to the pursuits of knowledge.

. . . .

How different is the view of past life in the man who has grown old in knowledge and wisdom from that of him who has grown old in ignorance and folly!

Shall I compare thee to a summer's day?
. . . .
Rough winds do shake the darling buds of May,
And summer's lease hath all too short a date.

D23 Use ellipsis periods to show that a sentence, while not abruptly interrupted, trails off with words left unsaid.

Trevor was there when the letter was stolen. Trevor was recognized by old Marsden, and now Marsden has been killed. Trevor spends a good deal of money but never seems to earn any. I'm beginning to wonder whether Mr. Trevor . . .

D24 Do not use any punctuation to mark the end of the lines in the various headings and addresses of a letter or envelope.[3]

The Donner Publishing Co.	709 Webster Street
1544 Banks Street	Pitt, Maine
Salem, Massachusetts	January 18, 1960

D25 Use a comma or a colon—but preferably a comma—after the salutation of an informal letter. (Use a colon after the salutation of a formal letter. See D84.)

Dear Joe,	Dear Father Raymond,
Dear Mother,	Dear Grandpa,

D26 Use a comma after the complimentary close of a letter.

Yours truly,	Sincerely yours,
Very truly yours,	Yours sincerely,

D27 Do not use a period or a comma at the end of a literary title that is set off on a line by itself (for example, at the beginning of a theme). You may use a question mark, or, if it is really needed, an exclamation point.

They Live on a Volcano

A Short Dissertation
On Buying Pigs in a Poke
By Norman Coles

Did Nero Burn Rome

Did Nero Burn Rome?

A Rat! A Rat!

The comma

D28 If substantives, attributive adjectives, adverbs, or dependent clauses occur in the form *a, b, c*—if, that is, there are no conjunctions between them—use commas between them.[4]

---

[3] It was formerly common to use a comma after every line except the last.

[4] A comma alone may be used in a series of independent clauses if they are short: "I came, I saw, I conquered."

The leaders in this movement are Kerry, Scott, Ryan.

A long, gleaming, two-edged knife stuck in the wall.

His words rang out coldly, sharply, threateningly.

This is a government of the people, by the people, for the people.

The charges against you are that you were driving without a license, that you were exceeding the speed limit, that you drove through a red light.

D29 If an *a, b, c* series of substantives, appositive adjectives, adverbs, or dependent clauses stands at the beginning of a sentence, use a comma after the last member of the series.

Kerry, Scott, Ryan, are the leaders in this movement.

We, you, they, want the same thing.

To work, to pray, to play, to rest, are most people's life.

Seeing what you see, hearing what you hear, doing what you do, are the way to peace and tranquillity of heart.

Long, gleaming, two-edged, a knife stuck in the wall.

Sharply, coldly, threateningly, his words rang out.

The prime minister cleverly, adroitly, accepted the issue.

That you were driving without a license, that you were exceeding the speed limit, that you drove through a red light, are the charges against you.

This rule does not apply to attributive adjectives. (See D28.)

A long, gleaming, two-edged knife stuck in the wall.

The one serviceable, safe, certain, remunerative, attainable quality in every study and in every pursuit is the quality of attention.

D30 Separate by a comma only adjectives equal in rank (co-ordinate adjectives). (They are equal in rank if they can be joined by *and*.)

> a truthful, courageous answer [truthful *and* courageous]
> a dingy, evil-smelling hallway [dingy *and* evil-smelling]
> [Wrong:] a variety of small, Alaskan salmon

D31 Often an adjective is so closely united to a noun that the two are equivalent to one word. If such an expression is preceded by another adjective, do not separate the two adjectives by a comma.

> fur coat—cheap fur coat
> white man—bearded white man
> brick house—new brick house

D32 If there is a conjunction between only the last two words, phrases, or dependent clauses in a row—if, that is, they occur in the form *a, b, and c*—separate them by commas, placing the last comma before the conjunction.[5] An exception to this rule is such an expression as "and so forth," "and so on," "et cetera," which is followed by a comma.

Were they red, yellow, *or* white roses?

She was always running from office to office, laughing uproariously at nothing, *and* shouting at the top of her voice.

If you are back here by four o'clock, if you have half of the money with you, *and* if you have a note from Mr. Farmer that he will take the rest from your wages, then you may have the drawing board and the compass and the dividers.

The comma, the semicolon, the dash, and so forth, are matters that concern editors.

Books, magazines, pamphlets, maps, and so on, are kept in the library.

Dogs, cats, parakeets, tropical fish, et cetera [etc.], can be bought at a pet shop.

D33 If all the words, phrases, or dependent clauses in a row are connected by conjunctions—if, that is, they occur in the form *a and b and c*—do not separate them by commas.

Men *and* women *and* children wandered through the ruins looking for scraps that might be sold to buy food.

If you mean that Heflin was negligent *or* that the radar was defective *or* that your information was incomplete, then we shall have to ask you for evidence.

D34 Where a conjunction makes one unit of two things, use no comma before the conjunction.

---

[5] This is not the only system used in the United States, but it seems to be the more common and has the advantage of clarity.

I ordered soup, salad, *ham and eggs.*	*Ham and eggs* is considered one dish, one unit.

Sink or swim, fail or succeed, and *live or die,* for all I care.

We traveled by the Pennsylvania, New York Central, and *Baltimore and Ohio* Railroads.

D35 Do not put a comma before a co-ordinating conjunction that connects only two words, two phrases, or two dependent clauses.

[Wrong:] To the end of the line he attached a wire leader, *and* a hook about two and a half inches long.

[Right:] To the end of the line he attached a wire leader *and* a hook about two and a half inches long.

[Wrong:] He was a tall, *and* gawky lad.
[Right:] He was a tall *and* gawky lad.

D36 Use a comma before a single co-ordinating conjunction whenever (*a*) it is preceded by a similar conjunction joining two parallel elements—for instance, two nouns—and (*b*) it itself is joining two other parallel elements—for instance, two verbs.

We begin our lives on earth in a world of glory *and* inexplicable wonder, *and* end them in a world that has grown sere and old.

We know Jules *and* Frances, *and* feel they would be good company.

I do not like spaghetti *or* sauerkraut, *or* want any beer.

D37 Do not separate the last attributive adjective of a series from the substantive it modifies.[6]

[Wrong:] The boatswain of the *Cleopatra* was a squat, shifty-eyed, *soft-spoken, fellow.*

[Right:] The boatswain of the *Cleopatra* was a squat, shifty-eyed, *soft-spoken fellow.*

[Wrong:] Hers is a merry, wholesome, *hearty, laugh* that makes you want to laugh too.

[Right:] Hers is a merry, wholesome, *hearty laugh* that makes you want to laugh too.

---

[6] Appositive adjectives that precede their substantive are separated from it by a comma: "*Humble, happy, and kind,* Philip brought out the best in all of us."

D38 Unless an interrupter occurs, do not separate a conjunction from what follows it.

[Wrong:] Ed was riding a sleek, young, *and,* spirited palomino.

[Right:] Ed was riding a sleek, young, *and* spirited palomino.

[Right:] Ed was riding a sleek, young, *and*—unless it was merely restless—spirited palomino.

[Wrong:] They said they wouldn't come, *but,* they did.

[Right:] They said they wouldn't come, *but* they did.

[Right:] They said they wouldn't come; *but,* if Alcide is to be believed, they did.

D39 Use commas to set off the second and subsequent items in a reference, a geographical name, a date,[7] an address, personal titles.[8]

Look up Shakespeare's *Hamlet,* Act III, scene 2, line 14.

Shreveport, Louisiana, is very different from New Orleans.

Earthquakes shook Los Angeles on Friday, November 14, 1941.

John Dickson lives at 2115 Pershing Drive, Watertown, Maryland, in a walk-up apartment on the second floor.

William Watson, Jr., will speak at the luncheon.

The Reverend John Blake, O.P., S.T.D., Ph.D.

D40 Do not use a comma before the first item of a series.

[Wrong:] Bilstein was thinking of, *driving home,* getting out of his wet clothes, taking a hot bath, and going directly to bed.

[Right:] Bilstein was thinking of *driving home,* getting out of his wet clothes, taking a hot bath, and going directly to bed.

[Wrong:] Graves grew up in, *Elsford,* Rhode Island.
[Right:] Graves grew up in *Elsford,* Rhode Island.

[Wrong:] All you have to do is, *dial this number,* ask for Mr. Scribner, and mention my name.

[Right:] All you have to do is *dial this number,* ask for Mr. Scribner, and mention my name.

---

[7] Usage is divided in cases where the year follows the month without the day: July 1955 *or* July, 1955.

[8] For semicolons with items in a series, see D75.

D41 Unless an interrupter occurs, do not use a comma to separate a subject from its predicate verb or a predicate verb from its complements or objects.

[Wrong:] *Fishing, swimming, and woodcraft, took* a lot of our time.

[Right:] *Fishing, swimming, and woodcraft took* a lot of our time.

[Right:] Fishing, swimming, and woodcraft, *all under the direction of the cabin counselors,* took a lot of our time.

[Wrong:] His particular aversions *are, work, study, and exercise.*

[Right:] His particular aversions *are work, study, and exercise.*

[Right:] His particular aversions are, *as you know,* work, study, and exercise.

D42 Use a comma before *and, or, nor, but,* and *for* when they join independent clauses of a compound sentence.[9] (But see D43.)

The siren cried out, *and* instantly a narrow lane was opened for the ambulance.

Neither was the coffee hot, *nor* were the doughnuts fresh.

D43 Use a semicolon rather than a comma before *and, or, nor, but,* and *for* in a compound sentence if—

A Either clause is long—say, three or four lines.

B Either clause contains commas or a colon, dash, or parentheses.

Ted was reared in the country and lived on a farm for eighteen years; but in spite of that he cannot recognize the common trees and flowers, and seems to know nothing of the care and feeding of livestock and poultry.

You may take the six-o'clock local train, slow-traveling but comfortable; or you may take the express, less convenient, perhaps, but faster.

It all came to one thing: mutiny; but some of the crew were not quite ready for that.

---

[9] Exception: you may omit the comma before *and, or, nor, but,* and *for* if both clauses are short—say, three or four words. For example, "I shall go but you must stay."

D44 Under three strict conditions a comma may be used even when *and, or, nor, but,* or *for* is not present: (*a*) if the clauses are short (say, three or four words); (*b*) if neither of them contains a comma, colon, dash, or parentheses; (*c*) if they are closely allied in thought and construction. For example, "United we stand, divided we fall" or "I came, I saw, I conquered," or "His voice trembled, his knees shook, his face paled."

D45 In a sentence beginning with a *that* clause from which the *that* is omitted, a comma is sufficient between the *that* clause and the principal clause.

Gerald has made himself sick, he played so hard.	[Usual phrasing:] Gerald played so hard that he has made himself sick.
Our vacation is over, I am sorry to say.	[Usual phrasing:] I am sorry to say that our vacation is over.
He will stay a week longer, he tells me.	[Usual phrasing:] He tells me that he will stay a week longer.
She did not understand a word of his talk, it could clearly be seen.	[Usual phrasing:] It could clearly be seen that she did not understand a word of his talk.
You are really not at fault, you know.	[Usual phrasing:] You know that you are really not at fault.

D46 Set off words in direct address by commas.

Dick, I want to apologize for what I said.
Come this way, *my friend,* to see the giraffe.
Here's a letter for you, *Harry.*

D47 Set off an ordinary nonrestrictive appositive by commas.[10]

The first letter of the alphabet, *a,* was all that Marko learned in the first eight weeks.
This is a bluebottle, *or buzzing,* fly.

---

[10] For dashes, especially with long nonrestrictive appositives or those that contain their own punctuation, see D91-96; for colons see D77; for parentheses see D100.

The Turkish government sternly forbade the wearing of the fez, *or tarboosh.*

This ambition you mentioned, *to make people notice you,* is selfish and will make you unhappy.

You are simply repeating the most important of all truths, *that there is a God.*

D48 Do not set off restrictive appositives.

I mean Churchill *the novelist,* not Churchill *the statesman.*
The word *affect* is often confused with the word *effect.*
He made the claim *that he was not responsible for his brother.*

D49 Do not set off appositives or adjectives that are part of a proper name.

Robert *the Strong* was a great warrior.
This is a statue of Alexander *the Great.*
We call him Wilfred *the Destroyer.*

D50 Set off ordinary nonrestrictive modifiers by commas.[11]

A young man, *tall and handsome,* waved to me from his table across the room.

There is no point in asking, *probably.*

Baker will be the first to avoid punishment, *begging off somehow.*

Mr. Pierce is as pleasant a man, *in his own way,* as you would care to meet.

The pilot, *as if he had gone mad,* headed the plane straight into the mountain.

There had been no Mass said in the town for fifty years, *although some sort of service was held on Sundays and holydays by a handful of Catholic laymen.*

D51 Before setting off a modifier, make sure that you intend it to be nonrestrictive. If you are in doubt, use no punctuation. Too many commas are worse than too few.

D52 Do not set off restrictive modifiers.

He entered *trembling with emotion.*
The woman *with the red stocking cap* is my wife.
Boys *that tell lies* should be whipped.

---

[11] For dashes and parentheses with nonrestrictive modifiers, see D96 and D100.

D53 Ordinarily use commas (or an exclamation point) with *oh* and other exclamatory or parenthetical words, phrases, and clauses.[12]

Oh, what's the use?

It was a deep, blue pool in a kind of grotto; and, *oh*, was the water cold.

If you don't have the car—*oh!* you do have it.

Well, that's just about it.

It seemed like a short swim; and, *well*, I certainly didn't want to seem a coward.

Next, there is a little matter of timing that I want to take up with the sound man.

Try the recipe for, *say*, a week.

Where, *pray tell*, are the keys?

Red, *to be sure*, never knew that he had been cheated.

You have a reason, *I suppose*, for the charges you make?

He would have come, *he explained*, if his aunt had not hidden his clothes.

Then you do agree with me, *don't you?*

John Hamilton, *Jr.*, is nauseated.

Father Basil, *O.F.M.*, is on the forum.

A James Peck, *M.A.*, *Ph.D.*, wants to sell you and me a carload of breakfast food.

The contracts, blueprints, *etc.*, call for a room without doors.

Flowers, magazines, ash trays, *and so on*, cluttered every available table and chair.

D54 Do not set off *O* (which is nowadays always capitalized and reserved for rather poetic use with nouns in direct address).

O Diana, these are your forests!

D55 Set off a nominative absolute by commas.

The danger signal ringing, we stopped the car.

I cannot tell you, *my parents being away*, whether I can go bowling or not.

---

[12] For dashes and parentheses with parenthetical expressions, see D88 and D99.

Nothing extra was served at dinner, *the supplies being lower than they had been for months.*

D56 When an adverb clause precedes an independent clause, set off the adverb clause by a comma.

Although the road was icy and snow was falling, the doctor got to our house in time.

Finally, *when order had been completely restored,* the cowardly judge crept from behind his desk.

While you are baiting my hook, I'll dig for more worms behind the boathouse.

The comma may be omitted, however, if the adverb clause is short and the meaning is clear and does not run into the independent clause, or if the subject of the adverb clause and the subject of the independent clause are the same.

Before the bus leaves ask the driver what time it is.

Since Mr. Crane came to Maryvale last year he has made many friends.

D57 If an introductory adverb clause is preceded by a co-ordinating conjunction, do not use a comma after the conjunction unless the clause is long.

And if you see your brother Fred, ask him to the party, too.

But before you both leave, your wife must register at the office.

Nor, unless the governor can be persuaded to use his full power and intervenes before the end of the month, can we have any hope of getting what we want.

D58 Use a comma after an introductory phrase or series of phrases unless it is short.

To see the West as it really is, drive your own car and spend several days in each place.

Returning from a walk late last night, I heard the angry voices of some neighbors quarreling in their back yard.

Quite a while before dark, bats began to dip, circle, and glide through the long avenue of oaks.

After dinner we plan to entertain you with some home movies.

D59 If an introductory phrase is preceded by a co-ordinating conjunction, do not use a comma after the conjunction unless the phrase is long.

And with the help and encouragement of all of you, the staff can finish the assignment in a short time.

But owing to heavy rains and bad roads, I was delayed a week in Arizona.

Nor, granted all the pleasant people you will meet and the multitude of things you can see and do, will you fail to enjoy yourself on the cruise.

D60 Use a comma after *namely, for example, for instance, that is,* and so on, when they introduce an appositive.

One city—*namely,* Brooklyn—was not represented.

Some social studies (*for example,* history and civics) are taught in all high schools.

Sammy paid the same fee; *that is,* five dollars.

D61 *Namely,* and so on, may be preceded by a comma, a semicolon, a colon, or a dash. The colon and dash are to be preferred when what follows *namely* is either emphatic or lengthy.

One city was not represented, *namely,* Brooklyn.

Sammy paid the same fee; *that is,* five dollars.

One kind of guest we do not want: *namely,* a person who is boisterous, loud, and careless.

D62 Use a comma after a conjunctive adverb.

The job had to be done; *consequently,* the Marines did it.

Whirligig beetles can skitter fast across the surface of the water; *furthermore,* they can dive.

Verano likes flattery; *indeed,* he thrives on it.

D63 Use a comma (or commas) with absolute expressions like *first, now, perhaps, thus,* and so on.

First, your comment was unsolicited; *second,* it lacks all pertinency.

Now, it is easier to talk about millions than to make them.

Mark will maintain, *perhaps,* that he does not want to die.

Thus, a child that has been burned is afraid of fire.

184

D64 Many words function either as conjunctive adverbs or as absolute expressions; and these same words can be adverbs in the strict sense. How they are used in a sentence determines whether they are to be punctuated or not.

First, your scheme is impractical. [Absolute expression]
First catch your rabbit; then cook him. [Adverb]

Now, it is easier to talk about millions than to make them. [Absolute expression]

Now comes a point that is hard to explain. [Adverb]

Ravelon, *however,* was not on time. [Absolute expression]

Ravelon promised to be here at ten; *however,* he was late. [Conjunctive adverb]

Ravelon cannot be on time, *however* hard he tries. [Adverb]

D65 Do not confuse a phrase that is really the subject or object with an introductory phrase.

Bringing wood into the house every evening is a sheer waste of time.	Subject of the sentence. No comma here.
Bringing wood into the house every evening, she used up what little strength and energy she had left.	Introductory phrase. Use a comma here.

D66 Set off by commas a contrasting expression introduced by *not, but not, certainly not, never,* and so on, if you want it read with a preceding or following pause.

Only a lawyer or a doctor, *but not a tradesman,* would so pepper his language with Latin expressions.

Because he had power, *not of course because he was astute,* Tag's word was received with respect by the Randall politicos.

I have decided to lend the car to Jim *but not to you.*

He is very kind *not because he is a king;* many a man has been a king and has not been kind.

D67 Use commas to set off a suspended expression.

During, *and for a long time after,* the famine, the people were desperately poor.

In his fright the man began swimming away from, *not toward,* the dock.

Joe looks like, *but is quite different from,* his twin brother.

Our old house was as large as, *but less conveniently arranged than,* this new one.

D68 Use a comma before a single, complete, directly quoted sentence that occurs within another sentence.

Herbert answered, "I don't know."

D69 Do not use a comma before an indirect quotation or an indirect question.

[Wrong:] Herbert answered, that he didn't know.
[Right:] Herbert answered that he didn't know.

[Wrong:] He asked, whether anybody else had noted a change in the frequency.
[Right:] He asked whether anybody else had noted a change in the frequency.

D70 Use a comma to separate those parts of a sentence that would be confusing if read together without pause.

Two hours before, the fire broke out.

Within, the box was lined with satin.

To fleas, fleas are not offensive.

Whatever is, is not necessarily right.

A man, that is what we need.

Instead of hundreds, thousands came.

To John, Matthew was always kind.

When the cyclone hit, the Ryans were away from home.

By striking, the members of the union forced a reluctant recognition of their rights.

To deceive, a man must go against his nature.

To escape, a small, enterprising mouse chewed his way through *Mrs. Rancy's Cookbook.*

Fifteen people loaded with Christmas presents and bustling about exchanging greetings and inquiries about friends, and five neighbors cutting sandwiches in the tiny kitchen crammed the capacity of the little cottage to bursting.

186

A man, not a mouse, is what we need.

He's going to go, crazy or not crazy.

There was a small, fluffy poodle with the attendant, barking in miniature frenzy.

D71 Do not use unnecessary commas; that is, commas for which you cannot cite a rule or give a good reason.

The semicolon

D72 Use a semicolon rather than a comma before *and, or, nor, but,* and *for* in a compound sentence if—

A Either clause is long—say, three or four lines.

B Either clause contains commas or a colon, dash, or parentheses.

Ted was reared in the country and lived on a farm for eighteen years; but in spite of that he cannot recognize the common trees and flowers, and seems to know nothing of the care and feeding of livestock and poultry.

You may take the six-o'clock local train, slow-traveling but comfortable; or you may take the express, less convenient, perhaps, but faster.

It all came to one thing: mutiny; but some of the crew were not quite ready for that.

The town—a little one-street affair suddenly cropping up on the prairie—was not the place to look for Reggie; nor did our first day of inquiry there achieve any results.

Millhaven has suffered a number of epidemics (see Gilchrist's *Terror in Millhaven*); and so it seemed an ideal place to begin our investigation.

D73 Use a semicolon before a conjunctive adverb that joins independent clauses.

Pat is the sort to plan a thing thoroughly; moreover, she has the personality to win support for the new constitution.

There was no point in taking a loss year after year; consequently, we sold the presses and the equipment in the bindery.

I bowled 225; however, I don't do that every day.

D74 Use a semicolon between independent clauses that have no connective between them.

John Karney was supposed to arrive this morning; he arrived last night instead.

I can't leave the house this morning; I have too much to do.

D75 Use a semicolon to set off the items of a series if the items contain commas.

The Dana Company has branch offices in Billings, Montana; Santa Fe, New Mexico; and Tucson, Arizona.

Tell what is significant about these dates in the life of Julian Randolph: January 4, 1900; September 27, 1902; March 1, 1904; and December 9, 1908.

D76 A semicolon may be used before *namely, for example, for instance,* and similar expressions when they introduce an appositive. (See D60.)

Chrysler introduced something new in 1951; *namely,* the spark plug in the center of the cylinder.

Rodent is a name that includes a number of little beasts besides rats; *for instance,* squirrels.

Tippy has quite redeemed himself; *for example,* he behaved like a human being at lunch today.

The colon

D77 Use a colon to formally introduce matter in apposition or to precede an extended explanation. Note that a dash might be substituted for the colon. (See D60 for the use of commas with appositives. See H12 for the use of capitals after a colon.)

All the difficulty is due to just one little man: *James Nelson.*

The headings of the report are these: *the cause of the flood in Fremont County, the damage done by the flood, and the help given to the farmers by the Red Cross.*

I have been trained in three skills: *double-entry bookkeeping, typing, and shorthand.*

188

The next question that came up for discussion was: *Are the requirements for membership strict enough?*

Everything was in good shape: *the paper stacked, the pencils sharpened, the chairs placed.*

Democracy presupposes two conditions: *that the majority of the people be informed and intelligent, and that the electors use their power fully and honestly.*

We all know the steady progress of the morning: *a sleepy cup of coffee, a glance at the headlines, a dull ride to work.*

She felt as you would expect: *worried, frightened, perplexed.*

D78 Use a colon to introduce a quotation of more than one sentence.

> Boswell wrote of Oliver Goldsmith:
>
> Goldsmith's incessant desire of being conspicuous in company was the occasion of his sometimes appearing to such disadvantage as one should hardly have supposed possible in a man of his genius. . . . One evening, in a circle of wits, he found fault with me for talking of Johnson as entitled to the honor of unquestionable superiority. "Sir," said he, "you are for making a monarchy of what should be a republic."

D79 A colon may be used before a short quotation (one sentence, for example) whenever the quotation is felt to be formally or emphatically introduced.

> The commander comments: "Your directions are clear and must be carried out fully and immediately."
>
> In his last letter—and note this carefully—he says: "The governor will hear no more talk whatever about a parole for Tompkins."

D80 Use a colon to introduce a clause that summarizes what has gone before. (A dash is perhaps more common in this use. See D87.)

> You are to appear at the Vendôme at precisely four o'clock; you are to select a table near the door; you are to leave at precisely four-fifteen: *these things you must do exactly and without fail.*
>
> A shred of wet, muddy tweed coat; a scrap of paper torn from a railroad timetable; a hat carefully placed on the head of the stone Audubon in the park: *that was all we had to go on.*

189

D81 Use a colon to introduce items that are indented like paragraphs, provided that the introductory statement could stand as a sentence by itself. If the introductory statement is incomplete, use a dash.

> These things should be kept in mind:
>
> We are not obliged to repress our intelligence and try to persuade ourselves that an evil man is a saint.
>
> On the other hand, we are obliged to make every effort to give him the benefit of any reasonable doubt when we are assessing his character.
>
> We must not decide for ourselves that he is certainly destined for heaven or hell.

> If it will help, we may divide the whole problem into these three topics for discussion:
>
> The usefulness of an electronics club.
>
> The difficulties of founding an electronics club.
>
> The usefulness weighed against the difficulties.

> To tabulate our reasons, Milton was admitted because—
>
> He has the draftsmanship we need.
>
> He is a worker.
>
> He can work with others.
>
> The charges made against him by Mosser were accompanied by not one solid bit of evidence.

D82 Use a colon to separate items that contain semicolons.

> Trains leave in the morning at seven, eight, and nine from the Euston Station; at seven, eight-fifteen, and ten from the Paddington Station: in the afternoon at one, two, and three from the Euston Station; at twelve-ten, one, three, and four-thirty from the Paddington Station.

D83 Use a colon to divide hours from minutes when time is written in figures.

> 10:20 A.M.   1:07 P.M.   5:00 P.M.

D84 Use a colon after the salutation of a formal letter.

> Dear Miss Smithers: Very Reverend and
> Gentlemen: dear Monsignor:
> Dear Sir: Dear Mr. Thorn:

D85 Use a colon to divide Psalm or chapter from verse when these numbers are indicated by figures alone.

Ps. 32:1 [meaning Psalm 32, verse 1]

II Cor. 5:1 [meaning the Second Epistle to the Corinthians, Chapter 5, verse 1]

The dash

D86 Use dashes to show that a sentence is broken up, interrupted, unfinished, or suddenly changed.[13]

Tell me—tell me the truth—are you my brother?

I came upstairs and entered the room to find—

When I think how your life has been spent—how old did you say you were?

D87 Use a dash before that part of a sentence which summarizes what has gone before.[14]

Mr. Micawber warned that a person will be worried and unhappy who, making ten pounds a week, spends fifteen; who buys clothes and flowers and theater tickets heedlessly; who spends tomorrow's salary today—*who, in short, lives beyond his income.*

D88 Dashes may be used for emphasis instead of commas to set off a parenthetical expression, and they are preferred if the construction of the parenthetical expression does not fit the rest of the sentence or itself contains punctuation.[15]

A man named Will Due—*what a name*—is waiting to see you.

Didn't Joe Cain—*he went to law school after college, you remember*—become a noted attorney in New York?

D89 If a parenthetical remark is a direct question or an exclamation, you may put a question mark or exclamation point before the final dash.

Joe Cain—he went to law school after college, *don't you remember?*—became a noted attorney in New York.

---

[13] See D23 for the use of ellipses to show that a sentence trails off with words left unsaid.

[14] A colon may be used in the same way but is somewhat more formal. See D80.

[15] See D99 for the use of parentheses with parenthetical expressions.

The second man—*plucky little fellow!*—was not to be intimidated by Mr. Robble's rumbling and grumbling.

D90 A dash may be used instead of a comma after a substantive appositive that stands at the beginning of a sentence. A dash should be used if the appositive is itself punctuated or long.

A man—that is what we need.

Food, clothing, shelter—these are the material needs of men.

Reading slowly for a full understanding and enjoyment of what is said—this is what should be aimed at.

D91 Dashes may be used to set off nonrestrictive appositives within the sentence more emphatically than commas do. They should be used if the appositives contain their own punctuation, or if they are long, or if they would otherwise be misread.

The first letter of the alphabet—*a*—was all that Marko learned in the first eight weeks.

Tod's brothers—*Jake, Harry, and Al*—are all as pleasant as he.

The plot of the play—*the story of a mortgage, a sick father, a beautiful daughter, and a villain*—is trite, unblushing melodrama; but the actors enjoy themselves.

Everything—*whatever he earned as wages and whatever came to him as tips*—went anonymously to the men he had wronged.

When you admit what I say—*that some kind of discipline in speaking and acting is necessary for every growing boy and girl*—then we can make plans together.

One thing—*fearless men*—is what we need for success.

D92 A dash may be used before an appositive at the end of a sentence. (In some instances a colon may be used in place of a dash.[16])

One thing I do not like—*spinach.*

A friend of mine telephoned me today, a man I haven't spoken to for ten years—*Jim Burke.*

---

[16] A dash is more emphatic than a comma but less formal than a colon at the end of a sentence. See D47 and D77.

D93 Use dashes to set off an appositive introduced by *namely, for example, that is,* and so on, within the sentence.[17]

One city—*namely, Brooklyn*—was not represented.

A salad of some kind—*for example, a tossed salad*—would be better with the steak.

D94 Use a dash before *namely, for example, that is,* and so on, to introduce an appositive at the end of a sentence.[18]

Sammy paid the same fee—*namely, five dollars.*

D95 Do not use dashes to set off an expression containing only figures.

[Wrong:] The year of the crash—1929—made no change in Paulinus.
[Right:] The year of the crash, 1929, made no change in Paulinus.
[Right:] The year of the crash (1929) made no change in Paulinus.

D96 Dashes may be used to set off nonrestrictive modifiers more emphatically than commas do, especially if the modifiers contain their own punctuation.

Mr. Pierce is as pleasant a man as you would care to meet—*in his own odd way.*

Agnes answered with a giggle—*which infuriated me, startled Higgins, and made Cleo guffaw*—but did not offer any useful information.

D97 Use a dash instead of a colon to introduce items that are indented like paragraphs when the introductory statement could not stand by itself as a complete sentence.[19]

To tabulate our reasons, Milton was admitted because—
He has the draftsmanship we need.
He is a worker.
He can work with others.
The charges made against him by Mosser were accompanied by not one solid bit of evidence.

D98 Use dashes sparingly. Their too-frequent use results in restless and childish writing.

---

[17] Parentheses may also be used here.
[18] A semicolon may also be used here. See D76.
[19] Do not apply this rule to outlines. See N35.

Parentheses and brackets

D99 Use parentheses to enclose a parenthetical remark, something that has only a comparatively remote connection in thought, or when the parenthetical expression already contains a dash, or when one or more independent sentences are parenthetical.

Enclosed please find my check for twelve dollars ($12).[20]

The author confuses James Mill (1773-1836) with his son, John Stuart Mill (1806-73).

One of the earliest detective stories (Collins's *The Moonstone*) is better constructed than many later examples.

The hero of my story (I write this for your private information) was not an honest man.

If the phrase is short (say, four or five words), the comma may be omitted.

The figures (78, 76, and 75—Roland adds 74, but no one else agrees with him) turned up 180 times in 4 hours.

Feuerbach tore the paper to shreds. (As we have said, he loves drama.) Then he burst into tears.

D100 Parentheses may be used to enclose a nonrestrictive appositive; they should be used when the appositive contains a dash.

The social studies (history, geography, and civics) are taught in all elementary schools.

We were offered some milk (which was fresh) and some wine (which was sour); there was no solid food in the inn.

Jonathan Crespy (a friend—and a loyal friend, I may say) reluctantly admitted that Julius should go.

D101 Place in parentheses letters or figures used to mark the divisions of an enumeration in a sentence, a paragraph, or other continuous text.[21]

---

[20] Use figures in parentheses only when extreme clarity or business style demands the repetition. See D103.

[21] Do not apply this rule to outlines. See N42 and N49.

I maintain (1) that Watson did not come to London; (2) that, even if he had come, he could not have met Holmes; and (3) that Watson's letter to Holmes was actually written by Vance.

There were two possibilities: (*a*) to go home and (*b*) to fight.

D102 Do not use periods with the figures or letters described in D101.

D103 In business letters and commercial and technical documents, figures are sometimes given in parentheses after written numbers.

Send me twenty-five (25) pairs of basketball shorts and a dozen (12) handballs.

Enclosed is my check for twelve dollars ($12).

D104 When a sentence in parentheses interrupts another sentence, do not capitalize the first word of the sentence in parentheses.

Though I have often been tempted to quit (such thoughts surely come to every man), the example of More's fortitude has always given me courage to go on.	Here the sentence in parentheses interrupts another sentence. No capitals.
They say he was a wealthy man. (That was in 1860, of course, when a dollar bought more than it buys now.) Whether or not he was is beside the point.	Here the sentence in parentheses does *not* interrupt another sentence.

D105 If a period, comma, semicolon, or dash is needed at the end of a parenthesis that interrupts a sentence, place the mark outside the parentheses.

Karen did not know (or so she said).

Here he gave his strange, though accurate (and handsomely delivered), account of the disaster.

Tilton was born the year of the flood (1894); he doesn't remember much about it.

D106 If a colon, question mark, or exclamation point belongs only to the parenthesis, place the mark inside the parentheses and end the sentence with another mark.

(Helen:) There is something you are forgetting!
Karen did not know (or did she?).
Yates absconded with my fishing tackle (the scoundrel!).

D107 If a colon, question mark, or exclamation point belongs only to the rest of the sentence or to both the parenthesis and the rest of the sentence, place the mark outside the parentheses.

Perón mentions three *ladrones* (robbers): Gonzales, Trega, and the nameless butcher.

Would you care to join us (in other words, will you take the dare)?

Chesterton said the most startling thing (on page 7)!

D108 Enclose independent parenthetical sentences in parentheses. They are punctuated and capitalized just like other sentences. The end punctuation, of course, is placed inside the parentheses.

I had just met the man. (Oldenburg insists I met him a year earlier. Oldenburg, however, remembers things more or less as he pleases.) We had been introduced at the club's annual dinner by Clesi, a mutual friend.

Staub took the floor. (It has never been explained how the chair happened to recognize him; no alert presiding officer would have done so.) He began a speech that ran three days and nights.

Staub took the floor. (Why did the chair recognize him? That has never been satisfactorily explained.) He began a speech that lasted three days and nights.

D109 Use brackets [ ] to enclose a remark that is inserted into a quotation.

"So they [that is, Christian and Hopeful] were forced to go, because he [Giant Despair] was stronger than they. They had also but little to say, for they knew themselves in a fault. The giant, therefore, drove them before him, and put them into his castle [Doubting Castle], into a very dark dungeon."

—BUNYAN

196

D110 Use brackets to enclose a parenthesis within a parenthesis.

You will find this passage in Albert the Great's commentary on the Gospel of St. Luke (in Albert the Great's collected works [in Latin], edited by Borgnet [Paris: Vives, 1890-99], Vol. XXII).

D111 Sometimes—especially in footnotes—a need seems to arise of putting a third parenthesis within the second. This might be done by using a French (or the larger German) quotation mark. Any such practice appears extravagant, however, and the footnote should be rewritten so as to require only one parenthesis within another.

(*Begriff* is translated by Mure as "notion" [cf. *An Introduction to Hegel* «Oxford: Oxford Univ. Press, 1940», p. 137].)

Quotation marks

D112 Put a direct quotation in double quotation marks.

"I have no intention of budging," he said.

He answered, "I have no intention of budging."

"I have no intention of budging," he answered, "until you have given me your promise."

Is "A penny saved is a penny earned" as old an adage as "If wishes were horses beggars would ride"?[22]

When I say "The urn is a vase," I simply state a fact.

His example is the sentence "Man is an animal."[22]

What is the meaning of the metaphor "Fame is a spur"?

Some people do not accept such principles as "Whatever is moved is moved by another."[23]

D113 Put in single quotation marks a quotation within a quotation.

"We must remember," said the orator, "the immortal words of a great patriot, 'Give me liberty or give me death!' "

---

[22] Do not use a comma before a quotation of this kind if the quotation is restrictive. Use a comma if the quotation is nonrestrictive: *Butler quoted a sentence,* "Man is an animal," *as his only reply.*

[23] Do not use a comma before the quotation when it is preceded by *as.*

D114 Do not use quotation marks if words are directed by a person to himself or are merely unexpressed thoughts (but capitalize the first word).

I thought to myself, They did not expéct me.
No doubt you have asked yourself, Why am I here?
He said to himself, Here we go again!
They were thinking, We will have to pay.
Why not send it on? he said to himself.

D115 Put an indirect quotation in double quotation marks if you want it unmistakable that you are using another's own words; if you do not want it so, then do not use quotation marks.

St. Paul declared that "our citizenship is in heaven."
St. Paul declared that our citizenship is in heaven.

It is an old saying that "a penny saved is a penny earned."
It is an old saying that a penny saved is a penny earned.

D116 In literary writing (such as fiction), put all sentences belonging to a single uninterrupted quotation in one set of quotation marks.[24]

Trafford replied: "I don't think you understand my position. I am not here to defraud you people. But I cannot return your money just now without defrauding others."

Erin warned me: "Don't you dare pass this time, partner. I made a demand bid, and you have to answer. I said two spades, and Eil said three clubs. Come on, you have to say something."

"Mickey and I want to go duckhunting in Scheller's slough today. May I go, and may I take Dad's shotgun, and may I stay out until five?" Richard asked.

D117 In literary writing (such as fiction), when a continuous quotation falls into paragraphs, place quotation marks at the beginning of each paragraph, but at the end of only the last.[24]

"I was ten years old at the time," began Joe Manning. "My brother and I lived in a shanty near the docks. I say 'lived,' but

---

[24] See D118.

really we only slept there; we lived in the streets. We ate when and where we could; we got money anyhow; and we made friends of vicious boys and girls as abandoned as we.

"Then one day I was taken to the hospital badly hurt. Mrs. Parkham saw me there, adopted me, and took me West to live. My whole life was changed. I never heard from my brother, never saw him again.

"All that happened twenty years ago. How can you expect me to recognize this murderer as my brother? It's some kind of trick to get money out of Mrs. Parkham."

D118 In professional and technical writing (such as magazine articles, reports, and theses) do not use quotation marks with a quotation of more than thirty-five words. Instead, set the quotation off by indentation.[25]

Now that we have seen some of the principles of description, we can profit by analyzing the following paragraphs from Dickens's *Pickwick Papers:*

It was a long room, with crimson-covered benches, and wax candles in glass chandeliers. The musicians were securely confined in an elevated den, and quadrilles were being systematically got through by two or three sets of dancers. Two card tables were made up in the adjoining card room, and two pairs of old ladies, and a corresponding number of stout gentlemen, were executing whist therein.

The finale concluded, the dancers promenaded the room, and Mr. Tupman and his companion stationed themselves in a corner to observe the company.

D119 In dialogue, use a new paragraph and a new set of quotation marks every time the speaker changes.

"It seems to me," said Dr. Nichols, "that you ought to sell the farm and buy yourself a college education. You want an education, don't you?"

"Yes, sir," I said; "but would the sale fetch enough money to pay all my expenses?"

"Why, yes, I should think so. As a matter of fact, I myself am prepared to offer you twenty thousand for the place. That's per-

---

[25] In typing it is well also to use single space instead of double or triple.

haps a bit more than you would get if you put it on the market. But we are good friends, and the property is worth it. Will you sell it to me?"

"No, sir," I said, "I wouldn't sell it to you unless you were the last person who wanted it."

"Why, my boy, you surprise and embarrass me. Why wouldn't you sell it to me?"

"Because you just front for a big syndicate that buys up farms, works the land to death with the same money crop for about ten years, and then moves on, leaving dead dust and Johnson grass. I'll sell my land to some man who respects the good earth and wants a home."

D120 Capitalize the first word of a directly quoted sentence when it appears within another sentence.

Cecil replied, "My mother is a very determined person."

"My mother," replied Cecil, "is a very determined person." [*Is* is not the first word of the directly quoted sentence.]

Then, "Don't you worry," she whispered. "For an old woman I'm feeling very fit indeed. Why, I've many a song in me yet and many a quarrel, too."

Is "A penny saved is a penny earned" as old an adage as "If wishes were horses beggars would ride"?

D121 Do not capitalize the first word of a directly quoted sentence fragment unless the fragment begins the sentence in which it stands.

Margaret won't speak to "those common Kellys," as she calls them.

He is always talking about "roughing it," by which he means putting up at a luxury cabin not more than ten miles from some interesting town.

"My mother," replied Cecil, "is a very determined person." [Note that *is* is not capitalized, since it is the first word of only a fragment, not of a sentence.]

She said, "For an old woman I'm feeling very fit indeed." But her "very fit" sounded unconvincing, spoken as it was in a rather feeble voice.

"Crazy as a loon," he called me.

"If wishes were horses," we could overtake Selwyn.

D122 Put periods and commas inside the second quotation mark.[26]

> As usual, the newspapers denounced the strikers as "roughnecks," "hoodlums," and "traitors."
>
> "It seems," said the traveler, "that there is nobody here."
>
> Packer replied glumly, "All he said to *me* was, 'No, I won't.'"
>
> No, you're thinking of the "Johnson Rag," not the "Tiger Rag."

D123 Put colons and semicolons outside the second quotation mark.

> These were included under "necessary expenses": theater tickets, four new novels, and a foot-long taxi bill.
>
> Curtiss said, "I don't think so"; but it was obvious that he *did* think so.

D124 Put question marks and exclamation points (*a*) inside the second quotation mark if they belong to the quoted matter or to both the quoted matter and the rest of the sentence; (*b*) outside, if they belong to the rest of the sentence only.

Pilate asked, "What is truth?"	These marks belong to the quoted matter only; hence, inside the quotation marks.
I thought of the famous cry, "They shall not pass!"	
Who asked "What is truth?"	These marks belong to both the quoted matter and the rest of the sentence; hence, inside.
How stupid of you to keep shouting "Police!"	
Who wrote "Miniver Cheevy"?	These marks belong to the rest of the sentence only; hence, outside.
Yet these men, thieves and murderers, prate of "decency"!	

D125 If a direct quotation is broken by an expression like *he said,* and if the part before the break would ordinarily be followed by a semicolon, use a comma instead and put the semicolon after the *he said* expression.

> "That was thoughtless—incredibly so," he said; "but I forgive you."

---

[26] The system here given of writing quotation marks with other marks of punctuation is common in the United States. British usage is different.

D126   Put in quotation marks (but do not italicize) the title of something that is mentioned as part of a larger work.[27]

"Hamlet" in *The Seven Greatest Tragedies*	"Hamlet" would ordinarily be italicized, since it is a play. But here it is put in quotation marks as part of a larger work that is also named.
Marquand's "The Late George Apley" in *A Marquand Reader*	"The Late George Apley" would ordinarily be italicized, since it is ordinarily published as a book by itself.

D127   Put in quotation marks (but do not italicize) the title of an article, short story, essay, chapter; or of a poem, musical work, or story that is not long enough to make a book by itself—whether or not these are mentioned as part of a larger work.[28]

"Ode to a Nightingale" in *The Oxford Book of English Verse*
"Ode to a Nightingale"

"On Leisure" from *Essays in Idleness*
"On Leisure"

"Summertime" from *Porgy and Bess*
"Summertime"

"St. Louis Blues"

D128   Put in quotation marks the title of a whole series of books.

G. K. Chesterton's *Robert Browning,* in the "English Men of Letters Series."

D129   Quotation marks may be used around the titles of motion pictures and television and radio programs. (Italics for such titles would seem to be preferred, however. See D139. Always be consistent in using the one or the other.)

"Gunsmoke"	"Nat 'King' Cole Show"
"Studio One"	"High Noon"
"Goodyear Playhouse"	"American in Paris"

---

[27] For italic with titles of books, see D139.
[28] For italic with titles of longer literary and musical works, see D139-47.

D130 Do not put in quotation marks (or italicize either) the titles of charters, acts, statutes, reports, and so on, or of alliances and treaties.

Act of Supremacy
Articles of Confederation
Declaration of Independence

Emancipation Proclamation
Stamp Act
Treaty of Versailles

D131 Do not put in quotation marks (or italicize either)—

A The names of the Bible, its books, parts, versions.

the Septuagint
the Synoptic Gospels
the Gospel according to St. John

the Book of Psalms
the Sermon on the Mount
the Lord's Prayer
the Reims-Douay Version

B The titles of prayers.

the Lord's Prayer

the Ave Maria

C The titles of the Breviary, Missal, Book of Common Prayer, or the parts of these books.

the Breviary
the Office
the Roman Missal
the Proper

the Book of Common Prayer
Lauds
the Canon
the Common

D The names of creeds, confessions of faith, and catechisms.

the Apostles' Creed
the Augsburg Confession

the Baltimore Catechism
the Thirty-nine Articles

E The names of the Mass or of any of its parts.

the Mass
the Asperges

the Gloria
the Preface

F The titles of church services and devotions.

Benediction
Novena of Grace

First Friday devotions
Forty Hours devotion

G The titles of the mysteries of the rosary.

The first joyful mystery is the Annunciation.

203

D132 Put in quotation marks words that need setting off for clearness.

"I said—incorrectly—that my brother and I 'lived' in a shanty near the docks."

"Ngaio Marsh" is not the name of an African swamp but of a woman detective-story writer.

What a gap there is between "ought" and "is"!

D133 Put in quotation marks the definition or explanation of a word or phrase.

Geometer means "a person skilled in geometry."

At your service signifies "the speaker is ready to obey orders."

D134 An occasional technical word or term, which can be misunderstood by the reader or which is unknown to him, may be put in quotation marks the first time that it occurs in a work.

The money was borrowed from the bank by an "entrepreneur."

D135 An expression on a different language level from that of the rest of the composition (for example, a slang expression in a rather formal context) may be put in quotation marks. (If you find yourself using this rule a great deal in the course of a theme, then you are probably changing language levels too often, or the language level is not what you think it is.)

The man had no residence, no employment, no prospect of it, and no desire for any of these things. He was a "bum."

D136 It is usually bad taste to put in quotation marks a word that is used ironically or given a forced meaning. It is all right to do so, however, when there is a real chance that intelligent readers might otherwise be misled.

For Brutus is an honorable man.	Not: For Brutus is an "honorable" man.

I have had quite enough of your remarkable "hospitality," Cyril.

D137 Use brackets [ ] to enclose a remark that is inserted into a quotation.

"So they [that is, Christian and Hopeful] were forced to go, because he [Giant Despair] was stronger than they. They had also but little to say, for they knew themselves in a fault. The giant, therefore, drove them before him, and put them into his castle [Doubting Castle], into a very dark dungeon."

—BUNYAN

Italic

D138 To indicate in typescript or manuscript that a word is italicized, draw a line under it.

D139 Although the titles of books, pamphlets, plays, motion pictures, and radio and television programs may be put in quotation marks, good usage prefers to write them in italic. (Be consistent in using the one or the other.)

> Thackeray's *Vanity Fair* [book]
> Lord's *I Can Read Anything* [pamphlet]
> Shakespeare's *The Tempest* [play]
> *The Birth of a Nation* [motion picture]
> *Invitation to Learning* [radio program]
> *Meet the Press* [television program]
> Milton's *Paradise Lost* [a long poem,
> often printed as a book]

D140 The title of a book may contain within itself a second title, the title of another book. There are two ways of handling the second title: either (*a*) put it in roman type or (*b*) italicize it and put it within single quotation marks. The second style is recommended.

> *Dickens's* Pickwick Papers *as History*
> *Dickens's 'Pickwick Papers' as History*

D141 Although the titles of papal bulls, encyclicals, *motu proprio*'s, as well as apostolic constitutions, may be put within quotation marks, good usage prefers to write them in italic. (Be consistent in using the one or the other.)

> *Apostolicae Curae* [bull]
> *Rerum Novarum* [encyclical]

205

Restoring the Christian Social Order [encyclical]
Sacram Communionem [*motu proprio*]
Christus Dominus [apostolic constitution]

D142 Do not italicize (or put in quotation marks either) the titles of dictionaries, encyclopedias, indexes, directories, almanacs, and similar reference works.

Webster's New Collegiate Dictionary	Information Please Almanac
	Americana Annual
Catholic Encyclopedia	the Roman Ritual
Cumulative Book Index	Reader's Guide
the Official Catholic Directory	Code of Canon Law
	Who's Who

D143 Do not italicize (or put in quotation marks either) the titles of charters, acts, statutes, reports, and so on, or of alliances and treaties.

Act of Supremacy	Emancipation Proclamation
Articles of Confederation	
Declaration of Independence	Stamp Act
	Treaty of Versailles

D144 Do not italicize (or put in quotation marks either)—

A The names of the Bible, its books, parts, versions.

the Septuagint	the Book of Psalms
the Synoptic Gospels	the Sermon on the Mount
the Gospel according to St. John	the Lord's Prayer
	the Reims-Douay Version

B The titles of prayers.

the Lord's Prayer	the Ave Maria

C The titles of the Breviary, Missal, Book of Common Prayer, or the parts of these books.

the Breviary	the Book of Common Prayer
the Office	Lauds
the Roman Missal	the Canon
the Proper	the Common

D The names of creeds, confessions of faith, and catechisms.

the Apostles' Creed	the Baltimore Catechism
the Augsburg Confession	the Thirty-nine Articles

E The names of the Mass or of any of its parts.

the Mass	the Gloria
the Asperges	the Preface

F The titles of church services and devotions.

Benediction	First Friday devotions
Novena of Grace	Forty Hours devotion

G The titles of the mysteries of the rosary.

The fourth glorious mystery is the Assumption of the Blessed Virgin Mary into Heaven.

D145 Italicize the titles of newspapers and magazines (but do not italicize or capitalize the initial article).

the St. Louis *Post-Dispatch*
the London *Times*
the *Queen's Work*
America
Fortune
Holiday
Variety

D146 Do not italicize the name of the city in which the newspaper or magazine is published.

the Baltimore *Sun*
the Omaha *World-Herald*
the Manila *Philippines Herald*
the Chicago *Tribune*
the Hankinson *News*

D147 Although the titles of works of art such as paintings, statues, and lengthy musical works, including operas and ballets, may be put in quotation marks, good usage prefers to write them in italic.

Raphael's *Sistine Madonna* [painting]
Praxiteles' *Hermes* [statue]
Beethoven's *Emperor Concerto* [lengthy musical work]
Gilbert and Sullivan's *Iolanthe* [opera]

Oklahoma! [musical comedy]
Swan Lake [ballet]

D148 Italicize the names of ships, aircraft, and trains (but do not italicize or capitalize the initial article).

the *Queen Mary* [ship]
the *China Clipper* [airplane]
the *Empire Builder* [train]
the *Flying Fish* [submarine]
the *Mary Ann* [rowboat]

D149 Do not italicize the name of a steamship line, airline, or railroad.

the Louisville and Nashville Railroad
the Cunard Steam-Ship Company
the Burlington *Zephyr*

D150 Italicize foreign words and phrases not yet adopted into English.

dolce far niente   *advocatus diaboli*
Mimosa pudica   *bon voyage*
passim   *supra*
op. cit.   *ibid.*
en passant   *enfant terrible*

D151 Italicize a word used only as a word, a letter used only as a letter, and a figure (number) used only as a figure.

Jimmy, spell *measles.*

Write *ought to be* where you have *is.*

Both *grammar* and *glamour,* curiously enough, came originally from the same word.

Your *os* and *as* look too much alike.

Use a capital *S* there.

All the *8s* on this page are in the wrong type.

D152 Do not italicize (or put in quotation marks either) letters used for names.

The house was sold by A to his brother, B.
Father L—— will say the Mass.
Who is the mysterious Mr. X?

208

D153 Use italic for emphasis very sparingly.

Menge has *not* been retaken.

The apostrophe

D154 Use *'s* to form the possessive of singular nouns (except those in D156).[29]

Edison's inventions	James's coat
Byrd's discoveries	man's shoes
Dickens's novels	fox's brush
Keats's sonnets	cow's horns

D155 Use *'s* to form the possessive of names that end in silent *s* or *x*.

Descartes's philosophy	Des Moines's population
Charlevoix's discoveries	Illinois's capitol

D156 Use the apostrophe (') alone to form the possessive singular of the following:

A The expressions *for conscience' sake, for acquaintance' sake, for goodness' sake.*

B Foreign names ending in *es,* like *Xerxes (Xerxes'), Socrates (Socrates'), Alcibiades (Alcibiades').*

C Our Saviour's name *(Jesus').*

D157 Use *'s* to form the possessive of plural nouns that do not end in *s*.

alumnae's card party	men's shoes
alumni's wishes	oxen's yoke
children's clothing	women's gloves

D158 Use only the apostrophe (') to form the possessive of plural nouns that end in *s*.

Davises' fence	boys' caps
Joneses' front yard	cows' horns
Smiths' garage	foxes' brushes

---

[29] There are other, equally common systems of showing possession. The one used in this book, however, has the advantage of simplicity, which seems to outweigh the disadvantage of an occasional awkward expression like *Dickens's novels.*

For the possessive case, see C182-83.

D159 Add the apostrophe or *'s* to the last word of compound words in the possessive. (Compound words follow D154-58 according as the last word of the compound is singular or plural, ends in *s* or not.)

your daughter-in-law's success   the herdsmen's cries
the emperor of Japan's palace   the master of ceremonies' jokes

D160 Add the apostrophe or *'s* to the last word of titles in the possessive case (except those in D162).

Pope Leo XIII's encyclicals
the district attorney's office
Henry VIII's disobedience
the Standard Oil Company's boats
the Lord Mayor of London's cat
the Guild of Goldsmiths' annual exhibit

D161 Use *'s* to form the possessive of abbreviations.

CBS's *Studio One*
Joshua Miller, Sr.'s, will
Daniel A. Lord, S.J.'s, pageants

D162 Some titles in the possessive case are "frozen"; they omit the apostrophe or *'s*.

Bankers Association   St. Marys, Kansas
Governors Island   Teachers College

D163 If two or more nouns possess something together (joint possession), add the apostrophe or *'s* to the last only.

Abercrombie and Fitch's clothing for men
Gilbert and Sullivan's operas
Beaumont and Fletcher's plays
the juniors and seniors' poor-relief work

D164 If two or more nouns possess something separately, add the apostrophe or *'s* to each.

Tom's, Dick's, and Harry's overcoats
Wordsworth's and Shelley's poetry

D165 Use an apostrophe or *'s* to form the possessive case of those indefinite and reciprocal pronouns that have a possessive case (except *who, which, what,* and their compounds).

another's idea	someone's umbrella
others' ideas	somebody else's
anyone's guess	each other's clothes
nobody's business	one another's eyes

D166 Do not use an apostrophe with the personal, interrogative, relative, and possessive pronouns or adjectives.

mine   ours   yours   his   hers   its   theirs   whose

D167 Use an apostrophe in a contracted word to indicate the omission of a letter or letters.

can't [*not* ca'nt]	ev'ry
doesn't [*not* does'nt]	he's
don't [*not* do'nt]	I'm
isn't [*not* is'nt]	o'
it's [*for* it is]	o'clock
who's [*for* who is]	th'

D168 In the number of a year, the first two numerals are sometimes replaced by an apostrophe.

the spirit of '76	the class of '48
vintage of '02	the events of '65
depression of '32	the Panic of '93

D169 Use either an unitalicized *s* or an unitalicized *'s* to form the plural of titles of books and magazines, foreign words, letters, figures, and words used as words.

Bring your *King Lear*s and *Commonweal*s to class.
Bring your *King Lear*'s and *Commonweal*'s to class.

The various *esse*s come to the same thing.
The various *esse*'s come to the same thing.

Mind your *p*s and *q*s.
Mind your *p*'s and *q*'s.

Your 7s look just like your 9s.
Your 7's look just like your 9's.

*I*s and *me*s are too prominent in your talk.
I's and *me*'s are too prominent in your talk.

211

D170 Except for the cases in D169, do not use the apostrophe to form the plural of a word.

        books   *snouts*

two ~~book's~~ on the table   long, pointed ~~snout's~~

D171 Do not use an apostrophe for which you cannot give a rule or solid precedent.

The hyphen

D172 When two nouns not ordinarily used in combination are used as one word, connect them with a hyphen.

Father Abram Ryan was the *poet-priest* of the South.
He is the only *philosopher-statesman* in Washington.
Some modern painters might be classified as *artist-salesmen.*

D173 Hyphen a compound modifier preceding a noun (except in those cases mentioned in D174-75).[30]

do-as-I-please manner	saber-toothed tiger
door-to-door canvass	so-called geniuses
eleventh-century art	well-phrased sentences

D174 Do not hyphen (*a*) compound proper adjectives or (*b*) compound proper nouns that are used as adjectives.

East Indian spices	New Orleans restaurants
Lake District scenery	North American savages

D175 Do not hyphen an adverb ending in *ly* and the adjective or adverb it modifies.

Mike's *badly swollen* hand pained him a great deal.
This factory was *extraordinarily well* planned.

D176 Do not hyphen a compound modifier following a noun.

[Preceding:] This is a *well-chosen* adverb.
[Following:] This adverb is *well chosen.*

D177 Use a hyphen after *re* where it will help to distinguish two words that might otherwise be easily confused.

---

[30] Note the difference in meaning between *red and white roses* (two kinds of roses) and *red-and-white roses* (one kind).

Mr. Antonescu *re-covered* the stolen chair.
Christianity could partly *re-create* the Garden of Eden.

D178 Use a hyphen between words when it will help to keep the reader from falsely combining them with other words.

Dr. Cox is president of the *insane-hospital* board.
Twelve *foot-soldiers* walked up the path.

D179 Hyphen compound numbers from twenty-one to ninety-nine.

I'll be *twenty-one* next Tuesday.

D180 Hyphen a fraction when it is used as an adjective or adverb.

Can I get lumber in *one-half* and *two-thirds* lengths?
The gas tank is *three-fourths* full.

D181 Do not hyphen a fraction when it is used as a noun. (If, however, the fraction contains a compound number from twenty-one to ninety-nine, that number must be hyphened according to D179.)

Crumbock lost *one half* of his savings.
Two thirds of the distance remains.
I was airsick for *three fourths* of the trip.

Five thirty-seconds is not very much of an error.
This bottle contains almost *twelve twenty-sevenths* of the acid.
Why, *twenty-one thirty-seconds* is more than half!

D182 No general rules can be given here for hyphening ordinary compound words, because usage varies so widely. Consult a recent dictionary.

D183 Whenever you doubt about a hyphen and these rules or a dictionary cannot help you, do not use the hyphen.

E Division of words

E1 The following rules apply chiefly to matter that is handwritten or typed, rather than to printed matter.

E2 Do not divide a word at the end of a line when it is at all possible and reasonable to avoid making such a division. Such divisions, though necessary in some cases, decrease readability.

E3 Use a dictionary in order to be sure what the syllables of a word are.

E4 If there seems to be no way to avoid dividing a word at the end of a line, be sure to make the division between syllables only.

> Autumn is the season of ~~frui-~~ *fruit-*
> ~~ffulness~~ *fulness*.

> His sickness is only an ~~ima-~~ *imag-*
> ~~ginary~~ *inary* ailment.

E5 If a word begins with a prefix, make the division after the prefix.

> Casey was said to be an ~~intrac-~~ *in-*
> ~~table~~ *tractable* young rebel.

E6 Do not divide (*a*) one-syllable words (like *golf, thought,* and *praised*) or (*b*) words of less than seven letters (like *inner, useful,* and *filial*).

E7 Do not divide a word after one letter.

> It seems that we live in ~~a~~
> ~~ventful~~ *eventful* days.

E8 Do not carry only two letters of a divided word to the next line.

> Mark has protested ~~violent-~~ *violently*
> ~~ly~~ to the chaplain.

214

E9 Do not divide the syllables of a proper noun or adjective.

Here is an issue of the ~~Atlan~~-

Atlantic

~~tic~~ *Monthly.*

F Abbreviations

F1 Abbreviate these Latin words: *id est (i.e.); exempli gratia (e.g.); et cetera (etc.); et alibi, et alii (et al.); ibidem (ibid.); opere citato (op. cit.); videlicet (viz.).* (It is now very common to write *that is* in place of *i.e.; for example* in place of *e.g.; and so forth* or *and so on* in place of *etc.; and others* or *and elsewhere* in place of *et al.;* and *namely* in place of *viz.*)

[Right:] We found paper, kindling, *etc.,* all laid ready for a fire.

[Better:] We found paper, kindling, *and so forth,* all laid ready for a fire.

F2 Abbreviate eras of time and A.M. (*or* a.m.) and P.M. (*or* p.m.) when these are accompanied by figures.[1]

There is not a scrap of evidence before 10 B.C.
There is not a scrap of evidence until ten years before Christ.

In A.D. 1300 the university was still rather small.
Anno Domini thirteen hundred dawned on a university that was still rather small.

The masking stops at 6:00 P.M.
The masking stops at six in the evening.

F3 Abbreviate these titles always and only when they precede proper names: *Mr., Messrs.; Mrs.; saint (St.), saints (Sts.); doctor (Dr.), doctors (Drs.).*

That must be *Mr.* Clark in the closet.
See here, *mister,* that's airline property.

---

[1] Spell out the time of day when A.M. or P.M. is not used (G8). Put in figures the hours of the day if A.M. or P.M. is used, except at the beginning of a sentence (G16).

According to you, *St.* Thomas must have been jolly just because he was fat.

The *saint* spent a peculiar week in Denver.

I can guarantee that *Drs.* Pell and Nive will find something wrong with you.

I'm sorry, but the *doctors* are both ill.

F4 Abbreviate *reverend* and *honorable* only in the addresses and headings of letters, and not even then if they are preceded by *the*.

Rev. Francis X. Clements
St. Ignatius Rectory
502 Seward Avenue
Clifton, North Carolina

We were harangued by the *Honorable* Cyrus R. Schumacher.

The Reverend Francis X. Clements
St. Ignatius Rectory
502 Seward Avenue
Clifton, North Carolina

F5 Abbreviate *junior, senior,* academic degrees, the names of religious orders, and like designations when they are used after a person's name, and set them off by commas.

Does anybody here know an Andrew Johnson, *Jr.?*
James B. Fall, *Ph.D.,* held us in his drowsy spell for four hours.
Father Patrick Donovan, *O.S.B.,* blessed the new fire engine.

F6 Except in technical lists, do not abbreviate first and last names but only middle names, unless the person himself uses initials.

Mr. ~~Chas.~~ *Charles* Dyke   ~~Geo.~~ *George* O. Pickton
~~Wm.~~ *William* Colgrave   ~~J.~~ *Joseph* R. Connaught

He signs his name *J. V.* Train.
The register is signed *M.* Moresby Mult.

F7 Except in technical lists or the headings and addresses of letters (where abbreviation is optional), do not abbreviate but spell out the names of the months and of the days of the week.

There is going to be a class night on ~~Tues., Feb.~~ *Tuesday, February* 9.

F8 Except in technical lists and references or the headings and addresses of letters (where abbreviation is optional), do not abbreviate but spell out such words as *street, boulevard, avenue, page, chapter, company, manufacturing, brothers, consolidated, limited, incorporated, building, university,* and *railroad.*

The first shift at Able Seal *Manufacturing Company* comprises about five hundred men.

The clubroom, a two-by-four affair on Wellston *Street,* could hold a typewriter and an upright hand press.

In *Chapter* 2, *page* 22, there is a remark that may indicate that the author is a Republican.

F9 Do not abbreviate the titles *Professor, Father, Brother,* or *Sister.*

Professor Collins	*Brother* Martin de Porres
Professors Collins and Egan	*Brothers* Anselm and Basil
Father LaFarge	*Sister* Teresa
Fathers Engstrom and Smith	*Sisters* Frances and Emilda

F10 Use a period after abbreviations, except the titles of government agencies, labor unions, athletic associations; the call letters of broadcasting stations; and those abbreviations like CARE, NATO, and UNESCO that are pronounced like words.[2]

At 9:00 P.M. there will be a cakewalk.

FBI	CIO	WAVES
NATO	AAU	WACS
AMG	WWL	SPARS
WDAY	NBC	CYO
FCC	SEC	

---

[2] There is an increasing tendency to use no period with abbreviations. Until this practice becomes more general, however, the above rule is the one to follow for correctness.

F11 Use no comma after the period of an abbreviation unless a comma is required for clarity or by one of the rules of punctuation listed elsewhere in this book.

[Wrong:] I have a 7:00 P.M., class.
[Right:] I have a 7:00 P.M. class.[3]

[Wrong:] In A.D., 64 Nero fiddled while Rome burned.
[Right:] In A.D. 64 Nero fiddled while Rome burned.

If the schedule says P.M., P.M. is what it means.	Here the comma is required for clarity.
Planes leave at 7:00 P.M., at 11:00 P.M., and at 1:00 A.M.	Here the commas are required by D32.
Pencils, sketching pads, binoculars, etc., will have to be provided by the bird watchers themselves.	*Etc.* is generally considered to be parenthetical, and so the comma is required by D53. See also D32.

F12 Except in the cases provided for in these rules and a few others for which you can find good authority, do not use abbreviations.

F13 For abbreviations in footnotes, see N77.

G Numbers

G1 Always spell out numbers at the beginning of a sentence.

Nineteen forty-three
~~1943~~ was not a bad year for wheat.

G2 When it would be awkward to spell out a number at the beginning of a sentence, recast the sentence.

Instead of—
Four million, two hundred and forty-six thousand, five hundred and forty-two dollars was the company's gross in the first five years of operation.

---

[3] While printed matter uses small capitals for the abbreviations A.M. and P.M., you may write and type them a.m. and p.m. if you like.

Write this—
In the first five years of operation, the company grossed $4,246,542.

G3 In general, spell out all numbers expressed in only one or two words, provided they are not affected by some other rule in this section.[1]

He was in the hospital *three* months and *seventeen* days.
With bones and feathers, this is about a *five*-pound chicken.
In *sixty-eight* cities, *ten thousand* people gave *two* dollars each.
At *seven-fifty* the *three* golf clubs were a bargain.

G4 Spell out numbers from 2,100 to 9,900 when they are expressed only in hundreds.[1]

[Wrong:] The auditorium held *two thousand one hundred* people.
[Right:] The auditorium held *twenty-one hundred* people.

[Right if intended to be read as *two thousand one hundred:*] The auditorium held 2,100 people.

[Wrong:] The auditorium held *twenty-three hundred and forty* people.
[Right:] The auditorium held 2,340 people.

G5 Spell out the numbers of streets up to twenty, of centuries, of sessions of Congress, of military bodies, and of political divisions and subdivisions.[1]

> East Twentieth Street
> the seventeenth century
> Eightieth Congress, second session
> One Hundred and Sixty-seventh Infantry
> Ninth Congressional District, Fifty-second Ward

G6 Spell out the ages of persons and things (except in the cases treated in G10).

> a one-hundred-and-four-year-old tree
> men between thirty and forty

G7 Spell out the names of particular decades and hundreds.[1]

Display was typical of the *nineties;* the *eighties* were not so lavish.
The *eighteen-hundreds* were years of savage economic warfare.

---

[1] See D179-80 for the use of hyphens in writing numbers.

G8 Spell out the time of day when A.M. or P.M. is not used.

I'll see you at *four-thirty* this afternoon [*but* at 4:30 P.M.].
We adjourned at *ten o'clock* [*but* at 10:00 P.M.].

G9 Spell out sums in cents up to one hundred (except for the cases treated in G10).

four cents   ninety-eight cents

G10 In technical, statistical, and business writing—where it is important that the reader be able to work with figures—put dimensions, degrees, distances, weights, measures, sums of money, and the like, in figures even though they could be expressed in one or two words. (But do not put these numbers in figures if they begin a sentence. See G1. Also see G17.)

Decimals and percentages: .05 of an inch, 7 per cent
Dimensions: 8 by 11 inches, 3 by 5 by 9 feet
Degrees: 70° F., 30° C.
Distances: 15 miles, 9 yards, 2 inches
Weights: 3 tons, 15 pounds, 5 ounces
Measures: 5 gallons, 2 pints, 50 bushels, 1 peck
Sums of money: $5.00, $43.85, $.85, 85¢
Ages: 18 years, 1 month, and 3 days

G11 In general, put in figures numbers expressed in more than two words, provided they are not affected by some other rule in this section.

1,556 hospitals	101 airplanes
1,250,000 people	514 pennies
123 times	28,634,878 Catholics
422 ships	134 countries

G12 Put years and dates in figures except for the case in G1 and except when, in text, the day precedes the month or the month is omitted.[2]

1820	June 3
March 1, 1820	April 1

---

[2] See D179-80 for the use of hyphens in writing numbers.

Nineteen forty-three was not a bad year for wheat.

The *fifth* of May is a day of much celebration in Mexico, for on the *fifth* the revolution is commemorated.

G13 Put in figures (roman or arabic as required) the page numbers, chapter numbers, and other divisions of books.

page 39	column 4	Volume III
pp. 39-72	line 18	Vol. 3
Chapter V	section 1	Book I
Chap. 5	verse 3	No. 16

G14 Put in figures the numbers of houses and of streets above twenty (except for the case in G1).

> 3648 Fifth Avenue
> 29 East 60th Street
> Fifteen [*or* 15] Rosalind Drive

G15 Put in figures the numbers in abbreviated measurements (except for the case in G1).

75 m.p.h.	700 ft/sec
8 mi.	2 ft., 9 in.

G16 Put in figures the hours of the day if A.M. or P.M.[3] is used (except for the case in G1).

6:00 P.M.	11:45 A.M.

G17 If similar numbers come under conflicting rules in the same sentence or in neighboring sentences, write them all in figures or spell them all out according to G1, G18, and G19, if you can do so without awkwardness.

G18 If all the numbers could be expressed in two words or less, spell all of them out or put them all in figures.[4]

[Wrong:] I arrived at 8:00 A.M. and began the operation about *nine o'clock.*

[Right:] I arrived at *eight* in the morning and began the operation about *nine.*

[Right:] I arrived at 8:00 A.M. and began to operate about 9:00.

---

[3] See F11, footnote 3.

[4] See G17.

G19 If some of the numbers would have to be expressed in more than two words, put them all in figures.[5]

[Wrong:] The number of accidents recorded in the three-year period were *fifty-five, seventy-three,* and 108, respectively.

[Wrong:] The number of accidents recorded in the three-year period were *fifty-five, seventy-three,* and *one hundred and eight,* respectively.

[Right:] The number of accidents recorded in the three-year period were 55, 73, and 108, respectively. [Note that *three* of "three-year" is not affected because it is not, according to the sense of the sentence, a number similar to the others.][5]

G20 In hyphening figures, omit hundreds from the second unless the first ends in two zeros or the hundreds change.[6]

7640-95 [*not* 7640-7695]
pp. 223-26 [*not* pp. 223-226]

But—
1900-1914 [because of the two zeros]
487-504 [because of the changing hundreds]

G21 In hyphening figures, if the second-last figure of the first number is zero, do not repeat it in the second number.[6]

pp. 1207-9 [*not* 1207-09]

G22 In hyphening dates before Christ, repeat the hundreds, since the numbers diminish rather than increase.

494-426 B.C. [*not* 494-26]

H Capitals

Line and sentence capitals

H1 Capitalize the first word of a sentence.

They say he was a wealthy man. (*That* was in 1860, of course, when a dollar bought more than it buys now.)

---

[5] See G17.
[6] See the rules for writing numbers in N78B.

H2 When a sentence in parentheses interrupts another sentence, do not capitalize the first word of the sentence in parentheses.

Though I have often been tempted to quit (*such* thoughts surely come to every man), the example of More's fortitude in spite of his circumstances gives me courage.

In this example the sentence in parentheses interrupts another sentence.

They say he was a wealthy man. (*That* was in 1860, of course, when a dollar bought more than it buys now.)

In this example the sentence in parentheses does *not* interrupt another sentence.

H3 Within a sentence you may capitalize, if you like, the first word of a question that is put in the form of a direct question but is not quoted.[1] The capital makes the question rather formal and emphatic.

The big question is, *Will* this help a man to reach his goal?
Miss Ford's invariable morning question was, *did* you sleep well?
He was always the first to ask, *when* are we going home?

H4 If words are directed by a person to himself or are merely unspoken thoughts, capitalize the first word. (Do not use quotation marks.)

I thought to myself, *Where* is all this going to end?
No doubt you have asked yourself, *Why* am I here?
She said to herself, *Here* we go again!

H5 Capitalize the first word of a directly quoted sentence, even when it appears within another sentence.[2]

Cecil replied, "*My* mother is a very determined person."

---

[1] A direct question is a question expressed in the words of the speaker; for example: "Where is the wampum?" An indirect question gives the sense of the speaker's question without quoting him; for example: "He asked where the wampum was." Indirect questions are frequently introduced by *whether* and by *if* in the sense of *whether*.

[2] A direct quotation is a quotation in the speaker's or writer's own words that is not introduced by the conjunctions *whether, if,* or *that* either expressed or implied.

"*My* mother," replied Cecil, "is a very determined person." [*Is* is not the first word of the directly quoted sentence.]

Then, "*Don't* you worry," she whispered. "*For* an old woman I'm feeling very fit indeed. *Why,* I've many a song in me yet, and many a quarrel, too."

H6 Do not capitalize the first word of a directly quoted sentence fragment, unless the fragment begins the sentence in which it stands.[3]

Margaret won't speak to "*those* common Kellys," as she calls them.

"My mother," replied Cecil, "*is* a very determined person." [Note that *is* is not capitalized, since it is not the first word of a sentence but of a fragment.]

She said, "For an old woman I'm feeling very fit indeed." But her "*very* fit" sounded unconvincing, spoken as it was in a rather feeble voice.

"*Crazy* as a loon," he called me.

"*If* wishes were horses," we could overtake Selwyn.

H7 Do not capitalize the first word of an indirect quotation, whether you use quotation marks around it or not.[4]

St. Paul declared that "*our* citizenship is in heaven."

St. Paul declared that *our* citizenship is in heaven.

H8 Capitalize the first word of every line of poetry.[5]

---

[3] Do not confuse a sentence fragment or half-sentence with an interrupted sentence or elliptical sentence. In the following, the quoted sentence is an interrupted sentence, not a sentence fragment, and hence is capitalized.

Margot was stopped just as she began to say, "Then you mean that the ghost isn't—"

In the following, the quoted portion is an elliptical sentence, not a sentence fragment, and hence is capitalized.

Shelley turned around and said very carefully, very deliberately, "Not a chance."

[4] See D115. An indirect quotation is a quotation introduced by the conjunctions *whether, if,* or *that* either expressed or implied.

[5] In some modern poetry this rule (as well as many others) does not apply. If you quote such poetry, follow copy exactly.

I am afraid, dear friend,
that something trivial will come
of men
with dollars.
—MICHEL CHAMBRE

See H9

Being your slave, what should I do but tend
Upon the hours and times of your desire?
I have no precious time at all to spend,
Nor services to do, till you require.

—SHAKESPEARE

H9 Do not capitalize a line of poetry that simply runs over from the preceding line for lack of room.

The cloud shadows of midnight possess their
    own repose,
    For the weary winds are silent, or the moon
    is in the deep;
Some respite to its turbulence unresting ocean
    knows;
    Whatever moves or toils or grieves hath its
    appointed sleep.

—SHELLEY

H10 When the beginning of a line of poetry is omitted, do not capitalize the first word.

. . . hast thou golden slumbers?
    O sweet content!
. . . is thy mind perplexed?
    O punishment!

—THOMAS DEKKER

H11 Capitalize the first word after a colon when the colon introduces a complete sentence or a quotation (see D77-79).[6]

My advice to you is this: *Stay* in bed Monday and Tuesday, and stay in the house at least until noon Saturday.

They asked me the same old tiresome question over and over again: *Where* were you, and with whom, last Thursday afternoon?

This is the problem we must talk over: *The* woman is old and getting feeble, has no money, cannot stay any longer at her niece's, and has gotten into trouble at the police station.

In his last letter—and note this carefully—he says: "The governor will hear no more talk whatever of a parole for Tompkins."

---

[6] There is really no consistent general practice in using capitals after a colon in a case like this. To use them is more conservative.

Boswell wrote of Oliver Goldsmith: "His incessant desire of being conspicuous in company was the occasion of his sometimes appearing to such disadvantage as one should hardly have supposed possible in a man of his genius."

H12 Do not capitalize the first word after a colon when the colon introduces merely a word, phrase, or clause—unless you want strong emphasis.

All the difficulty is due to just one little man: the boss.

His faults are these: temper, inexperience, awkwardness.

There is only one thing I want: to sit down and take these shoes off.

Democracy presupposes two conditions: that the majority of the people be informed and intelligent, and that the electors use their power fully and honestly.

Verdict: Not guilty.

H13 Capitalize the first word of each line in the heading and address of a letter.

The Narrows   The Shorthorn
Pawhasset, New York   Arlington State College
February 15, 1960   Arlington, Texas

The Roberts Family   The Debate Team
326 Westwood   Elspeth High School
Briarly, Maine   Wotan, Nevada

H14 Capitalize the first word in the salutation of a letter. Do not capitalize *dear* unless it is the first word.

Dear Sir: Reverend and dear Father:
Dear Aunt Marie,   Very Reverend and dear
My dear Aunt Marie,   Monsignor:

H15 Capitalize only the first word in the complimentary close.

Yours truly,   Sincerely yours,
Very truly yours,   Yours sincerely,

H16 When a title is set in two or more lines (for example, on a title page or at the beginning of a theme), capitalize the first word of each line.[7]

---

[7] For the capitalization of other words in titles, see H125.

A Short Dissertation
On Buying Pigs in a Poke

Marius
The King's Henchman

Proper nouns and adjectives

H17 In general, capitalize proper nouns—the particular names of particular persons, places, and things.

May I have an appointment with Mr. *Anthony Powers*, please?

Let's stop off at *Niagara Falls.*

The lobby of the *Statler Hotel* will be a good place to meet.

Wasn't *Man o' War* one of the greatest race horses?

On June 15, 1215, the king signed the *Magna Charta,* or *Great Charter.*

H18 In general, capitalize proper adjectives; that is, adjectives derived from proper nouns. (See H20.)

American	North Korean
Christian	Olympian
Napoleonic	South American

H19 Do not capitalize the combining forms *un, non, pro,* and *anti* when they are used with hyphens to join proper nouns and adjectives.

un-American	pro-British
non-Jewish	anti-Bolshevik

Is it *un-American* [adjective] to want God in the schools?

For a *non-Catholic* [noun] he shows a remarkable knowledge of the Mass.

H20 Do not capitalize words that, though derived from proper nouns, have lost almost all of the proper noun's original meaning.

apache [Parisian gangster], from Apache Indian
artesian well, from Artesium in ancient France
babel of opinion, from the Tower of Babel

227

bedlam [uproar, confusion], from Bedlam [Beṭhlehem] Hospital for lunatics

china [porcelain ware], from China

gothic type, from Gothic

italic type, from Italic, pertaining to ancient Italy

macadam [a road finishing], from John L. McAdam, Scots engineer

mulligan stew, from Mulligan

pasteurize, from Pasteur

quisling, from Vidkun Quisling

roman type, from Roman

venetian blinds, from Venetian, pertaining to Venice

watt [volt-ampere], from James Watt, Scots inventor

If you tear another *jersey,* you'll have to play in an overcoat.

The *bedlam* at Bedlam could never have been more wildly noisy than dinnertime at Miss Willick's school.

Religious terms

RELIGIOUS BOOKS, PRAYERS

H21 Capitalize the word *Bible* and its synonyms, and the titles of the sacred writings of all religions.[8] (Do not use italic or quotation marks.)

the Bible	Mishna
the Book of Life	Rig-Veda
God's Word	the Scriptures
the Holy Bible	the Talmud
Holy Writ	the Written Word
the Koran	

H22 Do not capitalize words derived from those in the preceding rule.

biblical	scriptural
koranic	talmudic
mishnaic	vedic

---

[8] Do not capitalize initial *the* or conjunctions, articles, prepositions, within such names or titles.

H23 Capitalize all texts, versions, and revisions of the Bible and all canons (that is, lists of inspired books).[9] (Do not use italic or quotation marks.)

the American Translation	the Roman Catholic Canon
the Confraternity Edition	the Septuagint
the King James Version	the Vulgate
the Reims-Douay Version	

H24 Capitalize all parts and books of the Bible.[9] (Do not use italic or quotation marks.)

the Acts of the Apostles	the New Testament
the Apocalypse	the Old Testament
the Book of Psalms	the Pentateuch
Deuteronomy	Proverbs
the Epistles	the Psalms
Genesis	the Psalter
the Letter to Philemon	the Synoptic Gospels

H25 Capitalize the nouns *gospel* and *gospels* when they refer to one or more of the first four books of the New Testament, but not otherwise.[9] Do not capitalize *revelation*. (Do not use italic or quotation marks.)

Everyone should read the Gospels and know them.
This passage is from the Gospel according to St. John.

Preach the *gospel* to every creature.
"Oh," he said, "big business has its own *gospel*."

The apostles gave Christ's *revelation* to the world.
The sources of knowledge of *revelation* are Scripture and tradition.

H26 Do not capitalize the adjective *gospel*.

Millions of men have never heard the *gospel* message.
Businessmen should act upon *gospel* principles.
I'm telling you the *gospel* truth.

H27 Do not capitalize *faith* or *holy faith*.

We must live according to our *(holy) faith*.

---

[9] Do not capitalize initial *the* or conjunctions, articles, prepositions, within such names or titles.

229

H28 Capitalize the titles of Christ's and others' discourses that are known by names equivalent to the titles of literary works.[10] (Do not use italic or quotation marks.)

> the Angelic Salutation'
> the Discourse at the Last Supper
> the Eight Beatitudes
> the Sermon on the Mount

The Sermon on the Mount and the Discourse at the Last Supper were addressed to different audiences.

But—
Our Lord gave a *discourse* at the Last Supper.
There are *eight beatitudes.*

H29 Capitalize the titles of Christ's parables.[10] (Do not use italic or quotation marks.)

> the Faithful Steward   the Ten Virgins
> the Five Talents   the Unjust Steward
> the Good Samaritan   the Unmerciful Servant

The Prodigal Son is one of the greatest of all short stories.

The *prodigal son* [the person, not the parable, here] asked for less than his father gave him.

H30 Capitalize the titles of prayers.[10] (Do not use italic or quotation marks.)

> Ave Maria   Litany of the Saints
> Benedictus   Lord's Prayer
> Gloria [Gloria Patri]   Magnificat
> Glory Be to the Father   Memorare
> Hail Mary   Pater Noster

We always recited the Memorare to ask for good weather on picnics and holidays.
Say the Glory Be to the Father at the end of each mystery.

Let *glory be to the Father,* not to me, for this day's manful work. [Not the title of a prayer here.]

---

[10] Do not capitalize initial *the* or conjunctions, articles, prepositions, within such names or titles.

H31 Do not capitalize *rosary* or *beads*.

The complete *rosary* has fifteen decades.

Most Catholics say their *beads* every day.

H32 Do not capitalize descriptive names of real or imaginary biblical characters.

The *good thief* was saved.

Repent as the *prodigal son* did.

The *faithful steward* was commended.

The *good samaritan* should be the model of all who wish to be good neighbors.

H33 Capitalize the words *Breviary* and *Missal* and the names of the parts of these books.[11] (Do not use italic or quotation marks.)

Breviary	Missal
Canon	Office
Compline	Office of the Dead
Divine Office	Preface
Lauds	Psalter
the Little Hours	Roman Missal
Matins	Second Nocturn

The new translation of the Psalms has made reading the Breviary a more pleasant and more intelligent duty than it was.

Is today's Office a double or a simple?

The prayers of the Canon say so much so beautifully that I should like to memorize them.

The Missal was almost as big as the altar boy.

St. Chrysostom says that (in his day) the priest would not proceed with the Mass until the people had responded to the Preface.

No, Alice, Matins is sung between midnight and dawn.

H34 Capitalize the names of all creeds, confessions of faith, and catechisms.[11] (Do not use italic or quotation marks.)

the Apostles' Creed	the Baltimore Catechism
the Augsburg Confession	the Thirty-nine Articles

---

[11] Do not capitalize initial *the* or conjunctions, articles, prepositions, within such names or titles.

NAMES OF GOD

H35 Capitalize the names of God.[12]

Allah	Jehovah
Christ	Jesus
Divine Persons	Logos
Father	Messias [Messiah]
First Person	Paraclete
God	Second Person
God-Man	Third Person
Holy Ghost	Trinity

H36 Capitalize the following names whenever they are used as proper names of God—whenever they are substitute names, that is.

Advocate	Lord (our Lord)
the Bread of Angels	the Lord of Lords
the Child Jesus	Maker
Comforter	Master
the Creator	the Prince of Peace
the Good Shepherd	the Redeemer
the Infant	the Sanctifier
the Infant Jesus	Saviour
the King of Heaven	the Son
the King of Kings	the Son of God
the Lamb of God	the Son of Man

Adore your *Maker*.

The *Son of God* is Jesus Christ.

Simeon was glad because he saw his *Redeemer* and *Saviour*.

H37 Do not capitalize names such as those in H36 when they are used simply as descriptive predicates or appositives.

God is our *maker*.

[But:] Adore your *Maker*.

Christ is the *son* of Mary.

[But:] The *Son of God* is Jesus Christ.

---

[12] Do not capitalize initial *the* or conjunctions, articles, prepositions, within such names or titles.

All nations have longed for a *redeemer*, a *savior*.
[But:] Simeon was glad because he saw his *Redeemer* and *Saviour*.

Christ came into the world as an *infant*.
[But:] The Magi adored the *Infant*.

Our Lord proved Himself the *master* of His enemies.
[But:] "Peace!" cried Martha. "The *Master* is coming."

Christ, the *good shepherd*, searched for the lost sheep.
[But:] Teach us, *Good Shepherd*, to be kind.

Jesus is the *lord* of the world.
[But:] You can heal me, *Lord*, if You will.

Christ, as *lord of lords* and *king of kings*, has all power.
[But:] Jesus, *King of Kings*, have mercy on me!

Jesus is the *bread of angels*.
[But:] O *Bread of Angels*, be our strength!

The Holy Ghost is our *comforter*.
[But:] Courage comes from the grace of the *Comforter*.

God is the one true *sanctifier* of souls.
[But:] Pray that the *Sanctifier* may give light to men's minds.

H38 Do not capitalize adjectives accompanying the names of God (unless the adjectives combine with the name to form a descriptive substitute name—an epithet, that is).[13]

all-wise Creator	loving Saviour
almighty God	merciful Father
eternal Father	our Lord
Father almighty	our Saviour

H39 Capitalize adjectives and adverbs in descriptive substitute names of God (in epithets for God, that is) whenever such names would lose their meaning if the adjective or adverb were left out.

the First Cause	the Most High
Immutable One	the Only Begotten

Such reasoning brings one back to the *First Cause*.
It is the *Only Begotten* who is altogether pleasing to His Father.

---

[13] See H39.

H40 Capitalize *divinity, providence,* and *deity* when they are used as names of God.

May the *Divinity* guide your steps!
Christ proved His *divinity* by His miracles.

Place your hope in *Providence.*
God's *providence* directs all things.

All men must worship the *Deity.*
The ancient Egyptians had their *deities.*

H41 Do not capitalize *name, holy name, fatherhood,* or *sonship.*

Judge with mercy, in the *name* of God!
Show reverence for the *holy name.*
The thought of God's *fatherhood* will comfort you.
Christ was conscious of His divine *sonship.*

H42 Capitalize *body* or *blood* only when it is a synonym for the Eucharist.

Every second day Eric received the *Body* of Christ.
Catholics always genuflect to the most precious *Body* and *Blood.*

The *body* of Christ in the tomb could be adored.
Christ gave His *blood* for us.

H43 Capitalize *heart* only in the name *Sacred Heart* or when it is used as an abbreviation for the name. Do not capitalize the words for any other part of Christ's body.

The *Sacred Heart* is our refuge and our hope.
His *Heart* is our refuge and our hope.

Jesus was meek and humble of *heart.*
They pierced His *hands* and His *feet;* they counted all His *bones.*

H44 Do not capitalize *humanity, hypostatic union, mystical body, mystical union, cross.*

We shall meditate on Christ's *humanity.*

What is meant by the *hypostatic union?*

We are all members of Christ's *mystical body.*

Some saints have been granted the unusual grace of *mystical union* with God.

In the *cross* of Christ is our salvation.

H45 Capitalize *he, his, him, himself, we, our, ours, us, ourselves, me, my, mine, myself, you, your, yourself, thee, thine, thy, thou, thyself, they, their, them,* and *themselves* when they refer to God.[14]

Christ went *Himself* to raise *His* friend Lazarus from the dead.

The Father and I are one, and *We* will keep *Our* faithful safe from the world.

All *My* sheep know *Me,* and I know *Mine.*

The three Persons of the Trinity are one in *Their* nature.

H46 Do not capitalize *it* when referring to God.

The Sacred Heart will bless all who trust in *it.*

H47 Do not capitalize *one, who, whose, whom, that* referring to God unless the reference to God would otherwise be obscure.

Our hope is in Christ, *who* redeemed us.

[If there is no other indication that *who* refers to God:] I know *Who* has care of me.

H48 Do not capitalize *god* when it refers to a false deity, or *gods, goddess,* and *goddesses.*

The Romans built a temple to Mars, the *god* of war.

Juno was queen of all the *gods* and *goddesses.*

NAMES OF THE BLESSED VIRGIN

H49 Capitalize the names of the Blessed Virgin; but do not capitalize *blessed* when it is preceded by another adjective and *and,* or by an adverb.

Blessed Virgin	our Lady
Blessed Virgin Mary	our Queen
Immaculate Conception	Queen
Lady	Virgin
Mother of Mercy	Virgin Mary

Let us pray to the *glorious and blessed* Virgin.

Let us pray to the *ever-blessed* Virgin.

---

[14] See H46-47.

H50 Do not capitalize *virgin* when it is not used as a proper name or part of a proper name.

Mary was a *virgin* before, during, and after the birth of her son.

H51 Capitalize the following names of the Blessed Virgin (and all such names as are found in the Litany of Loretto) whenever they are used as proper names—whenever they are descriptive substitute names (that is, epithets).

Mother of Christ	Refuge of Sinners
Immaculate Heart	Help of Christians

H52 Do not capitalize the names in H51 when they are used as simple descriptive predicates or appositives.

Mary, the *mother of Christ,* was also asked to the wedding.
[But:] O *Mother of Christ,* be my mother!

Mary has always been the *refuge of sinners.*
[But:] Let us pray to the *Refuge of Sinners.*

H53 Do not capitalize adjectives accompanying the names of the Blessed Virgin.[15]

What an ugly statue of *our* Lady!

Mary, *immaculate* and *holy,* never knew sin.

St. Bernard wrote many sermons in praise of his *gracious* and *loving* Queen.

H54 Capitalize *mother* when it is a substitute for the proper name of the Blessed Virgin or in the expression *His Mother,* not otherwise. Do not capitalize *motherhood.*

Then, *Mother,* pray for me.

Remember, Jesus worked His first recorded miracle at the suggestion of *His Mother.*

Jesus had a human *mother* but not a human father.

Mary was blessed in her *divine motherhood.*

Christ's *Mother* is our *mother* also.

---

[15] This rule does not apply to *blessed,* for which see H49.

There are a few "frozen" titles like *Our Lady of Good Counsel, Our Lady of Lourdes, Our Lady of Mercy,* in which the *our* is considered part of the title and is capitalized. Make use of this exception.

HOLY FAMILY, EVENTS OF THE REDEMPTION

H55 Capitalize *Holy Family.*

Quickly the *Holy Family* fled into Egypt.

H56 Do not capitalize the names of events and states of being in the life of our Lord and the Blessed Virgin except for the following, which long usage has decided should be capitalized.

the Advent [of Christ]	the Last Supper
the Ascension	the Nativity
the Assumption	the Passion
the Crucifixion	Pentecost
the Immaculate Conception	the Resurrection
the Incarnation	the Sermon on the Mount
the Last Judgment	the Visitation

The *flight* into Egypt took place during that part of our Lord's life of which we know almost nothing.

The *public life* of Christ lasted a scant three years.

Our *redemption* was accomplished with the death of the Redeemer.

The *descent* of the Holy Ghost was followed by the first general manifestation of the new Church to the world.

At the *circumcision* Jesus received His name.

Christ endured a *passion* all the more horrible because He was utterly innocent.

Surely, after the *Passion* Christ knows our sufferings very well.

Mary's *Immaculate Conception* sheds glory on us too when we are in the state of grace.

Note 1. Many terms similar to the ones listed in the columns above are not capitalized. When in doubt, consult the most recent edition of a good dictionary.

Note 2. Of course, when names not ordinarily capitalized fall under some other rule, they are capitalized. For example, *scourging at the pillar* is capitalized when it is used as the name of a mystery of the rosary; *circumcision* is capitalized when it is used as the name of a feast.

H57 When two or more of the names indicated in H56 are used together in the same sentence and one is not capitalized, do not capitalize the others.

It is surprising how many people confuse the *virgin birth* with the *immaculate conception.*

We read of the *passion, death,* and *resurrection* of Christ.

H58 Capitalize *redemption* when it is preceded by *the* and refers to the entire series of events constituting our redemption by Christ.

The second volume treats of *the Redemption.*
We should be grateful to God for our *redemption.*

ANGELS, HOLY SOULS, DEVILS

H59 Capitalize *angel, archangel,* and *guardian angel* only when they are used as titles in direct address in place of proper names, or as titles followed by proper names. Do not capitalize the classes of angels, like *seraphim* or *principalities.*

O *Archangel* Michael, defend us from evil!
Help and protect me, *Guardian Angel.*

Pray to your *guardian angel* every day.
I always think of the *seraphim* as bigger than the *cherubim.*

H60 Do not capitalize *holy souls, poor souls,* or *souls in purgatory.*

November is the month of the *holy souls.*
O *holy souls,* pray for us!
Mass will be said tomorrow morning for the *souls in purgatory.*

H61 Capitalize all synonyms for *Satan* except *devil.*[16]

the Archfiend	His Satanic Majesty
Beelzebub	Lucifer
the Evil One	the Prince of Darkness

The *devil* goes about like a roaring lion.

---

[16] Do not capitalize initial *the* or conjunctions, articles, prepositions, within such names or titles.

HEAVEN, HELL, PURGATORY

H62 Capitalize *Gehenna, Hades, Elysian Fields, Garden of Eden, Pearly Gates,* and *Tartarus,*[17] but not *Abraham's bosom, beatific vision, heaven, hell, purgatory, nether regions,* and *nirvana.*

Christ sometimes spoke of *hell* as *Gehenna.*

If we cannot be perfectly happy in *heaven* without football, then we shall have football in *heaven.*

H63 Capitalize *paradise* only when it is used as a synonym for *Garden of Eden.*

God talked familiarly with Adam in *Paradise.*
Everyone's hope is to reach *paradise* some day.

H64 Do not capitalize *kingdom of God* or *kingdom of heaven.*

There will be neither tears nor pain nor death in the *kingdom of heaven.*

CHURCHES, CHURCH MEMBERS, CHURCH

H65 Capitalize the names of all religions and their adherents.[17]

Anglican Church	Lutheran Church
Anglicans	Lutherans
Catholic Church	Protestantism
Catholicism	Protestants
Catholics	Roman Catholic Church

H66 Capitalize *church* standing alone when it means the Roman Catholic Church.[17]

A great many prominent persons have been received into the *Church* recently.

H67 Capitalize a synonym for the Church such as *Holy Mother (the) Church.* Do not capitalize a merely descriptive expression such as *our holy mother, the Church.*

---

[17] Do not capitalize initial *the* or conjunctions, articles, prepositions, within such names or titles.

Such are the teachings of *Holy Mother Church.*

All her children are the constant concern of *our holy mother, the Church.*

H68 Do not capitalize *church* standing alone when it indicates a building, when it is used as an adjective, or when it does not necessarily refer to the Roman Catholic Church. And do not capitalize it when it is used as part of the description, rather than as part of the proper name, of a building.

There seems to be a *church* on every corner.

It is *church* law that everyone must help support his pastor.

The question of *church* and state is much argued.

That is the Baptist *church.*	Here *church* is part of a description rather than part of a proper name.
On the corner is the First Baptist *Church.*	Here *church* is part of a proper, particular, name.

MASS, THE SACRAMENTS

H69 Capitalize *Mass* and all the parts of the Mass, even when used as adjectives.[18] (Do not use italic or quotation marks.)

Asperges	Introit
Canon	Ite Missa Est
Communion of the Priest	Last Gospel
Consecration	Offertory
Credo	Ordinary
Elevation [of the Host]	Postcommunion
Epistle	Proper

I went to early Mass this morning.

No one has put away the Mass vestments.

The congregation stands during the reading of the Gospel.

The storm struck while the priest was at the Offertory.

Look up the Collect in your Missal.

---

[18] Do not capitalize initial *the* or conjunctions, articles, prepositions, within such names or titles.

H70 Do not capitalize adjectives modifying *Mass.*

low Mass	requiem Mass
Missa cantata	solemn high Mass

H71 Do not capitalize *sacrament* or the names of the sacraments (except the Eucharist, for which see H72).

Ted has received the *sacrament* of *baptism,* but he has never received *confirmation.*

I have been given *extreme unction* five times.

Christ Himself instituted *penance;* that is, *confession.*

My uncle has returned to the *sacraments.*

H72 Capitalize the names of the Holy Eucharist and the Eucharistic Sacrifice.[19]

Blessed Eucharist	Holy Communion
Blessed Sacrament	Holy Sacrament
Communion	sacrament of the Eucharist
Eucharist	Viaticum

H73 Do not capitalize adjectives and adverbs modifying the terms listed in H72.

Every night there will be devotions in honor of the *most adorable* Sacrament of the Altar.

H74 Do not capitalize *real presence, host, sacred host, sacred species, transubstantiation.*[20]

All Catholics believe in the *real presence.*
Vandals scattered the *sacred species* all over the sanctuary.

SERVICES, DEVOTIONS

H75 Capitalize the following church services and devotions (but not *service* and *devotion*).[21]

---

[19] Do not capitalize initial *the* or conjunctions, articles, prepositions, within such names or titles.
See H73.

[20] Of course, the words should be capitalized if they come under some other rule; for example, *Elevation of the Host,* in accord with H69.

[21] See footnote 19, above.
See H76.

Benediction [of the Blessed Sacrament]	Mass
Compline	Novena of Grace [of the Sorrowful Mother, of the Sacred Heart, *and so on*]
Exposition [of the Blessed Sacrament]	Stations of the Cross
First Friday devotions	Tenebrae
Forty Hours devotion	Three Hours devotion
Holy Hour	Tre Ore [service, devotion]
Litany of Loretto [of the Sacred Heart, *and so on*]	Vespers
	Way of the Cross

There will be rosary and *Benediction* at 8:15 P.M.

Many churches still have *Vespers* on Sunday afternoon.

H76 Do not capitalize the following words except when they appear as part of the names in H75 or come under some other rule.

benediction	prayers
blessing	retreat
day of recollection	rosary
exposition	sermon
grace	thanksgiving
litany	triduum
novena	veneration

The priest raised his hand in *benediction* [blessing].

There will be a *sermon* and *prayers,* followed by *exposition* and *veneration* of the relic.

This *novena* is the Novena of Grace.

There will be *rosary* and Benediction at 8:15 P.M.

After the *litany* the clergy and the laity marched in procession to the bishop's house.

H77 Capitalize the titles of the mysteries of the rosary: the *Carrying of the Cross,* the *Crowning of the Blessed Virgin Mary,* the *Crowning with Thorns,* the *Crucifixion,* the *Descent of the Holy Spirit,* and so on.[22]

The fourth glorious mystery is the *Assumption of the Blessed Virgin Mary into Heaven.*

---

[22] Do not capitalize initial *the* or conjunctions, articles, prepositions, within such names or titles.

CLASSES AND ORDERS OF PEOPLE IN THE CHURCH

H78 Do not capitalize the names of classes of men such as *patriarchs, prophets, doctors* and *fathers of the Church, apostles,* and *disciples.*

The greatest of the *prophets* was John the Baptist.

St. Robert Bellarmine is a *doctor of the Church.*

Give me the name of the earliest church *father.*

The *apostles* were simple, not stupid, men.

Christ's grace produced Peter, the *apostle.*

There were all sorts of men among the *disciples.*

Name three famous *patriarchs* of Constantinople.

H79 Capitalize the names of religious orders and the names by which their members are known.[23]

Brothers of Mary	Benedictines
Christian Brothers	Cistercians
Daughters of Divine Charity	Dominicans
Institute of Charity	Eudists
Order of Preachers	Jesuits
Order of St. Benedict	Oblates
Society of Jesus	Trappists

H80 Do not capitalize *congregation, order,* and so on, unless they are used as part of an official title.

The Jesuit *order* [the Society of Jesus] considers the foreign missions one of its primary works.

The *Order of Preachers* was founded by St. Dominic.

This *congregation* numbers more than two thousand religious.

The *Congregation of the Missions,* whose members are known as Vincentians, has three parishes in our town.

Three *religious* were caught in the rain, and you should have seen what happened to those white things they wear.

She joined the *Religious of the Missions* and was sent to New York, and there she spent the rest of her life.

---

[23] Do not capitalize initial *the* or conjunctions, articles, prepositions, within such names or titles.

H81   Do not capitalize such words as *priest, monk, nun,* and so on, when they are used as common nouns; that is, not as a title or part of a title.

abbot	deacon	nun
archbishop	dean	pope
bishop	evangelist	priest
canon	friar	rabbi
cardinal	minister	religious
catechumen	monk	scholastic
cleric	novice	theologian

What is the difference between an *archbishop* and a *bishop?*
A *deacon,* unlike a *priest,* may not say Mass.
The *ministers* of the Mass will vest in the east sacristy.

APOSTOLIC SEE, PAPACY

H82   Capitalize *Apostolic See, Holy See,* and *Chair of Peter,* meaning the supreme governing authority of the Church.[24]

All Catholics must obey the *Apostolic See.*

The last two popes in the *Chair of Peter* understood America very well.

H83   Do not capitalize *papacy.*

The system of government in the Roman Catholic Church is known as the *papacy.*

Personal titles

H84   Capitalize all religious, civil, military, and social titles that are followed by a proper name.[24]

Pope Pius XII	Monsignor Fleckler
His Holiness, Pope John XXIII	Canon Appleby
Cardinal Spellman	Father Thomas Reid
His Eminence, Cardinal	Brother Jonathan
Meyer of Chicago	Mother Marie
Bishop Manning	Sister Mary Helen

---

[24] Do not capitalize initial *the* or conjunctions, articles, prepositions, within such names or titles.

Alderman Porter Smith	General Heath
Ambassador John J. Archer	Governor Herman Long
Chairman Kelly	Judge J. Robert Regan
Chief Justice Fred M. Vinson	Lieutenant Seldon Wadsworth
Commissioner Walker	Mayor James G. Fogarty
Director Cecil B. de Mille	Professor Walter Briggs
Mr. Rollins	Miss Helen McIntyre
Mrs. James B. Sellen	Master John Smithers

At this point *Bishop* Manning rose in protest.

The *Abbot* Marmion would hardly agree with *Miss* Kelly.

I believe the last speaker was *Ambassador* John J. Archer.

General Chennault urged that Chiang Kai-shek's forces be allowed to attack the Chinese on the mainland.

The lady in question is a *Mrs.* James B. Sellen.

H85 Capitalize titles indicating position or occupation when they are followed by a proper name.

Architect Riley	Designer Adrian
Catcher Hargrave	Halfback Steiner
Chairman Walker	Singer Mary Martin
Coach Wilson	Treasurer Lambert

His brief encounter with *Halfback* Steiner left him crippled for life.

As usual, there was some disagreement between *Architect* Riley and *Treasurer* J. Charles Lambert.

I hear that *Designer* Adrian is not going along with Paris this year.

H86 Do not capitalize words indicating position or occupation when they are not used as titles.

His brief encounter with the *halfback*, Steiner, left him crippled for life.

As usual, there was some disagreement between the *architect*, Riley, and the *treasurer*, J. Charles Lambert.

Do you mean the *poet* Wordsworth or the *poet* Longfellow?

H87 Except for those mentioned in H88, capitalize titles that are used in direct address. (Such titles are a substitute for a proper name and serve to identify the person who is being addressed.)

245

Please, *Mr. Secretary,* will you read the minutes of the last meeting?
Welcome, *Senator,* to our banquet.
Your position, *Judge,* is perfectly clear.
Will *Your Excellency* please sign this?
Be so kind, *Your Eminence,* as to sit over here.

H88 Do not capitalize *sir, madam,* and broad general terms (like *gentlemen, ladies,* and *children*) that can be applied to wide classes of persons, except when they are followed by a proper name or are used as part of the salutation of a letter.

Yes, *sir,* you'll find him in.
No, *madam;* the boat has sailed.
Listen carefully, *gentlemen,* to this hypocrite.
But, *lady,* that's the only hat I own!
See here, my dear *child,* that's my nose!

Dear Sir:	Gentlemen:
Dear Madam:	Dear Ladies:

H89 Do not capitalize *mister, master,* and *miss* when they are not followed by a proper name; nor terms of address used opprobriously, like *nitwit, slowpoke,* or *stupid.*

You don't know the half of it, *mister.*

Indeed, *master,* the third camel does have an irresponsible expression on its face.

You'll find flat silver on the third floor, *miss.*

Hurry up, *slowpoke!*

H90 In general, do not capitalize a title not followed by a proper name unless it is in direct address or is affected by another of the rules of capitals.

The *pope* spoke on the radio today.
The *cardinal* asked the *pope* what to do.
John XXIII was elected *pope* on October 28, 1958.
Henry IV, *king* of England, had not yet been heard from.
I'm sorry, but the *governor* will not see you.
Should the *president* carry his complaint to Congress?
Was Fred Vinson ever *chief justice* of the United States?
Cardinal Spellman, *archbishop* of New York, hurried to Rome.

246

H91 Always capitalize *father* (a priest) and *brother* and *sister* (religious), whether or not they are used in direct address or before a proper name.[25]

> Father Thomas Reid   Brother Jonathan   Sister Mary Helen

> I have two *Sisters* and a *Brother* in my class.
> Bucky has an uncle who is an Oblate *Father*.
> The *Fathers'* birettas are on the sedilia.

H92 Capitalize such titles as *His Holiness, His Eminence, His Excellency,* and *His Honor* even when they are used without the person's name.

> You have just heard a broadcast by *His Holiness*.
> I wasn't able to see *His Eminence*.
> I wasn't able to see *His Eminence*, the cardinal.
> Gentlemen, *His Honor* is detained.
> Gentlemen, *His Honor*, the mayor, is detained.
> Have you met *His Excellency*, the British ambassador?

H93 Capitalize all epithets and nicknames.[26]

> Apostle of the Gentiles   Lone Eagle
> Father of His Country   Maid of Orleans
> the Holy Father   Richard the Lionheart
> Iron Chancellor   St. Leo the Great
> Ivan the Terrible   Sunshine State
> Leo XIII, the Pope of Labor   William the Silent

H94 Capitalize *reverend* and *honorable* when they are used as titles; and always use them with a given name or initials as well as a surname.[26] They should not be used with a surname alone.[27]

> the Reverend Aloysius Benton
> the Honorable J. L. Byrne

H95 If an unhyphened compound title is to be capitalized, capitalize all the words in it.

---

[25] Do not abbreviate *Father, Brother,* or *Sister.*

[26] Do not capitalize initial *the* or conjunctions, articles, prepositions, within such names or titles.

[27] *Reverend* and *honorable* may be abbreviated within the heading and address of a letter. Within a sentence spell them out (F4).

Acting Secretary Smith	Recording Secretary Oglesby
Lieutenant Commander Hayes	Field Marshal Stitz
Radio Operator Tomlin	Chief Engineer Wilson
Rear Admiral Budde	Adjutant General Smally

H96 Capitalize only the first word of a hyphened compound title before a proper name, but do not capitalize *ex* and *pro*.

Actor-manager Gordon
Vice-president Alben W. Barkley
Governor-elect Shane

ex-President Hoover
pro-Ally August Romano

H97 Capitalize *Jr., Sr.,* and all other abbreviations of titles following a name.

Samuel Thompson, Sr.	Fletcher Stanton, Ph.D.
Samuel Thompson, Jr.	Lowell Winship, O.P.

H98 Capitalize *father, mother, brother, sister, uncle, aunt, cousin,* and other kinship names when they are used in direct address or as a substitute for a person's name or as part of a person's name.

In direct address or as a substitute for a person's name
You can't make *Mother* [that is, Mary or Mrs. Wilkes] rest.
That's *Dad's* [that is, James's or Mr. Wilkes's] umbrella.
See here, *Aunt* [that is, Agatha or Miss Wilkes], I love the girl.
Stay out of *Sister's* [that is, Betty's] room.
Is that *Junior* [that is, Harold or Harold Martin, Jr.] sitting there in the car?

As part of a person's name
His family calls him *Brother* George.
Here come *Aunt* Mary and *Uncle* Julian.
Is it true that *Cousin* John married in Kalupa?
This is *Mother* O'Meara, my wife's mother.

H99 Do not capitalize kinship names when they are used as common nouns; that is, not in direct address or as a substitute for a person's name or as part of a person's name.

248

Tell Walter's *father* to come to the phone.
Your *mother* certainly looks young.
A *sister* should not give away a *brother's* secrets.
The *uncle* is a director of some railroad or other.

H100 Sometimes you will have a kinship name that has a possessive in front of it and a person's name after it. In such cases capitalize the kinship name if you want to use it as a title, as part of the person's name; do not capitalize it if it simply means "uncle [or cousin, and so on] whose name is such-and-such."

You've met my *Grandfather* Monty, Gene; well, this is my *Grandfather* Ryan.

I've never gotten a kind word from my *grandfather* Monty [that is, from my grandfather whose name is Monty].

Our own dear *Cousin* Elbert has lentigo.

Our own dear *cousin* Elbert has lentigo [that is, cousin whose name is Elbert].

This will introduce my *Uncle* Henry, who wants to sell you a casket.

This will introduce my *uncle* Henry, who wants to sell you a casket [that is, uncle whose name is Henry].

My *sister* Nancy is a writer [that is, sister whose name is Nancy].

My *brother* Joe paints [that is, brother whose name is Joe].

Your *grandmother*, Sarah Green, and I are good friends [that is, grandmother, whose name is Sarah Green].

My *aunt*, Mrs. Willoughby Patterne, has trouble with poltergeists [that is, aunt, whose name is Mrs. Willoughby Patterne].

Your *uncle*, Commodore Squash, is seasick [that is, uncle, whose name is Commodore Squash].

Places, divisions, directions, buildings

H101 Capitalize the names of political and administrative divisions.[28]

---

[28] Do not capitalize initial *the* or conjunctions, articles, prepositions, within such names or titles.
See H102 and H106.

Alaska	the Northwest Territories
the Archdiocese of St. Louis	the Philippines
Baton Rouge	the Republic [United States]
the British Empire	Sioux City
City of Chicago	the State of New Mexico
Diocese of Lafayette	Tenth Congressional District
the Dominion of Canada	the Twelfth Precinct
Fourth Ward	the United Kingdom
the Helenburg Deanery	United States of America
Louisiana	Vatican City
the Netherlands	Warren Township

I live in *Sioux City.*

The *Clayton County* sheriff took office yesterday.

H102 Do not capitalize the ecclesiastical term *parish* when it occurs in names such as those listed in H101.

We belong to Sacred Heart *parish.*

The *parish* of St. Gertrude has an active and rather celebrated little-theater group.

H103 Capitalize the names of sections of states, cities, towns, and so on.[29]

Beacon Hill	Jackson Square
the Delta	the Left Bank
Fourth Ward	the Loop
the Gold Coast	the Seventh Precinct

We had a typical *Vieux Carré* meal.

Chicago also has a *Gold Coast.*

H104 Capitalize the names of streets, avenues, boulevards, and so on.[29]

Commercial Alley	Portland Place
Gracie Square	Regent Court
Highway 61	Sheridan Road
Lindell Boulevard	Sherman Parkway
Minnesota Avenue	Twelfth Street
Natchez Trace	U.S. Route 61

---

[29] Do not capitalize initial *the* or conjunctions, articles, prepositions, within such names or titles.

See H106.

Are trucks allowed on the *Lincoln Highway?*
Harry is a *Park Row* cowboy.

H105 Capitalize geographical names.[30]

Adirondack Mountains	Gulf of Mexico
Aleutians	Gulf Stream
Alton Lake	Isle of Man
Arctic Zone	Japanese Currents
Atlantic Coast	Lake Erie
Bad Lands	Marquette State Park
Cumberland Gap	Mississippi River
Death Valley	Mount Hood
English Channel	Pacific Ocean
the Equator	Pikes Peak
Fly Creek	Rocky Mountain National Park
Gonzaro Pass	Torrid Zone

The *Japanese Currents* warm California, don't they?
Yes, Cap really was a *Mississippi River* pilot.

H106 Do not capitalize *kingdom, empire, state, diocese, city, county, town, precinct, street, avenue, square, coast, stream, zone, island, mountain, lake, river, park, creek,* and like words unless they are used as part of a proper or official name.

Britain has liquidated her *empire.*
Our *ward* has suddenly gone Republican.
Tyrrell Street is really a broad *avenue.*
These *islands* cannot be the Aleutians.
This jagged, ugly *peak* is unlike anything in the Adirondacks.
Which is the largest of the three *lakes,* Lake Michigan?

The *State* of Illinois is prosecuting the murderers.
The *State* is prosecuting the murderers.
This is the Badger *State.*

The *state* of Idaho grows apples and other fruits.
Our *state* is not large, but it is progressive.
Totalitarianism believes in an all-powerful *state.*

---

[30] Do not capitalize initial *the* or conjunctions, articles, prepositions, within such names or titles.
See H106.

Make your check payable to the *City* of St. Louis.

Make your check payable to the *City*.

Not many *cities* have grown as rapidly as the *city* of Houston.

H107 Capitalize the nouns *north, south, east, west,* and their noun combinations and derivatives only when they refer to a region of the nation or of the world, but not when they refer to direction.[31]

The civilization of the *East* is older than that of the *West*.

The *South* is the nation's winter playground.

The temperament of the typical *Northerner* is different from that of the typical *Southerner*.

Out of the *Middle West* comes food for the world.

We traveled *southwest* from the ranch.

To the *north* lay the mountains; to the *west*, the sea.

Most of us up-state North Dakotans do not realize that more than ninety per cent of the wheat used to make spaghetti is raised to the *south* of us, in the region below Grand Forks.

H108 Capitalize the adjectives and adverbs *north, south, east, west,* and their combinations and derivatives when they refer to a region of the nation or of the world. Do not capitalize them when they refer to direction or the points of the compass.[32]

But *Eastern* civilization is older than *Western*.

He was naive enough to think that all *Southern* planters have large homes.

Springfield lies a few miles to the *east*.

I like the *northwest* section of the country.

The wind is *southerly*.

H109 Capitalize the names of bridges, buildings, churches, chapels, clubs, libraries, and monuments.[33]

---

[31] See H108.

[32] See H107.

[33] Do not capitalize initial *the* or conjunctions, articles, prepositions, within such names or titles.

See H110.

Hell Gate Bridge	St. Francis Xavier Church
Grand Central Station	Rogers Memorial Chapel
Humboldt Building	Racquet Club
Municipal Auditorium	Newberry Library
Museum of Modern Art	Lincoln Memorial
Yacht Club	Beth-El Temple

H110 Do not capitalize words like *bridge, building, church,*[34] *chapel, club, library, monument,* unless they are part of a proper name.

There should be a *bridge* near Southport.
Alice fell asleep in the *chapel.*

Countries and governments

H111 Capitalize the names of countries and governments.

United States	French Government
British Commonwealth	Balkan States
Swiss Confederation	Union of South Africa

H112 Do not capitalize *commonwealth, confederation,* and so on, unless they are used as part of a proper name or as a synonym for a proper name.

Queen Elizabeth made an official tour of the *Commonwealth.*
Britain's *commonwealth* is loosely held together.

H113 Capitalize *Republic, Nation, Union, Federal Government,* when they are a synonym for *United States.* Otherwise do not capitalize them.

Since 1776 the *Republic,* like other nations, has had its scoundrels in high office.

The *Federal Government* exercises control over interstate commerce.

In this great *republic* of ours each of us has a share.

Schools are being assisted by *federal* funds.

The *government* of the United States cannot be sued except under certain restrictions.

---

[34] For capitalizing *church* when it means the Roman Catholic Church, see H66.

H114 Capitalize the names of political parties and their adherents (but not the word *party*.)[35]

Democratic party	Democrats
Labor party	Laborites
Republican party	Republicans

Many a *Republican* holds the principles of the *Democratic party*.
Markoe is a *Labor party* hack.

H115 Capitalize such words as *democrat* and *republican* when they refer to the Democratic and Republican parties, but not when they are used in their general meaning.[36]

There's really not much difference between *Democratic* and *Republican* aims and promises in this election.

The king banished Lamberti because of his *republican* principles.
Fuller could be called an eighteenth-century *democrat*.

H116 Capitalize the names of all national, state, county, municipal, and town assemblies, departments, bureaus, commissions, offices, courts, and so on.[37]

Allen County Traffic Bureau	Hewesport Board of Aldermen
Bureau of Standards	House [of Representatives]
Cabinet	House of Commons
Circuit Court of Appeals	House of Lords
Civil Service Commission	Office of Education
Commons	Ohio House of Representatives
Congress	Parliament
Department of Public Works	Senate
Farm Labor Board	Senate Finance Committee
Federal Bureau of Investigation	State Department of Health
Foreign Office	Supreme Court

John Wesley Snyder was secretary of the *Treasury* in 1949.

Hiss had worked in the *Department of State* at the time.

You want to talk to the chairman of the *Board of Health*, a Dr. Gleason.

---

[35] See H115.
[36] See H114.
[37] Do not capitalize initial *the* or conjunctions, articles, prepositions, within such names or titles.
See H120.

Organizations, institutions, schools

H117 Capitalize the names of organizations, associations, foundations, societies, companies, railroads, and banks.[38]

American Association for the Advancement of Colored People	Knights of Columbus
	Legion of Decency
	New York Central Railroad
American Legion	Rockefeller Foundation
Bay Shore Traction	Society for the Prevention of Cruelty to Animals
Camera Club	
Catholic Rural Life Conference	Sock and Buskin
Chicago Community Trust	Station WEW
Eastman Kodak Company	Steuben Glass
First National Bank	Woods School Fathers' Club

Herrick is going to be nominated for the *National Honor Society*.
I remember hearing that Toolen is a *Hodiak Mills* vice-president.

H118 Capitalize the names of educational institutions and of their schools and departments.[38]

Loyola University	Temple Hall
Pennsylvania State Teachers College	Ladue Grammar School
	Public School No. 8
Eden Seminary	Century Business School
Harvard Medical School	Miss Drane's Secretarial School
Campion High School	Department of Philosophy of Fordham University
St. Benedict Academy	

Gonzaga High School refuses to recognize any of my credits in home economics.

The *Wilson High* glee club—it has a resounding name that I've forgotten—is not very good.

My aunt, Helen Merkle, is head of the *Latin Department* at *Marlin*.

H119 Do not capitalize *freshman, sophomore, junior,* or *senior.*

I'm a *freshman* at Parkham.
The *sophomore* class is having a meeting today.

---

[38] Do not capitalize initial *the* or conjunctions, articles, prepositions, within such names or titles.
See H120.

The *juniors* are giving a dance for the *seniors*.

On you, *seniors*, depends the quality of the student body.

H120   Do not capitalize words like *club, assembly, bureau, commission, association, foundation, corporation, company, railroad, bank, university, college, department,* or *school,* unless they are part of a proper name.

Put your money in the *bank*—any *bank*, even Stillson's Bank of Commerce.

The *university* is going to finish the stadium next spring.

The Wilson High glee *club*—it has a resounding name that I've forgotten—is not very good.

A *commission* was set up to investigate the shock effects of fresh air on city dwellers who go to the country too suddenly.

What's the name of that *college* in Moorhead?

Military groups

H121   Do not capitalize the nouns *army* or *navy* unless they refer to the United States Army or Navy.[39]

The *Army* has worn a variety of uniforms since Washington's day [meaning the United States Army].

The *Navy* is sometimes almost absurdly jealous of its traditions [meaning the United States Navy].

A career in the *army* was all that Russia could offer him then.

The Brazilian *army* was represented in the council by General Longino Finkler.

H122   Do not capitalize the adjectives *army* and *navy* when used without *United States,* and do not capitalize *naval.*

We spent the first three weeks in an *army* barracks in Hawaii, doing nothing but twiddling our thumbs and waiting.

Some years ago *navy* spokesmen were rather turbulent in protesting unification of the armed forces.

United States *naval* power has increased sharply since 1949.

---

[39] Do not capitalize initial *the* or conjunctions, articles, prepositions, within such names or titles.
See H122-23.

An unidentified *United States Army* spokesman was credited with starting the rumor.

United States Navy personnel reported to the consulate.

H123 Capitalize the names of military divisions, regiments, companies, and so on.[40]

This is a memorial to the dead of the *Rainbow Division.*

There is no word from *Company F.*

Jarkie had his share of experience in the *Medical Corps.*

The *Marine Corps* has not enough marines to chance an engagement of that scope.

Under orders, the *Eighth Army* held off for three days.[41]

H124 Do not capitalize words like *division, regiment, company* when they are not part of a proper name.

Three *divisions* were strung along the Rhine.

The *cavalry,* as a matter of fact, hasn't ridden horses in years.

Just how much air power could accomplish without *infantry* is something we do not intend to find out just now.

Titles of works and events

PUBLICATIONS, WORKS OF ART

H125 Capitalize the first word in the titles of books, magazines, newspapers, essays, articles, poems, plays, motion pictures, paintings, and so on. Capitalize all words within the titles except conjunctions, articles, and prepositions (C-A-P).[42]

---

[40] Do not capitalize initial *the* or conjunctions, articles, prepositions, within such names or titles.

See H124.

[41] *Army* is capitalized because it is part of the proper name of a military unit.

[42] For the capitalization of initial *the, a,* or *an* with such titles, see H126 and H157. For the capitalization of a conjunction, article, or preposition after a colon within a title, see H126. For the capitalization of a final conjunction, article, or preposition, see H127.

See also H129-31.

For italic with such titles, see D139-47. For quotation marks with such titles, see D126-31.

The Life of Dr. Samuel Johnson [book]
"On the Extinction of the Venetian Republic, 1802" [poem]
Washington Crossing the Delaware [painting]

H126 Capitalize a conjunction, article, or preposition when it occurs after a colon within the title.

Receding Frontiers: An Interpretation is the title of his dissertation.

Please send me a microfilm copy of Rudge's "Polynesian Days: Through the Islands in a Yawl."

H127 Capitalize a conjunction, article, or preposition when it occurs as the last word in a title.

Either Get Out—Or
"Various Meanings of *The*"
Truths to Live By

H128 Do not capitalize initial *the* in the titles of newspapers and magazines.

This is the December 16 issue of the *Saturday Evening Post.*
The story was carried by the *Times-Picayune.*

H129 If a hyphen occurs in the title of a book, poem, and so on, capitalize the word following the hyphen only if that word is ordinarily a noun or proper adjective.

Nineteenth-Century Science [noun]
"Some Thrills of Deep-Sea Fishing" [noun]
"This Year's All-American Team" [proper adjective]

H130 If a hyphen occurs in the title of a book, poem, and so on, do not capitalize the word following the hyphen if it is a common adjective or if the hyphen merely joins a prefix like *ultra, co,* or *self* to the following word.

"Thirty-second Street's New Look"	*Second* is a common adjective.
The Case of the Dark-green Shade	*Green* is a common adjective.
Lives of Little-known Saints	*Known* is a common adjective or participle.
"Why Co-operate?"	*Co* is a mere prefix.

The Ultra-ambitious Oyster	*Ultra* is a mere prefix here.
How to Be Self-reliant	*Self* is a mere prefix here.

H131 Capitalize the titles of dictionaries, encyclopedias, indexes, directories, almanacs, and similar reference works. (Do not use italic or quotation marks.)

Webster's New Collegiate Dictionary	Information Please Almanâc
Catholic Encyclopedia	Americana Annual
Cumulative Book Index	the Roman Ritual
the Official Catholic Directory	Reader's Guide
	Code of Canon Law
	Who's Who

EVENTS AND ERAS

H132 Capitalize the names of historical events and eras.[43]

American Revolution	Dark Ages
Industrial Revolution	Middle Ages
the Flood	Elizabethan Age
Reformation	Christian Era
Renaissance	Victorian era
Reign of Terror	Revolutionary period
Revolution	Colonial days
World War I	Atomic Age
Boxer Rebellion	

H133 Ordinarily do not capitalize *day, era, period, epoch,* and *century* in the names of H132 unless they begin the title or are capitalized in a dictionary.

H134 Capitalize the names of expositions, fairs, festivals, and so on,[43] but not the names of events that have only a very local and minor interest.

Century of Progress Exposition	amateur night
Humboldt County Fair	Mothers' Club card party
Olympic Games	our annual strawberry festival
Book Week	the turkey raffle

---

[43] Do not capitalize initial *the* or conjunctions, articles, prepositions, within such names or titles.

CHARTERS, ACTS, ALLIANCES, TREATIES

H135 Capitalize the titles of charters, acts, statutes, reports, and so on.[44] (Do not use italic or quotation marks.)

Act of Supremacy	Declaration of Independence
Atlantic Charter	Magna Charta
Constitution [of the United States]	Monroe Doctrine
	Stamp Act

H136 Capitalize the titles of alliances and treaties.[44] (Do not use italic or quotation marks.)

Articles of Confederation	Old Law
Balkan Pact	Quadruple Alliance
New Law	Treaty of Versailles

Languages, peoples, academic courses

H137 Capitalize the names of languages, peoples, races, and tribes, whether in noun or adjective form.[45]

Latin	Spanish	Bushmen
French	Caucasian	Iroquois
English	Indian	Mohawk
Spartan	Negro	Scandinavian

Howard thinks it incredible that the ancient *Romans* communicated in *Latin.*

I should like to take *Spanish* 3.

They used to converse in the *Greek* language—*Attic,* of course.

A *Frenchman,* Lauras, told me that *Russian* is the most euphonious of languages.

Crane studied *Romance* languages at Oxford.

As a child Sheila learned the *Cherokee* dialect—or is it a language?

There is good *Italian* cooking to be had here.

---

[44] Do not capitalize initial *the* or conjunctions, articles, prepositions, within such names or titles.

[45] Do not capitalize initial *the* or conjunctions, articles, prepositions, within such names or titles.

See H138-39.

H138 Do not capitalize general terms that can be applied to several races or peoples.[46]

| aborigine | half-breed | redskin |
| gypsy | mulatto | whites |

There will be no segregation of *whites* from Negroes in heaven.
In Memphis there are Irish *gypsies* known as the Travelers.
In those days the *white man* was not very welcome in Japan.

H139 Do not capitalize *language, people, race, tribe,* and so on.[47]

Why not take a *language?*
Up there the Indians speak their own Taos *dialect.*
What's the origin of the French *language?*
The American *people* will stand for it.
These songs were produced by the Negro *race.*
Several *tribes* made up the Iroquois *nation.*

H140 Do not capitalize such words as *history, mathematics, chemistry, physics, religion,* and *algebra* unless they are used with a number to designate a specific course.

This year I'm taking *history* and *geometry,* but not Latin or *physics.*
I'm taking *History* 6 and *Chemistry* 1.
I used to think *religion* a dull subject, but *Religion* 4 has begun to interest me.

Days, months, seasons, festivals

H141 Capitalize the names of the days of the week, the months of the year, holidays, holydays, and ecclesiastical seasons, feast days, and fast days.[48] (Do not use italic or quotation marks.)

Tuesday	Easter
January	Pentecost
Fourth of July	Advent
the Fourth	Feast of St. Agnes

---

[46] See H137.

[47] See H137-38.

[48] Do not capitalize initial *the* or conjunctions, articles, prepositions, within such names or titles.
See H142-43.

Halloween	Gaudete Sunday
Labor Day	Holy Thursday
Lincoln's Birthday	Octave of the Feast
New Year's Eve	of St. John
Rosh Hashana	Rogation Days
Thanksgiving	Shrove Tuesday
All Saints' Day	Ash Wednesday
Ascension Thursday	Day of Atonement
Assumption	Ember Days
Christmas	Vigil of Pentecost

H142 Do not capitalize *day* when the name of a holyday or holiday makes sense without it.

Ed Buono's birthday is on Christmas *day*.	*Day* is not necessary.
March 25 is Lady *Day*, the Feast of the Annunciation.	*Day* is necessary.

H143 Do not capitalize *day, week, month, year, century, era, epoch, aeon, period, age,* and so on, when they are not used as part of a title.[49]

Bills flood in with the mail every *day* of the *week*.

There have been many revolutions during the *month* of July.

Terence spouts glibly about the eighteenth *century* but says nothing of the present *year*.

Our *era* is quite properly called the Christian Era.

Beowulf is not an *epoch;* it's an epic.

During that *period* of the Stone Age, I imagine, dress design was sharply limited by the materials available.

In an *age* when everyone runs with the herd, Monica is quite content to please God and, incidentally, herself.

H144 Do not capitalize *spring, summer, winter, autumn,* and *fall* unless they are personified.

Mrs. Williams and the children go to Maine in the late *spring,* stay all *summer,* and return in the *fall*.

We must get ready for Old Man *Winter*.

---

[49] Quite often these terms are not capitalized even when they are part of a title. See H133 and H142.

262

Miscellaneous capitals

H145 Capitalize names that are clearly short forms of titles that must be capitalized.

The *Church* [the Roman Catholic Church] is a society.

The best place in the world to live is the *States* [the United States].

The *Street* [Wall Street] was in panic.

The *Terror* [the Reign of Terror] lasted from about March, 1793, to July, 1794.

The *Republic* was born in 1776.

At first he lived near Riverside Drive and then, later, on the *Drive* itself.

The *High School* [St. Benet's High School] cordially welcomes your Excellency.

H146 With the exception of those listed in H147, capitalize any word or its abbreviation that is followed by a numeral or a letter.

Act III	Lesson 7
Answer 10	List A
Appendix V	Number (No.) 7
Article II	Part IV
Book I	Question 6
Chapter V (5)	Room 16 (Room B)
Chart XVI	Rule 18
Exercise 19	Volume III (Vol. 3)

H147 Do not capitalize the following minor subdivisions.[50]

page 39	footnote 7
pp. 39-51	letter *b*
column 4	stanza 3
paragraph *a*	verse 3
line 18	v. 2
note 7	scene 2

H148 Capitalize the special adjective in a trade name, but not the common name it modifies.

---

[50] See H146.

Blue Label tomatoes	RCA radios
Café du Monde coffee	Stetson hats
Camel cigarettes	Sunrise bacon
Ivory soap flakes	Wrigley's gum

H149 Capitalize the names of ships, aircraft, trains, and so on.[51]

the *Queen Mary* [ship]
the *China Clipper* [airplane]
the *Empire Builder* [train]

H150 Capitalize *I* and *O*.[52]

I came; *I* saw; *I* conquered.
Hear me, *O* my friends!

H151 Do not capitalize *yes, no, oh, good-by, good morning, amen,* and so on, unless they begin a sentence.

Oh, Mike has a most pleasant way of saying *yes.*
A gentleman can always say *no* courteously.
I said *good-by* without regret.
Janice always added a smile to her *good morning.*
To that prayer we add a hearty *amen.*

In a faltering voice Grandpa answered, "*Yes.*"

H152 Capitalize and italicize *whereas* and *resolved* in resolutions, and capitalize the first word following them.

Whereas, The fourth day of . . .
Resolved [or, *Be it resolved*], That the members . . .

H153 You may capitalize words for which special, usually humorous, emphasis is wanted. (Use this capitalization only very rarely.)

He looked with the greatest disdain upon the *Common Herd.*
She fell into theosophy on her way to the *Higher Things* in life.

H154 Capitalize words that are personified.

Man in the Moon   the Reaper

---

[51] Do not capitalize initial *the* or conjunctions, articles, prepositions, within such names or titles.

[52] *O* (nowadays reserved for direct address in rather poetic language) is always capitalized and never followed by a comma. *Oh* is not capitalized and is usually followed by a comma.

We must get ready for *Old Man River*.

The *Chair* recognizes the delegate from Puerto Rico.

> . . . bring with thee
> Jest and youthful Jollity,
>
> .   .   .   .
>
> Sport that wrinkled Care derides
> And Laughter holding both his sides.
>   —MILTON

H155 Capitalize the names of the heavenly bodies and the signs of the zodiac, but not *sun* and *moon*.

Big Dipper	Saturn
Milky Way	sun
moon	Taurus

It is impossible to see the *Southern Cross* from here.

A circle with a dot in the center is the symbol for the *sun.*

H156 Do not capitalize conjunctions, articles, or prepositions (C-A-P) within titles, except as in H126 and H127.

The preacher's sermon was on the Discourse *at the* Last Supper.

Let me read you the parable of the Friend Coming *in the* Night.

The article was entitled "Ups *and* Downs *of an* Elevator Man."

Mr. Sidney H. Coleman was then the executive vice-president of the Society *for the* Prevention *of* Cruelty *to* Animals.

I have returned *Costume throughout the Ages* to the library.

H157 Except for the cases in H125-27, H158-60, do not capitalize *the, a,* or *an* when it precedes a title or proper name. The article is not regarded as part of the title or name.

In *the* Bible are *the* Old Testament and *the* New Testament.

Let's say *a* Hail Mary.

When a priest says he's saying *the* Office, he means he's reading *the* Breviary.

Every Catholic is familiar with *the* Baltimore Catechism.

There in the stable *the* Magi found *the* Infant and adored Him.

Sister Mary had great devotion to *the* Sacred Heart.

June's father has been received into *the* Church.

The first part of *the* Mass, from the beginning to *the* Offertory, is called *the* Mass of the Catechumens.

Tonight *the* Holy Hour begins at half-past seven.

March 25 is Lady Day, *the* Feast of the Annunciation.

This article was written by *the* Reverend E. Irvin Burns, S.J.

Tell me who *the* Apostle of the Gentiles was.

Bob works for *the* Department of Commerce.

Where is *the* First National Bank?

It was dark when the men reached *the* Cumberland Gap.

Side by side on my desk are *the* American College Dictionary and *the* Concise Oxford Dictionary.

Describe *the* Industrial Revolution.

Today, *the* Fourth of July, is a great holiday.

H158 Capitalize *the* when it is the first word in the heading or address of a letter.

H159 Capitalize *the* in a certain few place names. (They will be found in a dictionary or gazetteer.)

While in the Netherlands we made a trip to *The Hague.*
East of Portland is the city of *The Dalles.*

H160 Capitalize *the* (as well as any demonstrative) preceding a noun when they form a kind of proper name or title.

For Siger of Brabant, Aristotle is *The* Philosopher.
They call me *The* Worm.
To June's parents, he was *That* Actor.

I Spelling

In general[1]

I1 Practically every rule of spelling has exceptions. But the following rules hold often enough to make them useful.

---

[1] For the proper spelling and punctuation of the possessive case of nouns and pronouns, see D154-66.

I2 When in doubt about the spelling of a word, consult a dictionary. Only the dictionary habit ensures correctness.

I3 American usage, in some instances, is different from British usage. British usage is best for Britons, American usage for Americans.

British usage	American usage
judgement	judgment
colour	color
analyse	analyze

THE PLURAL OF NOUNS²

I4 Form the plural of most nouns by adding *s*.

alley—alleys	chair—chairs
baboon—baboons	crowd—crowds

I5 When the singular of a noun ends in *ch*, *sh*, *s*, or *x*, add *es* to form the plural.

bench—benches	genius—geniuses
church—churches	Mass—Masses
crash—crashes	fox—foxes
rush—rushes	hoax—hoaxes

I6 When the singular of a noun ends in *y* preceded by a consonant, change *y* to *i* and add *es*.³

ally—allies	library—libraries
army—armies	mercy—mercies
lady—ladies	sky—skies

I7 When the singular of a noun ends in *y* preceded by a vowel, add *s*.⁴

---

² For the plural of pronouns, see A28, A31, A37, and A55. For the plural of verbs, see A63-64.

³ A consonant can be defined as a letter of the alphabet that is not *a, e, i, o,* or *u*. (More technically, it is a letter that cannot be named unless a vowel is pronounced with it; for example, *t* cannot be named without an *e* sound.) *U* preceded by *q* is considered a consonant: so the plural of *colloquy* is not *colloquys* but *colloquies*.

⁴ The vowels are *a, e, i, o, u* (and, in some words, *w* and *y*). They are letters that can be sounded without the help of another letter.

alley—alleys   key—keys
alloy—alloys   monkey—monkeys
essay—essays   play—plays

I8 When a compound noun is written as one word, form the plural of the last word.

bathhouse—bathhouses   teaspoonful—teaspoonfuls

I9 Generally, when a compound noun is written with hyphens, form the plural of the first word. The rule, however, does not hold where it would make for awkwardness or absurdity of pronunciation.

brother-in-law—brothers-in-law
passer-by—passers-by

But—
good-for-nothing—   *Goods-for-nothing* would be
   good-for-nothings   awkward.

two-year-old—two-year-olds   *Twos-year-old* is absurd.

I10 For the plural of nouns not covered by the rules, see a dictionary. The following is a list of some that may give you trouble:

A Words ending in *o:*

cameo—cameos   piano—pianos
curio—curios   solo—solos
dynamo—dynamos   soprano—sopranos

echo—echoes   potato—potatoes
mosquito—mosquitoes   tornado—tornadoes
Negro—Negroes   torpedo—torpedoes

banjo—banjos, banjoes   halo—halos, haloes
buffalo—buffalos, buffaloes   hobo—hobos, hoboes
cargo—cargos, cargoes   volcano—volcanos, volcanoes

B Words that still keep a foreign ending:

alumna—alumnae[5]   appendix—appendixes,
alumnus—alumni[6]   appendices

---

[5] Rhymes with "a bum knee."
[6] Rhymes with "a bum eye."

beau—beaux, beaus
chateau—chateaux
ciborium—ciboria
crisis—crises
curriculum—curricula,
   curriculums

index—indexes, indices
oasis—oases
parenthesis—parentheses
synopsis—synopses
tableau—tableaux, tableaus
thesis—theses

c Words that end in *f, fe,* or *ff:*

belief—beliefs
chief—chiefs
dwarf—dwarfs

fife—fifes
grief—griefs
tariff—tariffs

beef—beeves, beefs
elf—elves
half—halves
hoof—hoofs, hooves
knife—knives
leaf—leaves

life—lives
loaf—loaves
self—selves
thief—thieves
wharf—wharfs, wharves
wolf—wolves

d *Child, ox,* and words that change the root:

child—children
gentleman—gentlemen
goose—geese
louse—lice

man—men
mouse—mice
ox—oxen
woman—women

IE AND EI

111 When spelling words with *ie* and *ei* in them, make use
of the rhyme—

     I before *e*
     Except after *c*
     Or when sounded like *a*
     As in *neighbor* and *weigh.*

After letters other than c:

achieve	brief	grief	siege
apiece	chief	niece	sieve
belief	field	relieve	thief
believe	fierce	shield	yield

[Some exceptions:] *leisure, neither, seize,* and *weird*

269

After c:

ceiling	conceive	perceive
conceited	deceive	receive

When sounded like a:

freight	neighbor	rein	veil
heinous	reign	their	weigh

CEED, CEDE, AND SEDE

I12 Memorize the spelling of these verbs:

Ceed:

exceed	proceed	succeed

Cede:

accede	intercede	recede
cede	precede	secede
concede		

Sede:

	supersede	

PREFIXES

I13 A prefix is a syllable or a word added at the beginning of a word or root to change its meaning.

admit   readmit [admit again]

I14 When adding a prefix to a word or root, do not double letters or drop letters.

antisocial	discharge	readmit
belabor	misshapen	re-enter
bemoan	misstate	reinforce
coerce	mistake	uncertain
coherent	occur	underrate
co-operate	overrun	understand
debase	oversee	unnatural
demonstrate	pre-eminent	withhold
disable	prelection	withstand

[Exception:] *all: already, although, altogether, always*

270

SUFFIXES

115 A suffix is a syllable or a word added at the end of a word or root to change its meaning.

cold   colder [more cold]

116 When adding a suffix to a word ending in a consonant, double the final consonant of the word if—

A The word is accented on the last syllable.[7]

bag   be*gin*

B The final consonant is preceded by a single vowel short in sound.

b*a*g   beg*i*n

C The suffix begins with a vowel.

-age	*-ing*
bag–baggage	occur–occurred
begin–beginning	plan–planned
big–biggest	rebel–rebelled
clan–clannish	refer–referred
control–controlled	run–running
get–getting	sad–saddening
grab–grabbing	sit–sitting
hot–hotter	wed–wedding
impel–impelled	wit–witty
infer–inferred	

[Some exceptions:] *gaseous, transferable*

117 When adding a suffix to a word that ends in a double consonant, keep the double consonant.

add–added	full–fullness [*also* fulness]
address–addresses	odd–oddly
butt–butted	puff–puffy
dull–dullness [*also* dulness]	shrill–shrilly
ebb–ebbing	stiff–stiffness
embarrass–embarrassment	will–willful [*also* wilful]

---

[7] One-syllable words, of course, are accented on the last (the only) syllable.

I18 Keep final *l* before a suffix beginning with *l*.

accidental—accidentally occasional—occasionally
cool—coolly soul—soulless
final—finally usual—usually

I19 Except for the cases in I16, American usage does not double final *l* before a suffix that begins with a vowel.

equal—equaled travel—traveled

I20 Keep *n* before the suffix *ness*.

barren—barrenness sudden—suddenness

I21 Keep silent *e* before a suffix that begins with a consonant.

docile—docilely manage—management
hate—hateful pale—paleness

[Some exceptions:] *acknowledgment, argument, judgment, truly*

I22 Keep silent *e* if it both—

A Follows soft *c* or *g*.

peace advantage

B Precedes the suffix *able* or *ous*.

peaceable advantageous

change—changeable notice—noticeable
courage—courageous outrage—outrageous
manage—manageable service—serviceable

I23 Change final *ie* to *y* before the suffix *ing*.

die—dying lie—lying tie—tying

I24 In all cases not covered by I22-23, omit silent final *e* before a suffix that begins with a vowel.

argue—arguing hope—hoping
arrive—arriving please—pleasant
desire—desirable plume—plumage
force—forcible purple—purplish
give—given true—truer
guide—guidance type—typing

[Some exceptions:] *dyeing* (tinting with dye), *hoeing, singeing* (burning slightly, as feathers), *tingeing* (staining)

272

125 If a word ends in *y* preceded by a consonant, change the *y* to *i* (unless the suffix begins with *i*).

anarchy—anarchical
body—bodily
bounty—bountiful
busy—busier
cry—cried
dry—drily [*also* dryly]

duty—dutiful
hardy—hardiness
mercy—merciless
sly—slily [*better* slyly]
study—studious
whinny—whinnied

[Exceptions:] Words formed from one-syllable adjectives like *dry*, *sly*, and *spry*: *dryness, slyness, spryly,* and *spryness*

126 If a word ends in *y* preceded by a vowel, keep the *y* before the suffix.

allay—allayed
annoy—annoyance
buy—buying
gay—gayer

gay—gayety [*better* gaiety]
gay—gayly [*better* gaily]
joy—joyful
obey—obeying

[Some exceptions:] *daily, laid, lain, paid, said, slain*

127 Add *k* to final *c* before the suffixes *ing, ed,* and *er*.

frolic—frolicking, frolicked, frolicker
picnic—picnicking, picnicked, picnicker
mimic—mimicking, mimicked
panic—panicking, panicked

128 Words ending in the sound *ize* are generally, in American usage, spelt *ize*.

Americanize
apologize
baptize
canonize
catechize
characterize
civilize
criticize
devitalize
dramatize

galvanize
harmonize
homogenize
modernize
organize
pasteurize
pulverize
recognize
specialize
sympathize

[Some exceptions:] *advertise, advise, chastise, compromise, despise, devise, enterprise, supervise, surprise; analyze*

Graded spelling lists

I

I29 This list of 250 words is partly the result of fifteen years of noting and checking the words most often misspelled. Fifty of the words have asterisks before them. According to Easley S. Jones,[8] if you master these you will eliminate about sixteen per cent of your spelling errors.

1	accept[9]	3	argument	5	chosen
	accidentally		around		coarse[14]
	*accommodate		article		college
	accumulate		*athletic		committed
	acquaintance		author		committee
	*across		awkward		conscience
	adjective		because		convenience
	advice[10]		becoming		couldn't
	affect[11]		*before		deceive
	against		*beginning		*decided
2	*all right	4	*believed	6	decision
	almost		*benefited		declarative
	already		blasphemy		*definite
	altogether[12]		breath[13]		dependent
	always		breathe[13]		describe
	among		*business		*description
	anyone		can't		desirable
	anything		certainly		despair
	*appearance		characteristic		desperate
	aren't		choose		determine

---

[8] Easley S. Jones, *Practice Handbook in English*, p. 167. Copyrighted 1935 by Easley S. Jones. By permission of Appleton-Century-Crofts, Inc. Jones's complete list comprises one hundred spelling demons, the remaining fifty of which, with some exceptions, are dispersed through the rest of the lists in this book.

[9] *To receive with consent.* Do not confuse with *except.*

[10] Noun. Do not confuse with the verb *advise.*

[11] *To influence; to feign or pretend.* Do not confuse with *effect.*

[12] *Entirely.* Do not confuse with *all together.*

[13] *Breath,* noun; *breathe,* verb.

[14] *Unrefined, rough.* Do not confuse with *course.*

7   develop
    development
    device[15]
    didn't
    different
    dining[16]
    *disappeared
    doctor
    doesn't
    dollar

8   don't
    during
    dying[17]
    *effect[18]
    eighth
    embarrass
    especially
    Eucharist
    everybody
    everything

9   exaggerate
    excellent

    *existence
    *experience
    extraordinary
    familiar
    fatigue
    finally
    forgiveness
    *forty

10 forward
    four
    friend
    gallery
    genuine
    government
    *grammar
    group
    guardian
    hadn't

11 hasn't
    haven't
    *height
    hoping[19]

    humility
    idle[20]
    *imagination
    imagine
    *immediately
    *independent

12 instead
    *interesting
    isn't
    *its[21]
    it's[22]
    jealous
    knowledge
    laboratory
    laid[23]
    lead[24]

13 *led[25]
    library
    license[26]
    lightening[27]
    lightning[28]
    loose[29]

[15] Noun. Do not confuse with the verb *devise*.

[16] Present participle of *dine (to take dinner)*. Do not confuse with *dinning* (from *din*).

[17] Present participle of *die (to cease to live)*. Do not confuse with *dyeing* (present participle of *dye*).

[18] Noun, *result;* verb, *to bring about, accomplish*. Do not confuse with *affect*.

[19] Present participle of *hope*. Do not confuse with *hopping* (from *hop*).

[20] Adjective, *useless, inactive;* also a verb. Do not confuse with *idol* or *idyll*, both nouns.

[21] Possessive case of *it*.

[22] Contraction of *it is*.

[23] Past and past participle of *lay (to set [something] down)*.

[24] Noun, the metal; pronounced to rhyme with *head*. Verb, present, *to conduct, to go ahead of those who follow;* rhymes with *need*.

[25] Past and past participle of *lead (to conduct, to go ahead of those who follow)*. Do not confuse with *lead*, noun, the metal, which is pronounced the same way.

[26] *License* and *licence* are almost equally common as verbs. *License* is distinctly preferred to *licence* as a noun.

[27] Present participle of *lighten*.

[28] An *electrical discharge as during a storm*.

[29] Adjective, *not fastened;* verb, *to undo*.

*lose[30]
lying[31]
many
meant

14 meddle
*minutes
morning[32]
mountain
mystery
*necessary
neighbor
night
noticeable
noun

15 nowadays
nuisance
*occasion
*occurred
occurrence
often
omitted
*opinion
*opportunity
opposite

16 original
paid
passed
past
peculiar

perform
perhaps
personally
persuade
pleasant

17 *possess
possible
preceding
preferred
present
*principal[33]
*principle[34]
*privilege
probably
procedure

18 proceed
professor
prominent
publicly
pursue
quantity
quarter
quiet[35]
quite[36]
really

19 *received
recognize
recommend
relief

religious
repetition
sacrament
sacrilege
sanctifying
scream

20 sense
sentence
*separate
shining
shriek
similar
since
sincerely
solemn
species

21 speech
stopped
stories
*stretched
studying
success
*successful
surely
*surprise
suspense

22 terrible
terrific
*their[37]

[30] Verb, *to fail to keep.*
[31] Present participle of *lie,* either sense.
[32] *Early part of the day.* Do not confuse with *mourning (sorrow, expression of grief).*
[33] Adjective, *chief, main;* noun, *official in a school, money drawing interest,* and so on.
[34] *A fundamental truth; rule of conduct.*
[35] *Free from noise or disturbance.*
[36] *Completely; exactly.*
[37] *Belonging to them.*

there[38]	two[44]	*weird
therefore	*until	where
they're[39]	useful	
thorough	using	25 *whether
threw[40]		which
through[41]	24 *usually	who's[48]
title	village	whose[49]
	villain	winning
23 to[42]	visitor	within
*together	wasn't	without
*too[43]	waste[45]	wouldn't
trait	weak[46]	writing
tries	weather[47]	you're[50]
*truly		

II

I30 This list is made up of 250 words, of which about a dozen are either newcomers to the language, born of the advances in technology, medicine, and so on, or else old words that have acquired a new prominence or a new twist of meaning to express new discoveries. Nearly all the words on the list are in your active vocabulary, which means they turn up regularly in what you write.

1 ability	accelerator[51]	addresses
abundance	achieve	advertise[52]

---

[38] *In that place.*
[39] Contraction of *they are.*
[40] Past of *throw.*
[41] Preposition, *in at one side and out at the opposite side of.*
[42] Preposition, *in the direction of.*
[43] Adverb, *also; more than enough.*
[44] Adjective and pronoun, *twice one.*
[45] Do not confuse with *waist (the part of the body located between the chest and the hips).*
[46] Do not confuse with *week (a period of seven days).*
[47] Do not confuse with the conjunction *whether.*
[48] Contraction of *who is.*
[49] The possessive of *who* and *which.*
[50] Contraction of *you are.* Do not confuse with *your,* the possessive of *you.*
[51] *The foot-operated throttle of an automobile.*
[52] The spelling *advertise* is distinctly preferable to *advertize.*

	advise[53]	4	busier		deal[62]
	agriculture		buying		despise
	air-borne		carburetor		difficult
	allergy		casually		disable
			ceiling		disappoint
2	alley[54]		cellophane		discharge
	alleys[55]		chastisement		
	allies[56]		chief	7	distributor
	ally[57]		chiseled[59]		dramatize
	aluminum		chuckle		dyeing
	apiece				echo
	apologize	5	comfortable		echoes
	appendixes[58]		coming		elf
	appliance		comparison		elves
	arguing		compromise		embarrassment
			conceive		encouragement
3	armies		controlled		encyclopedia[63]
	authorize		convertible		
	baggage		coolly	8	enterprise[64]
	balloon		corpuscles		equaled[65]
	baptize		courageous		essays
	belief				exceed
	believe	6	crises[60]		field
	biology		criticize[61]		fierce
	bodily		cruise		foul[66]
	brief		daily		fowl[67]

---

[53] *Advise,* verb; *advice,* noun.
[54] *A very narrow street.*
[55] Plural of *alley.*
[56] Plural of *ally.*
[57] *Partner nation in a war.*
[58] Also *appendices.*
[59] *Chiselled* is acceptable American, and preferred British, spelling.
[60] Plural of *crisis.*
[61] *Criticise* is acceptable American, and preferred British, spelling.
[62] *Distribution of the cards in cardplaying;* also *a bargain.*
[63] Also *encyclopaedia.*
[64] *An undertaking; readiness to undertake things.*
[65] *Equalled* is acceptable American, and preferred British, spelling.
[66] *Very dirty; wicked.* When applied to weather, as in Shakespeare's "So foul and fair a day I have not seen," *foul* means foggy, rainy, or generally unpleasant. As a noun *foul* is used to name violations of the rules of an athletic contest.
[67] Singular or plural; *rooster, hen,* and so on.

	freight		hydrogen		lively
	frolicked		hymn		lives[74]
9	frolicking	12	indexes[70]	15	loaves
	frontier		industrial		lonely
	funeral		inquiry		loving
	garage		insurance		luxury
	gardener		interrupt		management
	gaseous		invisible		masses
	generous		island		medicine
	getting		jackknife		mercies
	ghost		jewel		miracle
	glasses		jeweler		mirror
10	gleam	13	joyful	16	mischief
	glimpse		judging		mistake
	gown		judgment[71]		monkeys
	grief		juice		mortgage
	grieve		keys		mosquitoes
	guidance		kindle		movement
	guide		kindred		negotiate
	guilty		knight		Negroes
	hair[68]		knitting		nephew
	handkerchief		labeled[72]		nervous
11	hasten	14	ladies	17	nevertheless
	hedge		lasso		niece
	heir[69]		laughter		noisy
	helicopter		lawyer		nostril
	heroes		leaves[73]		notable
	hesitate		leisure		nourish
	horizon		libraries		nursery
	hotter		liquor		obeying

---

[68] *The natural covering of the human head.*
[69] *One who inherits.* The *h* is not pronounced.
[70] Also *indices.*
[71] *Judgement* is acceptable American, and preferred British, spelling.
[72] *Labelled* is acceptable American, and preferred British, spelling.
[73] Verb, *departs;* noun, plural of *leaf.*
[74] Verb *(is alive* or *dwells),* rhymes with *gives;* noun (plural of *life),* rhymes with *wives.*

	occasionally		quaint	theological
	oddly		qualified	thief
			quartz	thieves
18	organize		quench	tobacco
	originally		quietly	tomatoes
	ornament			torpedoes
	outrageous	21	quit[77]	transferred
	overwhelm		quote	traveled[83]
	oxygen		reconnaissance	
	oyster		referred	24 traveler[83]
	palm		reign	traveling[83]
	parentheses[75]		relieve	truer
	patience[76]		rifle	tying
			rivaled	uncertain
19	peaceable		rout[78]	understand
	penance		route[79]	utensil
	perceive			valiant
	phase	22	said	valley
	phenomenon		seize	vault
	physician		shield	
	pianos		should've[80]	25 veil
	picnicked		signaled[81]	vilely
	picnicking		singular	visible
	pierce		slain	weigh
			sonar[82]	wheel
20	pigeon		squadron	willful
	playwright		succeed	witty
	potatoes			wolves
	precede	23	sugar	writhe
	psychiatry		surname	yield

---

[75] Plural of *parenthesis*.

[76] *The virtue of suffering quietly and cheerfully.* Do not confuse with *patients* (*persons under medical treatment*).

[77] *Stop* or *leave*. Do not confuse with *quite* or *quiet*.

[78] Rhymes with *out*. Verb, *to force out;* noun, *a disorderly retreat.* Do not confuse with *route*.

[79] Rhymes with either *boot* or *bout*. Verb, *to send along a certain road;* noun, *road, way to go.* Do not confuse with *rout*.

[80] Contraction of *should have*.

[81] *Signalled* is acceptable American, and preferred British, spelling.

[82] *A device for submarine detection.*

[83] *Travelled, traveller,* and *travelling,* are acceptable American, and preferred British, spelling.

III

131 This list is made up of 250 words, some of which are a little more difficult, but no less common, than the words in the two preceding spelling lists.

1 absurd
   accident
   accustomed
   achievement
   acquire
   acquitted
   address
   aerial
   aggravate
   airplane

2 altar[84]
   alter[84]
   amount
   amusement
   ancestor
   answer
   anxious
   apology
   apparently
   appetite

3 approaching
   arrange
   arrangement
   arrival
   arrive

   assistance
   assistant
   association
   athlete
   attacked

4 audience
   authority
   awful
   balance
   barren
   based
   beautiful
   believer
   boundary
   bouquet

5 brilliant
   burglar
   buried
   candidate
   canoe
   canvas[85]
   captain
   career
   carrying
   centigrade

6 changing
   choice
   clothes
   colonel
   column
   common
   compel
   compelled
   complement[86]
   completely

7 compliment[87]
   comrade
   concern
   confidence
   confident
   conquer
   conqueror
   considered
   control
   countries

8 course[88]
   cries
   crowd
   cruelty
   dealt

---

[84] *A structure on which sacrifices are offered.* Do not confuse with the verb *alter (to change)*.

[85] *A coarse cloth.* Do not confuse with *canvass*, which may be used as a verb *(to go through a city or district asking for votes, orders,* and so on).

[86] Noun, *that which fills up or completes; the full number.* Verb, *to supply a lack.* Do not confuse with *compliment*.

[87] Noun, *an expression of approval;* verb, *to express approval of (someone).* Do not confuse with *complement*.

[88] Noun, *a track; part of a meal; series of studies;* and so on. Do not confuse with the adjective *coarse (unrefined, rough)*.

debt
debtor
defendant
definition
depth

9 destroyer
dictionary
digging
discipline
discussed
discussion
disease
divide
divine
divisible

10 division
efficiency
efficient
emphasis
emphasize
encyclical
endeavor
enemies
entrance
espionage

11 evident
except
exercise
expense
expensive
explanation

Fahrenheit
February
forcibly
foreigner

12 forfeit
formally
formerly
forth[89]
fourth[90]
freshman
fulfill[91]
governor
guarantee
guess

13 handle
handsome
having
hear[92]
history
hungry
hurrying
imaginary
imitation
immense

14 immigration
incident
incidentally
independence
indispensable
innocent
instance

instant
interfere
invitation

15 itself
knew
know
known
later[93]
latter[93]
lieutenant
literature
magazine
maintain

16 maintenance
maritime
material
mathematics
merely
millionaire
mischievous
monkey
murmur
muscle

17 mysterious
naturally
necessity
neither
nickel
obedience
obedient
obliging

---

[89] *Forward.* Do not confuse with *fourth.*
[90] *Between third and fifth.* Do not confuse with *forth.*
[91] *Fulfil* is acceptable American, and preferred British, spelling.
[92] *To perceive by the ear, listen.* Do not confuse with the adverb *here.*
[93] The comparative of *late.* Do not confuse with *latter,* the opposite of *former.* (Some grammars and dictionaries, if superficially read, give the impression that *latter* is a synonym for *later* in certain circumstances. The impression is incorrect. Do not use *latter* as the comparative form of *late.*)

	o'clock		Protestant		strange
	officer		proved		strength
			pursuing		striking
18	oneself[94]		realize		suggestion
	operator		receiver		surround
	ostracize				tendency
	parallel	21	recollect		testimony
	particularly		recollection		till
	partner		relative		
	peace[95]		religion	24	tired
	perseverance		replies		toward
	persistent		representative		Tuesday
	perspiration		restaurant		twelfth
			ridiculous		typical
19	physical		sacrifice		undoubtedly
	physically		sacrificing		university
	piece[96]				unnatural
	plain[97]	22	safety		unnecessarily
	positive		scarcely		valuable
	possession		secretary		
	practice[98]		servant	25	varied
	preference		severely		variety
	premier		siege		vegetable
	preparation		smooth		velocity
			soldier		view
20	presence[99]		sophomore		violence
	priority		source		violet
	prisoner				Wednesday
	professional	23	speaking		woman
	pronunciation		statistics		women

[94] Also *one's self.*

[95] *A state of quiet or tranquillity.* Do not confuse with *piece (a part).*

[96] *A part.* Do not confuse with *peace.*

[97] *Clear.* Do not confuse with *plane (flat).* When using the words as nouns, remember that a level expanse of terrain is spelled *plain,* whereas the surface named in geometry or in rather scientific descriptions of objects is spelled *plane.*

[98] Sole spelling of the noun. The verb may also be spelled *practise.* For convenience' sake, it is a good idea to use the spelling *practice* invariably; for then you will never be troubled by having to notice whether you are using the noun or the verb and by having to remember which spelling or spellings are common for each.

[99] Singular noun, *state of being present.* Do not confuse with the plural noun *presents (gifts).*

IV

132 The 250 words in this spelling list are all words that you can reasonably be expected to use and to spell properly. They are more difficult than the words in the other lists, but these words are necessary for the expression of adult ideas and concepts.

1		3		5	
	absence		appreciation		buoy
	abundant		appropriate		bureau
	accompanied		arithmetic		cafeteria
	achieved		aroused		calendar
	acquainted		ascend		capital[4]
	acquittal		ascension		capitol[4]
	actor		ascent		cemetery
	addressed		assurance		censure
	aisle[1]		attendance		chaperon[5]
	alliance		attraction		chauffeur
2		4		6	
	amateur		auxiliary		climbed
	ambassador		bachelor		commercial
	analysis		banana		commissioner
	analyze[2]		barbarous		comparative
	annual		bearing[3]		competent
	anonymous		beggar		competitive
	antarctic		Britain		competitor
	anxiety		British		conceit
	apparatus		Briton		concentration
	appreciate		bulletin		conscientious

---

[1] *A space or passageway between chairs or benches.* Do not confuse with *isle* (*a small island*).

[2] Also *analyse.*

[3] *Carrying; enduring; bringing forth offspring.* Do not confuse with *baring* (*uncovering, exposing*).

[4] Adjective, *of primary importance, initial;* noun, *accumulated wealth, chief city,* and so on. Do not confuse with *capitol (statehouse).* The easiest way to avoid confusion and consequent mistakes in spelling is to remember that *capitol,* meaning statehouse, is spelled with an *o,* and that in every other meaning you should use an *a.* This will give you only one thing to remember instead of dozens. Make use of this same simplifying principle whenever you come across words which are related either in sound or meaning and which have only one exceptional spelling.

[5] Also *chaperone.*

7 conscious
continually
continuous
copies
council[6]
councilor[7]
counsel
counselor
courteous
courtesy

8 criticism
crystal
curiosity
deceit
deceitful
descend
descendant
descent
desert[8]
dessert[8]

9 diphtheria
disaster
disastrous
disobedience
dissatisfaction
dissatisfied
dissipate
dormitories
ecstasy
eligible

10 eliminated
emigrant[9]

eminent
environment
equivalent
essential
excel
excellence
exhausted
exhilarate

11 fiery
financial
fragrant
frantically
fraternities
fundamental
furniture
gallant
gambling
gauge

12 generally
genius
geyser
goddess
grandeur
grievance
grievous
harass
hindrance
humorous

13 hundredths
hurriedly
hypocrisy
hypocrite

illiterate
immigrant[10]
increase
incredible
infinite
influence

14 influential
intelligence
intelligent
intentionally
interpreted
irresistible
lacquer
legitimate
liable
literally

15 livelihood
loneliness
loyalty
manual
marriage
marries
melancholy
meringue
metal
miniature

16 miscellaneous
momentous
mournful
nauseate
nineteenth
ninety

[6] *An assembly.* Do not confuse with *counsel (advice).*

[7] *Member of a council.* Do not confuse with *counselor (an adviser). Councillor* and *councillor* are acceptable American, and preferred British, spelling.

[8] Noun, *due reward or punishment;* verb, *to abandon;* accented like *avert.* Noun, *arid region,* accented like *culvert. Dessert, last course at a meal,* accented like *avert.*

[9] *One who leaves one country to live in another.* Do not confuse with *immigrant.*

[10] *One who comes into a foreign country to live.* Do not confuse with *emigrant.*

ninth

obstacle

offender

omission

17 opponent

optimism

optimistic

pageant

pamphlet

paralysis

paralyzed

parliament

pastime

perilous

18 permanence

permanent

perpendicular

personnel[11]

pneumonia

politician

politics

porch

possessor

practically

19 prairie

precedence

precedent

prejudiced

prevalence[12]

primitive

proffered

propeller

prophecy[13]

prophesied

20 prophesy[14]

psychology

purchaser

questionnaire

receipt

reference

remembrance

reservoir

respectability

rheumatism

21 rhyme[15]

rhythm

righteous

sacrilegious

sandwich

scenery

schedule

science

scientific

sentinel

22 sergeant[16]

shepherd

shone[17]

shown[18]

significance

significant

site[19]

specifically

specimen

stationary[20]

23 stationery[21]

strategy

streaking

suffrage

summarize

summit

superintendent

susceptible

syllable

symmetrical

24 synonym

technical

temperament

temperature

threshold

tragedy

traitor

transferred

translate

treasurer

---

[11] *A body of persons employed in some service.* Do not confuse with *personal.*

[12] *Frequent occurrence; general acceptance.* From the verb *to prevail.*

[13] Noun, *prediction.* The *cy* rhymes with *sea.*

[14] Verb, *to predict.* The *sy* rhymes with *sigh.*

[15] Also *rime.*

[16] Also *serjeant.*

[17] Past and past participle of *shine.*

[18] Past participle of *show.*

[19] *A location.* Do not confuse with *cite (to quote)* or with *sight (vision).*

[20] *Not moving.*

[21] *Paper for writing.*

25 tyrannically	vigilance	welcome
unconscious	vigilant	welfare
vacancy	warrant	wondrous
vengeance		

J Diagraming

In general

J1 A diagram of a sentence is a picture that shows the inter-relation of the words, phrases, and clauses. Diagrams are a good way to analyze the structure of a sentence. They will frequently, though by no means always, reveal the grammatical flaw in a bad sentence; and they will untangle a complicated sentence so that one can see, for example, whether *who* or *whom* is required.

Diagraming simple sentences

SUBJECT NOUN AND PREDICATE VERB

J2 Diagram a subject noun or pronoun and a predicate verb like this:

MODEL

People are singing.

J3 Diagram a compound subject like this:

MODEL

Johnson and *Powers* disappeared.

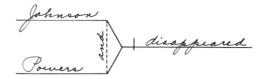

Either *Bill* or *John*, hardly   The diagram stresses the con-
Kenneth, will do.   nective force of *hardly*.

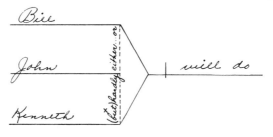

Either *Bill* or *John*, hardly   The diagram stresses the ad-
Kenneth, will do.   verbial force of *hardly*. (Com-
                                      pound elliptical sentence.)

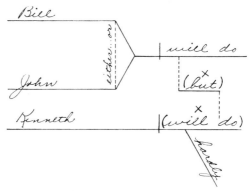

I, not *you*, am responsible.

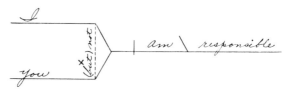

288

My *friend* and *neighbor*, Kittredge, is celebrating.

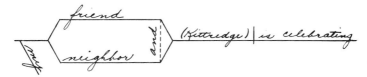

Raisins, peanuts, and *jelly* will mix.

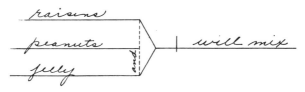

J4 Diagram a compound predicate like this:

Fairbanks *turned* and *ran.*

Fairbanks not only *turned* and *ran* but also *screamed.*

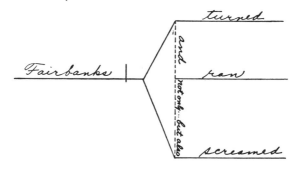

Fairbanks and Schlegel *turned* and *ran.*

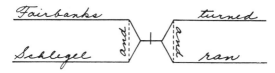

EXPLETIVE

J5 An expletive:

MODEL

Expletive

subject noun | *predicate verb*

It is painful to be burned.

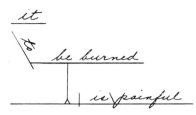

There came a man from afar.

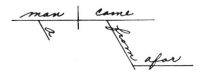

DIRECT OBJECTS

J6 A direct object:

MODEL

subject noun | *predicate verb* | *direct object*

Hilary is playing *golf*.

Hilary | *is playing* | *golf*

Mirabel likes *parades* and *pageants*.

J7 Two direct objects (not a compound direct object):

MODEL

Mr. Claudel teaches *Adrian algebra*.

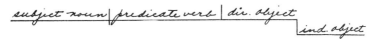

Hear *me* my *lessons*.

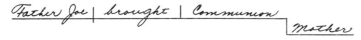

INDIRECT OBJECTS

J8 An indirect object:

MODEL

Father Joe brought *Mother* Communion.

Dad got *Arnold* and *me* jobs.

COMPLEMENTS

J9 A predicate noun, pronoun, or adjective:

MODEL

subject noun | predicate verb \ pred. noun or adjective

This is *milk*.

this | is \ milk

This is *milky*.

this | is \ milky

Raeburn is getting *tired* and *angry*.

Pitkin was named and was elected *chairman*.

J10 An objective complement:

MODEL

subject noun | predicate verb | dir. object / obj. complement

Boykin appointed Fleisch *administrator*.

Boykin | appointed | Fleisch / administrator

292

I call that *ungrateful* as well as *selfish*.

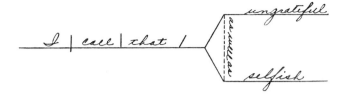

RETAINED OBJECTS

J11 A retained object:

MODEL

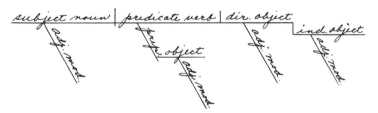

Vengarte has been given *money*.

MODIFYING ADJECTIVE

J12 A modifying adjective:

MODEL

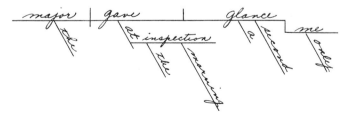

At *the morning* inspection *the* major gave *only* me *a second* glance.

Whimpering and *barking,* the dog circled the porcupine.

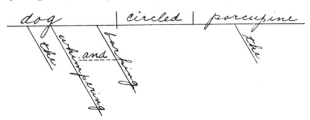

ADVERBS AND ADVERBIAL NOUNS

J13 An adverb:

MODEL

Very inexpensive books are *nowadays nearly everywhere* available.

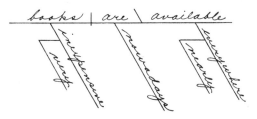

Hats get *more* and *more* absurd.

Friedel, groping *blindly* and *awkwardly,* *finally* found the light cord.

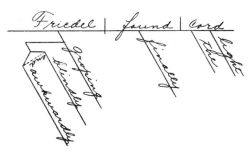

J14 An adverbial noun:

Dougherty went *home yester-* *day morning.*

Home, yesterday, and *morning* are adverbial nouns.

PHRASES IN GENERAL

J15 The subject noun or pronoun of a verbal is set off from the verbal by the same perpendicular line, extended a little below the horizontal line, that is used to set off a subject noun or pronoun from a predicate verb (J2). The direct and indirect objects, predicate complements, retained objects, and objective complements of verbals are diagramed just like those of predicate verbs (J6-11).

NOUN PHRASES

J16 Prepositional noun phrases are not very common; but, when they occur, diagram them like this:

Over the fence is out.

The smoke is coming from *under the house*.

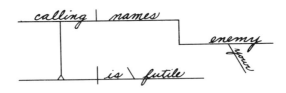

J17 A gerund noun phrase:

MODELS

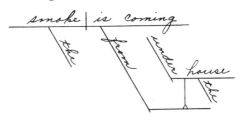

Calling your enemy names is futile.

Becoming a man takes a lot of doing.

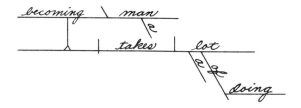

The older children enjoy *shocking sorghum*.

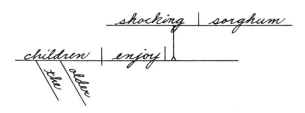

Arguing with Linda is *fighting the wind*.

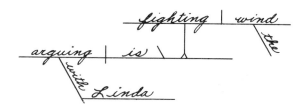

Your snubbing me and playing deaf only make me persistent.

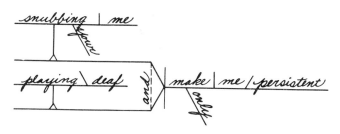

His swimming and Janet's won the meet.

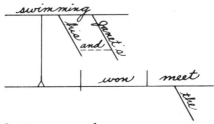

J18 An infinitive noun phrase:

MODEL

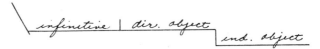

We asked the waiter *to bring Laury a bib*.

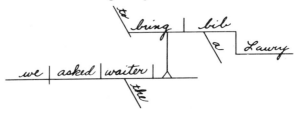

To object is reasonable this time.

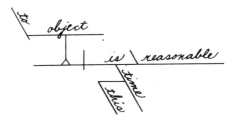

The girls are *to dress as Ubangis.*

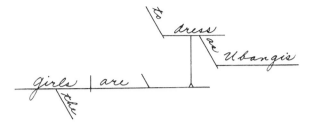

Someone ought *to tie the bell on.*

MODEL

We know *him to be a reader.*

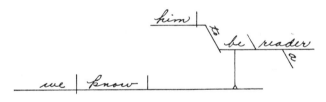

For her to object is unusual.

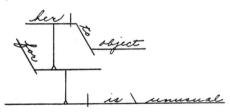

Your brother seems *to be restless.*

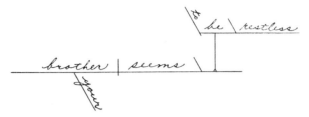

It is useless *to whine, to plead, or to argue with me.*

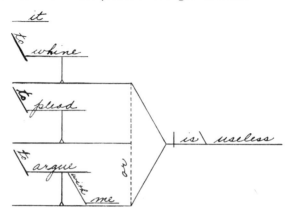

PREPOSITIONAL ADJECTIVE AND ADVERB PHRASES

J19 A prepositional adjective phrase:

MODEL

I prefer one *with a head.*

300

The chance *of surviving* seemed small indeed.

J20 A prepositional adverb phrase:

We swam daily *near the mouth.*

Gene plunged forward, sinking *to his knees.*

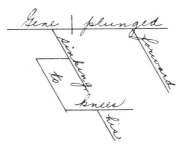

Who's afraid *of a striped kitten?*

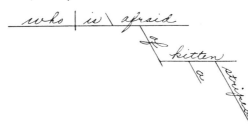

INFINITIVE ADJECTIVE AND ADVERB PHRASES

J21   An infinitive adjective phrase:

You appear *to be troubled.*

The will *to win* can be important.

J22   An infinitive adverb phrase:

Put the pot on the stove *to boil.*

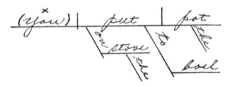

Is everyone ready *to return* to the surface?

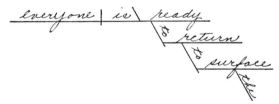

Afraid *to destroy the map,* I dropped it out the window.

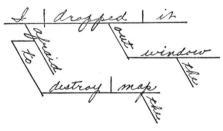

The beggar was too surprised *to say thanks or speak at all.*

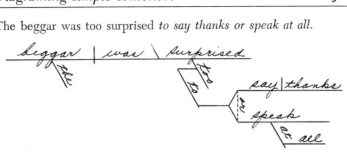

PARTICIPIAL ADJECTIVE PHRASES

J23 A participial adjective phrase:

MODEL

Having given me another sly look, Mr. Snipe departed.

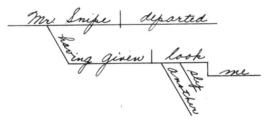

MODEL

I noticed hundreds of men *standing idle.*

Quarak, *screeching a warning and beckoning wildly,* swung away to the treetops.

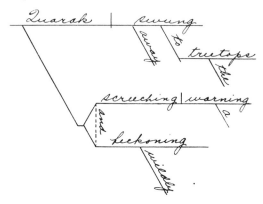

APPOSITIVES

J24   Place appositive nouns after and next to the head word in the diagram and enclose them in parentheses.

MODEL

head word (appositive)

My friend *Henry* is the man to see.

I have given years to my favorite occupation, *talking.*

304

The manager's nephews—*Clem, Lem,* and young *Bartholomew*—have good jobs.

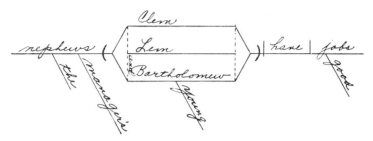

The regional sport, *racing jack rabbits,* is strenuous.

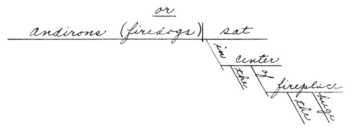

Andirons, or *firedogs,* sat in the center of the huge fireplace.

Or merely stresses the appositive and helps the rhythm.

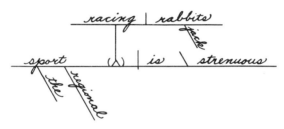

Another fact—namely, your *absence*—is against you.

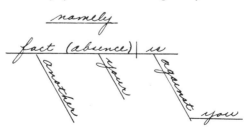

305

MODIFYING POSSESSIVES

J25 Possessives are often adjectives. When they are so, diagram them like adjectives.

Calvin's doctrine is terrible.

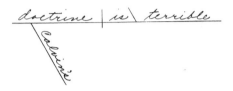

INDEPENDENT ELEMENTS

J26 Since independent elements have no grammatical connection with the rest of the sentence, they are diagramed by themselves, above or below the sentence or clause in which they appear.

J27 Independent words, phrases, or clauses are diagramed just like other words, phrases, or clauses.

J28 A nominative absolute:

MODELS

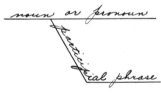

The battle won, the tanks retired.

306

I'm glad, *no one needing the house,* to let you stay in it.

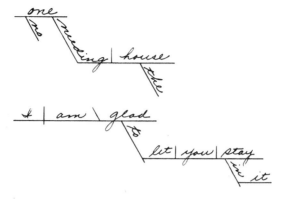

His mouth open in astonishment, the actor stood stock-still.

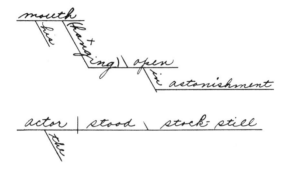

J29 A noun in direct address:

Mr. Froebes, have you anything to say?

Gentlemen, be seated.

J30 An exclamatory word:

Golly, I like the looks of the cowboy riding Terror!

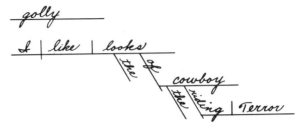

J31 An absolute word, phrase, or clause:

Fetch me the candle snuffer, *please.*

Granting your facts, have you a solution?

By the way, has anyone found a license plate with an automobile attached?

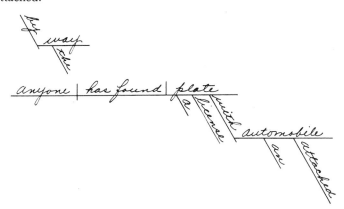

We all, *to be sure,* need mercy.

Who *do you suppose* ate the icing?

Consider *do you suppose* in this case to be merely thrown into the sentence. If it were not, it would be the independent clause with the *who* clause as its object.

This is the man whom *I imagine* we were to avoid.   Complex sentence.

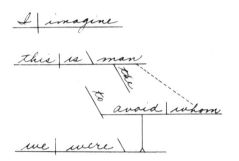

We found abalones among the rocks; *that is*, ear shells.

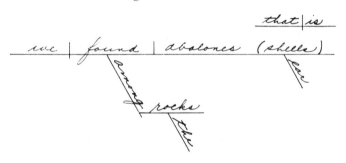

Helmer was a hero; *that is to say*, he did not let his fear rule him.   Compound sentence.

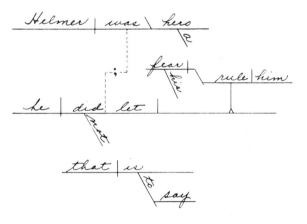

Fergen was a hobo or, *shall we say*, a gentleman of the road.

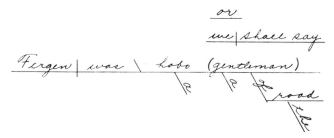

WORDS OMITTED

J32 In diagraming, replace an omitted word or group of words. Enclose it in parentheses, and put an x above it.

Bring me no more reports.

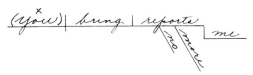

You are not so sensitive as I.   Complex sentence.

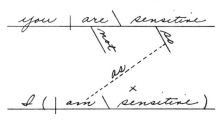

Diagraming compound sentences

J33 A compound sentence is made up of two or more clauses that could stand alone as simple sentences. So the diagraming of a compound sentence adds nothing to the diagraming of a simple sentence (J2-32) except the showing of connection between the clauses.

311

J34 When *and, or, nor, but,* or *for* is omitted between the
clauses of a compound sentence, put a semicolon between
them in the diagram, like this:

Everybody talks about the weather; nobody does anything about it.

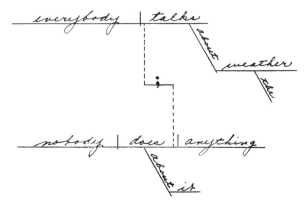

Everybody talks about the weather; still [conjunctive adverb],
nobody does anything about it.

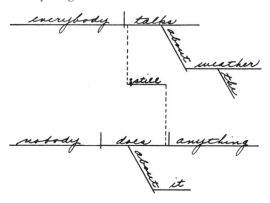

312

J35 When *and, or, nor, but,* or *for* is used between the clauses of a compound sentence, diagram the sentence like this:

Everybody talks about the weather, *but* nobody does anything about it.

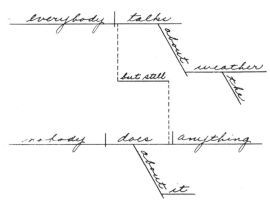

Everybody talks about the weather, *but* still nobody does anything about it.

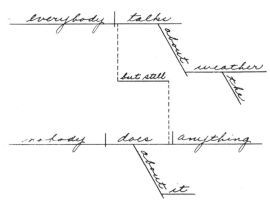

313

The Kenwigs family was not proud, *but* the neighbors ought to know about Morleena's French lessons; so she was told to mention them very humbly.

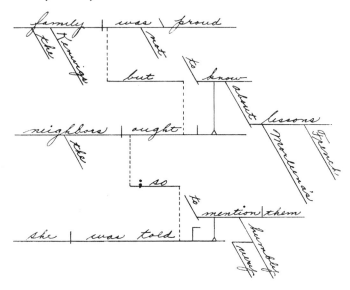

Diagraming complex sentences

NOUN CLAUSES

J36 Put a noun clause on a stilt.

MODEL

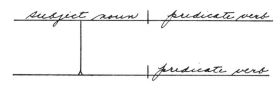

Sentences with subject noun clauses—
Whoever buys this car buys trash.

314

It was foretold in the Old Testament *that the Messias would be born in Bethlehem.*

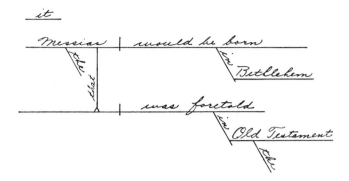

Where you have been and *what you bought there* are nobody's business.

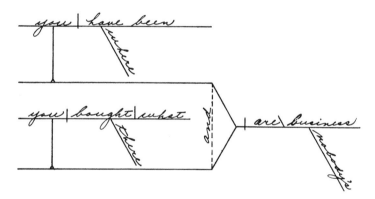

Sentences with object noun clauses—
Tell me *whether you will return in time.*

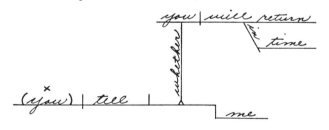

315

It is a question of *how we can raise the money* and *when we can have the hall.*

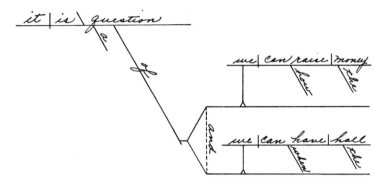

Ted, knowing only *what was required,* did not make a good record at college.

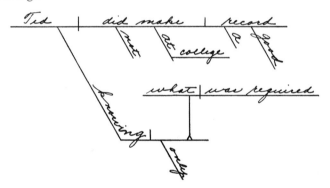

We had an argument about *whose snapshot should be submitted.*

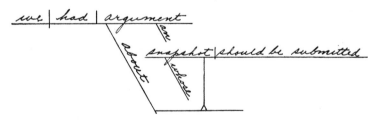

Sentences with noun-clause complements—

Holiness is *what we are striving for.*

Rose discovered Mullen to be *what she least expected*—intelligent.

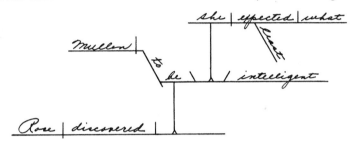

The question is, *who has the chipmunk.*

Sentences with noun-clause appositives—

Don's excuse, *that he had a flat tire,* sounded a bit thin.

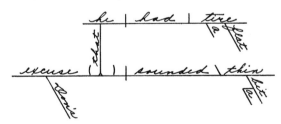

317

Everything—*whatever he earned* and *whatever came to him as tips*—he gave to his mother.

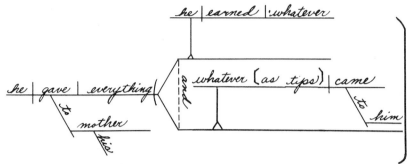

My Protestant friend is deterred by one difficulty; namely, *how can confession be necessary and good?*

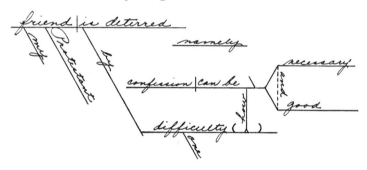

ADJECTIVE CLAUSES

J37 Draw a dotted line from the relative word in the adjective clause to the antecedent in the other clause. (Do not put the relative word on the dotted line.)

The Battle of Lepanto, *which Chesterton made the subject of this poem,* saved Europe from the Turks.

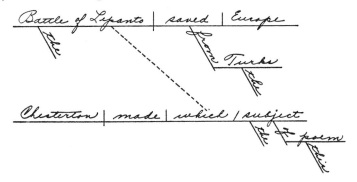

The sultan put his army through tactics *that would check the enemy's latest move.*

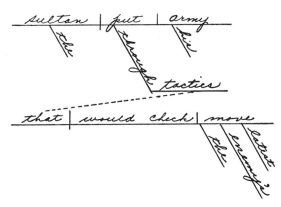

319

Conrad, *whose novel you just read,* died in 1924.

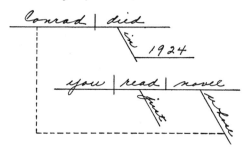

Holt told us the reason *why the fan belt had broken.*

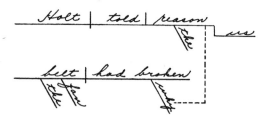

Tim is a man *who* we know *will fight for us.*

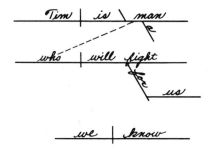

This is the lacquer *that we were waiting for* and *that arrived too late for use on our biggest contract.*

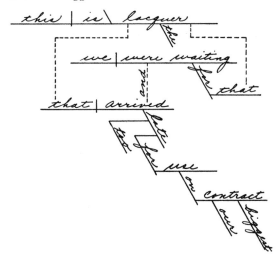

Alfredo is the uncle of Jake, *who is the cousin of Dubar, who in turn is my uncle.*

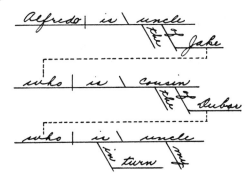

J38 On those rather rare occasions when a whole clause rather
than an individual word or phrase is the antecedent of an
adjective clause, draw the dotted line from the relative
word in the adjective clause to the line under the predicate verb of the other clause.

Margaret threw away my pipe with the broken stem, *which an-*
noyed me very much.

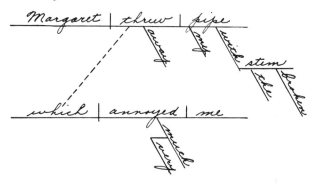

ADVERB CLAUSES

J39 Draw a dotted line from the predicate verb of the adverb
clause to the word that the adverb clause modifies. On
this dotted line, write the subordinating conjunction.

The latch was on *when I tried the door.*

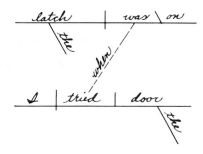

Charles behaved so badly *that we had to put him into a strait jacket.*

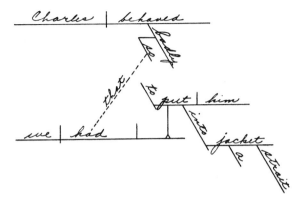

A diamond is harder *than any other precious stone.*

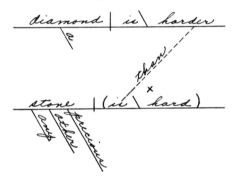

He sometimes acts *as though he were demented.*

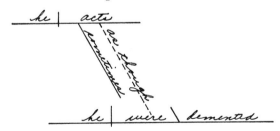

Had I the right, I would abolish advertising.

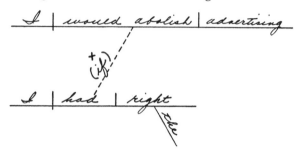

When one is tired and longs for rest, he can find repose at Slump-haven—*if he can pay for it.*

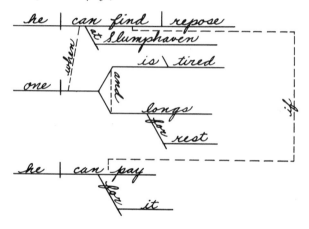

Where a million people blacken the sand like bees swarming thick on a limb and *where every one of the million is in motion,* there I lie and try to get a sun tan.

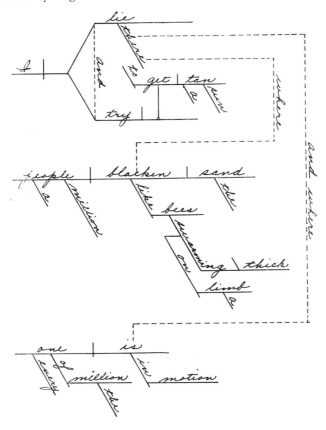

When Jason and I arrived at school and *then I remembered my books at home, seven miles away,* then I got a little upset—like a volcano.

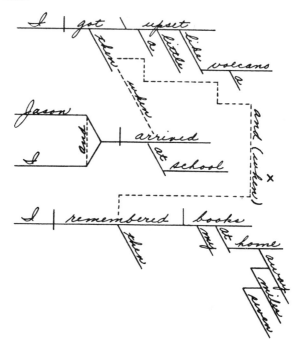

MIXED DEPENDENT CLAUSES

J40 It often happens that you will find a noun and an adjective, a noun and an adverb, or all three kinds of clauses together in one sentence. When this happens, diagram each kind according to its own form and rules. (Diagrams such as those in J40-41 are really virtuoso stunts, included in this book chiefly to convince the skeptical that complicated sentences can be diagramed. They are not, as a matter of fact, very useful, since their very complication makes them difficult to follow and the relationships the diagrams are meant to point up become obscure. Ordinarily one has little need to diagram more than one or two clauses at a time.)

The fact *that Renard was a journalist with whom I had become acquainted while I was taking a vacation in Santa Fe* was written down in my report.

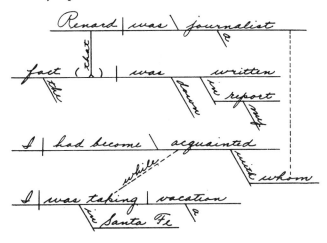

Diagraming compound-complex sentences

J41 A compound-complex sentence:

Don waited patiently for news; but, when they returned, the men had nothing to report about Miggy.

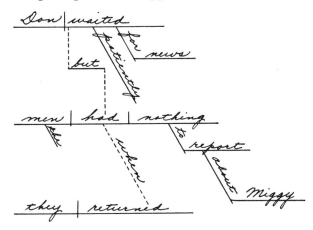

While Rome burned, Nero fiddled and his courtiers laughed.

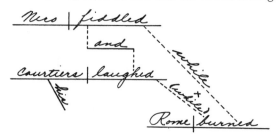

Vittorio fairly jigged with irritation when the bagpipes struck up, but McTavish seemed to enjoy the music.

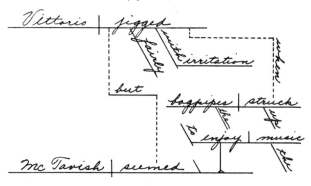

Magellan was killed in the Philippines; nevertheless, his companions, eager to prove that the world is round, continued their westward journey until their ships at length cast anchor off the coast of Spain.

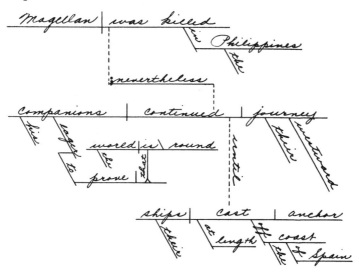

Among the pioneers in the modern French school of music was
Cesar Franck, the greatest and most famous composer that Belgium
has produced; in fact, musicians so esteemed him that they made
a cult of him and his music even before he died.

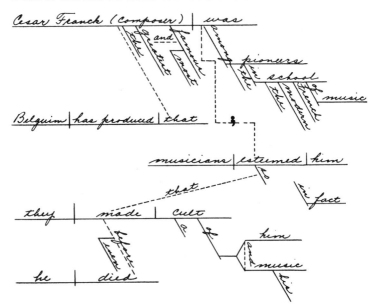

Diagraming direct quotations

J42 If a direct quotation is a half-sentence that can be considered part of the sentence or clause in which it stands,
diagram it as part of the sentence or clause.

Mr. Moulton shouted loudly that he was "plenty peeved!"

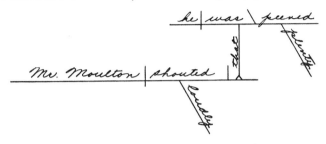

J43 If a direct quotation is not a half-sentence but a sentence,
diagram it as you would any other sentence. Diagram
the *he said* portion of the sentence independently of the
quotation.

"My people," said the chief, "do not wish to fight your people."

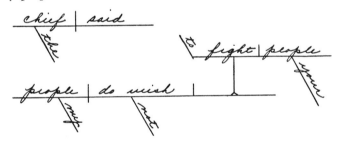

K

"Give us back our self-respect," shouted Tomanski, teetering on a rickety old chair, but maintaining his position above the crowd.

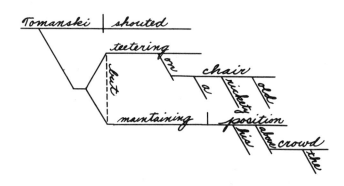

K The sentence—rhetoric

K

Unity in the sentence[1]

K1 Unity means oneness. In composition, unity is the principle that requires that there be only one main thought and that all the other thoughts and words in a sentence, paragraph, or theme directly or indirectly reinforce the one main thought.

K2 Put into separate sentences ideas that are not plainly related. (Be careful, however, to avoid a choppy style.)

Franklin D. Roosevelt had infantile paralysis and was president when the base at Pearl Harbor was attacked.

There is no relationship between the paralysis and the attack. So put the two ideas into separate sentences.

---

[1] For the definition of a sentence and for sentences according to use and structure, see B1-18.

Franklin D. Roosevelt had infantile paralysis.

Franklin D. Roosevelt was president when the base at Pearl Harbor was attacked.

At the banquet of the Good Neighbor Club the toasts were in Spanish, the rest of the evening being spent in dancing.	There is no relationship between the toasts and the dancing. These two ideas should, therefore, be handled in two separate sentences.

At the banquet of the Good Neighbor Club the toasts were in Spanish. Once the toasts were over, there was dancing the rest of the evening.

K3 **If the sentence does not become unwieldy or cluttered, put into it all ideas that are closely related.**

On the second floor, above the chapel, is the library. It contains about a hundred thousand books. It also subscribes to and circulates most of the current periodicals.	Let us suppose that the writer wants to say that there is a large library on the second floor. All of that can be put into one sentence with considerable gain in unity of impression. Below, the fragments are knit together into one clear and unified statement of the facts.

On the second floor, above the chapel, is a library that houses about a hundred thousand books and nearly all the current periodicals.

K4 **Do not write rambling, talkative sentences that include too many details.**

When the wheezy old Ford had gasped its way up the dirt road of Mohawk Mound and then, with clanks and jolts, had tottered down the other side, through the cool dawn, into the valley through which the Saco Creek flowed, we piled together, beneath a big white oak where the Ford was	Although this sentence is talking about a lot of pleasant things of interest to everyone, the reader learns to hate it before it closes. It contains too many details. It rambles. It becomes a maze, a labyrinth. See how clear it becomes in the next example, where it is broken up into three sentences.

left, our tent, duffel bags, cooking equipment, radio, fishing rods, and baskets, preparatory to taking a mile-and-a-half hike through thick, thorny underbrush to our camp site on the Creek where we were to fish for a long week end.

Through the cool dawn the wheezy old Ford gasped its way up the dirt road of Mohawk Mound and then, with clanks and jolts, tottered down the other side into the valley where flowed the Saco Creek. Beneath a big white oak, under which the Ford was left, we piled together our tent, duffel bags, cooking equipment, radio, fishing rods, and baskets. Our camp site on the Creek, where we were to spend a long week end fishing, was a mile and a half away through thick, thorny underbrush.

K5   Do not write tag-at-the-end sentences.

Summer is the time when the outdoors is most inviting, at least in good weather.	Just when the reader thinks he has the thought clear, the sentence reverses itself a little and confuses him. Give him the qualifying *at least* phrase early in the sentence where he is conditioned to expect it.

Summer—at least in good weather—is the time when the outdoors is most inviting.

K6   Save the independent clause of a sentence for the main idea; and do not put two ideas into two independent clauses unless the ideas are of equal or very nearly equal importance.

I entered the room, and Forhan was still sitting and staring at nothing.	Suppose that what Forhan was doing is the one main idea. Turn the first independent clause into something subordinate; say, a dependent modifying clause. That will make the independent clause, sitting and staring at nothing, stand out clearly.

When I entered the room, Forhan was still sitting and staring at nothing.

334

You are not permitted to kill a woman who has wronged you, but nothing forbids you to reflect that she is growing older every minute.[2]	In this sentence the writer wants to set forth two main ideas for the sake of humor: you may not kill a woman physically, but you may torture her mentally. It was most effective to put these two ideas into two independent clauses.

Coherence in the sentence

K7 Coherence is the principle of composition that requires that, for the sake of clarity, ideas and words follow one another in an orderly manner and that the connections between parts be made clear.

K8 If there is a reasonable chance that the relationship between ideas and words may be mistaken, the sentence, paragraph, or theme is incoherent.

K9 Coherence in the sentence means that the parts of a sentence—words, phrases, and clauses—are rightly put together.

K10 The principal enemies of coherence in the sentence are misplaced (dangling) and squinting modifiers; unparallel structure for parallel ideas; faulty connectives and connections; and illogical expressions.

MODIFIERS

K11 Place modifying words, phrases, and clauses as near as you reasonably can to the words which they are modifying; and do not make use of misplaced (dangling) or squinting modifiers.[3]

---

[2] *The Collected Works of Ambrose Bierce* (New York: Neale Pub. Co., 1911), VIII, p. 379.
[3] See C308-13.

PARALLEL STRUCTURES

K12 Where you can do so without forcing or awkwardness, express like ideas in like words and like constructions.

Here are like ideas, but they are expressed in unlike words:

Just as Suarez High School is distinguished for its dramatics, so the students of Aquinas High School have become prominent in debating.

⌈ Suarez High School
  the students of Aquinas High School ⌊

⌈ is distinguished for its dramatics
  have become prominent in debating ⌊

Parallel ideas are given parallel expression:

Just as Suarez High School is distinguished for dramatics, so Aquinas High School is distinguished for debating.

⌈ Suarez High School
  Aquinas High School ⌊

⌈ is distinguished for dramatics
  is distinguished for debating ⌊

Just as the students of Suarez High School have become distinguished for dramatics, so the students of Aquinas High School have become distinguished for debating.

⌈ the students . . . School
  the students . . . School ⌊

⌈ have become distinguished for dramatics
  have become distinguished for debating ⌊

K13 Keep sentence parts parallel when they are joined by *and, or, nor, but,* and other co-ordinating conjunctions.

He was notified that he was drafted by the Army and to report for duty.

This sentence is incoherent. For no reason *and* is made to connect a dependent clause with an infinitive phrase. See how much cleaner an impression the sentence makes below, where *and* connects two dependent noun clauses.

He was notified that he was drafted by the Army and that he should report for duty.

Tommy rode not only through the city but also rode over the little rustic bridge.

This sentence is incoherent. *Not only . . . but also* is made to connect *through the city* and *rode*—a phrase and a predicate verb that are unlike not only in construction but also in thought. The sentence is more coherent below, where the conjunction connects two phrases and ideas that are somewhat alike.

Tommy rode not only through the city but also over the little rustic bridge.

For Denis, who had to regain his inn without attracting notice, there was real danger as well as merely feeling uncomfortable in the walk; and he went warily and with boldness at once, and at every corner pausing to make an observation.

This sentence is incoherent and, as a result, somewhat unclear. *As well as* connects the noun *danger* with the gerund phrase *feeling uncomfortable.* It is all right to connect a noun with a noun phrase when there is no noun ready to hand that will carry the thought. But here there is a noun ready to hand, and the reader is vaguely aware of the fact. Again, *and* is made to connect the adverb *warily* with the prepositional phrase *with boldness.* It is not a blunder to connect an adverb with an adverb phrase; but see how the sentence gains in sharp clarity below where two adverbs are used. Lastly, *and* is made to connect the predicate verb *went* with the participle *pausing;* and that is an out-and-out blunder that makes the sentence unpleasant and, to some degree, confusing.

337

For Denis, who had to regain his inn without attracting notice, there was real danger as well as mere discomfort in the walk; and he went warily and boldly at once, and at every corner paused to make an observation.[4]

K14 Do not use *and, or, nor, but,* and other co-ordinating conjunctions between sentence parts that are not parallel in thought.

I was punished for breaking silence and a cup.	True, *silence* and *cup* are both nouns. But the meaning of *break silence* and the meaning of *break a cup* are so divergent that they should not be connected as they are here. The sentence had better be rephrased as below. (This sort of expression, however, is sometimes justified rhetorically. The figure of speech is called "zeugma.")

I was punished for talking at the wrong time and for breaking a cup.

A man, tall and with a key, came up the stairs and let us in.	*Tall* is an adjective and *with a key* is an adjective phrase, but their meaning is so divergent that they should not be connected as they are here. The sentence had better be rephrased as below.

A tall man came up the stairs and let us in with his key.

Between the silver ribbon of morning and the green glittering ribbon of sea, the boat touched Harwich and let loose a swarm of folk like flies, among whom the man we must	*[Whom] we must follow* and *who wore a beard* are both adjective clauses, but their meaning is so divergent that they should not be connected as they are here. The connec-

[4] Robert Louis Stevenson, "The Sire de Malétroit's Door," *New Arabian Nights* (New York: Charles Scribner's Sons, 1895), p. 319.

338

follow and who wore a beard
was by no means conspicu-
ous—nor wished to be.

tion is not natural. *Bearded
man we must follow* would
solve the difficulty nicely; or
the beard could be saved for
a completely separate sentence, as below.

Between the silver ribbon of morning and the green glittering ribbon of sea, the boat touched Harwich and let loose a swarm of
folk like flies, among whom the man we must follow was by no
means conspicuous—nor wished to be. . . . His lean face was dark
. . . and ended in a curt, black beard that looked Spanish and suggested an Elizabethan ruff.[5]

K15 Do not shift the idea in the subject needlessly.

Bravely the little boy spoke to
the maid; but, instead of getting a reply, she slammed the
door in his face.

The idea in the first subject is
the boy; in the second it is the
maid *(she)*. The sentence can
be made to read much more
smoothly (and, incidentally,
the misplaced phrase can be
avoided) if the idea in the
subjects is kept the same.

Bravely the little boy spoke to the maid; but, instead of getting a
reply, he saw the door slammed in his face.

He was the sort of man whom
anybody could lead on a string
to the North Pole; it was not
surprising that an actor like
Flambeau, dressed as another
priest, could lead him to
Hampstead Heath.[6]

Here the idea in the subject
changes frequently, but with
good enough cause. Very awkward constructions and weak
passives would result if the
subject stayed the same. The
sentence is coherent, the subjects are not confusing.

K16 Do not shift voice needlessly.

Killian brought us food and
medicines; but, best of all, we

The change to passive voice
(were given) is scarcely neces-

---

[5] G. K. Chesterton, "The Blue Cross," *The Innocence of Father Brown* (New
York: Dodd, Mead & Co., 1911), p. 1. By permission.

[6] *Ibid.*, p. 22. By permission.

were given news of the rescue sleds by him.

sary or helpful; and the sentence reads very much more smoothly (much more coherently) below, where the active voice is used in both clauses of the sentence and the idea of the first subject is retained throughout.

Killian brought us food and medicines; but, best of all, he gave us news of the rescue sleds.

K17 Do not shift person or number needlessly.

Well, I like history because people interest me; and certainly history provides you with people of every imaginable type and class.

The shift from *I* and *me* to *you* is unnecessary, troublesome, and incoherent. The sentence is a good deal smoother and clearer when it is rewritten in the ways shown below.

[Good:] Well, I like history because people interest me; and certainly history provides me with people of every imaginable type and class.

[Even better:] Well, I like history because I like to analyze people; and in history I certainly find people of every imaginable type and class.

One went in, not as into most shops, in the mood of: "Please serve me, and let me go!" but restfully, as you enter a church; and, sitting on the single wooden chair, waited—for there was never anybody there.

You distracts. The sentence is more coherent below.

One went in, not as into most shops, in the mood of: "Please serve me, and let me go!" but restfully, as one enters a church; and, sitting on the single wooden chair, waited—for there was never anybody there.[7]

---

[7] John Galsworthy, "Quality," *The Inn of Tranquillity* (New York: Charles Scribner's Sons, 1912), p. 16. By permission.

K18 Do not shift present and past time needlessly.

When at last I find him, Vla-dinov is very happy to see me, assures me that he can get papers for me and can smug-gle me across the border without attracting notice, but wanted more money than he had already been paid.

The writer is using the "vivid present," which is quite all right—a good device if not overworked. But the shift to the past in *wanted* is unneces-sary, jarring, distracting—inco-herent. Say *wants more money than he has* . . .

He caught hold of a springy young sapling and to it he fastens his hunting knife, with the blade pointing down the trail; with a bit of wild grape-vine he tied back the sapling.

The shift to the present in *fastens* is needless and dis-tracting. Richard Connell's sentence, below, is very much better.

He caught hold of a springy young sapling and to it he fastened his hunting knife, with the blade pointing down the trail; with a bit of wild grapevine he tied back the sapling.[8]

CONNECTIVES AND CONNECTIONS

K19 Use connectives that express your meaning precisely.

Andrew is slow, and he leads his class.

And hardly expresses the writ-er's idea plainly; and so there is a chance that the reader may be puzzled or annoyed.

Andrew is slow, but he leads his class.

But makes good sense and rules out misunderstanding.

Andrew is slow, and yet he leads his class.

And yet makes good sense and rules out misunderstanding.

I always felt a deep sympathy for the students, though I knew only their names; yet none of them was without trials and humiliations.

A faulty connective, *yet*, makes nonsense of an otherwise sen-sible sentence.

---

[8] Richard Connell, "The Most Dangerous Game," *Golden Book*, XII, 49 (Oct. 1930). Copyright renewed 1952 by Louise Fox Connell. By permission.

| I always felt a deep sympathy for the students, though I knew only their names; for none of them was without trials and humiliations. | *For* makes the last clause the reason for the sympathy and pulls the meaning of the sentence together—makes the sentence coherent. |
| On the brown face of Velvet Pants there was not the slightest trace of fear, as he was smiling a slight, amused smile. | The meaning of *as* is not clear. Does it mean *while?* Does it perhaps mean *because?* As a matter of fact, neither *while* nor *because* makes perfect sense here. The meaning intended is much clearer in the sentence below. |

On the brown face of Velvet Pants there was not the slightest trace of fear: indeed, he was smiling a slight, amused smile.[9]

K20 Occasionally *and* can be used without obscurity in the sense of *and yet* or *but*. For example, if a father said to his son, "I never heard of anyone your age camping out alone," the son might reply with perfect clarity, "Joe Bergen is only twelve, and he camps out alone." Ordinarily, however, *and* is not an adequate substitute for *and yet* or *but*.

K21 Do not omit a word that is important to the clear and easy expression of your thought.[10]

| They sell crabs at the Fulton Fish Market. | In this sentence *they* does not mean "people in general." It should be either given an antecedent, replaced by a noun, or eliminated altogether as in the construction below. |

Crabs are sold at the Fulton Fish Market.

| Hurried radio calls were sent out to all state policemen to | Which were too late, the calls or the policemen? *They* does |

9 Richard Connell, "The Unfamiliar," *Century,* CVI, 74 (Sept. 1923). Copyright renewed 1951 by Louise Fox Connell. By permission.
10 See C222-25, C258, C283-84, C286-87, C291, C293, C296, and C315-16.

stop the maroon convertible, but they were too late.

not say which. The point is of no great consequence in this sentence; yet such little obscurities mark the incoherent—and unread—writer.

Hurried radio calls were sent out to all state policemen to stop the maroon convertible, but the calls were too late.

The elder Legruy seemed eager to get rid but not to pay for my services.

The sense is clear; but an important word has been annoyingly omitted.

The elder Legruy seemed eager to get rid of my services but not to pay for them.

My friend Mrs. Lummy has more fascinating ailments, like rushes of blood to the elbow, than anybody I know.

The sentence is absurd. Since Mrs. Lummy is "my friend," I must know her; yet the sentence says that I do not, since she has more ailments than "anybody I know."

My friend Mrs. Lummy has more fascinating ailments, like rushes of blood to the elbow, than anybody else I know.

LOGICAL PHRASING

K22 Phrase your sentences thoughtfully and logically so that they make sense and can have only one meaning.

Make yourself comfortable until half-past ten, when the moderator will begin his talk.

Grammatically this sentence is quite all right; nonetheless it is incoherent, thoughtlessly phrased. For it may mean simply that one should wait until the speech begins, or it may imply that once the speech begins all comfort will be at an end. As phrased below, the sentence does not insult the moderator.

Since the moderator's talk does not begin until half-past ten, you may as well make yourself comfortable during the wait.

343

The fireplace, which had not yet been lighted, made the room seem colder.	The fact that the fireplace held no fire is pushed into a subordinate nonrestrictive clause. This focuses attention on the independent clause—*the fireplace made the room seem colder.* That idea seems illogical. The sentence below would not puzzle the reader even for a moment.

The cold, black, fireless hearth only made the room seem colder.

The garret windows were opened, and pails were emptied, and there goes a new suit of clothes!	The writer of this became so carried away that he omitted a step or two from his narrative—a step or two that the reader would like to have; namely, that the clothes are on a man in the street below. In the sentence below, Macaulay writes a more coherent, if less lively, sentence.

The garret windows were opened, and pails were emptied, with little regard to those who were passing below.[11]

K23 Do not use *first* when no other items follow.

K24 Do not use *finally* when other items follow.

K25 Do not use *therefore, consequently,* and so on, when what follows is not even in a wide sense a conclusion from what preceded it. Say *and now* or something of the sort.

Therefore, in conclusion let me say that it has been a pleasure to address such an intelligent and attentive audience.	*Therefore* is wrong here unless the speaker has been arguing to prove that he has enjoyed speaking to this audience— which is hardly likely. *And now* would be much better.

---

[11] Thomas Babington Macaulay, *History of England from the Accession of James II* (Philadelphia, Porter & Coates), I, 281.

Emphasis in the sentence

K26 Emphasis means relative stress. In writing, emphasis is the principle that requires that more important thoughts be made to stand out from less important thoughts. Your writing is properly emphatic when your reader knows, without thinking the matter over, which thoughts you consider most important, which less, and which least important.

K27 Save the independent clause of a sentence for the main idea; and do not put two ideas into two independent clauses unless the ideas are of equal or very nearly equal importance.

I entered the room, and Forhan was still sitting and staring at nothing.	Suppose that what Forhan was doing is the one main idea. Turn the first independent clause into something subordinate; say, a dependent clause for proper emphasis.

When I entered the room, Forhan was still sitting and staring at nothing.

You are not permitted to kill a woman who has wronged you, but nothing forbids you to reflect that she is growing older every minute.[12]	In this sentence the writer wants to set forth two main ideas for the sake of humor: you may not kill a woman physically, but you may torture her mentally. He does well to put these two ideas into two independent clauses.

K28 Put emphasis in a sentence by arranging a series in the order of climax: important idea, more important idea, most important idea.

Willard is highly accomplished: he can dance, play	Unless the writer is striving for humor, this sentence is

---

[12] *The Collected Works of Ambrose Bierce* (New York: Neale Pub. Co., 1911), VIII, 379.

345

Mozart well on the piano, and wiggle his ears.

weak, unemphatic. The sentence below is emphatic—it distributes stress properly, arranging Willard's accomplishments in some sort of ascending scale.

Willard is highly accomplished: he can wiggle his ears, dance, and play Mozart well on the piano.

I came; I saw; I conquered.

This sentence of Julius Caesar's is so handsomely emphatic that, though worn out by frequent quotation and parody, it remains an excellent example of climax.

K29 Do not admit a word by which a sentence does not gain in clarity.

[Unemphatic:] In a manner of speaking and, indeed, to put the thing plainly and as briefly as possible, the pie is truly and undeniably delicious, Mrs. Crane.

[Emphatic:] Mrs. Crane, the pie is delicious.

[Less emphatic:] Sunlight is poured out even on those who are wicked.

[More emphatic:] The sun shines even on the wicked.

[Emphatic, for every word works:] Especially was he beloved by the pretty girls along the Connecticut, whose favor he used to court by presents of the best smoking tobacco in his stock, knowing well that the country lasses of New England are generally great performers on pipes.[13]

Dog bit boy.

This is clear and emphatic enough, but it is unpleasantly curt. The mind dislikes waste, but it does not like poverty of expression. *The dog bit the boy* is much better.

---

[13] Nathaniel Hawthorne, "Mr. Higginbotham's Catastrophe," *Twice-Told Tales* (Boston: Houghton Mifflin Co., 1885), p. 127.

K30 Occasionally, but not regularly, give emphasis to an idea by saying in so many words that it is important.[14]

I have a skillet and a bass to fry in it.	This sentence is clear. It may be made even clearer and more pleasant by the addition of *what is more important.*

I have a skillet and, what is more important, a bass to fry in it.

The house had a tall, narrow stone face pierced only by a door at street level and two eyelike windows under the roof with bars on them.	If the writer intends to make the bars on the windows an important part of his story, he had better emphasize them with two or three underscoring words, as below.

The house had a tall, narrow stone face pierced only by a door at street level and two eyelike windows under the roof with—remarkable fact—bars on them.

K31 Occasionally, but not regularly, give emphasis to a word or an expression by taking it out of its usual place in a sentence or clause and placing it at the beginning or at the end.[15] Take care to do this without awkwardness or loss of clarity.

Go I must and will; stay I cannot.	The usual order of such a sentence is *I must and will go; I cannot stay.* Place *go* and *stay* at the beginning of their clauses and you call attention to them, emphasize them.

I am a reasonable man, but this I will not tolerate.	The usual order of such a sentence is *I am a reasonable man, but I will not tolerate this.* Putting the object pronoun *this* before the subject pronoun gives it prominence and emphasis.

---

[14] See K34.
[15] See K32 and K34.

Relentlessly the dentist drilled into Blake's tooth.	The usual order is *The dentist drilled relentlessly into Blake's tooth.* Putting *relentlessly* first gives it great prominence and strong emphasis.
Boundless and constant is the mercy of God.	The usual order: *The mercy of God is boundless and constant.*
An excellent athlete and a good scholar is Jonathan.	The usual order: *Jonathan is an excellent athlete and a good scholar.*
There had quietly entered the room a tall, poised, handsome woman—Lady Hitchcock.	The usual order: *A tall, poised, handsome woman, Lady Hitchcock, had quietly entered the room.* Placing the name last gives it prominence.

K32 There is a strong literary flavor about many inverted sentence orders.[16] In very natural, informal, conversational, or matter-of-fact writing, be careful to use only those that do not sound grand—too big for the subject matter, the mood of the piece, or the audience.

K33 Emphasize thoughts by repeating them; but do this only sparingly.

Kroner was hated throughout the ship, hated by the captain, hated by the second mate, and hated especially by the crew that he disciplined and worked without mercy.	In this sentence, *hated* receives great stress by being repeated four times.
"You are behaving ridiculously, quite ridiculously," he said with quiet venom.	The repetition implies that the speaker thinks the matter over and still reaches the same verdict. This lends force.
It's useless, useless, I tell you; it's completely useless.	Here the repetition of *useless* makes a very heavy sentence, with a note of despair.

---

[16] See K31.

First in war, first in peace, and first in the hearts of his countrymen, he was second to none in the humble and endearing scenes of private life . . .

These are the famous opening words of Henry Lee's funeral oration in honor of George Washington. Here emphasis is achieved by the repetition of the words *first in* three times.

Alone, alone, all, all alone,
Alone on a wide, wide sea!

These two lines—an elliptical sentence from "The Ancient Mariner"—contain a multiple repetition.

K34 The devices described in K30-31 and K33 should not be used in sentence after sentence. Ordinarily give your reader time to forget that you have used them before you use them again.

SUSPENSE SENTENCES

K35 Suspense could be defined as a state in which a person does not yet know, but wants to know, and feels that he will get to know. Its effect is to sharpen the impact, the importance, the appeal of the thing that one wants to know.

K36 Occasionally write a rather long sentence in which you do not release the predicate verb or (in the case of a complex sentence) the independent clause until the end or nearly the end of the sentence.

Under the brilliant lights of the marquee, huddling out of the rain after the play and waiting for his Cadillac to draw up to the curb, the fabulous Mr. Endacre was shot and killed.

Notice that you could not place a period at any point in this sentence until after the word *shot*, which occurs near the end. This is a suspense sentence. Compare it with the sentence below, which could be stopped very soon after it is begun and which consequently does not arouse much suspense in the reader.

349

The fabulous Mr. Endacre was shot and killed under the brilliant lights of the marquee, huddling out of the rain after the play and waiting for his Cadillac to draw up to the curb.	There is no suspense in this sentence. The important information is released in the first six or seven words, before the reader's expectation and desire to know have been aroused. As a result, *the fabulous Mr. Endacre was shot and killed* does not here receive the prominence it does in the sentence just above.

K37 A periodic sentence is a very long suspense sentence, usually rather grand and emotional in tone and ordinarily about something important.

To bring under one yoke, after the manner of old Rome, a hundred discordant peoples; to maintain each of them in its own privileges within its legitimate range of action; to allow them severally the indulgence of national feelings, and the stimulus of rival interests; and yet withal to blend them into one great social establishment, and to pledge them to the perpetuity of the one imperial power;— this is an achievement which carries with it the unequivocal token of genius in the race which effects it.[17]

K38 A semisuspense sentence is a sentence that employs a suspense structure for a good part of the sentence and then adds further remarks. Semisuspense sentences are very useful.

Near the mouth of the stream, at the foot of the cliff on Mount Durion, Jud the Trapper held his strange school, where Jason spent ten years learning to wrestle, to box, to hunt, to play the fiddle, and to make the great pharmacy of the woods yield him its medicines to cure his hurts.	Suspense construction is used down through *strange school*.

---

[17] John Henry Newman, *The Idea of a University* (New York: America Press, 1941), pp. 437-38.

K39 To get suspense in the structure of a sentence—

A Begin with modifiers—adjectives, adverbs, adjective and adverb phrases and clauses—or noun clauses.

On the twelfth day of the search, near the head of the lake, in a kind of hollow, well screened from the shore by a growth of spruce, the McAllisters found the remains of a fire, and a message, still clear, scrawled in the dirt.

Adjective and adverb phrases.

Whenever I find myself growing grim about the mouth; whenever it is damp, drizzly November in my soul; whenever I find myself involuntarily pausing before coffin warehouses and bringing up the rear of every funeral I meet; and especially whenever my temper gets such an upper hand of me that it requires a strong moral principle to prevent me from deliberately stepping into the street and methodically knocking people's hats off—then I account it high time to get to sea as soon as I can.[18]

If skillfully written, dependent clauses (adverb, adjective, and noun) can hold off the point of a sentence quite a while. It is possible to pile up a good number of them before releasing the independent clause. Some of the dependent clauses themselves can be rather long, provided that they remain clear. In this selection the adverbial *whenever* clauses and the other dependent clauses that they contain postpone the release of the independent clause until considerable suspense has been built up.

B Begin with an accumulation of subject nouns (and noun phrases or clauses) with or without modifiers.

The chair facing the door expectantly, the kettle steaming on the hob, the cups and silver laid ready for tea, the bread with one or two slices already cut and lying at the end of the loaf, the book open on the table—everything in the room seemed to be waiting, waiting—but not for me.

---

[18] Adapted from Herman Melville, *Moby Dick* (New York: Dodd, Mead & Co., 1934), p. 1.

That a child of five should be lecturing their guests on geopolitics, that one of the adults of the family should be cutting out little dolls of paper and putting them to sleep with songs, that the ice cream should be kept in the oven, the car on the porch, the chickens in the master bedroom, and the guest of honor in the garage didn't seem at all strange to the strange McSwivverns.

c Begin with nominative absolutes.

The greatest prudes often being the greatest hypocrites and Fowler clearly being a great prude, it is little wonder that he gave everyone about him the devil of an itch to prick the outer bubble of his pietism and disclose his fraud.

d Begin with direct objects.

The England that he loved so much, the England that had hunted him and tried its best to break his body on the rack, the England where a handful of Catholics stood firm in the sea of scorn and danger that lapped them round, the England that was home—that England Father Gerard would never see again.

e Put modifiers or appositives between the subject noun and the predicate verb.

And this corrupt politician, petty, in love with the dollar, faithless to every trust that has ever been given him, is now to decide what shall be law and what shall not?

A man, a stranger to me but very affable, really charming, who said he was an old friend of yours from your days at Wallace High, borrowed your car.

K40 A loose sentence is the opposite of a suspense sentence. It is a sentence of some length that could be stopped by a period a good deal before its end. (There are borderline sentences which might be described as either loose or suspense sentences.)

The fabulous Mr. Endacre was shot | and killed | under the brilliant lights of the marquee, | huddling out of the rain | after the play | and waiting | for his Cadillac | to draw up to the curb.

The sentence at left could be stopped by a period at any of the points indicated by the division lines. It is clearly a loose sentence.

| Whenever there is time, I stop at Mrs. Welker's \| on my way home \| to exchange news \| with her \| and to find out how her arthritis is treating her. | This is predominantly a loose sentence, but the adverbial clause lends just enough suspense to make it a troublesome borderline case. |

K41 A loose sentence is not inferior to a suspense sentence and may be every bit as soundly and as artfully constructed. The loose sentence is the backbone of most writing. Only when it is used over and over again without the relief of an occasional suspense sentence is it bad.

Sentence development

K42 Two qualities, chiefly, make a style adult: clearness and variety. Provided one's thought is clear, one's writing will also be clear if it has unity, coherence, and emphasis. The following rules will help toward variety.

K43 Put variety into your writing by carefully mixing sentence patterns. Do not always write sentences of the same length and kind.

COMBINING SENTENCES

K44 When sentences or independent clauses fall into a monotonous pattern because of uniform length and structure, the pattern can often be broken by combining some of the sentences or independent clauses according to the rules that follow.

K45 When two or more dull sentences or clauses have predicates that are identical or nearly identical in thought, combine them into one sentence or clause by using a compound subject.

| The Williamses have people over from the city every week end. The Carbanks have people over too. But Dad says we | None of the sentences at left is bad in itself. But the first four work the same pattern to death for no reason. They |

come to Florida to get away from people. Mother agrees with him. It's all very difficult for a nineteen-year-old daughter who must see men if she is to marry one some day.

are all short and choppy in rhythm. The brevity and choppiness do not echo the thought or serve any other purpose. In the next version below, a compound subject combines the first two sentences nicely and breaks up the monotony. (The second and third sentences also could easily be combined if it seemed desirable.)

The Williamses and the Carbanks have people over from the city every week end. But Dad says we come to Florida to get away from people. Mother agrees with him. It's all very difficult for a nineteen-year-old daughter who must see men if she is to marry one some day.

K46 When two or more dull sentences or clauses have subjects that are identical or nearly identical in thought, combine them into one sentence or clause by using a compound predicate.

Fowler was hesitant. He was indecisive. He was afraid to talk in public. But he was very intelligent. Clark was aggressive. He always knew what he wanted. He loved an audience. But he was not precisely a thinker. The two men were born partners.

There is no reason for releasing the thought to the reader in these driblets or for wearying him with so many sentences of the same length. By combining predicates, in the version below, the writer produces a pleasing arrangement of two long sentences and one short one.

Fowler was hesitant, indecisive, afraid to talk in public, but very intelligent. Clark was aggressive, always knew what he wanted, loved an audience, but was not precisely a thinker. The two men were born partners.

K47 When one dull sentence explains a noun or pronoun in another dull sentence, turn the explanatory sentence into an appositive. (Use the same technique with dull independent clauses.)

Everyone else was happy. Everyone else had friends. But nobody noticed Benito. He was a hungry dreamer and a jailbird.

These sentences are so nearly uniform that monotony develops by the end of the paragraph. Turn the last sentence into an appositive.

Everyone else was happy. Everyone else had friends. But nobody noticed Benito—hungry dreamer and jailbird.

The boss of any business worries a lot. He feels it his duty to worry. No one can help him. But I heard a strange rumor today. There is a new machine to do his worrying for him.

An appositive noun clause can break the monotonous pattern at left.

The boss of any business worries a lot. He feels it his duty to worry. No one can help him. But today I heard the strange rumor that there is a new machine to do his worrying for him.

K48 Combine two or more dull sentences or independent clauses by means of the expletive construction.

[Monotonous:] You have made up your mind. That is obvious. You are going to sing. No one can stop you. But the orchestra will not play.

[Better:] It is obvious that you have made up your mind to sing. No one can stop you. But the orchestra will not play.

K49 Combine two or more dull sentences or independent clauses by turning the less important into a nominative absolute.[19]

[Monotonous:] The Chrysler skidded up to the barrier. Its horn was blaring, and its tires were screaming. The driver jumped out.

[Better:] Horn blaring and tires screaming, the Chrysler skidded up to the barrier. The driver jumped out.

K50 Do not put the more important of two thoughts in a nominative absolute. The nominative absolute is a humble frame suitable only to secondary thoughts.

---

[19] See K50-51.

K51 It takes a trained eye and ear to discriminate between an awkward nominative absolute and one that is at home in its sentence. So (*a*) use nominative absolutes sparingly; (*b*) read your sentences aloud to detect awkward sound or rhythm; and (*c*) note, when you read good authors, how they use nominative absolutes effectively.

K52 If one of a series of dull sentences or independent clauses tells when, where, how, or why, turn it into an adverb, an adverb phrase, or an adverb clause.[20]

[Monotonous:] One moment we were all standing around the skunk. It happened suddenly. The skunk was alone.

[Better:] One moment we were all standing around the skunk. Suddenly the skunk was alone.

[Monotonous:] The infantry had a difficult time. They crawled through Huertgen's mud and mines. They crawled for endless, slow, and costly miles.

[Better:] The infantry had a difficult time. For endless, slow, and costly miles, they crawled through Huertgen's mud and mines.

[Monotonous:] Tucker was timid, and he was reluctant. Somehow he got himself up on the stage.

[Better:] Though Tucker was timid and reluctant, he somehow got himself up on the stage.

K53 Sometimes one or more of a series of dull sentences or independent clauses can be turned into an adjective, an adjective phrase, or an adjective clause.[20]

[Monotonous:] Toward the northeast, at daybreak, loomed Gibraltar. It was large. It was grand and gray.

There could be a reason in some contexts for breaking up the thought into such tiny fragments; for example, humor. But ordinarily such a pattern is irritating.

[Better:] Toward the northeast, at daybreak, loomed Gibraltar, large, grand, and gray.

---

[20] Subordinate only secondary thoughts in this way. Unity and emphasis require that, as far as possible, the independent clause or the subject noun and predicate verb of a simple sentence be reserved for the more important idea.

[Monotonous:] This is an account of Mrs. Wendell Morgan. She is an elderly woman. She is known familiarly to all of lower Howard Avenue. She is of frowzy appearance, vague manner, and undiscerning look.

[Better:] This is an account of Mrs. Wendell Morgan. Elderly, of frowzy appearance, vague manner, and undiscerning look, she is known familiarly to all of lower Howard Avenue.

[Monotonous:] In my henhouse are two jumpy hens. At the slightest disturbance they panic the rest of the flock. Last night this proved fortunate. It saved my hens.

[Better:] In my henhouse are two jumpy hens that, at the slightest disturbance, panic the rest of the flock. Last night this proved fortunate. It saved my hens.

K54 In order to avoid monotony, develop the main ideas of sentences in a variety of ways—by enumeration, by giving circumstances, by comparison and contrast, by giving causes and effects, by giving examples, and by repetition.

ENUMERATION IN THE SENTENCE

K55 Develop a sentence thought by dividing an idea in the subject or predicate into its parts.

[Thought:] Jerome Kern wrote some masterpieces of modern popular music.

[Development:] Jerome Kern, master of melody and boss of tricky rhythms, wrote some masterpieces of modern popular music.	The idea in the subject, Jerome Kern, is divided into parts, broken up into several notions that come to mind when one says "Jerome Kern."

[Thought:] Jerome Kern wrote some masterpieces of modern popular music.

[Development:] Jerome Kern wrote some masterpieces of modern popular music: "Ol' Man River," "Smoke Gets in Your Eyes," and "Long Ago and Far Away."	An idea in the predicate, masterpieces, is divided into parts, into a list of song titles—broken up into what comes to mind when one says "masterpieces of modern popular music."

357

[Thought:] I shan't easily forget that time aboard the *Nanette*.

| [Development:] I shan't easily forget that time aboard the *Nanette,* when we ran for a glorious week before a spanking breeze, when the days were gold and blue and white, when the stars at night lay in the sky like diamonds bedded lightly in soot, and when, in shocking contrast, I lived in constant, nauseating terror of Captain Twilliger's great, hard fists. | An idea in the predicate, "that time," is divided into parts, sliced into the several concrete, individual things that made up the time spent aboard the *Nanette.* |

CIRCUMSTANCES IN THE SENTENCE

K56 Develop a sentence thought by giving the circumstances related to it—by answering the question *When, where, how,* or *why is this?*

[Thought:] Be ready to come in the morning.

| [Development:] Be ready to come in the morning, whenever you get the signal from Alexis. | The adverb clause answers the question *When in the morning?* |

[Thought:] I'm afraid Tarky doesn't like me.

| [Development:] I'm afraid Tarky doesn't like me, for I caught him in my closet putting ants and a caramel into the pocket of my coveralls. | The independent clause introduced by *for* answers the question *Why am I afraid?* |

COMPARISON AND CONTRAST IN THE SENTENCE

K57 Comparison consists of bringing out points of similarity between two or more things.

K58 Contrast consists of bringing out points of dissimilarity between two or more things.

K59 A contrast may be made only between things in which there are also some points of similarity obvious to the reader. It would be silly to say "Joe is not like the letter *r*," since the reader does not expect Joe to be like the letter *r*. But it is quite all right to say "Joe is not like Jim," because the reader knows that Joe is like Jim in many ways.

K60 In nontechnical talk the word *comparison* is frequently used to include contrast and to mean the showing of points of dissimilarity as well as similarity between two or more things.

K61 Develop a sentence thought by using comparison, contrast, or both.

[Thought:] Hugh Bright is a flashy dresser.

[Development:] Hugh Bright is a flashy dresser, who, with his green hats, lemon ties, purple shirts, and fancy oxfords, looks like something out of a Technicolor nightmare.

Hugh Bright is compared to something out of a Technicolor nightmare.

[Thought:] Jack Dempsey was a fighter, not a boxer.

[Development:] Jack Dempsey was a fighter, not a boxer, who asked only to stand toe-to-toe and slug—unlike Joe Louis, who, by footwork, by strategy, and by tactical retreat, gained time to study and to wear down his adversary.

Jack Dempsey is contrasted with Joe Louis.

[Thought:] The ricksha is an oriental vehicle.

[Development:] The ricksha is an oriental vehicle that resembles a wheel chair, though, unlike a wheel chair, it has shafts like a carriage, with a man instead of a horse between them.

The ricksha is both compared to, and contrasted with, first a wheel chair and then a horse-drawn carriage.

CAUSE AND EFFECT IN THE SENTENCE

K62 Develop a sentence thought by stating some of the effects or consequences of the truth or event in the sentence.

[Thought:] A great tree on the bank suddenly tottered and crashed to earth.

[Development:] A great tree on the bank suddenly tottered and crashed to earth, shattering the night quiet, with the result that Mack, startled, lurched heavily away from the noise, overbalancing the canoe and sending us, our clothes, provisions, guns, and the tent into the black, icy river.

The effects of the crash—the shattering of the quiet, the tipping of the canoe, the loss of the baggage, and the icy plunge—are used to build a very nice sentence.

K63 Develop a sentence thought by stating some of the causes of, or reasons for, the truth or event in the sentence.

[Thought:] The place was called Township—a confusing name.

[Development:] The place was called Township—a confusing name—not because anyone thought the word useful or musical, but because an Alvin J. Township, lumberman, had built most of its public buildings out of his profits and had desired to stamp his generosity with his trade-mark.

The original thought is developed by dismissing one reason for the rather odd name and giving another.

EXAMPLES IN THE SENTENCE

K64 Develop a sentence thought by giving particular instances or concrete examples of the general or abstract truth in the sentence.

[Thought:] Man is always eager to blind himself to what is unpleasant.

[Development:] Man is always eager to blind himself

The general and abstract notion *man* is made particular

to what is unpleasant; for example, after World War II, Americans put on rose-colored glasses to look at Russia and cried, "What a friendly democracy she is."

and concrete by the example of Americans in the development, and the eagerness to blind oneself to unpleasant things is reduced to a particular example of what Americans did once World War II was safely concluded.

K65 It is by no means always necessary to use an expression like *for example* or *for instance* when developing a thought by giving examples.

REPETITION IN THE SENTENCE

K66 Develop a sentence topic by repeating an idea in the subject or predicate in different words and with greater clarity or force.

[Thought:] Paul Adams was no sycophant.

[Development:] Paul Adams was no sycophant, not the sort to trail behind campus playboys, waiting his chance to pat them on the back, not the sort to flatter their feeble wit with loud guffaws.

An idea in the predicate, sycophant, is repeated in a descriptive definition that to most readers will be clearer than the word itself.

L The paragraph

L1 A paragraph is a sentence or a group of sentences separated by indention or by a similar device from other sentences in the same piece of writing.[1]

This is a paragraph. The first line is, as you see, indented, set back a little from the left-hand margin formed by the other lines. It is the technical essential of a paragraph that it be set off by

---

[1] For paragraphs in dialogue see D119.

indention or by some other device from the rest of the piece of writing. But, as other rules will indicate, a paragraph ordinarily corresponds to a unit of thought. In fact, the reason for the indention and, consequently, for the paragraphing is to set off one unit of thought from another. Thus the reader is prevented from mixing up things that should be kept separate, and the mind is given little rests between units.

L2 In continuous composition, a good paragraph is a group of sentences that all develop a single topic thought (although occasionally a paragraph will consist of only one sentence by itself).

> Write your name and address in the upper right-hand corner of the page. In the center of the first line, write the title of your story. Skip two line-spaces and then indent for the first paragraph. Leave margins of an inch and a half at the sides and the bottom of the page.

The topic thought of the paragraph: *Here is the style your paper must follow.*

> And now let us leave the style of the paper for a moment and consider its content.

This is a one-sentence paragraph, used as a bridge between parts of the theme.

L3 Occasionally a paragraph is complete in itself, and there results a one-paragraph composition like the ones to be found in some newspaper editorials or in the writings of some columnists. A paragraph, however, is generally a part—a new side or phase, a step forward: in brief, a division or a subdivision—of a larger composition.

L4 Except in the block form of typed letters, in outlines, in printed displays, and in certain kinds of technical writing, the first line of every paragraph should be indented; that is, the first line should be set in a little from the left-hand margin. When indention is not used, paragraphs are indicated in some other way, usually by the insertion of extra space between them.

362

L5 The first line of a handwritten paragraph should be indented about one inch; of a typewritten paragraph, from three to eight characters.

L6 The first lines of all paragraphs in the same composition should be indented uniformly.

> The indention of this first paragraph will govern the indention of those that follow.
>
> This paragraph, as you see, is indented uniformly with the one immediately above. So with any others in the same theme.

Unity in the paragraph

L7 Unity means oneness. In composition, unity is the principle that requires that there be only one main thought and that all the other thoughts and words in a sentence, paragraph, or theme directly or indirectly reinforce the one main thought.

L8 The topic thought of a paragraph is the one clear, rather brief thought that answers the question *What is the paragraph about?*

> Write your name and address in the upper right-hand corner of the page. In the center of the first line, write the title of your story. Skip two line-spaces and then indent for the first paragraph. Leave margins of an inch and a half at the sides and the bottom of the page. Do not let words wander into the margins.

> The topic thought of the paragraph: *Here is the style your paper must follow.*

L9 Put one, and only one, topic thought into each paragraph.

> It was Miss Murdstone who was arrived, and a gloomy-looking lady she was; dark, like her brother, whom she

> As it is given here, this paragraph has two topic thoughts: (1) *Miss Murdstone was an unpleasant-appearing woman.*

greatly resembled in face and voice, and with very heavy eyebrows, nearly meeting over her large nose . . . She brought with her two uncompromising hard black boxes, with her initials on the lids in hard brass nails. When she paid the coachman she took her money

(2) *Murdstone was an unpleasant name.* When a paragraph is given to each topic thought, as in the presentation of the passage below, each paragraph gains in unity of impression.

out of a hard steel purse, and she kept the purse in a very gaol of a bag which hung upon her arm by a heavy chain and shut up like a bite. I had never, at that time, seen such a metallic lady altogether as Miss Murdstone was. Murdstone—I thought this an odd name, one that sounded dark and forbidding. It was not a familiar English name, and I have never heard it since. It filled me with fear and made me, beforehand, uneasy about meeting its bearer.

It was Miss Murdstone who was arrived, and a gloomy-looking lady she was; dark, like her brother, whom she greatly resembled in face and voice, and with very heavy eyebrows, nearly meeting over her large nose . . . She brought with her two uncompromising hard black boxes, with her initials on the lids in hard brass nails. When she paid the coachman she took her money out of a hard steel purse, and she kept the purse in a very gaol of a bag which hung upon her arm by a heavy chain and shut up like a bite. I had never, at that time, seen such a metallic lady altogether as Miss Murdstone was.[2]

Murdstone—I thought this an odd name, one that sounded dark and forbidding. It was not a familiar English name, and I have never heard it since. It filled me with fear and made me, beforehand, uneasy about meeting its bearer.

L10 Make each sentence of a paragraph develop the topic thought either directly or indirectly.

Mr. Claudius had a very elaborate funeral. There were great banks of flowers. I my-

This is not a good paragraph. The topic thought, not fully expressed in any one sentence,

---

[2] Charles Dickens, *The Personal History of David Copperfield* (Chicago, Weeks Pub. Co.), p. 56.

self have never cared much for flowers at a funeral. At funerals they seem to raise a cloying sweetness that infects the good clean air. There were a great many mourners, enough to fill the great church. The music was of the finest, for the uncertain singers of the parish had made way for surer, grander voices hired for the occasion. The cortege was piloted to the cemetery by a whole platoon of motorcycle policemen. It all seemed singularly inappropriate to the character of Mr. Claudius, who

is: *Mr. Claudius's grand funeral did not fit him.* But the third and fourth sentences do not develop this topic thought either directly or indirectly. They should be put into another paragraph, if they are worth keeping, or dropped entirely. At the very least they should be put in parentheses—but only if they are very much worth keeping—to show that they interrupt the progress of the paragraph and are an aside, a digression.

had tried so hard all his life for plainness and simplicity, only to have pomp thrust upon him at the very end.

L11 If the paragraph does not become unwieldy or cluttered, put into it all the ideas that develop one topic thought.

My first glimpse of Europe was the shore of Spain.

Since we got into the Mediterranean, we have been becalmed for some days within easy view of it. All along are fine mountains, brown all day, and with a bloom on them at sunset like that of a ripe plum.

Here and there at their feet little white towns are sprin-

The false stop after each paragraph here makes the reader think that the writer has done with the topic thought. He is consequently thrown off to find the writer taking it up again and again. The treatment in the passage below is much clearer.

kled along the edge of the water, like the grains of rice dropped by the princess in the story. Sometimes we see larger buildings on the mountain slopes, probably convents.

I sit and wonder whether the farther peaks may not be the Sierra Morena (the rusty saw) of Don Quixote. I resolve that they shall be, and am content. Surely latitude and longitude never showed me any particular respect, that I should be over-scrupulous with them.

My first glimpse of Europe was the shore of Spain. Since we got into the Mediterranean, we have been becalmed for some days within easy view of it. All along are fine mountains, brown all day, and with a bloom on them at sunset like that of a ripe plum. Here and there at their feet little white towns are sprinkled along the edge of the water, like the grains of rice dropped by the princess in the story. Sometimes we see larger buildings on the mountain slopes, probably convents. I sit and wonder whether the farther peaks may not be the Sierra Morena (the rusty saw) of Don Quixote. I resolve that they shall be, and am content. Surely latitude and longitude never showed me any particular respect, that I should be over-scrupulous with them.[3]

L12 A topic sentence is the topic thought of a paragraph expressed in one sentence of the paragraph itself. (The topic thought may use up the whole sentence or it may take up only part of it.) While every paragraph has a topic thought, not all paragraphs have a topic sentence.

He is a swarthy browned man of fifty, well-made and good-looking, with crisp dark hair, bright eyes, and a broad chest. His sinewy and powerful hands, as sunburnt as his face, have evidently been used to a pretty tough life. What is curious about him is that he sits forward on his chair as if he were, from long habit, allowing space for some dress or accoutrements that he has altogether laid aside. His step too is measured and heavy, and would go well with a weighty clash and jingle of spurs. He is close-shaved now, but his mouth is set as if his upper lip had been for years familiar with a great mustache; and his manner of occasionally laying the open palm of his broad brown hand upon it, is to the same effect. *Altogether, one might guess Mr. George to have been a trooper once upon a time.*[4]

L13 Ordinarily express the topic thought of a paragraph in a topic sentence—unless, that is, doing so would hurt the paragraph. (For example, a topic sentence would be a mistake if it would give away too soon the secret that is creating suspense in a story.)

---

[3] James Russell Lowell, "Leaves from My Journal in Italy and Elsewhere," *Fireside Travels* (Boston: Houghton Mifflin Co., 1892), pp. 157-58.
[4] Charles Dickens, *Bleak House* (Chicago, Weeks Pub. Co.), p. 352.

L14 Ordinarily put the topic sentence at the beginning of a
paragraph; occasionally—for, say, suspense or variety—put
it at the end.

From her father Queen
Elizabeth inherited her frank
and hearty address, her love
of popularity and of free intercourse with the people, her
dauntless courage and her
amazing self-confidence. Her
harsh, manlike voice, her impetuous will, her pride, her
furious outbursts of anger
came to her with her Tudor
blood. She rated great nobles
as if they were schoolboys; she

The topic sentence is: *But she
was at once the daughter of
Henry and of Anne Boleyn.*
Buried as it is at left in the
middle of the paragraph, it
does not contribute much to
clearness. At the beginning of
the paragraph, as in Green's
original treatment below, it
makes a sharper impression on
the reader's mind.

met the insolence of Essex with a box on the ear; she would break
now and then into the gravest deliberations to swear at her counselors like a fishwife. But she was at once the daughter of Henry
and of Anne Boleyn. Strangely in contrast with the violent outlines
of her Tudor temper stood the sensuous self-indulgent nature she
derived from Anne Boleyn. Splendour and pleasure were with
Elizabeth the very air she breathed. Her delight was to move in
perpetual progresses from castle to castle through a series of gorgeous pageants, fanciful and extravagant as a caliph's dream. She
loved gaiety and laughter and wit. A happy retort or a finished
compliment never failed to win her favour.

Queen Elizabeth was at once the daughter of Henry and of
Anne Boleyn. From her father she inherited her frank and hearty
address, her love of popularity and of free intercourse with the
people, her dauntless courage and her amazing self-confidence. Her
harsh, manlike voice, her impetuous will, her pride, her furious
outbursts of anger came to her with her Tudor blood. She rated
great nobles as if they were schoolboys; she met the insolence of
Essex with a box on the ear; she would break now and then into
the gravest deliberations to swear at her counselors like a fishwife.
But strangely in contrast with the violent outlines of her Tudor
temper stood the sensuous self-indulgent nature she derived from
Anne Boleyn. Splendour and pleasure were with Elizabeth the very
air she breathed. Her delight was to move in perpetual progresses

from castle to castle through a series of gorgeous pageants, fanciful and extravagant as a caliph's dream. She loved gaiety and laughter and wit. A happy retort or a finished compliment never failed to win her favour.[5]

When I reached the Franklin place and walked up the path to the porch, there was no one about. The door hung by one hinge, and loosed its hold of that when I touched it, crashing to the floor with a clatter that sounded awful after the sunny stillness of the farmstead. I entered the living-dining room. The long trestle table had been flung over on its side. What little furniture there had been—the two long benches, the fragile whatnot with sea shells and such in the corner, the one or two chairs—had all been toppled or smashed. Glass from the broken windows littered the floor. It was obvious that the raiders had gotten to the Franklins' before me.

Here the topic sentence, *It was obvious that the raiders had gotten to the Franklins' before me*, is placed last in the paragraph with good effect. It rounds off the ideas of the paragraph like a little summary, and a certain amount of suspense is generated by saving it till the end. This sort of thing happens oftener in narratives than in other writing.

L15 In some paragraphs the topic sentence is understood, not expressed; the paragraphs cannot be expected to have a topic sentence. That is true of technical, dialogue paragraphs. It is true also of some narrative paragraphs where the topic sentence would often have to be something like *Here is what happened in the next ten minutes.*

Coherence in the paragraph

L16 Coherence is the principle of composition that requires that, for the sake of clarity, ideas and words follow one another in an orderly manner and that the connections between parts be made clear.

---

[5] John Richard Green, *A Short History of the English People* (New York: American Book Co., 1916), p. 370. By permission.

L17 Coherence in the paragraph means that the sentences of the paragraph are rightly put together and properly connected.

L18 When you are moving from sentence to sentence, keep the same voice, person, number, and time, and the same subject, unless the thought requires a change.

L19 Establish clear connections where they are needed between sentences; and make sure that connectives are used with precision.

The rifle seemed to be in good condition. The bore was pitted with rust.

One could speak these two sentences and, by bearing down heavily on *seemed,* make the meaning of the paragraph clear. But when one puts them in writing, something is needed to bridge the gap between them. The two versions of the sentence given below will be clearer to readers.

At first the rifle seemed to be in good condition. However, the bore was pitted with rust.

At first alerts the reader for the change of thought in the second sentence; then *however* makes certain that he will not miss it.

At first glance the rifle seemed to be in good condition. On closer inspection its bore proved to be pitted with rust.

This is even clearer. *At first glance* and *on closer inspection* make the relationship of the two sentences altogether unmistakable.

The pilgrims wound their way up the mountainside slowly, chanting the rosary and singing hymns. The way was long and the incline steep, but all of them kept up the steady pace and prayed and sang as though they had breath and to spare. In the mean-

The writer does well to put a connective phrase at the beginning of the last sentence. One is needed, since there is a shift from the main body of the procession to the bishop at its end. But *in the meantime* does not express the relationship so precisely as the

time, the elderly bishop strode firmly along, carrying the heavy monstrance.

connective below. The bishop could be in another part of the state.

The pilgrims wound their way up the mountainside slowly, chanting the rosary and singing hymns. The way was long and the incline steep, but all of them kept up the steady pace and prayed and sang as though they had breath and to spare. At the end of the procession, the elderly bishop strode firmly along, carrying the heavy monstrance.

Hepner and Wolfram thrust aside the two retainers who guarded the door, strode into the center of the hall, and, standing back to back between the two rows of tables, smilingly faced the chieftains and lords, who had half risen from the benches and half stretched tentative fingers toward swords and knives. Then casually, quietly, he said, "My comrade and I will lop the first hand that touches a hilt."

The paragraph reads clearly enough until the fourth word (*he*) of the second sentence. Then the reader would like to know whether Hepner or Wolfram is doing the talking.

Hepner and Wolfram thrust aside the two retainers who guarded the door, strode into the center of the hall, and, standing back to back between the two rows of tables, smilingly faced the chieftains and lords, who had half risen from the benches and half stretched tentative fingers toward swords and knives. Then casually, quietly, Hepner said, "My comrade and I will lop the first hand that touches a hilt."

L20 When relating a series of events, put first what happened first, second what happened second, and so on.

Serra and Portolá were right in thinking that their countrymen were at hand. The approaching Indians brought them the good tidings that San Diego was but a two-days'

The time sequence of the paragraph at left is badly scrambled. Do not be surprised that it sounds as if it makes sense and yet confuses badly. See how much clearer, more pleas-

370

journey even for Portolá's tired men and still more tired beasts. The next day they were met by ten soldiers whom the *co-mandante,* Rivera y Moncada, had sent to escort them to ant, more interesting it is in the paragraph next below, where the events follow the order of time.

their destination. The colonization of California had begun. The Indians had said that both ships were in port, that the first land expedition had arrived long since, and that there were many friars on the spot. Cheered and heartened, the company pushed on over a country so broken and rock-strewn that Serra—always a truth-teller—feared his heart would stop beating from sheer fright. It was the next day that the ten soldiers mentioned above met them. Under their guidance they encamped for the last night on level ground by running water, and in the morning, July 1st, 1769, they reached a gentle eminence from which they could see the ships riding at anchor, and the Spanish flag flying in the breeze. Portolá's soldiers fired a salute which was answered joyously from land and sea. The sacred expedition of Galvez had entered the promised land.

[Serra and Portolá were right in thinking that their countrymen were at hand.] The approaching Indians brought them the good tidings that San Diego was but a two-days' journey even for Portolá's tired men and still more tired beasts. They said that both ships were in port, that the first land expedition had arrived long since, and that there were many friars on the spot. Cheered and heartened, the company pushed on over a country so broken and rock-strewn that Serra—always a truth-teller—feared his heart would stop beating from sheer fright. The next day they were met by ten soldiers whom the *comandante,* Rivera y Moncada, had sent to escort them to their destination. Under their guidance they encamped for the last night on level ground by running water, and in the morning, July 1st, 1769, they reached a gentle eminence from which they could see the ships riding at anchor, and the Spanish flag flying in the breeze. Portolá's soldiers fired a salute which was answered joyously from land and sea. The sacred expedition of Galvez had entered the promised land. The colonization of California had begun.[6]

---

[6] Agnes Repplier, *Junípero Serra,* pp. 67-68. Copyrighted 1931 by Agnes Repplier. By permission of Doubleday & Co.

L21 When you are treating a series of things that can be located, start at the bottom and go to the top, or start at the top and go to the bottom, or start at the right and go to the left, and so on; or start at one end and go to the other, and so on; that is, proceed in an orderly fashion.

One sock drooped about the heel of his left brogue; the other sock was not visible, having no doubt slipped under the arch of his foot and bunched there uncomfortably. His nose was a mere indication, a reminder of what a nose is ordinarily like. A great rip in the seat of his trousers caused him some understandable concern; and this rip he was at pains to hold together with his unoccupied right hand, with a pathetic pretense of not noticing what he was doing, in the hope that no one else would notice, either. The top of one shoe had torn away from the sole and now presented the parody of an open mouth disclosing a thick brown tongue—his grimy big toe. In his left arm he cradled a shaggy, dispirited, dry-nosed, small dog—of a black that was partly brown and a white that was gray. His eyes were the eyes of a boy twelve years old, which is to say that they were beautiful—as yet unglazed by the hardness and the fixity that comes with looking out always for the main chance. He wore no shirt despite the bite of the air, and so his cramped rib cage showed sickly white along the bones and sickly blue in the little hollows between them. Occasionally the dog would squirm and attempt to lick his face. One of the dog's hind legs was splinted and bandaged, and that rather expertly.

This paragraph is annoyingly disordered. It is clear enough, for the subject being described is not difficult; but the reader's mind is made to return over and over again to a part of the boy's body (or to the dog) which should have been finished with once and for all. The mind's eye is jerked from shoe to nose to trousers to shoe to dog to eyes to torso to dog to shoes to dog. If this sort of thing continued for any length of time, any reader would soon weary of the effort to follow the writer. In the reorganization given on the next page, the writer selects a natural, coherent order (he might have used any one of several) and proceeds from bottom to top without any annoying and confusing twists, turns, and returns.

The top of one stringless shoe had torn away from the sole and now presented the parody of an open mouth disclosing a thick brown tongue—the boy's grimy big toe. One sock drooped about the heel of his left brogue; the other sock was not visible, having no doubt slipped under the arch of his foot and bunched there uncomfortably. A great rip in the seat of his trousers caused him some understandable concern; and this rip he was at pains to hold together with his unoccupied right hand, with a pathetic pretense of not noticing what he was doing, in the hope that no one else would notice, either. In his left arm he cradled a shaggy, dispirited, dry-nosed, small dog—of a black that was partly brown and a white that was gray. One of the dog's hind legs was splinted and band-aged, and that rather expertly. Occasionally the dog would squirm and attempt to lick the boy's face. The boy wore no shirt despite the bite of the air, and so his cramped rib cage showed sickly white along the bones and sickly blue in the little hollows between them. His nose was a mere indication, a reminder of what a nose is ordinarily like. His eyes were the eyes of a boy twelve years old, which is to say that they were beautiful—as yet unglazed by the hardness and the fixity that comes with looking out always for the main chance.

The sand-hills here run down to the sea, and end in two spits of rock jutting out opposite each other, till you lose sight of them in the water. One is called the North Spit and one the South. Between the two, shifting backward and forward at certain seasons of the year, lies the most horrible quicksand on the shores of Yorkshire. At the turn of the tide something goes on in the unknown deeps below, which sets the whole face of the quicksand quivering and trembling in a manner most remarkable to see, and which has given to it, among the people in our parts, the name of the Shivering Sand. A great bank, half a mile out, nigh the mouth of the bay, breaks the force of the main ocean coming in from the offing. Winter and summer, when the tide flows over the quick-sand, the sea seems to leave the waves behind it on the bank, and

Collins, the author of this passage, follows an easy order of place. He takes the reader's eye out along two parallel hills that can both be seen at once, to the quicksand between them, and out to the barrier that hems in the sand and walls out the sea.

373

rolls its waters in smoothly with a heave, and covers the sand in silence. A lonesome and horrid retreat I can tell you! No boat ventures into this bay. No children from our fishing-village, called Cobb's Hole, ever come here to play. The very birds of the air, as it seems to me, give the Shivering Sand a wide berth.[7]

L22 In a paragraph in which neither events nor localized things are discussed, it is impossible to use the order of time or place. In such a paragraph it is good to use the order of interest or importance.

L23 After the topic sentence, if there is one, begin with the least interesting or important idea, go on to a more interesting or important idea, and so on, and end with the most interesting or important idea.

Your drums are the blusterers in conversation, who, with a loud laugh, unnatural mirth, and a torrent of noise, domineer in public gatherings, overbear sensible people, stun their companions, and fill the place they are in with a rattling sound that has seldom any humor, wit, or good manners in it. The drum, notwithstanding, by this boisterous vivacity, is very apt to impose upon the ignorant and, in conversation with the uneducated, often passes for a man of learning and wit and for extremely pleasant company. I need not observe that the emptiness of the drum very much contributes to its noise.[8]

Addison is here comparing men who bluster and bully in conversation to the drums in an orchestra. He mentions three ways in which the blustering talker is like the drum: in making a lot of noise, in impressing uneducated people, and in being empty. The first idea is the simplest and most obvious one. The second idea is more complicated, for it shows more thought and reflection. The third idea is the most important—loud talkers are empty-headed people with nothing to say.

---

[7] Wilkie Collins, *The Moonstone* (New York: Modern Library, 1937), p. 24. By permission of Random House, Inc.

[8] Adapted from Joseph Addison in the *Tatler*, No. 153 (Saturday, April 1, 1710).

L24 When you are in control of the order, as in a story, you can frequently make two or more of the orders of time, of place, and of importance or interest coincide, with consequent gain in clarity and interest.

> The new foreman of the road gang, Black Scott, was a stupid and cruel man. As the weeks of June passed, the road gang, fed to the teeth with his tyrannical way and vile tongue, grew ·lazier and lazier: the men loitered long at the water barrel, spent half hours cleaning their shovels and picks, continually rested what they claimed were strained backs and blistered hands, and often spent the day lying "sick" in their bunks. At mealtime, when Black Scott was with them, they said nothing, only asking for food in a mutter or with a sneer. After meals and at night, they gathered in little groups and cursed the food, the job, the weather—and especially Black Scott and his cruel, domineering ways. Thus passed June and July, the men simmering in a surly rage; and by the end of August hatred had rotted their hearts and evil taken full possession of their minds. Black Scott was in danger of his life.

L25 Most of the time it is quite justifiable to subordinate the order of time or the order of place to the order of interest or importance in those paragraphs where the various orders are combined. But do not use an order or combination of orders that is not clear.[9]

Emphasis in the paragraph

L26 Emphasis means relative stress. In writing, emphasis is the principle that requires that more important thoughts be made to stand out from less important thoughts. Your writing is properly emphatic when your reader knows, without thinking the matter over, which thoughts you consider most important, which less, and which least important.

L27 Ordinarily place an important idea at the beginning or the end of a paragraph.

---

[9] The treatment given in the preceding numbers considers some of the obvious orders of presentation. But any order may be used that will be clear and easy.

[The spring of 1846] was a busy season in the city of St. Louis. Not only were emigrants from every part of the country preparing for the journey to Oregon and California, but an unusual number of traders were making ready their wagons and outfits for Santa Fé. Many of the emigrants, especially of those bound for California, were persons of wealth and standing. The hotels were crowded, and the gunsmiths and saddlers were kept constantly at work in providing arms and equipment for the different parties of travelers. Steamboats were leaving the levee and passing up the Missouri, crowded with passengers on their way to the frontier.[10]

In the first sentence of this paragraph, Parkman puts the important thought of the whole paragraph.

While still warming my hands, inspecting the cartridges, and standing with the gun leaning against my stomach, I was suddenly conscious that an elephant was almost on top of me. I have no knowledge of how the warning came. I have no mental record of hearing him, seeing him, or of any warning from the gun boy who faced me and who must have seen the elephant as he came down on me from behind. There must have been some definite signal, but it was not recorded in my mind. I only know that as I picked up my gun and wheeled about I tried to shove the safety catch forward. It refused to budge, and I remember the thought that perhaps I had left the catch forward when I inspected the gun and that if not I must pull the triggers hard enough to fire the gun anyway. This is an impossibility, but I remember the determination to do it, for the all-powerful impulse in my mind was that I must shoot instantly. Then something happened that dazed me. I don't know whether I shot or not. My next mental record is of a tusk right at my chest. I grabbed it with my left hand, the other one with my right hand, and swinging in between them went to the

In this paragraph Akeley considers that his most important point is to explain how he happened to react almost instinctively in the crisis described. This point he states in the last sentence.

---

[10] Francis Parkman, Jr., *The Oregon Trail* (New York: Rinehart & Co., 1931), p. 3. By permission.

376

ground on my back. This swinging in between the tusks was purely automatic. It was the result of many a time on the trails imagining myself caught by an elephant's rush and planning what I would do, and a very profitable planning, too; for I am convinced that if a man imagines such a crisis and plans what he would do, he will, when the occasion occurs, automatically do what he planned. Anyway, I firmly believe that my imaginings along the trail saved my life.[11]

L28 Put a series of ideas within a paragraph in the order of climax—least important or interesting, more important or interesting, still more important or interesting, most important or interesting.[12]

Warren Hastings was born on December 6, 1732. His mother died a few days later, and he was left dependent upon his impoverished grandfather. The child was early sent to the village school, where he learned his letters at the same desk as the sons of the peasants; nor did anything in his clothes or training indicate that his life was to be widely different from that of the farm boys with whom he studied and played. But no cloud could overcast the dawn of Hastings's genius and ambition. The farm boys noticed, and long remembered, how eagerly young Hastings took to books. The daily sight of the lands that his ancestors had possessed and that had passed into the hands of strangers, filled his young brain with wild fancies and projects.

In this paragraph Macaulay describes the young Warren Hastings. Macaulay's chief interest in him is his ambition to be "Hastings of Daylesford"—his determination to become a wealthy and important man. Consequently Macaulay first writes a few sentences about Hastings's birth and early training, and then gives the greater part of the paragraph to discussing Hastings's ambition. This interest, this importance, not only comes last in the paragraph but is given by far the greater detail.

---

[11] Carl E. Akeley, *In Brightest Africa* (Garden City: Garden City Pub. Co., 1925), p. 47. Reprinted by permission of Mary L. Jobe Akeley.

[12] When applying this principle to a paragraph that begins with a topic sentence, use the order of climax in the sentences that follow the topic sentence—insofar as it is reasonable to do so.

He loved to hear stories of the wealth and greatness of his ancestors, of their splendid estates, their loyalty to the government, and their valor. One bright summer day, Hastings, then just seven years old, lay on the bank of the stream that flows through the old domain of the Hastings family. There and then, as he told the tale seventy years later, there rose in his mind the scheme that, through all the turns of his eventful career, was never abandoned. He would recover the lands that had belonged to his ancestors. He would be Hastings of Daylesford. This purpose, formed in boyhood and poverty, grew stronger as his mind developed and as his fortunes improved. He pursued his purpose with that calm but indomitable force of will that was the most striking peculiarity of his character. When, under a tropical sun, he ruled fifty millions of Asiatics, his hopes, amidst all the cares of war, finance, and legislation, still pointed to Daylesford. And when his long public life, so singularly checkered with good and evil, with glory and blame, had at length closed forever, it was to Daylesford that he retired to die.[13]

L29   Occasionally emphasize an important idea by repeating it within a paragraph. Ordinarily repeat it in somewhat different words; rarely in the very same words.

Finally, oppressed by the clatter, the blatting of the orchestra, the tinkle of insincere conversation, Fleurin made his way across the dance floor, through the French doors that gave on the lawn, across the lawn, across the highway, to the sea wall. Peace, he thought —I must find peace. Not the peace of emptiness, for that is only silence and silence can be fear. I must have the peace of fullness, and that means the peace of love. There can be love without peace, but there can be no peace without love. One must love the things that fill, not the things that empty, and then one will have peace.

The repetition of the words *love* and *peace*, and of the ideas of emptiness, fullness, and so on, in this paragraph seems justified and effective. For somehow the repetition conveys a bit of Fleurin's desperate hunger for a meaning and a purpose in life. The paragraph below, which does not use repetition, loses in clarity and effect.

---

[13] Adapted from Thomas Babington Macaulay, "Warren Hastings," *Critical and Miscellaneous Essays* (new and rev. ed. New York: D. Appleton & Co., 1856), IV, 77.

Finally, oppressed by the clatter, the blatting of the orchestra, the tinkle of insincere conversation, Fleurin made his way across the dance floor, through the French doors that gave on the lawn, across the lawn, across the highway, to the sea wall. Peace, he thought—I must find something to quiet my mind. But I don't want emptiness. I want fullness. That means that I want love. There can be some kinds of affection without rest of soul, but there can be no real tranquillity unless the heart has fastened on something. But if I love the things that enrich a man, not the things that beggar him, then I may find satisfaction.

Great sin need not keep a man from finally getting to heaven. There was St. Peter, the chief of the apostles, for instance, who three times denied that he knew Christ—swore that he did not know Him at the very time when Christ, having been arrested, needed His friends. Then there was the Good Thief, St. Dismas, who had led, probably, a gangster's life. Another example is St. Augustine, who, as a young man—until he was thirty-three—lived a highly immoral life and defended heresy. Still others are St. John of God and St. Camillus of Lellis. St. John spent eighteen adventurous years as a free-lance trooper, hardened in body and soul; and St. Camillus, an Italian soldier, was for a long time a rakehell gambler. No; great sin does not prevent a man from getting to heaven, so long as he repents, walks away from evil, and turns at last to God.

This paragraph uses one of the most emphatic repetition devices that there are. A thought is stated at the beginning. Then, after the point has been developed, the same thought is repeated—sometimes in the very same words; sometimes, as here, in slightly different words—at the end of the paragraph. This gives the same thought the benefit of the two most striking positions in the paragraph. What is more, it forges the paragraph together into one compact, sharp blade of thought that can hardly fail to penetrate the mind and leave an impression there.

L30 Occasionally put the idea that you wish to emphasize into a very brief sentence, and all the other ideas into rather long sentences. Place the brief sentence at the beginning or, often better, at the end of the paragraph. The difference in the length of the sentences will call attention sharply to the idea in the short one.

The torrential rain made an infernal racket on the dry palmettos that roofed the fragile half-shelter—roofed it so imperfectly, however, that little cascades of cold water often found the neck of a man's poncho and ran down his back, drenching him and leaving him shivering. What water missed the neck of one's poncho dripped, or ran, or somehow found its way to the ground, and there joined with the soft earth to make first a soupy gumbo and then a muddy lake most uncomfortable to sit in—and, of course, it was either sit in the muddy lake or stand up on the broken leg. All in all, Felito felt miserable.

All in all, Felito felt miserable gains considerable emphasis because it is a short sentence coming after two very long ones. Notice that the paragraph next below, which ends with a long sentence, fails to make so sharp an impression, even though it is a good paragraph.

The torrential rain made an infernal racket on the dry palmettos that roofed the fragile half-shelter—roofed it so imperfectly, however, that little cascades of cold water often found the neck of a man's poncho and ran down his back, drenching him and leaving him shivering. What water missed the neck of one's poncho dripped, or ran, or somehow found its way to the ground, and there joined with the soft earth to make first a soupy gumbo and then a muddy lake most uncomfortable to sit in—and, of course, it was either sit in the muddy lake or stand up on the broken leg. With all of these things to contend with and no means of contending with them except patience, poor Felito felt very miserable indeed and longed for some change, almost any change, in his circumstances.

Poor Felito felt very miserable is smothered a bit in this version, though not so badly that the thought is obscured.

It was half-way through the morning, and he had not breakfasted; the slight litter of other breakfasts stood about

He had put salt in it gathers a great deal of emphasis from the contrast between its length and that of most of the senon the table to remind him of his hunger; and adding a poached egg to his order, he proceeded musingly to shake some white sugar into his coffee, thinking all the time about Flambeau. He remembered how Flambeau had escaped, once by a pair of nail scissors, and once by a house on fire; once by having to pay for an unstamped letter, and once by getting people to look through tences that have gone before. In fact, the sentence gains such emphasis that the reader would feel cheated if the salt turned out to be unimportant to the story. (It turns out to be important; for it is one of a trail of clues left by Flambeau's victim for the detective to follow, and it leads to Flambeau's capture.)

a telescope at a comet that might destroy the world. He thought his detective brain as good as the criminal's, which was true. But he fully realized the disadvantage. "The criminal is the creative artist; the detective only the critic," he said with a sour smile, and lifted his coffee cup to his lips slowly, and put it down very quickly. He had put salt in it.[14]

Paragraph development

L31 Put variety into your paragraphs by developing the topic thoughts in different ways—by enumeration, by giving circumstances, by comparison and contrast, by giving causes and effects, by giving examples, and by repetition.

ENUMERATION IN THE PARAGRAPH

L32 Develop a topic thought by dividing an idea in the subject or predicate into its parts.

[Topic thought:] Jerome Kern wrote some masterpieces of modern popular music.

[Development:] *Jerome Kern wrote some masterpieces of* An idea in the topic sentence,[15] "masterpieces of modern popu-

---

[14] G. K. Chesterton, "The Blue Cross," *The Innocence of Father Brown* (New York: Dodd, Mead & Co., 1911), pp. 8-9. By permission.

[15] A topic sentence is the topic thought of a paragraph expressed in one sentence of the paragraph itself. In the column at left, it is the sentence in italic.

modern popular music. "Ol' Man River," for instance, seems fated not to die, though it has been mangled by singers who do not understand it; indeed, the artiest critics don't mind admitting that it deserves to live. "Smoke Gets in Your Eyes," though its lyrics are the sort to cloy after a time, is such good music that it survived even the lush treatment that Kostelanetz used to give it; and its appeal reaches lovers of Basin Street as well as those whose taste is just a little sentimental. "Long Ago and Far Away" has the quality frequently described as "haunting" and "elusive," with this difference, that it continues to haunt and to elude after comparable songs have begun to bore. These three songs are outstanding, of course; but almost nothing that Kern wrote can be easily dismissed. People are likely to be humming his tunes when they can no longer remember who wrote them.

CIRCUMSTANCES IN THE PARAGRAPH

L33 Develop a topic thought by giving the circumstances related to it—by answering the question *When, where, how,* or *why is this?*

[Topic thought:] There is a new boy on our block.

[Development:] *There is a new boy on our block!* He arrived yesterday—he and his family—with a big moving van carrying a lot of furniture and (believe me; I saw it) a beautiful mahogany-and-white lake cruiser with a compact marine engine. He is going to live in the Lyons house, the one with the big side yard hidden away behind hedges. He arrived just in time; for, when the Lyonses moved, the neighborhood could no longer use the tree

The first sentence (after the topic sentence), *He arrived yesterday . . . marine engine,* tells when and how. The second sentence, *He is going to live . . . behind hedges,* tells where. The last sentences, *He arrived just . . . has not expired,* tell when.

382

house in the yard nor the basement clubroom; and so the gang on the block was breaking up and joining other groups, having no place to get together. Now we'll be able to reorganize—and my term as president has not expired.

COMPARISON AND CONTRAST IN THE PARAGRAPH

L34 Develop a topic thought by using comparison, contrast, or both.

[Topic thought:] Reading a historical novel is like traveling in a foreign country.

[Development:] Reading any good historical novel is like traveling in a foreign country. The reader, as if he were a tourist, is carried to a new land entirely. He sees men and women dressed in what would be considered a very queer way in his own neighborhood; he hears them talk wisdom and nonsense in expressions new to him. He finds, to his wonder, that people can live—and quite happily, too, it appears—without electric lights or automobiles or moving pictures or streamline trains or any of the things he is used to. And like the wise tourist, who has seen ordinary foreign people going about their ordinary business and pleasure, the wise reader conceives a sympathy for these "foreigners." He realizes that, though they are outwardly so different from himself, they are not a strange breed, after all. Under the surface they are human beings exactly like himself!

The comparison of reading a historical novel to traveling in a foreign country makes clear what we learn from both—that, in spite of differences in clothes and conveniences, all human beings are alike.

[Topic thought:] The campus of Faber High is very quiet in the summer.

[Development:] The campus of Faber High is a very different thing in the winter from what it is in the summer. In the winter—from fall until late spring—it is a busy place, with five hundred boys milling over it all day long. Early in the morning they come, yelling and shoving,

The campus in summer is contrasted with the campus in winter.

383

and spill over the lawns and sidewalks and playing fields. At recess, at noontime, and during the long afternoon, they're playing football, basketball, baseball, handball, and games without a name; they're getting into fights and shouting themselves hoarse. But the summer —how different. There is nothing on the campus then but the trees and the sunshine. The grass on the lawns gets thick and green; the weeds grow high on the football field and around the handball courts. The gymnasium, the auditorium, the swimming pool—all are empty caverns. And there is no sound, only silence all day long, deep and continuous silence, strange and out of place, silence that is startled by the sleepy chirp of a sparrow, the hum of a bee, or the slap of the flag rope against the metal pole.

CAUSE AND EFFECT IN THE PARAGRAPH

L35 Develop a topic thought by stating some of the effects or consequences of the truth or event it relates.

[Topic thought:] A twig snapped in the brush along the bank.

[Development:] *A twig snapped in the brush along the bank.* The frogs fell silent as if on signal. The three boys on the houseboat sat up rigid in their bunks, listening intently. Then Rob threw off his blanket, dropped noiselessly

The effects of the twig's snapping—the silence of the frogs and the actions and fear of the boys—are used to round out the topic thought into an effective paragraph.

from his upper berth to the floor and, taking the shotgun from its hooks over the door, broke and loaded it with two shells from the box in the cupboard. Cleg and Hart joined him; and all stood silently trying to read reassurance in one another's faces, shivering a little because they were clad only in shorts and, a bit more, because they were frightened, and listening tensely for the next noise from shore.

L36 Develop a topic thought by stating some of the causes of, or reasons for, the truth or event it relates.

[Topic thought:] The twig snapped.

[Development:] The man had been careful to avoid any

The causes of the twig's snapping—the snake, the position

384

alarm that could alert the boys on the houseboat; and he had been skillful about it, too. But what is one to do when one steps on a snake and cannot tell, in the dark, whether or not it is a moccasin? He stepped back swiftly, of course, and in doing so placed the heel of a boot on a dry twig lying across a little hollow in the ground. *The twig snapped* with a noise as sharp as that of a small firecracker in the silent forest.

of the twig, the man's impulsive action—are used to develop the topic thought.

EXAMPLES IN THE PARAGRAPH

L37 Develop a topic thought by giving particular instances or concrete examples of the general or abstract truth that it relates.

[Topic thought:] It occasionally happens that, while a boy is in high school, he offers no accurate indication of his chances for the future.

[Development:] *It occasionally happens that, while a boy is in high school, he offers no accurate indication of his chances for the future.* G. K. Chesterton's experience is a case in point. He was considered very dull and phlegmatic by his masters, one of whom delivered the crushing verdict that the boy's talent for English writing was negligible. Don Bosco is said to have been another who did not promise much in his early studies, except perhaps tenacity of purpose. And Vianney, the celebrated Curé d'Ars, was to all appearances such a numskull that he was ordained almost with reluctance and misgivings. No doubt their teachers should have been more alert to their capabilities. But the most alert teacher cannot always penetrate the defenses of a bashful student, and it would require a special insight to be able to say that a dullard like Jean Vianney would be transformed into a Curé d'Ars. Or that a clumsy, dull English schoolboy would be the creator of the delightful Father Brown.

The general truth in the topic statement is developed by naming three men who were rather striking examples of it: G. K. Chesterton, Don Bosco, and Jean Vianney.

REPETITION IN THE PARAGRAPH

L38 Develop a topic thought by repeating an idea in the subject or predicate in different words and with greater clarity or force.

[Topic thought:] Mountains are to the earth's bulk what big muscles are to a man's body.

[Development:] *Mountains are to the earth's bulk what big muscles are to a man's body.* The earth's muscles and tendons and sinews are, in the mountain, brought out with fierce and knotted energy, full of expression, passion, and strength. The plains and the low hills are the earth at rest, with its muscles relaxed and concealed under curving, smooth skin. This is one of the first truths about the make-up of earth. The spirit of the mountains is action, strength, energy; the spirit of the plains is rest. The plains are asleep; the mountains lift up their giant faces to the heavens, crying triumphantly, "I live forever!"

The second sentence repeats, more vividly, the notion that mountains are the result of muscular activity. The third sentence repeats the very same thing, but negatively, by a contrast. The fourth, fifth, and sixth sentences repeat the same notion, each with new clarity or force.

M The theme

M1 A theme is a group of paragraphs that all contribute to the development of one topic.[1] (Sometimes a theme will consist of only one paragraph. One-paragraph themes, however, are rare except in such compositions as editorials, jokes, columns, and advertisements. Sometimes, on the other hand, a theme will be as long as an average-sized book.)

---

[1] See also exposition, N3-99; description, O2; narration, P2-43; and argument, Q3-41.

386

The introduction

M2 Do not use an introduction unless it will accomplish some useful purpose. The topic paragraph, especially in short themes, is often the best introduction in itself. Wordiness or a reluctance to get down to business will only bore the reader. Ordinarily, the introduction amounts to about one fifth of the whole composition.

M3 Use an introductory paragraph or so—

A To put your audience or readers in a receptive mood.

[Doubtful:] We have a very poor spirit in this club of ours. I have given the club a lot of thought, and I believe I can tell you what is wrong with us and what we can do about it.

It may not be prudent to begin with this topic paragraph. The topic involves criticism, which few men take kindly unless it is softened. The audience or readers may be prejudiced from the start. Use an introductory paragraph or two, as just below.

[Better:] I think all of you know my record—how little I have done to make this club of ours what it could be. For example, you remember, I imagine, when I failed to have our annual report printed in time for the last meeting of the year—and simply because I was too lazy to get it ready. You may recall that, until a month ago, I had not attended a single meeting this year. Oh, I've been no asset. Well, I've been doing some thinking (you have every right to laugh), and I've decided to do things differently. I believe you'll take some plain talk from me, since you know that I am talking to myself just as much as to you.

We have a very poor spirit in this club of ours. I have given the subject a lot of thought, and I believe I can tell you what is wrong with us and what we can do about it.

B To interest your audience or readers and make them want the rest of the theme.

[Doubtful:] The effects of the Ten Commandments are not negative; they are positive.

This sounds very dull indeed, unless the audience or reader guesses at the implication.

387

[Better:] If you are like most people, you think of the Ten Commandments as a series of frowning *don'ts* that restrict a man's liberty. But have you ever found yourself wondering what this world would be like if the Ten Commandments were simply disregarded? One day I fell to speculating about this, and the speculation startled me. I found that the Ten Commandments are the basis of liberty, that the Ten Commandments set men free.

Put it this way: the Ten Commandments are really not negative; they are positive.

c To avoid an unpleasantly abrupt beginning.

[Doubtful:] Three things in our organization cause me a good deal of concern.

This would be a rather harsh and abrupt opening under most circumstances.

[Better:] I know that you will excuse me if I do not this time pay my debt of praise to an organization to which I owe as much as any of you. We are met for a different purpose now—not to congratulate ourselves on what we have, but to discover what we lack.

Three things in our organization cause me a good deal of concern.

d To settle the doubts of the audience or readers about bringing up such a subject at such a time.

[Doubtful:] Mallophaga, or bird lice, have some peculiar traits, several of which I shall discuss in this paper.

One can hear the groan of the audience or readers and the angry murmur: "Why bring *that* up?" Not everybody is automatically interested in bird lice. This is a very unfortunate opening.

[Better:] Ordinarily I should not think of annoying you with the health problems of semidomestic fowl. But since we are planning to raise pigeons and sell squabs to bring in some extra money, I think I'll find you interested in Mallophaga.

Mallophaga, or bird lice, have some peculiar traits, several of which I shall discuss in this paper.

e To supply information that the audience or readers need at the very beginning of the theme.

[Doubtful:] Insofar as it assumes that man is purely ma-

Many readers would not understand this sentence because

terial, cybernetics is doomed to failure.

of the terms *cybernetics* and *material*. It is important, therefore, that before the theme goes very far these terms be explained; otherwise the author can write off his early paragraphs as total loss.

[Better:] There is a science—if one may use that word loosely—that has been attracting public notice of recent years in America: the science of cybernetics. "Cybernetics" is the comparative study of complex calculating machines and the human nervous system, with the hope that more may be learned about the operation of the human brain. Disciples of this science are fond of talking about machines as though they were human and about men as though they were machines. Some of these people apparently think that there is nothing essentially different between men and machines—that both are material only, that neither is partly spiritual.

Now, what I intend to try to show is that cybernetics, insofar as it assumes that man is purely material and not partly spiritual, is doomed to failure.

M4 It is a good idea to know exactly what you are introducing before you introduce it. Ordinarily, therefore, write the introduction last. It often happens, however, that an excellent introduction pops into one's mind before the theme itself is drafted. When this happens, write the introduction down on a separate piece of paper while it is still "hot." Then proceed to write the theme. Afterwards, read the introduction to see if it still fits. If it does, then use it. If it does not, jettison it and write another—if an introduction is needed.

M5 Unless there is good reason to the contrary, an introduction should answer all or some of these questions:[2]

---

[2] When it is a case of writing an atmospheric introduction to a story, a suspense-creating advertisement, or something of the kind, these questions—with the possible exception of the first—will not prove very helpful. But in the general run of informational and argumentative papers, they may help you to write an introduction that is organically connected with the theme. Use them where they help you and neglect them where they hinder you.

A What (and who) is going to be talked about? (This is answered when the theme topic is included in the introduction or is itself used as the introduction.)

B Why is it going to be talked about?'

C Who is going to talk about it?

D What is he going to say about it?

E Why is he saying it to this particular audience or at this particular time, and so on?

F How is he going to talk about it? What divisions of the subject is he going to make, what is he going to include or exclude, and so on?

The conclusion

M6 Often a theme does well to come to a close where its development stops. Do not use concluding paragraphs unless they will accomplish some useful purpose. Wordiness or a reluctance to finish will only bore the reader and may spoil the effect of an otherwise good theme. Ordinarily, the conclusion amounts to about one tenth of the composition.

M7 It sometimes helps to use a concluding paragraph or so—

A To summarize the main points made in the body of the theme and leave them fresh in the reader's mind right at the very end.

Well, now, our time is up. This has been a lengthy and complicated discussion. Much that we have talked about needs further treatment. But two conclusions of major importance have been reached and should have immediate effect on our conduct: first, that discipline is a necessary condition of happiness and, second, that a man must forget himself to a large extent if he is to be himself to any extent at all.

B To avoid an impression of abruptness or inconclusiveness, to keep the reader from asking, "What! Is that the end?"

[Too abrupt:] ". . . If Horace is here, then I am saved," she cried, turning to Mr. Klusterblum.

[Better:] ". . . If Horace is here, then I am saved," she cried, turning to Mr. Klusterblum.

And so indeed she was saved, though not from Horace. For this story ended as all such stories must. She and Horace were married and quarreled happily ever after. And the moral of this epic is: If you must climb cliffs, use a ladder.

c To finish on a rousing note and reinforce the persuasiveness of the whole theme.

Carry yourselves, then, like the American soldiers that you are, and fear nothing but yourselves. Remember that America depends upon your fortitude, that she has no defense but you, that she entrusts herself to you as to sons. Fight, then, like warrior sons of America.

d To lower the reader gently from a highly emotional state and ease him back into a calmer world.

. . . as the bullet slammed into his chest.

So died, violently, a man who hated violence. Life has its ironies, has it not? And hardly a man dies without some little irony at the end to make a cynic mock—and a good man smile with understanding of the divine humor and the divine unexpectedness in things.

Unity in the theme

IN GENERAL

M8 Unity means oneness. In composition, unity is the principle that requires that there be only one main thought and that all the other thoughts and words in a sentence, paragraph, or theme directly or indirectly reinforce the main thought.

M9 The theme topic is the subject matter of the theme, the one clear, rather brief thought that answers the question *What is the theme about?*

M10 A good theme has one and only one theme topic.

M11 Make sure that the theme topic is itself unified. If it contains more than one idea, make sure either that they are very closely related or that there is only one main idea to which the others are subordinate.

[Faulty:] The skyscraper capitol of Louisiana is in Baton Rouge, and the Standard Oil Company has an enormous plant there.

There conceivably could be something that relates the capitol and the plant more closely than does the fact that they are both in the same city. But, as far as one can tell here, the theme would profit if one or the other idea were dropped entirely.

[Good:] The skyscraper capitol of Louisiana is in Baton Rouge.

[Good:] The Standard Oil Company has an enormous plant in Baton Rouge.

[Faulty:] Boys enjoy making pocket money in many ways, but baby sitting is certainly not one of them.

This could lead the writer to develop two distinct topics without relating them: (1) *Boys enjoy making pocket money in many ways.* (2) *Boys do not enjoy baby sitting.*

[Good:] Baby sitting is not one of the ways in which boys enjoy making pocket money.

This theme topic will lead the writer to develop only one thought.

[Faulty:] Dickens was a great writer, but he failed to make a success of his family life.

This theme topic may lead the writer to develop two topics rather fully, when either of the topics would be more than sufficient for a theme of some considerable length.

[Good:] Dickens, the famous writer, failed to make a success of his family life.

Phrased thus, the theme topic will lead the writer to give no more than passing mention to Dickens's fame and to concentrate on his family life.

M12 It often starts both reader and writer off well to state the theme topic in a topic paragraph near the beginning of the theme.

392

Educators are sharply divided on whether every high-school graduate or only a very few should be permitted to go to college.

Some people think that any control imposed on the press is a violation of freedom of the press; others maintain that freedom, even freedom of the press, can only be had where some control is imposed.

Some political theorists say that even an interim dictatorship over countries occupied by America after a war violates the spirit of the Declaration of Independence and of the Constitution; others say that such temporary undemocratic government is essential to the creation of true democracy later on.

It is very difficult for the reader to guess what central idea holds these paragraphs together. The first talks about education; the second, the press; the third, defeated countries; the fourth, minorities; the fifth, raising children. Yet there is one main thought in these varied paragraphs. The puzzlement would disappear if the theme began with this topic paragraph: *Americans today are troubled by this question: How much control is healthy for people?*

When they are in power, some politicians call for the suppression of any group that happens to criticize their foreign policy, on the ground that such criticism gives aid and comfort to the enemy. Some pundits and jurists, however, maintain that even parties like the Communists should not be curbed, much less suppressed, lest the freedom of minorities to exist and to become majorities should suffer injury.

Some parents seem to feel that they infringe the rights of their children if they punish them for neglect or disobedience. Others act as if children should never, under any circumstances, be allowed even to discuss a decision made by their elders, but should obey without any question whatever [and so on].

M13 Make every sentence develop its paragraph topic; make every paragraph develop the theme topic.[3]

M14 It is not always possible and is never necessary that every paragraph develop the theme topic *directly*. Paragraph A, for example, may develop the theme topic, and para-

---

[3] See M14.

graphs B and C may develop paragraph A. But do not carry such indirect development to the point where the reader loses the trail.

DIGRESSIONS

M15 In long and leisurely themes, it is all right to indulge in an occasional digression, provided that—

A There is some good reason for the digression, such as an attempt to put the reader in the mood to accept what you have to say.

B The reader is told in one way or another just when you leave the theme and when you come back to it.

C The digressions are relatively few and brief. (One digression of a sentence or so is about the maximum for a three- to five-hundred-word theme.)

INTRODUCTIONS

M16 Make sure that your introduction is closely connected with the rest of the theme and naturally leads into it.

Thank you, John Edlegurt, for "them kind words."

Ladies and gentlemen, I'm supposed to speak to you tonight on family allowances to supplement the living wage. Well, that reminds me. There was an old muskrat trapper (ha-ha) living along Bayou Bourboux down in old Louisiana who decided to "hire him a helper." Well, the helper

This introduction is very poor. It is connected with a theme on family allowances only in word and not in thought. Moreover, it is artificially introduced—does not grow out of the theme itself or out of the speaker's situation or any of the things naturally connected with the theme.

was a boy with "nimble fingers." Pretty soon the old trapper noticed that some of his pelts were disappearing, and it didn't take him long to make the obvious connection. When the boy came at the end of the month to collect his money, the trapper handed him about a tenth of what they had agreed upon. "Why," says the boy, "that ain't a livin' wage. You're supposed to pay me a livin' wage."

"Yeah?" answers the trapper. "You look in the Bible, son, and see what it says *there* about the wages of *sin!*"

I think all of you know my record—how little I have done to make this club of ours what it could be. For example, you remember, I imagine, when I failed to have our annual report printed in time for the last meeting of the year—and simply because I was too lazy to get it ready. You may recall that, until a month ago, I had not attended a single meeting this year. Oh, I've been no asset. Well, I've been doing some thinking (you have every right to laugh), and I've decided to do things differently. I believe you'll take some plain talk from me, since you know that I am talking to myself just as much as to you.

This is a good introduction, closely and naturally connected with the rest of the theme.

We have a very poor spirit in this club of ours. I have given the subject a lot of thought, and I believe I can tell you what is wrong with us and what we can do about it.

M17 Ordinarily an introduction will tend to be closely connected with the rest of the theme and to lead into it naturally if it answers all or some of these questions:[4]

A What (and who) is going to be talked about? (This is answered when the theme topic is included in the introduction or is itself used as the introduction.)

B Why is it going to be talked about?

C Who is going to talk about it?

D What is he going to say about it?

E Why is he saying it to this particular audience or at this particular time, and so on?

F How is he going to talk about it? What divisions of the subject is he going to make, what is he going to include or exclude, and so on?

---

[4] When it is a case of writing an atmospheric introduction to a story, a suspense-creating advertisement, or something of the kind, these questions—with the possible exception of the first—will not prove very helpful. But in the general run of informational and argumentative papers, they may help you to write an introduction that is organically connected with the theme. Use them where they help you and neglect them where they hinder you; but never fail to keep the general rule of introduction, M16.

Coherence in the theme

M18 Coherence is the principle of composition that requires that, for the sake of clarity, ideas and words follow one another in an orderly manner and that the connections between parts be made clear.

M19 Coherence in the theme means that the words, sentences, paragraphs, chapters, and parts of the theme are rightly put together and properly connected.[5]

M20 Arrange the main and subordinate parts of a theme in one of the following or similar orders:

A *The order of time.* First tell what happened first; second, tell what happened after that; third, tell what happened after that; and so on. (This order is particularly useful in narratives.)[6]

From the time that he left Alva, Wyck's progress was much more rapid than he had expected it to be. For once, reconnaissance had been wrong in the right way; the roads turned out to be in much better condition than reports had indicated. Moreover, the motorized units proceeded without the mechanical breakdowns so usual that commanding officers come to consider them inevitable—breakdowns that can snarl traffic for hours on narrow byways.

At 3:00 P.M., however, Wyck did run into trouble. A small party of Fascists fighting for the Germans—less than fifty—held up the advance for a little less than an hour with four machine guns, two of which swept the road where it passed through a narrow defile. They were finally cleared out without the loss of one American or allied soldier; and Wyck proceeded on his way, still well ahead of schedule.

The roads continued good; and so Wyck arrived at the southwestern approach to Templi well before his time, deployed his forces, and entered battle at precisely 8:00 A.M. the next day.

Within an hour it was apparent that he was meeting the full resistance of Templi. No one was creating a diversion at the eastern

---

[5] See also narration, P13-15 and P39-41.
[6] See P1-2.

end of the little town. Hard pressed for a decision, Wyck fanned his men out in a quarter circle in the southwest and did what he could with what he had [and so on].

B *The order of place.* Start at the bottom and go to the top, or start at the top and go to the bottom, or start at the right and go to the left, and so on; or start at one end and go to the other, and so on. (This order is particularly useful in descriptions.)[7]

I was told to look for Mr. Forous on Salinas Street.

Salinas Street is a long, dirty, festering wound running through the south flank of Claymore from the river to the open prairie west of town.

At the river end it presents a pair of saloons, like gatehouses, on either side of the street. Dives they are, and look it; but they are the soundest edifices on the whole street and do not prepare one for the incredible squalor beyond.

After the saloons come two rows of hovels, gaping slack-jawed at each other across the wide, pitted, trash-strewn thoroughfare. "Hovels" has too grand a sound to describe the unbelievable jungle of drunken, staggering, slouching structures thrown together with wire, packing cases, sections of rusted metal culvert, cardboard, and old license plates nailed to overlap in pathetic parody of shingles and clapboard. These are the homes of the "Salinas Street Slush-Eaters," as the rest of Claymore cynically calls them—these foul and rickety nightmares that do not shelter the inmates from so much as a curious glance.

After several hundred yards of these, on the north side of the street there is a little clearing in the center of which rises—but not very high—Father Andreas's church: a shed, roofed with tin, open on three sides, and floored with dirt except for the platform under the "sanctuary" [and so on].

C *The order of interest or importance.* Start with the least important or interesting thought and move by degrees to the most interesting or important.

As a matter of fact, it was rather a full day. I spent several hours getting the dummy for the *Colombière Clarion* ready for the

---

[7] See O1.

printer and another forty minutes working out that silly exercise in emphasis for English class tomorrow.

I spent another three hours doing something rather interesting: watching the men at D'Astignac Studios painting a backdrop for the school's production of *Everyman*. I found it amazing that they could work so quickly. Watching them slap paint on—mostly with ten-inch brushes—you would imagine that the result was going to look like something my manic-depressive little sister thinks up out of her water-color kit. On the contrary, they achieved a perfect copy of Laury's design and got it on a canvas twenty by forty feet in less than three hours.

But the thing that will make it a day to remember was something that happened down at the printer's. I was helping Mr. Shelton lay out our copy according to the dummy, when a rather fat, bald, tired-looking man came out of the office and walked over to the shop table where we were working. When he picked up a sheaf of *Clarion* copy and started reading through it, I felt rather annoyed that he hadn't asked anybody's permission. But I didn't say anything. He took advantage of a pause in the discussion I was having with Shelton to ask very curtly, "Who wrote this thing on the prize debates at Colombière?"

"I did," I said without looking up.

"You, eh?"

"Uh-huh."

"Well, son, when you finish high school and college, if you're still fool enough to like newspaper work, come down and get a job from me."

"Yes?" I said; "and who are you, mister?"

"Priestly," he answered; "R. C. Priestly, city editor, Wichita *Herald*. Darned good paper, and an excellent city editor."

D *The logical order.* Follow a series of causes and effects, circumstances and results, and so on.

It must not be understood that Joe was more of a coward than most boys. He could take a reasonable amount of physical punishment with a reasonable amount of suppressed whimpering. Joe's difficulty was pride.

Until the time that he was ten, he had lived in a rural area where he got his schooling at home and had the companionship of only two or three boys. He had learned to hunt, but not to shoot baskets. He had learned to plow a field, but not to field a ball. At the age of ten he came to live in the city and found that he was an ignoramus in all the sciences at which city boys excel. He could have learned them even then, but he was too proud. Pride kept him from courting the laughs and jeers that greet the late beginner. He pretended that he did not care for sports and spent his time watching the others and joining them only in those diversions at which they were no less green than he.

He had a glib and entertaining tongue; he was generous enough not only with possessions but with praise; and so he never lacked companions, friends, invitations. Indeed, whole days might pass during which he would account himself happy; but then would come one of those embarrassing incidents that he had learned to dread.

There was the time, for instance, when the coach, a kindly man with no knowledge of Joe's frame of mind, had tried to shame him, in front of a number of the school heroes, into going out for baseball. The coach was not entirely to be blamed. Joe did look like a ballplayer, and the technique of shaming a boy is not altogether bad pedagogy in some circumstances.

There were other embarrassing moments, too, when, for example, he had to pretend not to see a football that bounced his way, lest he should betray his girlish awkwardness in throwing it back to the players. Little by little he had learned a trick that absorbed the scorn of schoolmates and turned their jibes to friendly raillery. The trick was to anticipate the laugh against himself, to play for it. If he could not avoid returning a ball, he shouted: "Watch out! Here comes my spit ball." He would make elaborate show of spitting delicately on his finger tips. "It's illegal, but it's tricky. You'd better back up!" His wild and feeble peg would be greeted with mild merriment; and the impression would circulate that he could really do much better if he were not such a clown [and so on].

E *The psychological order.* Follow the order that will make your matter more interesting, easier to understand, or more acceptable to a particular audience.

ANTONY: Friends, Romans, countrymen, lend me your ears;

I come to bury Caesar, not to praise him.

At the beginning of this speech the crowd is hostile to Antony and the dead Caesar. Antony does not dare to give them his thesis right at the beginning,

399

The evil that men do lives after them;
The good is oft interred with their bones.
So let it be with Caesar. The noble Brutus
Hath told you Caesar was ambitious:
If it were so, it was a grievous fault;
And grievously hath Caesar answer'd it.
Here, under leave of Brutus and the rest
(For Brutus is an honourable man;
So are they all, all honourable men,)
Come I to speak in Caesar's funeral.
He was my friend, faithful and just to me:
But Brutus says he was ambitious;
And Brutus is an honourable man.
He hath brought many captives home to Rome,
Whose ransoms did the general coffers fill:
Did this in Caesar seem ambitious?
When that the poor have cried, Caesar hath wept:
Ambition should be made of sterner stuff:
Yet Brutus says he was ambitious;
And Brutus is an honourable man.

does not dare to say that Caesar was a great and just ruler and that he has been foully murdered. He would never get a hearing. He therefore begins most modestly. He carefully balances every item of praise of Caesar with the charge of ambition brought against him. He mentions traits of character that the crowd can accept without feeling disloyal to Brutus. Then he skillfully begins to set before them more sentimental facts, leading their emotions inch by inch, then foot by foot, then yard by yard away from the convictions that Brutus has planted in them a scant few minutes before. When he has got them weeping with him, he shocks them with the sudden sight of Caesar's shredded body. Then (near the end of the speech, not given here) he caps everything with what he has saved till the last—the poorest argument against ambition, but the argument that will mean most to the crowd—the fact that Caesar has left a little money to every Roman citizen and has willed his private estates as public parks. The money and the parks buy the mob for Antony, and he sets it to burning down Rome and lynching his enemies. Had he

You all did see that on the Lupercal
I thrice presented him a kingly crown,
Which he did thrice refuse: was this ambition?
Yet Brutus says he was ambitious;
And, sure, he is an honourable man.
I speak not to disprove what Brutus spoke,
But here I am to speak what I do know.
You all did love him once, not without cause:
What cause withholds you, then, to mourn for him?
O judgment, thou art fled to brutish beasts,
And men have lost their reason!—Bear with me;
My heart is in the coffin there with Caesar,
And I must pause till it come back to me.
FIRST CITIZEN: Methinks there is much reason in his sayings.
SECOND CITIZEN: If thou consider rightly of the matter,
Caesar has had great wrong.
THIRD CITIZEN: Has he, masters?
I fear there will a worse come in his place.
FOURTH CITIZEN: Mark'd ye his words? He would not take the crown;
Therefore 'tis certain he was not ambitious.
FIRST CITIZEN: If it be found so, some will dear abide it.
SECOND CITIZEN: Poor soul! his eyes are red as fire with weeping.
THIRD CITIZEN: There's not a nobler man in Rome than Antony.
FOURTH CITIZEN: Now mark him, he begins again to speak.
ANTONY: But yesterday, the word of Caesar might
Have stood against the world; now, lies he there,
And none so poor to do him reverence.
O masters! if I were dispos'd to stir
Your hearts and minds to mutiny and rage,
I should do Brutus wrong, and Cassius wrong,
Who, you all know, are honourable men:
I will not do them wrong; I rather choose
To wrong the dead, to wrong myself, and you,
Than I will wrong such honourable men.
But here's a parchment with the seal of Caesar,
I found it in his closet; 'tis his will:
Let but the commons hear this testament,

proceeded in any other way, he would soon have lost his hearing and possibly his head. He used a psychological order, adapted to his audience.

401

(Which, pardon me, I do not mean to read,)
And they would go and kiss dead Caesar's wounds,
And dip their napkins in his sacred blood;
Yea, beg a hair of him for memory,
And, dying, mention it within their wills,
Bequeathing it, as a rich legacy,
Unto their issue.

FOURTH CITIZEN: We'll hear the will: read it, Mark Antony.

CITIZENS: The will, the will! we will hear Caesar's will.

ANTONY: Have patience, gentle friends, I must not read it;
It is not meet you know how Caesar loved you.
You are not wood, you are not stones, but men;
And, being men, hearing the will of Caesar,
It will inflame you, it will make you mad:
'Tis good you know not that you are his heirs;
For if you should, O, what would come of it!

FOURTH CITIZEN: Read the will; we'll hear it, Antony;
You shall read us the will; Caesar's will.

ANTONY: Will you be patient? Will you stay a while?
I have o'ershot myself to tell you of it:
I fear I wrong the honourable men,
Whose daggers have stabb'd Caesar; I do fear it.

FOURTH CITIZEN: They were traitors: honourable men!

CITIZENS: The will! The testament!

SECOND CITIZEN: They were villains, murderers: the will; read the
      will.

ANTONY: You will compel me, then, to read the will?
Then make a ring about the corse of Caesar,
And let me show you him that made the will.
Shall I descend? and will you give me leave?

CITIZENS: Come down.

SECOND CITIZEN: Descend. [*Antony comes down.*]

THIRD CITIZEN: You shall have leave.

FOURTH CITIZEN: A ring; stand round.

FIRST CITIZEN: Stand from the hearse, stand from the body.

SECOND CITIZEN: Room for Antony, most noble Antony!

ANTONY: Nay, press not so upon me; stand far off.

CITIZENS: Stand back; room: bear back.

ANTONY: If you have tears, prepare to shed them now.
You all do know this mantle: I remember
The first time ever Caesar put it on;

'Twas on a summer's evening, in his tent,
That day he overcame the Nervii—
Look, in this place, ran Cassius' dagger through:
See what a rent the envious Casca made:
Through this the well-beloved Brutus stabb'd;
And, as he pluck'd his cursed steel away,
Mark how the blood of Caesar follow'd it,
As rushing out of doors, to be resolv'd
If Brutus so unkindly knock'd, or no;
For Brutus, as you know, was Caesar's angel:
Judge, O you gods, how dearly Caesar lov'd him!
This was the most unkindest cut of all;
For when the noble Caesar saw him stab,
Ingratitude, more strong than traitors' arms,
Quite vanquish'd him: then burst his mighty heart;
And, in his mantle muffling up his face,
Even at the base of Pompey's statue,
Which all the while ran blood, great Caesar fell.
O, what a fall was there, my countrymen!
Then I, and you, and all of us fell down,
Whilst bloody treason flourish'd over us.
O, now you weep; and, I perceive, you feel
The dint of pity: these are gracious drops.
Kind souls, what, weep you when you but behold
Our Caesar's vesture wounded? Look you here,
Here is himself, marr'd, as you see, with traitors.
FIRST CITIZEN: O piteous spectacle!
SECOND CITIZEN: O noble Caesar!
THIRD CITIZEN: O woful day!
FOURTH CITIZEN: O traitors, villains!
FIRST CITIZEN: O most bloody sight!
SECOND CITIZEN: We will be revenged: revenge—about—seek—burn
—fire—kill—slay—let not a traitor live[8] [and so on].

M21 It happens often enough that one of the other orders listed in M20 is also the best psychological order for a certain audience under certain circumstances.

M22 Do not use the psychological order as an excuse to throw away all order. Make sure first that you yourself have a

---

[8] William Shakespeare, *Julius Caesar*, Act III, scene 2.

plan that you can explain on demand and then take care that the reader always knows where he is, what is happening, and can see the connections between the parts of your theme.

M23 Supply the reader with all the information he needs for an easy following of the thought.

One fine day in late March, when it looked as if spring had decided to stay, Mark Hokins cut himself a generous slice from the flitch that hung in his smokehouse, took a loaf of bread from the box in the kitchen cupboard, filled a bottle with water, and set out at a good pace across the valley toward the mountains and the village of Little Rawlings.

What makes the passage at left incoherent is the omission of one little bit of information that is important to the good order of the composition. In the revision below, the missing information is supplied at the beginning of the second paragraph.

The supplies would hardly have been adequate for anyone else. But Hokins had taught himself to do with little—had even taught himself to enjoy doing with little. Looking at his tall leanness and the set of his jaw, you sensed immediately that this man was an ascetic, keeping himself in training against a day to come.

One fine day in late March, when it looked as if spring had decided to stay, Mark Hokins cut himself a generous slice from the flitch that hung in his smokehouse, took a loaf of bread from the box in the kitchen cupboard, filled a bottle with water, and set out at a good pace across the valley toward the mountains and the village of Little Rawlings.

Since Little Rawlings was three days of good walking away, the supplies would hardly have been adequate for anyone else. But Hokins had taught himself to do with little—had even taught himself to enjoy doing with little. Looking at his tall leanness and the set of his jaw, you sensed immediately that this man was an ascetic, keeping himself in training against a day to come.

M24 Supply necessary information when or before the reader needs it. Do not use devices like *I forgot to tell you* or *it should have been mentioned earlier that* . . .

This is incoherent

Terrence McFarlane looked at the people around him. There were about thirty of them altogether, most of them dozing, lulled by the rhythmic sway as well as by the want of fresh air. McFarlane could stare at them without seeming impolite. Like everybody else over twenty-five, he enjoyed looking at people and trying to guess what sort they were and what had made them like that.

That sailor, for instance, had an interesting face. Even in sleep, which usually relaxes a man's features, the sailor looked hard. He was the youngest person on the │bus│ and yet the bitterest-looking of the lot.

This is coherent

Terrence McFarlane looked at the people around him. There were about thirty of them altogether, most of them dozing, lulled by the rhythmic sway of the │bus│ as well as by the want of fresh air. Mc-Farlane could stare at them without seeming impolite. Like everybody else over twenty-five, he enjoyed looking at people and trying to guess what sort they were and what had made them like that.

That sailor, for instance, had an interesting face. Even in sleep, which usually relaxes a man's features, the sailor looked hard. He was the youngest person on the bus and yet the bitterest-looking of the lot.

M25 To supply missing connections, to make vague ones more definite, and to smooth out abrupt transitions, use bridge words, phrases, sentences, and paragraphs.

Without bridge words, phrases, sentences, or paragraphs

Anyone looking at Tim Peltier would have set him down as one of the most cheerful, generous hands that ever shouldered a big fat sack of cattle feed.

He had an easy way of talking through a constant grin, which made everything he said seem pleasant when you were looking at him. He put

With bridge words, phrases, sentences, and paragraphs

Anyone looking at Tim Peltier would have set him down as one of the most cheerful, generous hands that ever shouldered a big fat sack of cattle feed.

He had an easy way of talking through a constant grin, which made everything he said seem pleasant when you were looking at him. He put

405

his hand on your shoulder when he asked you to do something for him, and you found yourself complimented by the gesture.

He was the laziest, most malicious, and most calculating coyote it has ever been my misfortune to bunk with.

Tucker Langwood had a face always drawn into a scowl. His mouth seemed to remember dinner without relish. He had a beady pair of eyes, one of which swung well out to the left from time to time even when he was looking straight ahead.

Tucker Langwood was a fine man, the rare kind of hand that picks the worst bunk in the shack and acts as if he had the best.

"Peltier," said the boss, "Sherrod's through. He turned up drunk again this morning. That makes you foreman. I expect you to get more work out of the men than Sherrod did" [and so on].

his hand on your shoulder when he asked you to do something for him, and you found yourself complimented by the gesture.

That was Tim Peltier to look at. And Tim Peltier to live with—?

He was, *as a matter of fact,* the laziest, most malicious, and most calculating coyote it has ever been my misfortune to bunk with.

Tucker Langwood was in most respects Peltier's direct opposite. He had a face always drawn into a scowl. His mouth seemed to remember dinner without relish. He had a beady pair of eyes, one of which swung well out to the left from time to time even when he was looking straight ahead.

But Tucker Langwood was a fine man, the rare kind of hand that picks the worst bunk in the shack and acts as if he had the best.

Peltier and Langwood might never have tangled—for Langwood was not a tangler—if Peltier had not been made foreman just before the last spring roundup.

"Peltier," said the boss, "Sherrod's through. He turned up drunk again this morning. That makes you foreman. I expect you to get more work out of the men than Sherrod did" [and so on].

406

M26 Some common bridge words are *this, that; but, still, yet, however; then, next, first (second* or *secondly, third* or *thirdly,* and so on); *while, finally, meanwhile, afterward;* and *so, therefore, consequently.*

M27 *Meanwhile* and similar connectives are very helpful in holding the reader on the track when the writer is keeping two or more series of events going at once.

M28 Do not use *so* when a mere time connection or no connection at all exists between parts.

. . . told me to dress for dinner since she was having guests.

at
~~So at~~ eight o'clock the guests began to arrive [and so on].

. . . that finishes everything I have to say.

Well,
~~So~~ it has been fun chatting with you by mail [and so on].

M29 When using *this, that, he,* and other pronouns as bridge words, take care that it is always clear just what each one's antecedent is. When this is not clear, drop the pronoun in favor of some other word or phrase whose reference is not vague.

Preston took his place at my left, Henri at my right, and Piggot directly in front of me.

Piggot
~~He~~ snarled at me: "Dirty little sneak! What are you doing in a school with decent fellows?"

The boulder-strewn roads that wound over the ugly mountains were very hard on the jeeps, rattling them into junk heaps in two months or less. The altitude, also, seemed to affect the operation of the sturdy little cars. But perhaps the Greeks, with no touch at all for mechanical things and no skill in driving, caused more damage and breakdowns than the terrain and the altitude together.

These difficulties
~~This~~ finally made Major Shellabarger decide to call a conference of the American observers and General Karapopoloumenos's staff.

M30 Some common bridge phrases are *this* and *that* plus a noun, *on the other hand, on the contrary, after that, in* *the second place, in the last part, in the next part, in the meantime, as a consequence,* and *as a result.*

> Murca, we discovered, was fond of a noisome cheese that he had brought with him in considerable quantity.
> *This peculiarity* did not endear him to the others [and so on].

M31 Do not use bridge words, phrases, sentences, or paragraphs where they are not needed to make clear the connection and relationship between the parts of the theme. If you load your writing with unnecessary transitional expressions, you will slow its pace and make it sound windy.

Emphasis in the theme

M32 Emphasis means relative stress. In writing, emphasis is the principle that requires that more important thoughts be made to stand out from less important thoughts. Your writing is properly emphatic when your reader knows, without thinking the matter over, which thoughts you consider most important, which less, and which least important.

M33 Make clear the relative importance of thoughts in a theme.

M34 Give the most important thoughts the most space, the less important thoughts less space, and so on.

M35 It sometimes happens that an important idea is so persuasive and so easy to understand in itself that to give it fuller treatment than less important ideas would be to blow it up with empty verbiage. When this happens, ignore M34 and use some other emphasis device.

M36 The introduction and the conclusion should be short in comparison with the body of the theme. In general, make the introduction and conclusion together one third or less of the whole theme.

M37 Put important thoughts in emphatic positions.

M38 The most emphatic position in a theme is ordinarily near the end. The end of the theme is often, therefore, a good place (*a*) to restate the theme topic, (*b*) to summarize the main points of the theme, (*c*) to use your most telling argument or most striking presentation, (*d*) to introduce your most interesting incident, or (*e*) to release the reader from the suspense that has been building up by finally telling him what you want him to know.

M39 The second most emphatic position in a theme is ordinarily near the beginning. For this reason it is often good to use the opening paragraphs to state the theme topic and to say something about it that will make the reader want to see it developed.

M40 After the topic paragraph, if there is one, start with the least important or interesting thought and move by degrees to the most interesting or important.

As a matter of fact, it was rather a full day. I spent several hours getting the dummy for the *Colombière Clarion* ready for the printer and another forty minutes working out that silly exercise in emphasis for English class tomorrow.

I spent another three hours doing something rather interesting: watching the men at D'Astignac Studios painting a backdrop for the school's production of *Everyman*. I found it amazing that they could work so quickly. Watching them slap paint on—mostly with ten-inch brushes—you would imagine that the result was going to look like something my manic-depressive little sister thinks up out of her water-color kit. On the contrary, they achieved a perfect copy of Laury's design and got it on a canvas twenty by forty feet in less than three hours.

But the thing that will make it a day to remember was something that happened down at the printer's. I was helping Mr. Shelton lay out our copy according to the dummy, when a rather fat, bald, tired-looking man came out of the office and walked over to the shop table where we were working. When he picked up a sheaf of *Clarion* copy and started reading through it, I felt rather annoyed that he hadn't asked anybody's permission. But I didn't say anything. He took advantage of a pause in the discussion I was having with Shelton to ask very curtly, "Who wrote this thing on the prize debates at Colombière?"

"I did," I said without looking up.

"You, eh?"

"Uh-huh."

"Well, son, when you finish high school and college, if you're still fool enough to like newspaper work, come down and get a job from me."

"Yes?" I said; "and who are you, mister?"

"Priestly," he answered; "R. C. Priestly, city editor, Wichita *Herald*. Darned good paper, and an excellent city editor."

M41   Sometimes clarity or some other important consideration makes it inadvisable to follow M37-40. For example, there are circumstances in which it is good to have a very unemphatic, gentle opening that promises very little. In such cases, use some other emphatic device.

M42   Get emphasis for a thought by contrasting its treatment with the treatment of the other thoughts around it.

M43   Rarely, use visual devices like the setting off of a single brief statement in a paragraph by itself.

It was obvious that a single extra division would turn the tide for us. We were doing well. We were holding Klavic's army longer than anybody had thought we could.

A single extra division would have given our left flank the

The sentence *But Tarleton never came* receives some emphasis in the first version as the last sentence in its paragraph, but more in the second as a paragraph by itself.

strength it needed to advance. We all knew that that extra division, under Aubrey Tarleton, had been ordered up since the night before. We were all waiting tensely for it, hour after hour. But Tarleton never came.

It was Tarleton's unexplainable absence that finally broke [and so on].

It was obvious that a single extra division would turn the tide for us. We were doing well. We were holding Klavic's army longer than anybody had thought we could.

A single extra division would have given our left flank the strength it needed to advance. We all knew that that extra division, under Aubrey Tarleton, had been ordered up since the night before. We were all waiting tensely for it, hour after hour.

But Tarleton never came.

It was Tarleton's unexplainable absence that finally broke [and so on].

M44 Modern writers of the "popular" sort overwork the visual-contrast trick of M43. It is an obvious form of emphasis, and the reader does not like obvious tricks. So never use visual contrast to the point where the reader may come to notice what you are doing.

M45 Occasionally emphasize a thought by introducing it with an abrupt change of mood or atmosphere.

It was a mournful evening. Sheila sat in the window seat, staring out into the night. There was not enough light in the room behind her to make reflections on the panes, and so she could see out quite well; and what she saw was

The man and the boy are given importance and their entrance is pointed up sharply by the abrupt change of mood and atmosphere between the first and second paragraphs.

melancholy enough: a few giant cypresses starting up, stark and bare and grotesque, out of the black water of the swamp and gesticulating in silhouette against the faintly luminous sky. They shuddered a little when the wind came raging at them and howled on past the house and the window from which Sheila was looking out. Once she thought she saw something move in the dark water under the cypresses, but she could not be sure.

"Blow me for an empty bag," cried a voice behind her. "Here's a good room with a fine fire laid. Let's make port and drop anchor in here, Jackie—if, of course, the young lady over there in the window doesn't mind sharing this snuggery with us. The *pretty* young lady, I *should* say, Jackie; for the girl is pretty, though you're too young to notice—or are you, lad?" Sheila turned to find a great stout man and a boy in his teens standing in the doorway, both with their mouths open—the man's because he was talking and the boy's because he was gawking.

411

M46 Occasionally emphasize a thought by changes in rhythm, sound, sentence structure, and so on.

Laugh! Laugh loud! Be brittle and staccato. What you do, do quickly. Move along. Do, do, do. Never think. Achieve; win things; acquire things; fight for things; hold on to things. Never look at yourself. You won't like what you see. It will disturb you. Just get things for yourself. Pad yourself around with them. Insulate yourself against biting winds. And drink; above all, drink. Drink the sharp sting out of life. Soften the blinding light of life by looking at it through the bottom of a bottle.

Notice that in the first paragraph nearly all the sentences are brief and that the only two long sentences are loose sentences. Many of the words—for example, *brittle, do, think, fight*—have a sharp sound. The second paragraph is a long periodic sentence, containing a good many mouth-filling words of long, full, liquid, sonorous, or softened sound—for example, *overwhelm, drown, hush, rolls, flows, intones.*

But a quiet voice, a voice welling up in serenity to engulf the world's madness, to overwhelm it and drown it and hush it forever, a voice whose tide rolls out and laps the shores of eternity, a voice that flows some day into every heart, a voice raised in Galilee intones: "Thou fool, this night do they require thy soul of thee."

M47 Occasionally emphasize a thought by repeating it in the course of a theme. Sometimes, in very oratorical and emphatic themes, the thought may be repeated several times in exactly the same words. But usually the repetition must be dressed up a bit if it is to please and not seem too naked a device.

Drivers of automobiles do not think enough.

At a time when safety councils, police, and automobile clubs use all kinds of publicity—posters, advertisements, markers—to make streets and highways safe, drivers of automobiles never seem to realize that they are being alerted, never seem to question what they do behind the wheel of a car.

Recently a national magazine published photographs of automobile accidents, cars smashed and wrenched into junk, bloody and battered bodies lying on the highway. All of the accidents were due to some foolishness on the part of the drivers, who were going too fast or neglected warning signs or passed other cars when they should not have.

Readers of the magazine were appalled—and rightly—at what they saw, but how many of them asked whether they did not themselves often drive just as foolishly? They did not stop to think.

Before every major holiday the newspapers, with frightening accuracy, will foretell the number of automobile accidents that will occur on that holiday. Readers are shocked, deplore all this carelessness (which other people, of course, are guilty of), and no doubt murmur, "Something ought to be done." But they are never led to examine what they do as drivers themselves, whether they drive too fast, ignore traffic regulations, or take needless chances.

Drivers of automobiles do not think enough.

M48 Occasionally get emphasis by stating that a thought is important, interesting, or something of the kind.

> And now we come to the most practical solution that I have to offer, an idea that I am sure is worth all my other suggestions put together . . .

M49 Of all the ways of getting emphasis, this by express statement (M48) is the most annoying when it is abused. The writer who abuses it is somewhat like the wit who ruins jokes by always saying, "I want to tell you a story that will simply slay you. You'll die laughing." Keep in mind the principles in M50-51.

M50 Do not say that a thought is important, interesting, or anything of the kind unless you are sure that it is; and do not say that a thought is more important, interesting, and so on, than it actually is.

> [An insult to the intelligence of reader or listener:] And now to the question that all America is asking: What cigarette guarantees the safest smoking enjoyment?

M51 Even if you have several very important or interesting points, do not *state* that more than one or two of them are important or interesting. Use other emphasis devices for the rest.

Variety of development

M52 Some of the more serviceable ways of developing the main ideas of themes are enumeration, giving circumstances, comparison and contrast, giving causes and effects, giving examples, and repetition.

ENUMERATION IN THE THEME

M53 Develop a theme topic by dividing an idea in the subject or predicate into its parts.

[Theme topic:] Jerome Kern wrote some masterpieces of modern popular music.

When Jerome Kern died not so long ago, the news of his death was news of a loss to	Topic paragraph.[9]

America. Kern had not won a war, and he had not established peace; but he had paid rent for the time he had lodged on earth by making a rather substantial contribution to the fund of things that can pleasure a man's heart without poisoning it. For Jerome Kern wrote some masterpieces of modern popular music.

Take his "Ol' Man River." Compare it with the flood of noise about the Mississippi that has welled up in tin-pan alley in the last thirty years or so, rolled over America for a while, and then subsided, to the relief of everyone but the composers. Kern, of course, is no Schubert; and the score of "Ol' Man River" would scarcely sweep Toscanini into	The first paragraph of the development takes up the first division of masterpieces of modern popular music. This first division is "Ol' Man River." The topic thought of this paragraph is *In comparison with many other popular songs, "Ol' Man River" is a masterpiece.*

ecstasy. But as a certain kind of song it is a masterpiece, ranking

---

[9] The theme topic is the subject matter of the theme, the one clear, rather brief thought that answers the question *What is the theme about?* A topic paragraph is a paragraph that contains an explicit statement of the theme topic.

414

with the rare best of its sort and rolling on to fuller and fuller popularity long after its rivals have quite trickled out.

Again, "Smoke Gets in Your Eyes" shows what Kern could do with the romantic sort of thing that others botch so badly. Here is swirling melody that triumphs over the lamentable pattern that many modern songs have fallen into—

The second paragraph takes up a second division. The topic thought: *In comparison with many other popular songs, "Smoke Gets in Your Eyes". is a masterpiece.*

strain, strain-repeat, break-strain, repeat. Its excellence is clearly proved by the fact that it can be sung by really good singers without reducing them to musical slummers and without itself sounding shoddy—something that cannot be said for the majority of pieces that make the *Hit Parade.*

As with these two songs, so it is with almost everything that Kern wrote. It is a pity

Conclusion.

that his work is not to be carried forward by anyone. With Berlin and Cole Porter aging, the great Gershwin gone, and the masters of jazz and Dixieland now just names in the history of music, the prospects of modern popular song are not so bright as they might be. There is no doubt about it, America will miss Kern.

CIRCUMSTANCES IN THE THEME

M54 Develop a theme topic by giving the circumstances related to it.

[Theme topic:] Rear Admiral Jesse B. Oldendorf annihilated Nishimura's fleet.

Though it is not often that a classic textbook problem in naval warfare comes to life in actual battle, it certainly did happen once in recent times, when Rear Admiral Jesse B. Oldendorf annihilated Nishimura's fleet.

Topic paragraph.

415

The action took place on
October 25-26, 1944, soon
after MacArthur's return to the
Philippines, at a time when a
breakthrough by Nishimura
would have jeopardized our
chances of winning the war in
the Pacific.

Oldendorf's fleet was plug-
ging the gap between Surigao
Strait and the part of Leyte
Gulf where American landing
operations were proceeding under the protection of a number
of inadequate old warships.

Nishimura, who might have
skirted Surigao Strait and,
going around on the outside
of the islands, bottled up the
whole American operation in
Leyte Gulf and blasted it at
will, chose rather to string out
his fleet single file in the long
narrow alley of Surigao. He
lacked anything worthy the
name of reconnaissance and
did not suspect that the Americans lay athwart the end of
the strait. Thus it happened
that he steamed straight up
to the center of Oldendorf's
battle line and created the
T-formation in which the perpendicular is subject to mur-
derous cross fire.

Because of the annihilation
that followed, the Pacific war
went to the Americans; and
the tacticians will have something to talk about for years
to come.

COMPARISON AND CONTRAST IN THE THEME

M55 Develop a theme topic by using comparison, contrast, or both.

[Introduction:][10] It is said that there are only three cities in the United States that have an atmosphere and character all their own. They are New York, San Francisco, and New Orleans.

[Topic paragraph:] For many people, New Orleans, the smallest of these three cities, is the most attractive.

[Paragraph of comparison:] New Orleans, like New York and San Francisco, has excellent hotels and restaurants, a great variety of places to visit and things to see.

[Paragraph of contrast:] New Orleans has a unique attraction, the French Quarter, which has remained intact from the early days and is like a European city. New York and San Francisco have nothing of the kind to show.

[Paragraph of comparison:] New Orleans has a cosmopolitan population, as have New York and San Francisco, residents and visitors that represent almost every nation on the globe.

[Paragraph of contrast:] New Orleans has a unique cultural atmosphere, which derives from its Spanish-French beginnings, a Latin atmosphere more French, however, than Spanish. New York, on the other hand, has a cultural atmosphere less clearly noticeable, since the city has retained little that was characteristic of its Dutch and English beginnings; and San Francisco is not markedly Spanish.

[Conclusion:] New Orleans attracts people who like to take life in a leisurely, easygoing way that has much of the Continental in it.

M56 In the example in M55 a theme topic is developed by a series of comparisons and contrasts. Another form of development is one long comparison or contrast running through a number or all of the paragraphs of a theme.

CAUSE AND EFFECT IN THE THEME

M57 Develop a theme topic by stating some of the effects or consequences of the truth or event it relates.

---

[10] Only skeletal development of this theme is given here.

[Introduction:]¹¹ In its relatively brief history, the United States Weather Bureau has recorded some sensational items.

[Topic paragraph:] In December, 1947, New York City was smothered under more than twenty-five inches of snow.

[Paragraph:] Traffic was strangled.

[Paragraph:] A fearful fire hazard was created (fire engines were snowed up in their garages).

[Paragraph:] Normal city life was in great part paralyzed.

[Paragraph:] The removal of the snow cost the city $232,170 for each inch of snow, or about $6,000,000 altogether.

[Paragraph:] But of course there were many who squeezed some fun out of the queer state of affairs.

M58 Develop a theme topic by stating some of the causes of, or reasons for, the truth or event it relates.

[Topic paragraph:]¹¹ Brown, Lovett, and Driscoll do look a little weary this morning.

[Paragraph:] It seems that they attended the game last night in Driscoll's Model-A Ford—not a restful equipage.

[Paragraph:] Moreover, on the way home, the Ford began to disintegrate.

[Paragraph:] The boys left it and walked seven stumbling dark miles to a farm, where they rented a horse.

[Paragraph:] The horse, a spavined hack not up to pulling automobiles, soon collapsed and had to be put on top of the car to rest.

[Paragraph:] The boys pushed the car and the horse the remaining five miles to Houston.

[Paragraph:] In Houston they were arrested for trucking livestock without a license.

[Paragraph:] At 6:00 A.M. Driscoll's father bailed them out—just in time to get ready for school.

[Conclusion:] What wonderful times we have when we are young—and how tired we get having them.

EXAMPLES IN THE THEME

M59 Develop a theme topic by giving concrete examples of the general or abstract truth that it relates.

---

¹¹ Only skeletal development of this theme is given here.

[Introduction:][12] Those who say (with foolish pride) that they never take anything "on faith" should notice what they are doing daily.

[Topic paragraph:] A man cannot prove everything; he must live by faith.

[Paragraph:] It is only by faith in the testimony of witnesses that many of us know that there actually was a George Washington, president of the United States.

[Paragraph:] We should all starve to death or go slowly mad if we did not believe that our restaurants and cooks use salt for seasoning, and not arsenic, when they say they use salt.

[Paragraph:] One who buys or sells stocks would be reduced to gibbering paralysis if he did not believe the quotations that come to him over the wires or in the newspapers.

[Paragraph:] Even the ordinary affairs of everyday life would become a nightmare if one did not accept on faith much of what others tell him.

[Conclusion:] If we believe so much and act—rationally indeed—upon that belief, then let us not preen ourselves on having a "scientific" mind that must have a demonstration of everything.

REPETITION IN THE THEME

M60 Develop a theme topic by repeating it with greater clarity or from a more interesting angle as the topic thought of subsequent paragraphs.

[Introduction:][12] Too many people spend almost the whole of their brief lives before they discover a basic fact about human happiness.

[Topic paragraph:] We must love what is good or else we will be unhappy.

[Paragraph:] To love evil is to be unhappy.

[Paragraph:] All human joy worthy of the name is founded in loving what is good.

[Paragraph:] If we do not love what is good, we really do not love anything, including ourselves.

[Paragraph:] If we do not love what is good, the universe is a shrieking nightmare or a cold waste.

---

[12] Only skeletal development of this theme is given here.

[Conclusion:] Do not be dismayed; for to love what is good is to love and to get—now or later—everything that can satisfy and thrill the human heart.

M61 Greater care must be used with repetition than with the other methods of developing sentences, paragraphs, and themes; for cold, bald, useless repetition will bore a reader to death.

COMBINATION OF METHODS

M62 A combination of two or more of the methods explained in M53-61 can often be used effectively in developing a sentence, a paragraph, or a theme. Indeed, a combination of methods is more common than a single method in the development of themes, since continued use of one method would ordinarily produce monotony.

Introduction:[13] I was a witness to what happened at Tecky Mills last month.

Theme topic: One day "Mr. Smoothy" drifted into the plant.

Development by giving circumstances
[Paragraph (when?):] He turned up right after the union at Tecky Mills had negotiated a fair contract with the management.

[Paragraph (how?):] He slipped right in without a stir at the router that old Jim Cabo had vacated when he was pensioned and retired.

Development by enumeration
[Paragraph:] "Mr. Smoothy" was a quiet fellow, rather well-mannered, whose real name was Joel Tollern.

[Paragraph:] He made friends easily.

Development by repetition
[Paragraph:] Yes; one day "Mr. Smoothy" drifted into Tecky Mills. [This is an effect paragraph, used to produce an atmosphere of suspense and slight foreboding, as well as to refocus the reader's attention.]

Development by giving effects
[Paragraph:] The atmosphere of the Mills began to change.

---

[13] Only skeletal development of this theme is given here.

[Paragraph:] The men began to change.

[Paragraph:] Things began to happen to the work—annoying things, dangerous things.

Development by comparison

[Paragraph:] It was as though a kind of corruption had begun to stir and bubble in the Mills.

Development by giving causes

[Paragraph:] Why had "Mr. Smoothy" come?

Conclusion: What has "Mr. Smoothy" taught me?

N Exposition

In general

N1 Exposition is that form of writing or talking whose purpose is to explain or inform.[1]

Common examples of exposition are most textbooks, histories, college themes, term papers, and research papers.

N2 A good exposition must have clarity, economy, accuracy.

    A Clarity—because the purpose of an exposition is to give light, explanation, information.

    B Economy—because the reader's mind easily becomes clogged with too many details, and thus he misses what the writer is trying to explain.

    c Accuracy—because misinformation or inexact information will either mislead your reader or cost you his respect.

N

---

[1] Almost always, the four forms of discourse (exposition, narration, description, and argument) are mingled in a composition of any length at all. Thus it happens that an exposition may contain narration, and so on.

If you wish to classify a whole theme, look at its main purpose. If its purpose is to relate a series of events, it is not exposition; if its purpose is to make a reader see, feel, or hear something just in order to entertain him, the piece is not exposition; if to convince or persuade him, not exposition. But if the main purpose is to explain something to him or to give him information, then the theme is exposition. The same thing holds true for portions of themes.

The expository theme (term paper, research paper)

N3   An expository theme is a theme whose purpose is to explain or inform.[2]

CHOOSING THE GENERAL SUBJECT

N4   The subject need not, and ordinarily will not, be new. The treatment may well be. There are very few new subjects under the sun; but the approaches to any given subject are practically limitless.

N5   When you have little time for study,[3] write about what you know.

N6   When you have sufficient time for study, you may choose some subject that you would enjoy learning something more about.

N7   Keep your readers in mind when you choose your subject. Will they be interested? Interested or not, will they benefit from being told something about this subject?

N8   Keep yourself in mind when you choose your subject. Will you be interested? Interested or not, will you benefit by writing about it? Will your teachers accept a treatment of this subject coming from you?

For example, it might not be acceptable for a sophomore to choose "The Seniors Are Morons" as the subject of an editorial.

N9   Keep the occasion in mind when you choose your subject. Is it tactful or beneficial to bring up this subject at this time, under these circumstances, for these readers? (Benefit outweighs tact.)

---

[2] Two very useful books on this topic are these: Meta Riley Emberger and Marian Ross Hall, *Scientific Writing* (New York: Harcourt, Brace & Co., 1955) and Jacques Barzun and Henry F. Graff, *The Modern Researcher* (New York: Harcourt, Brace & Co., 1957).

[3] The word *study* is here taken to include reading, interviews, experiments, experiences, and so on—research.

N10 Once you have chosen the general subject of an expository theme, this is ordinarily the best order to follow:

Step 1. Jot down what you yourself know about the general subject (N11-12).

Step 2. When you have finished jotting, put your notes in order, grouping them under appropriate headings (N13).

Step 3. Whenever necessary, fill out your knowledge of a general subject by means of interviews and reading (N14-21).

Step 4. Select a theme topic (N26-31).

Step 5. Outline the theme (N32-56).

Step 6. Write the rough draft of the theme (N57-86).

Step 7. Write the final copy of the theme (N87-99).

STEP 1. JOTTING

N11 Before you do any research, outlining, or composing, jot down what you yourself know about the theme topic.

N12 Write these preliminary notes just as they occur to you, so that nothing may obstruct the free flow of your thought and nothing may distract your memory from the associations it is making.

STEP 2. PUTTING NOTES IN ORDER

N13 Put the notes of N12 in order, grouping related ideas under appropriate headings.

STEP 3. READING

N14 The notes of N11-13 will ordinarily bring to light weaknesses and shortcomings in your knowledge, proof, or authorities. Whenever necessary, fill out your knowledge of a general subject by means of interviews or reading.

N15   Learn how to use the library intelligently. The librarian will help you find your way to using the three important tools in the library: (*a*) reference books, (*b*) guides to books and periodicals, and (*c*) card catalogues. Rely on the librarian to acquaint you with the full resources of the library.

N16   Here are some standard reference works. Find out where these books are kept (they may not all be in the same place). Find out what reference books the library has. Become familiar with the contents and arrangement of the books; look through them and find out for yourself what they contain.

Encyclopedias

AMERICAN PEOPLES ENCYCLOPEDIA, Sears, Roebuck and Company

BRITANNICA JUNIOR, Encyclopaedia Britannica Company

CATHOLIC ENCYCLOPEDIA, Robert Appleton

COLUMBIA ENCYCLOPEDIA, Columbia University Press

COMPTON'S PICTURED ENCYCLOPEDIA AND FACT INDEX, F. E. Compton and Company

ENCYCLOPAEDIA BRITANNICA, Encyclopaedia Britannica Company

ENCYCLOPEDIA AMERICANA, Americana Corporation

LINCOLN LIBRARY OF ESSENTIAL INFORMATION, Frontier Press

NEW INTERNATIONAL ENCYCLOPEDIA, Funk and Wagnalls Company

WORLD BOOK ENCYCLOPEDIA, Field Enterprises, Inc.

Yearbooks and almanacs

AMERICANA ANNUAL, Americana Corporation

BRITANNICA BOOK OF THE YEAR, Encyclopaedia Britannica Company

FUNK AND WAGNALLS NEW STANDARD ENCYCLOPEDIA YEARBOOK, Funk and Wagnalls Company

NEW INTERNATIONAL YEAR BOOK, Funk and Wagnalls Company

WORLD BOOK ENCYCLOPEDIA ANNUAL SUPPLEMENT, Field Enterprises, Inc.

THE AMERICAN YEAR-BOOK, Thomas Nelson and Sons

ECONOMIC ALMANAC, National Industrial Conference Board

INFORMATION PLEASE ALMANAC, The Macmillan Company

NATIONAL CATHOLIC ALMANAC, Saint Anthony Guild

Biographical dictionaries

AMERICAN CATHOLIC WHO'S WHO, Walter Romig

BOOK OF CATHOLIC AUTHORS, Walter Romig

CURRENT BIOGRAPHY: WHO'S NEWS AND WHY, H. W. Wilson Company

DICTIONARY OF AMERICAN BIOGRAPHY, Charles Scribner's Sons

DICTIONARY OF NATIONAL BIOGRAPHY, Oxford University Press

Thomas, Joseph, UNIVERSAL PRONOUNCING DICTIONARY OF BIOGRAPHY AND MYTHOLOGY, J. B. Lippincott Company

WEBSTER'S BIOGRAPHICAL DICTIONARY, G. and C. Merriam Company

WHO WAS WHO IN AMERICA, Vol. 1, 1897-1942; Vol. 2, 1943-1950; A. N. Marquis Company

WHO'S WHO (1848 to date), A. and C. Black, Ltd., London

WHO'S WHO IN AMERICA (1899 to date), A. N. Marquis Company

Dictionaries and books of synonyms

AMERICAN COLLEGE DICTIONARY, Harper and Brothers

CATHOLIC DICTIONARY, The Macmillan Company

CONCISE CATHOLIC DICTIONARY, The Bruce Publishing Company

CONCISE OXFORD DICTIONARY OF CURRENT ENGLISH, Oxford University Press

Evans, Bergen and Cornelia, A DICTIONARY OF CONTEMPORARY AMERICAN USAGE, Random House

Fowler, H. W., A DICTIONARY OF MODERN ENGLISH USAGE, Oxford University Press

NEW CENTURY DICTIONARY OF THE ENGLISH LANGUAGE, Appleton-Century-Crofts Company, Inc.

NEW OXFORD DICTIONARY (Murray's, N.E.D., New English Dictionary), Oxford University Press

NEW PRACTICAL STANDARD DICTIONARY OF THE ENGLISH LANGUAGE, Funk and Wagnalls Company

ROGET'S INTERNATIONAL THESAURUS, Thomas Y. Crowell Company

THORNDIKE-BARNHART COMPREHENSIVE DESK DICTIONARY, Doubleday and Company

WEBSTER'S DICTIONARY OF SYNONYMS, G. and C. Merriam Company

WEBSTER'S NEW INTERNATIONAL DICTIONARY OF THE ENGLISH LANGUAGE, G. and C. Merriam Company

Gazetteers and atlases

LIPPINCOTT'S COMPLETE PRONOUNCING GAZETTEER OR GEOGRAPHICAL DICTIONARY OF THE WORLD, J. B. Lippincott Company

WEBSTER'S GEOGRAPHICAL DICTIONARY, G. and C. Merriam Company

WORLD ATLAS, Encyclopaedia Britannica Press
WORLD ATLAS, Rand McNally Company

Histories of literature and similar books
CAMBRIDGE HISTORY OF AMERICAN LITERATURE, The Macmillan Company
CONCISE CAMBRIDGE HISTORY OF ENGLISH LITERATURE, The Macmillan Company
OUTLINE HISTORY OF AMERICAN LITERATURE, Barnes and Noble, Inc.
OUTLINE HISTORY OF ENGLISH LITERATURE, Barnes and Noble, Inc.
OXFORD COMPANION TO AMERICAN LITERATURE, Oxford University Press
OXFORD COMPANION TO CLASSICAL LITERATURE, Oxford University Press
OXFORD COMPANION TO ENGLISH LITERATURE, Oxford University Press
READER'S ENCYCLOPEDIA OF WORLD LITERATURE AND THE ARTS, Thomas Y. Crowell Company

Mythology and antiquities
Gayley, Charles M., CLASSIC MYTHS IN ENGLISH LITERATURE AND IN ART, Ginn and Company
Hamilton, Edith, MYTHOLOGY, Little, Brown and Company
Peck, Harry T., HARPER'S DICTIONARY OF CLASSICAL ANTIQUITIES, American Book Company

Books of quotations
Everett, Christopher and Louella, BARTLETT'S FAMILIAR QUOTATIONS, Little, Brown and Company
Mencken, H. L., A NEW DICTIONARY OF QUOTATIONS ON HISTORICAL PRINCIPLES FROM ANCIENT AND MODERN SOURCES, Alfred A. Knopf, Inc.

Indexes to books and periodicals
CUMULATIVE BOOK INDEX (1928 to date), H. W. Wilson Company
GUIDE TO CATHOLIC LITERATURE, Walter Romig
THE UNITED STATES CATALOG (books in print January 1, 1928), H. W. Wilson Company
ANNUAL MAGAZINE SUBJECT INDEX, F. W. Faxon Company
CATHOLIC PERIODICAL INDEX, H. W. Wilson Company
INTERNATIONAL INDEX TO PERIODICALS (1907 to date), H. W. Wilson Company

Reader's Guide to Periodical Literature (1900 to date), H. W. Wilson Company

N17 Familiarize yourself with the card catalogue in the library. Find out whether or not the catalogue is complete, with three sets of index cards—author cards, title cards, and subject cards. Study them, for they can give you a lot of information, sometimes enough for you to tell definitely whether you want to call for the book or not.

Shown below are three typical index cards, printed and sold by the Library of Congress.

813
P834f
       Porter, Katherine Anne, 1894–   2, 3

        Flowering Judas and other stories, by Katherine Anne Porter. New York, Harcourt, Brace and   4 company [c1935]

          4 p. l., 3-285 p. 21 cm.   5

          Contents.—María Concepción.—Magic.—Rope.—He.—Theft.—That tree.—The jilting of Granny Weatherall.— 6 Flowering Judas.—The cracked looking-glass.—Hacienda.

         I. Title.   7

        PZ3.P8315Fn   35–19672 8, 9

        Library of Congress   [56p½]   10

1 (top right corner)

---

1 This is the call number, the Dewey classification number above (813, American fiction) and the Cutter author number below. Together they tell what section of the library the book is in and where the book can be found in that section.

2 This is the full name of the author.

3 This is the year of the author's birth. If an author is deceased, the year of his death will be noted.

4 This is bibliographical information—the place of publication, the name of the publisher, and the year the book was copyrighted.

The year of copyright is found on the reverse of the title page
of a book. The catalogue card always prints the copyright date
as it is given here.

When the year of publication is printed on the title page, that
date is shown on the catalogue card without *c* and brackets.

When no date is given or is uncertain—either the date of publication or the copyright date—*n.d.* ("no date") is printed on
the catalogue card.

5 This tells you that the book contains four preliminary leaves,
that the contents run from page 3 to page 285, and that the
book is 21 centimeters high. (A leaf is printed on only one
side; a page is printed on both sides.)

6 This is a complete list of the contents of the book, the titles of
all the stories it contains.

7 This indicates that the library catalogue has a card for the book
under its title. (Notice that the numeral is a roman numeral.
See No. 12 below.)

8 This is the Library of Congress's own classification number for
the book. (This classification system is different from the
Dewey system.)

9 This shows the date when the card was printed by the Library
of Congress (1935) and the number of the card (No. 19672).
Sometimes this number is followed by a double dagger, as on
the card just below, or some other symbol.

10 This is a Library of Congress code number referring to the
number of cards printed.

539.7
T238o

    Teller, Edward, 1908–

        Our nuclear future; facts, dangers, and oppor-
tunities, by Edward Teller and Albert L. Latter.
New York, Criterion Books [c1958]

        184 p. illus. 22 cm.   11

        1. Atomic energy—Popular works. 2. Radioactivity—
Physiological effects. 3. Atomic weapons.   ɪ. Latter, 12
Albert L., joint author. ɪɪ. Title.

        QC778.T4   *539.76   58–8783 ⸸ 13
        Library of Congress   [58r58c⁴30]

---

11 Besides giving you the number of pages and the height of the book, this tells you that the book is illustrated.

12 This gives you the other headings under which cards will be found in the catalogue for the book: the topics treated (1, 2, and 3); and the name of the joint author and the title of the book (I and II).

13 This is the classification number for the book according to the Dewey system. (Library of Congress cards do not all carry the Dewey number.)

933
P249s

Parrot, André, 1901—

Samaria, the capital of the kingdom of Israel. [Translated by S. H. Hooke from the French] New York, Philosophical Library [1958]

143 p.   illus., maps, plans.   19 cm.   (Studies in Biblical archaeology, no. 7)

Bibliography: p. 138-143.

Translation of *his* Samarie capitale du royaume d'Israël.

1. Samaria—Hist.   i. Title.   ii. Title: Samarie capitale du royaume d'Israël.   iii. Series.

DS110.S3P313   933   58—14899

Library of Congress   [5]

This card gives you, besides the kind of information found on the cards above, the French title of the original work. It tells you that the book contains a bibliography and that cards can be found under the subject, the English and French titles, and the name of the series.

N18   The three cards shown in N17 are author cards (in library circles they are referred to as "unit cards"). The same kind of card is used for the title index and the subject index.

N19   Title cards will have the title of the book typed across the top of the card, and the title index will lead you to a book when you know its name but not the author's name.

429

N20 Subject cards will have the subject typed across the top of the card, and the subject index will tell you in a short time what books the library has on the subject you are interested in.

Do not be satisfied with looking under only one subject. You might want a book on nineteenth-century American poetry, for instance. You will probably find cards under "Poetry," "Poetry—American," "American Poetry—Nineteenth Century," and "Nineteenth Century."

N21 If there is a great deal of material available on your general subject, choose one aspect of the subject and read with that as a guide. Select articles that seem likely, from their listing in the index and from other indications, to treat your angle of the subject. Omit or read quickly portions of books that do not treat your angle.

N22 When making notes—either of what you know about a subject or of what you read—make them all in a uniform way. This makes for easy reference and easy final arranging. Use index cards of one size—either 3 x 5 inches or 4 x 6 or 5 x 8.

N23 Ideally, make only one note on any one card. Always write on only one side of a card. If your note is long, use more than one card and number them 1, 2, 3, and so on. In one of the upper corners of the card put a key word—or index word—so that you can readily assemble related cards in making the outline of the paper.

N24 When you note a fact or make a quotation from a printed source, at the same time always copy out full bibliographical information. These are the various forms:

For reference to books
Name of author
Title of the book, underlined
Place of publication, publisher, and date of publication (or—if that is missing—the date of copyright may be given). Enclose all these in one set of parentheses followed by a period.

Page number where the fact or quotation can be found
Library call number

---

childhood

Hilaire Belloc, <u>Joan of Arc</u> (London:
Cassell & Co., 1929).

Pp. 7-10.

BJ 572 Be

For reference to magazine articles
Author of the article (if the name is given)
Title of the article, in quotation marks
Name of the magazine, underlined; the volume; the date between
parentheses; the pages; a period following the last item
Page number where the fact or quotation can be found

---

illness

Herbert Elliston, "Jim Forrestal, a
Portrait in Politics," <u>Atlantic Monthly</u>,
CLXXXVIII (Nov., 1951), 73-80.

P. 78.

For reference to newspaper articles
Headline or title of the article, in quotation marks
Name of the city (and state, if necessary) in which paper is published; name of paper, underlined; date; page; column; a period following the last item

subsidies

"Educational TV? 20-Odd Colleges Plan Own Stations," New York, <u>Wall Street Journal</u>, June 5, 1952, p. 1, col. 1.

For reference to articles in encyclopedias
Author of the article (if you can find his name)
Title of the article, in quotation marks
Title of the encyclopedia, without underlining or quotation marks; the year or edition between parentheses if either is important; the volume; the pages; a period following the last item
Page number where the fact or quotation can be found

climate

Frederick Barton Maurice, "Lee, Robert Edward," Encyclopaedia Britannica (1950), XIII, 862-64.

P. 862.

N25 It is best to make out the cards in N22-24 immediately, while you are working through indexes, guides, and bibliographies, whenever you find a likely looking article or book. It is well to put references to printed material in proper footnote or bibliography form. (See N69-84.) Even if you do not use the cards directly in your theme, they will furnish you with a bibliography.

STEP 4. SELECTING A THEME TOPIC

N26 Select a theme topic and write it out.

N27 Writing out the theme topic often exposes weaknesses in it. A written theme topic, moreover, lying on your desk before your eyes, is a constant reminder of what the theme is supposed to be about and keeps you from straying off into useless digressions.

N28 If it is at all possible to do so—and it almost always is—state your theme topic in a single, uncomplicated, declarative sentence:

A A single, uncomplicated sentence, because the briefer and less complicated the theme topic, the easier it is to develop it coherently.

B A declarative sentence, because questions do not indicate and limit development. There are innumerable developments possible if the theme topic is "How did Denton beat Plainville?" But the two chief parts of the theme are already plain if the theme topic is "Denton beat Plainville by using a modified T and concentrating on Joe Jacoby."

C A complete sentence, because half-sentences and very elliptical sentences cause the same trouble that questions do.

N29 Limit the general subject sharply when stating the theme topic.

For example, if a student has Russia as his general subject, he will get into difficulties if he makes his theme topic "The history of Soviet Russia is interesting." The development could easily run to many volumes. The student will probably write a hop-skip-and-jump theme in which he touches many topics and handles none of them well or an unfinished theme with only "The End" to show that he meant to conclude it. He would do much better to use a topic like this, "At the United Nations during 1950, Russia acted on the principle that truth means whatever may help the Communist party."

N30 Avoid extravagant and superlative terms when stating the theme topic.

For example, it is easy to show that Da Vinci's *Last Supper* is a well-beloved masterpiece. It would be very difficult indeed to show that it is the greatest painting in the world.

N31 Make the theme topic as definite as you reasonably can.

[Vague, leading to uncertain planning and development:] There are several steps in cracking petroleum.

[Definite, leading to clear-cut planning and development:] There are five steps in cracking petroleum.

STEP 5. OUTLINING

N32 An outline is a sketch showing the theme topic and the main points of its development.[4]

N33 The outline is not merely a helpful adjunct to the writing of expository themes; it is also a useful form of exposition in its own right. It is sometimes the clearest way in which first to present a difficult subject to a reader, since it gives him an uncomplicated, over-all view. It offers a convenient set of hooks on which to hang an extempore talk. Lastly, an outline can be a help to study. When, for example, you have to put great masses of matter into your head to pass an examination, you would do well to outline the material, to organize it into a unified whole, and then study the outline.

---

[4] In this book *outline* is a technical term reserved for exposition. The outline sketch of a narrative from which the final form is written is called a plan or plot, and the sketch of an argument or persuasive speech is called a brief. (In popular speech *outline* is often used for all three of these forms and even for summaries and condensations.)

N34 Two kinds of outline are particularly useful in planning an expository theme: the topic outline (N35-52) and the sentence outline (N53-54).

N35 A topic outline is a list of the points a theme will discuss, arranged to show their equal or unequal importance and expressed (with the exception of the theme topic) in incomplete sentences.

Theme topic.—Interscholastic football is not the sport for four classes of boys.
    I. Some boys occupied with more important things
   II. Some boys unfit physically
  III. Some boys unfit intellectually
  IV. Some boys unfit emotionally

Except in the case of very short themes without much development, an outline such as the one just above, which gives only the main heads, does not serve very well. Usually subheads are needed, as shown below.

Theme topic.—Interscholastic football is not the sport for four classes of boys.
    I. Some boys occupied with more important things
      A. Earning their education
      B. Developing intellectual abilities
   II. Some boys unfit physically
      A. Injuries and diseases
      B. Slow co-ordination
  III. Some boys unfit intellectually
      A. From viewpoint of the team
      B. From viewpoint of the boy
         1. Cannot spare time from studies
           a) Long practice
           b) Utter weariness
           c) Constant distraction
         2. Cannot keep football in its proper place
         3. Cannot get benefits of training
  IV. Some boys unfit emotionally
      A. From viewpoint of the team
         1. Irresponsible
         2. Indecisive

B. From viewpoint of the boy
  1. Strain
  2. Abnormal reactions
    a) Depression
    b) Elation
    c) Fear
      (1) However, football sometimes a diagnosis
      (2) However, football sometimes a cure
        (a) Much depends on coach
        (b) Much depends on other boys
        (c) Much depends on boy himself

Note that by no means must all heads have subheads or sub-subheads. Only so many should be used as the author wishes or the matter requires.

N36 If you wish, you may indicate the introduction or the conclusion or both in the outline.

Theme topic.—Interscholastic football is not the sport for four classes of boys.
Introduction.—This article necessary though unpopular
  I. Some boys occupied with more important things
  II. Some boys unfit physically
    A. Injuries and diseases
    B. Slow co-ordination
  III. Some boys unfit intellectually
  IV. Some boys unfit emotionally
Conclusion.—This article is intended to be a help, not to stir up controversy.

N37 Do not use any letters or figures with the headings "theme topic," "introduction," and "conclusion." But you must italicize them and follow them with a period and a dash.

N38 Do not bother to use the heading "body." The roman numerals are sufficient indication of the body of the theme, and "body" would only clutter the outline.

N39 Ordinarily the headings "introduction" and "conclusion" should be written in last; otherwise you may give in to the inclination to conceive a brilliant introduction and make the rest of the theme fit it, instead of the other way round as good sense requires.

N40   Begin each heading of an outline with a capital.

N41   Do not use a period after the headings of a topic outline unless they make complete sentences.[5] You may use a question mark or an exclamation point if either is needed for clarity.

N42   Label the heads and subheads of an outline with these alternating figures and letters in the following order: I. II. III.; A. B. C.; 1. 2. 3.; a) b) c); (1) (2) (3); (a) (b) (c); i. ii. iii.

N43   Put a period after all the letters and figures in N42 that are not followed by a mark of parenthesis.

N44   Do not put a period after the letters and figures in N42 that are followed by a mark of parenthesis.

N45   The heads in each series marked with the same kind of letter or figure should be of equal or nearly equal importance. For example, Head II should be equal or nearly equal to Head I; Head B under Head I should be equal or nearly equal to Head A, but not equal to Head I; and so on.

N46   Whenever it can reasonably be done, begin each head in the same series with the same or an equivalent part of speech.[6] This verbal parallelism aids the mind in remembering the headings and in perceiving immediately which are of parallel importance.

   I. Noun . . . .
      A. Verb . . . .
         1. Preposition . . . .
         2. Preposition . . . .
      B. Verb . . . .

---

[5] See the second example under N35.

[6] Gerunds and pronouns may be considered parallel with nouns, adjectival participles with adjectives, and so on.

```
II. Noun . . . . . . . . . . . . . . . . . . . . . .
    A. Adverb . . . . . . . . . . . . . . . . . . .
    B. Adverb . . . . . . . . . . . . . . . . . . .
       1. Verb . . . . . . . . . . • . . . . . . . .
       2. Verb . . . . . . . . . . . . . . . . . . .
```

Note that all roman-numeral heads are in the same series. A and B under Head I are in one series; A and B under Head II are in another; and so on.

N47 Whenever you can easily carry parallelism beyond the first word of a heading, do so.

N48 Do not cling to parallel form at the expense of clarity or efficiency.

N49 Indent heads labeled A, B, C; indent 1, 2, 3, more deeply than A, B, C; and so on. Line up vertically all heads that have the same kind of a number or letter.

```
I.
    A.
    B.
       1.
       2.
          a)
          b)
             (1)
             (2)
                (a)
                (b)
                   i.
                   ii.
II.
    A.
    B.
       1.
       2.
```

N50 Do not ordinarily use a single subhead under any head. A single subhead can usually be combined with its head, with benefit to the arrangement and logic of the outline.

Wrong	*Right*
I. The panic	I. The panic, July, 1742
A. July, 1742	II. The rebellion
II. The rebellion	

N51 Make each head and subhead as definite as you can without being wordy. Use statements instead of questions. Do not give details.

Wrong	*Right*
I. The loss of Balny	I. The loss of Balny
A. When?	A. At the beginning of the war
B. How?	B. Through Marvin's treachery
C. By whom?	C. By General Jasper Clark

N52 The heads of the outline may in some cases coincide with the topic thought of paragraphs written from the outline. But there need not be one paragraph or only one paragraph for each head or subhead of the outline.

N53 A sentence outline is a list of the points a theme will discuss, arranged to show their equal or unequal importance and expressed in sentences.

Theme topic.—Interscholastic football is not the sport for four classes of boys.

Introduction.—This article is necessary though it will probably be unpopular.

    I. Some boys are occupied with more important things.
      A. Some are earning their education.
      B. Some are developing their intellectual abilities.
   II. Some boys are unfit physically.
      A. Injuries and diseases disable some.
      B. Slow co-ordination hinders others.
  III. Some boys are unfit intellectually.
      A. Some are unfit from the viewpoint of the team.
      B. Others are unfit from the viewpoint of the boy.
        1. They cannot spare time from their studies.
          a) Long practice fights study.
          b) Utter weariness fights study.
          c) Constant distraction fights study.
        2. They cannot keep football in its proper place.
        3. They cannot get the benefits of the training.

IV. Some boys are unfit emotionally.
    A. Some are unfit from the viewpoint of the team.
        1. They are irresponsible.
        2. They are indecisive.
        3. They are too self-centered.
    B. Others are unfit from the viewpoint of the boy.
        1. They undergo too much strain.
        2. They experience abnormal reactions.
            a) They experience depression.
            b) They experience elation.
            c) They experience fear.
                (1) However, football sometimes diagnoses fear.
                (2) However, football sometimes cures fear.
                    (a) Much depends on the coach.
                    (b) Much depends on the other boys.
                    (c) Much depends on the boy himself.

Conclusion.—This article is intended to be a help, not to stir up controversy.

N54 The statements in N36-40 and N42-52 apply to both topic and sentence outlines.

N55 Remember that a very few headings in an outline can turn into a very long theme.

N56 Do not hesitate to alter the outline while you are writing the theme, but show the alterations on paper; and do not work without a written outline.

STEP 6. THE ROUGH DRAFT

N57 When you have completed your outline, write a rough draft of the expository theme.

N58 Space the lines of the rough draft very widely and leave abundant margins at the top, bottom, and sides for corrections and insertions. If you are using lined paper, it is usually a good idea to skip every other line. Double space a typewritten rough draft. A crowded and messy rough draft can treble your work and lead to disorganized writing.

N59 When you transfer to the rough draft a quotation or a fact or an idea from the notes described in N22-25, put after it a reference to the card you have used.

> "The King's Men played on no bare boards; the throne of Denmark was no chair. Renaissance stagecraft was quite elaborate. It included nearly everything that the lighting and machinery of those days could produce." Staging, card 2

QUOTATIONS

N60 Direct prose quotations, except for those mentioned in N61, should be inserted right into the text of the theme and enclosed in double quotation marks. (See D21-22 for the use of ellipsis periods with quotations which are not complete.)

N61 When a direct prose quotation runs to more than thirty-five words, it should be indented in its entirety eight typewriter characters from the left-hand margin and typed single-space. Paragraphs should be indicated by indenting the first line an additional three typewriter characters. No quotation marks should be used except those that are in the original text. (See D118.)

> it became quite clear that he was interested in the transfer only because it meant a saving of some thousands of dollars to his firm of importers. In the signed minutes of the meeting held on January 2, 1948, the stenographer reports Bullock directly as saying--
>
>> Frankly, I don't care whether these children are returned to Frankfort or not. I want the use of my warehouse, and I want someone else to take over the task of feeding them. Each of them is costing us from fifty cents to a dollar a day for food. You can talk all you want about "the Christian attitude," as Mr. Pollet so beautifully puts it; I'm a hardheaded businessman, and I just don't put out money where none comes in.[26]
>
> It was at this point that Mr. Pollet, seconded by the delegate from England, made a motion to expel Mr. Bullock from

441

It is permissible (indeed, some college style sheets require it) to indent long quotations an equal distance from the left- and right-hand margins.

N62 Quotations of only one line of poetry should be inserted right into the text of the theme and enclosed in double quotation marks.

N63 Quotations of more than one line of poetry should be set off from the text by single-spacing and centered between the left and right margins. No quotation marks should be used other than those that are already present in the original poem.

NOTES

N64 Unless your theme is very informal indeed, you will want to acknowledge the source of any direct quotation in it and also of ideas and information not directly quoted but nonetheless borrowed from some other writer.

The acknowledgment called for here is not ordinarily made right in the text itself. It is made either in notes at the end of the theme[7] or in footnotes at the bottom of the same page on which the end of the quotation or borrowed material appears.[8] The purpose of these separate acknowledgments is to avoid interrupting the text with dull and complicated references.

N65 At the place in the text where you wish to introduce a note or a footnote, write a superior figure. On an ordinary typewriter a superior figure is written by turning the platen back half a space and holding it there with the left hand and striking the number key with a finger of the right hand. Be sure to place the superior figure always immediately after the quotation or words to which the footnote belongs.[9]

[7] For notes at the end of the theme, see N68.
[8] For footnotes see N69-85.
[9] See N66-67.

N66 The first superior figure to appear in the theme should be *1*, the second should be *2*, and so on down through the theme.[10]

N67 A superior figure in the text should be placed immediately after a word, with no intervening space, unless punctuation follows the word. If punctuation follows the word, the figure should be placed immediately after the punctuation, with no intervening space.

```
The second book9 had not yet been published.
```

```
As a friendly critic of Mr. Danesly's theories insists,

"Danesly always expressed himself badly. He was not so

foolish as his writing makes him seem."10
```

N68 When footnotes are not used,[11] but rather all the notes are grouped together at the end of the theme—

   A Do not start these notes on the page on which the theme ends but on the next page.

   B On the first line under the top margin write *Notes* with a capital and small letters and underline it. Center the word between the left and right margins.

   C After the title *Notes,* skip two line-spaces, indent as for paragraph, and then write the number of the first note. (Write the number on the line; do not turn the platen back half a space as for a superior figure.) Follow the number with a period. Hit the space bar once and then

---

[10] When you are using footnotes (rather than notes grouped together at the end of the theme), it is permissible to start over with superior-figure *1* on each page. For the sake of uniformity, however, number your notes consecutively throughout the theme.

In many books, footnote numbers begin again at *1* with each chapter or section. The object is to make sure that footnote numbers never go above 99. Three-figure numbers are rather noticeable. They tend to interrupt the text and make a page of type matter look less pleasant.

[11] Readers do not like to turn back and forth to relate notes and text. They much prefer to find a note at the bottom of the page to which it is pertinent. For this reason, many college stylebooks instruct the student to use footnotes instead of a note section at the end of a theme.

copy the note from the card. Do the same for subsequent notes.

D Single-space the notes.

E Skip a line-space between notes.

14

Notes

1. Hilaire Belloc, Joan of Arc (London: Cassell & Co., Ltd., 1929), pp. 7-10.

2. Herbert Elliston, "Jim Forrestal, a Portrait in Politics," Atlantic Monthly, CLXXXIII (Nov., 1951), pp. 73-80.

FOOTNOTES

N69 When footnotes are used—

A Make sure that the footnotes do not run into the bottom margin of the page. When footnotes and text cannot be perfectly fitted, it is better to let the text fall short than to invade the margins.

B Separate the first footnote from the text by a line twenty typewriter characters long.

C Separate the first footnote from the line mentioned in B, just above, by a line-space.

D Separate one footnote from another on the same page by a line-space.

E Single-space each footnote.

F Before writing the superior figure at the beginning of each footnote, indent the same number of spaces as for a standard paragraph of the text. Then turn the platen back half a space and write the footnote number. The first word of the footnote follows the number immediately, without intervening space.

N70 There are several standard ways of writing footnotes. Some publishers have their own stylebooks that typesetters and proofreaders are obliged to follow. One of these has been widely used since 1893—Horace Hart's

Rules for Compositors and Readers at the University Press, Oxford (36th ed. Oxford Univ. Press, 1954). Some magazines and reviews have their own stylebooks, like that used by the law reviews of Columbia, Harvard, the University of Pennsylvania, and Yale (*A Uniform System of Citation, Form of Citation and Abbreviations* [8th ed. Harvard Law Review Association, 1949]). Another association that has its own stylebook is the Modern Language Association (*The MLA Style Sheet*, compiled by William Riley Parker [Modern Language Association, 1951]). Furthermore, many departments—science, history, languages— of colleges and universities have style sheets that writers of theses for these departments are obliged to follow.

Aside from these specialized norms for writing footnotes, there are general works that are useful and handy for any writer who is free to settle his own footnote forms. One of them is the *Style Manual* of the United States Government Printing Office (rev. ed. Washington, 1953); another is the University of Chicago Press's *A Manual of Style* (11th ed. Chicago, 1949). Both of these books are long, running to almost 500 pages each. A shorter stylebook (it contains only 82 pages), a condensation of the Chicago rules, is Kate L. Turabian's *A Manual for Writers of Term Papers, Theses, and Dissertations* (rev. ed. Chicago, 1949).

N71 The first principle in writing footnotes is completeness. Always give enough information for the reader to be able to trace the reference, whether he wants to either look up the book in a library or order a copy of it from a bookseller. Give the author's correct and complete name, the full and exact title of the book, and the facts of publication—where, by whom, and when the book was printed. In the case of an article, give the name of the publication in which the article was printed, the volume number of the publication (or else the date of publication or both), and page numbers.

The second principle in writing footnotes is consistency. Always be consistent in the form of your footnotes, what-

ever that form may be. If you find that, because of the
nature of what you are referring to, you must deviate from
the form, try to keep the deviation to a minimum.

Sometimes you may find that you must refer to such
things as legal documents, scientific works, ancient and
medieval manuscripts, and early printed books of complicated make-up. For such references the ordinary rules
for footnote forms often cannot be applied. In this case
examine books and periodicals that make use of these
sources; study the footnotes and follow them as a guide,
making your own forms as you read.

BOOKS

N72 A A footnote should give the name of the author (or
authors), if known. (For an editor's name, see E below.)
A comma follows the author's name.

> Sherman Kent, *Writing History* (New York: Appleton-
> Century-Crofts, 1954), p. 59.
>
> Robert Graves and Alan Hodge, *The Reader over Your
> Shoulder* (New York: Macmillan Co., 1943), p. 104.

B If there are more than two authors, write the names in
one of two ways:

> Herbert H. Hyman *et al.*, [*or* Herbert H. Hyman and Others,]
> *Interviewing in Social Research* (Chicago: Univ. of Chicago
> Press, 1954), pp. 143-57.

C If the book has been published under a pseudonym—or
under a pseudonym with the author's name supplied—
write it in this way:

> Denis Sept-Isles, [*or* Denis Sept-Isles (Robert Sherwood),]
> *The Final Invasion* (Paris: Henri Fils, 1918), p. 39.

D If the book has been published anonymously—or anonymously with the name supplied—write the footnote in
one of these ways:

> *After You, My Dear* (Edinburgh: Sanders, 1933), p. 116.

446

Anon., *After You, My Dear* (Edinburgh: Sanders, 1933), p. 116.

[John Murchison,] *After You, My Dear* (Edinburgh: Sanders, 1933), p. 116.

E If a book has been published under only an editor's name, the footnote may be written in one of two ways:

Alfred C. Ewing (ed.), *The Idealist Tradition from Berkeley to Blanshard* (Glencoe: Free Press, 1957), p. 357.

The Idealist Tradition from Berkeley to Blanshard, ed. Alfred C. Ewing (Glencoe: Free Press, 1957), p. 357.

F Sometimes the name of an association or society will take the place of an author's or editor's name:

Social Science Research Council, *Theory and Practice in Historical Study: A Report of the Committee on Historiography* (New York: Social Science Research Council, 1946), p. 98.

N73 A footnote should report the full title of a book (title and subtitle) as it occurs on the title page. No punctuation is used after the title whenever the facts of publication follow in parentheses.

John Hersey, *Hiroshima* (New York: Alfred A. Knopf, 1946), p. 44.

Mary Barnett Gilson, *What's Past Is Prologue, Reflections on My Industrial Experience* (New York: Harper & Bros., 1940), p. 207.

N74 When a footnote lists the name of the author of a work plus the name of an editor of the work, put a comma after the title and follow it with *ed.* and the editor's name.

Christopher Dawson, *The Dynamics of World History,* ed. John J. Mulloy (New York: Sheed & Ward, 1957), p. 79.

If *ed.* is followed by a phrase like "with an introduction," do not use only *ed.* Write *ed. . . . by.*

Henry David Thoreau, *Walden and Other Writings,* ed. with an introd. by Brooks Atkinson (New York, Modern Lib.), p. 210.

N75 When the footnote lists the name of the author of a work plus the name of a translator of that work, put a comma after the title and follow it with *trans.* and the translator's name.

Ludwig Wittgenstein, *Remarks on the Foundations of Mathematics,* trans. G. E. M. Anscombe (New York: Macmillan Co., 1956), p. 102.

If *trans.* is followed by a phrase like "from the German," do not use only *trans.* Write *trans. . . . by.*

G. Révész, *The Origins and Prehistory of Language,* trans. from the German by J. Butler (New York, Philosophical Lib.), p. 129.

N76 Often a book will carry miscellaneous information after the title about the introduction, the edition, the illustrations, the preface, and so on. In such a case, write the footnote in accordance with the samples below.

Alexander Smith, *Dreamthorp, with Selections from 'Last Leaves,'* with an introd. by Hugh Walker ("The World's Classics." Oxford, Oxford Univ. Press), p. 25.

Lyle Saxon, *Fabulous New Orleans,* illustrated by E. H. Suydam (New York: D. Appleton-Century Co., 1939), p. 175.

Peter Abelard, *Dialectica,* first complete ed. of the Parisian manuscript by L. M. de Rijk (New York: Gregory Lounz, 1957), pp. 577-79.

Plotinus, *The Enneads,* trans. from the Greek by Stephen MacKenna, revised by B. S. Page, foreword by E. R. Dodds, introd. by Paul Henry (2nd ed. New York: Pantheon Books, 1957), p. 343.

N77 Details of publication—all the information, that is, about the physical production of a book—are given in parentheses after the author, title, editor, and so on.

These details, which will vary from book to book according to circumstances and are not all found in every book, are as follows:

A The number of volumes in a work.

A *Cycle of Adams Letters, 1861-1865,* ed. Worthington Chauncey Ford, with illustrations (2 vols. Boston: Houghton Mifflin Co., 1920), I, 9.

B The edition of a book—second, third, and so on; revised, enlarged, and so on.

> Albert R. Chandler, *The Clash of Political Ideals* (3rd ed. New York: Appleton-Century-Crofts, 1957), p. 202.

C The series to which the book belongs.

> A. M. Henry, O.P., *The Virtues and States of Life* ("Theology Library," Vol. IV. Chicago: Fides, 1957), p. 10.

Notice that the volume number is not within the quotation marks. The reason is that the number is not a part of the name of the series.

D The place of publication.

> Harrison E. Salisbury, *The Shook-up Generation* (New York: Harper & Bros., 1958), p. 112.

The punctuation after the place-name will vary, being either a comma, a semicolon, or a colon. (1) Use a comma after a place-name when you have only the place-name and the publisher's name, neither of them being internally punctuated—(Philadelphia, Dorrance & Co.). (2) Use a semicolon after a place-name when you have a place-name and a publisher's name, one of them (or both) being internally punctuated—(San Marino, Cal.; Huntington Lib.), (New York; Harcourt, Brace & Co.). (3) Use a colon after a place-name when you have a place-name, a publisher's name, and a date—as in the footnote examples above in N76.

E The date.
Put the date after the publisher's name.

> (St. Louis: B. Herder Book Co., 1955)

Sometimes no date is printed on the title page. In this case, (1) you may use the copyright date, which is usually printed on the reverse of the title page—for instance, c1941; (2) you may use *n.d.* ("no date") if the copyright date is not given; (3) you may use a date in brackets if that date is known from sources other than the book itself—for instance, [1854].

Infrequently, a book will have, say, only the place-name and the date, only the publisher's name and the date, or only the place-name and the publisher's name.

(Glasgow, 1782)
(Craig the Bookseller, 1803)
(Glasgow, Craig the Bookseller)

N78 After the details of publication the footnote should show the volume number of the book[12] (if the work is more than a single volume) and the page number of the reference.

A Put the volume number in capital roman numerals without *Volume* or *Vol.*

A Cycle of Adams Letters, 1861-1865, ed. Worthington Chauncey Ford, with illustrations (2 vols. Boston: Houghton Mifflin Co., 1920), II, 122.

The example above refers to a work whose two volumes were both published in the same year. Sometimes you will want to refer to a work of several volumes that were published during a period of two years or more. If it is not important to emphasize the date of the particular volume you are referring to, indicate the dates of the complete work in the usual way.

Antoine Laval, *Louisiana Old and New* (3 vols. New Orleans: Vieux Carré Pub. Co., 1939-41), III, 57-84.

If it is important to emphasize the date of the particular volume you are referring to, write the footnote in the following way (omitting the total number of volumes).

Antoine Laval, *Louisiana Old and New* (New Orleans: Vieux Carré Pub. Co., 1941), III, 57-84.

B Put page numbers in arabic numerals (but use small roman numerals for such introductory matter in the book as prefaces, introductions, forewords, and so on).

---

[12] See N79, special rules.

A Cycle of Adams Letters, 1861-1865, ed. Worthington Chauncey Ford, with illustrations (2 vols. Boston: Houghton Mifflin Co., 1920), II, 122 [*or* I, xiii].

When your reference or quotation runs from one page to another and when the page numbers each contain three numerals of the same hundred, omit the first numeral from the second number.[13] (See G20-22.)

[pp.] 142-49 (This means, for instance, that the quotation runs from page 142 to page 149.)

There are two exceptions to this rule. If the first number ends in two zeros, use three numerals in the second number: [pp.] 500-503, [pp.] 500-512. If the second numeral of both the first and second numbers is a zero, use only one numeral in the second: [pp.] 501-7. When a reference or quotation runs between pages of different hundreds, use three numerals for each page number: [pp.] 299-311.

c If you want to note a section of the book in addition to the volume and the page, indicate it clearly.[14]

The Monument, ed. John Evans (2 vols. Dublin: G. Moore, 1900), I, Part IV, 17.

Works published in more than one volume sometimes do not refer to the individual books as volumes but as books or parts. In this case, use *Book* or *Part* in place of *Vol.,* and use *p.* or *pp.* before the page number.

A. E. Main, *Journey to Athens* (St. Louis: Pine Co., 1927), Book II, pp. 200-202.

If a column number (or some like designation) is used in place of a page number, use both *Vol.* and *col.*

E. Marek, *Chronicles of Central Europe* (10 vols. New York: Hule Merom Co., 1889), Vol. IX, col. 315.

---

[13] Page numbers of four numerals are rare. Treat them, however, according to the rules for page numbers of three numerals. These same rules apply to writing dates.
[14] For capitals and numbers with terms referring to parts of a book, see H146-47 and G13. For handling special cases that involves titles and volume numbers, see N79.

N79 You will often find that the bibliographical details of the book you are referring to cannot be arranged in the ordinary pattern given for writing footnotes. The book has unusual and distinctive features about it that call for individual treatment. In this case, follow the footnote norms and rules in a general way, supplying all the information that is necessary to identify the book and help the reader find it easily. Study the sample footnotes below.

The following footnote refers to a book that is (*a*) one of several volumes all (*b*) by the same author and (*c*) published under one general title; but (*d*) each volume has its own separate title.

> Antoine Laval, *Louisiana Old and New*, Vol. II: *Louisiana in the Nineteenth Century* (New Orleans: Vieux Carré Pub. Co., 1940), p. 78.

The following footnote refers to a book that is one of several volumes that all (*a*) have the same general title and (*b*) are edited by one person; but each book has (*c*) its own separate title and (*d*) its own individual author.

> A. P. English, *Aristotle the Philosopher*, Vol. II of *Great Philosophers*, ed. Henry David (15 vols. San Francisco: Wade & Co., 1918), p. 101.

ESSAYS, ARTICLES, AND UNPUBLISHED MATERIAL

N80 Footnotes for essays, articles, and unpublished material follow, in a general way, the form of footnotes for books (see N69-79). And the same general principle obtains: Give complete and accurate information so that the reader can easily check the reference.

A When referring to an essay in a collection, give (1) the name of the author, if it is known; (2) the title of the essay; (3) the title of the book; (4) the name of the editor, if there is one; and (5) the pertinent details of publication, as called for in N69-79.

E. B. White, "Children's Books," *One Man's Meat* (new and enlarged ed. New York, Harper & Bros.), pp. 23-29.

Matthew Arnold, "Dante and Beatrice," *A Book of English Essays (1600-1900)*, selected by Stanley V. Makower and Basil H. Blackford ("The World's Classics." Oxford, Oxford Univ. Press), p. 331.

B When referring to an article in a quarterly or monthly magazine, give (1) the name of the author, if it is known; (2) the title of the article; (3) the name of the magazine; (4) the volume number and page number of the magazine. Sometimes the date of the magazine is given in parentheses after the volume number; sometimes the number of the magazine or the date alone (or both) is given without the volume number.

Mario Pei, "Who Said Latin Is Dead?" *Holiday*, XXIV (Nov., 1958), 32.

Victor S. Frank, "A Russian Hamlet: Boris Pasternak's Novel," *Dublin Review*, No. 477 (autumn, 1958), p. 212.

When referring to an article in a weekly or semimonthly magazine, or to a newspaper, do not give the volume number.

Joseph Wechsberg, "Metamorphosis," *New Yorker*, Nov. 1, 1958, pp. 47-83.

"The Kind Reviewer," the London *Times Literary Supplement*, Oct. 10, 1958, p. 577.

"The Trouble in Pakestan," the St. Louis *Post-Dispatch*, April 2, 1956, p. 2C.

c When referring to a book review, give (1) the name of the reviewer, (2) the name and author of the book reviewed, and (3) the pertinent bibliographical details, as above.

Alden L. Fisher, review of *Feeling and Form* by Susanne K. Langer, *Modern Schoolman*, XXXI, 155-58.

D When referring to an article in an encyclopedia, give (1) the name of the author, if it is known; (2) the title of the article; (3) the name of the encyclopedia; (4) the name of the editor, unless the reference is to one of the big, well-known encyclopedias that have had many editors; and (5) the volume and page number.

"Cheese," Encyclopedia of Food and Wines, ed. A. Gourmet, II, 74-93.

J [Joseph Jacobs], "Spinoza," Jewish Encyclopedia, XI, 511-20.

E When referring to unpublished theses, notes, or documents, identify clearly (1) the reference and (2) the source.

Charles Molyneux, "The Rhythm of Mrs. Meynell's Prose" (unpublished M.A. thesis, Dept. of English, St. Louis Univ., 1931), p. 26.

R. G. Fisher, "The Effect of Northern Climate on the Individual" (mimeographed notes, Dept. of Social Investigation, Univ. of Alaska, 1956), p. 9.

Letter from Mrs. Elizabeth Higgs to Miss Sarah Nubian, June 27, 1818 (Fremont County Archives; Whitefalls, Cal.).

BIBLICAL AND CLASSICAL REFERENCES

N81 In footnote references to the Bible, use abbreviations like those listed below for both the books and the versions of the Bible. (There is no universally accepted set of abbreviations for biblical references. The editors of Bibles and Scripture handbooks generally compose their own rules, as do the editors of dictionaries.)

Ps. 32:1 (Psalm 32, verse 1)
II Cor. 5:1 (Second Epistle to the Corinthians, Chapter 5, verse 1)

The Bible
N.T.—New Testament
O.T.—Old Testament
Gen.—Genesis
Num.—Numbers
Isa.—Isaias
Acts—Acts of the Apostles
Rev.—Revelation (the Apocalypse)

Versions of the Bible
A.V.—Authorized Version (King James Bible)
C.A.T.—Chicago American Translation
D.V.—Douay Version
Sept.—Septuagint
W.V.—Westminster Version of the New Testament
Vulg.—Vulgate
Vulg. (Knox)—Msgr. Knox's translation of the Vulgate

N82 Footnotes for references to the Greek and Roman classics should show the name of the author, the name of the work, and the section of the work referred to.[15]

Italicize the title of the work. Use no punctuation after the name of the author or the title. Use small roman numerals to indicate the book (that is, the division of the work).[16] Use arabic numerals for all other numbers.

Aristotle *Rhetoric* iii. 2. 1412a9-11.
Plato *Republic* iv. 432.
Cicero *Disputationes Tusculanae* x. 2. 29.

ABBREVIATIONS

N83 Abbreviations are much used in footnotes, since abbreviations save space on the printed page and, being a kind of shorthand, a technical device, that the reader can comprehend at a glance, do not divert his attention too long from the important thing, the book or article he is reading.

---

[15] The classical departments of most colleges and universities—and most publishers of classical works—have their own footnote style.

It might be said here, by way of parenthesis, that no specific directions can be given for writing footnotes referring to the works of men who wrote between classical and modern times. These works, usually in Latin, are complicated in their structure and division, which differ even from work to work of the same author; besides, in many instances—as in the case of St. Thomas Aquinas—editions of a work have been published at different times, in different places, and with different arrangements of the same material. To compose footnote references to such books, follow the general norms and principles stated and exemplified in N69-79 and N84, and study the footnotes in the learned publications that have their own style in referring to these early works.

[16] There are exceptions to this. The books of Aristotle's *Metaphysics*, for example, are not numbered but are lettered with capital Greek letters thus: Aristotle *Metaphysics* Δ. 1. 1013a29.

The following abbreviations are those most commonly used in footnotes. (See H146-47 for the use of capitals and small letters with words which designate parts of a book.)

Bk. (Bks.)	book (books)
Bros.	brothers
cf.	compare; confer; see
Chap. (Chaps.)	chapter (chapters)
Co.	company
col. (cols.)	column (columns)
Dept.	department
ed. (eds.)	edition (editions); editor (editors); edited by
1st ed., 2nd ed.	first edition, second edition (and so on)
et al.	*et alii,* "and others"
f.	following
ibid.	*ibidem,* "in the same place"
idem	"the same"
l. (ll.)	line (lines)
loc. cit.	*loco citato,* "in the place cited"[17]
n. (nn.)	note (notes)
n.d.	no date
No. (Nos.)	number (numbers)
op. cit.	*opere citato,* "in the work cited"[17]
p. (pp.)	page (pages)
pp. 5 f.	page 5 and the following page
pp. 5 ff.	page 5 and the following pages
Pt. (Pts.)	part (parts)
Pub.	publishing
Pubns.	publications
rev.	revised, revised by
sec. (secs.)	section (sections)
trans.	translation, translator, translated by
Univ.	university
Vol. (Vols.)	volume (volumes)

Use an ampersand (&) for *and* in publishers' names: Harper & Bros.

---

[17] Never use *loc. cit.* or *op. cit.*, for they irritate the reader, making him backtrack—often through several pages—to discover what the place or work is that has been cited. Use an abbreviated title instead. See N84.

SECOND REFERENCES

N84 The footnote forms shown in N69-82 are the ones for a first reference to a book, article, and so on. Footnotes that afterward refer to a work already fully identified should not repeat the bibliographical details of the first reference. It is enough to use either *ibid.* or an abbreviated reference.[18] (Never use *loc. cit.* or *op. cit.* in a second reference. See footnote 17, under N83.)

A *Ibid.* is an abbreviation of *ibidem* and means "in the same place."

When references to the same work, even though they are separated by several pages, follow one another in succession, use *ibid.* in the second (and subsequent) footnote.[19]

[1] Ira Fleck, *Suburbia* (Boston: Houser Press, 1954), p. 201. [First reference]

[2] *Ibid.* [The reference here is exactly the same as the one which is above.]

[3] *Ibid.*, p. 209. [The reference here is to the same work, but the page number is different.]

[1] Eric Montgomery, *The Inner Passage* (Vancouver: Columbia Books, 1955), I, 98. [First reference]

[2] *Ibid.*, 115. [The work and volume number are the same; the page number is different.]

[3] *Ibid.*, III, 276. [The work is the same; the volume is different.]

B When a second or further reference is made to a work already cited in complete form, use an abbreviated reference whenever *ibid.* cannot be used—whenever,

---

[18] *Idem,* "the same person," is sometimes used when two different books by the same author follow each other in a footnote:

[1] James Murray, *Elizabethan Lyrics* (New York: Morris Co., 1943), p. 47.

[2] *Idem, The Songs of Marlowe* (New York: Morris Co., 1945), p. 60.

The use of *idem* is not recommended. Repeat the author's name.

[19] If you feel that the references are separated by too many pages, then, for the sake of clarity, you may use an abbreviated reference in place of *ibid.* in the second footnote.

that is, another reference intervenes between these first and second references.

[1] George Decatur, *A Preface to the Philosophy of Being* (rev. ed. New York: Appleton-Century-Crofts, 1955), p. 125.

[2] Etienne Gilson, *The Spirit of Mediaeval Philosophy*, trans. A. H. C. Downes (New York: Chas. Scribner's Sons, 1936), p. 60.

[3] Decatur, *Philosophy of Being*, p. 38.

[4] *Ibid.*, p. 137.

[5] Meyrich H. Carré, "Pierre Gassendi and the New Philosophy," *Philosophy*, XXXIII (1958), 112.

[6] Gilson, *Mediaeval Philosophy*, p. 63.

[7] Carré, "Gassendi," 113-15.

[8] Decatur, *Philosophy of Being*, p. 130.

OTHER FOOTNOTES

N85 Footnotes are not reserved exclusively for bibliographical reference. They may be used for editorial comment or for information that should not be allowed to interrupt the text and yet may be useful to the reader. In the ordinary theme, however, there should not be many nonbibliographical footnotes; for footnotes irritate some readers, who cannot resist reading them and yet find them distracting. If, therefore, there is any doubt about the usefulness of a nonbibliographical footnote, omit it. For every reader that it pleases, there will probably be three others that it will irritate. In matter that is not intended to be read consecutively—such, for example, as the rules in this book—abundant footnotes are not a hazard; indeed, they are welcomed if, by cross references and similar apparatus, they help the reader to find what he wants. Examples of nonbibliographical footnotes are illustrated below.

[1] This passage is printed with the kind permission of the author.

[2] The only known copy of the work that M. Rubinoff quotes so often is in a lamasery in Tibet.

[3] Never use *loc. cit.* or *op. cit.*, for they irritate the reader, making him backtrack—often through several pages—to discover what the

place or work is that has been cited. Use an abbreviated title instead.

BIBLIOGRAPHY

N86 A bibliography, as the word is used here in connection with a theme, is a list of books and articles used in preparing a theme, a list of sources that the writer consulted for information.

A bibliography of one kind may give all the sources, books, and articles, alphabetically arranged in a single list; a bibliography of another kind may give the sources alphabetically arranged in separate lists of books first and then articles. Again, a bibliography may separate the primary sources (books and articles by a particular author) from the secondary sources (books and articles about an author), making the further subdivisions under each, especially if the bibliography is a long one, of books first and then articles. (The short sample bibliography at the end of this section divides the sources into primary and secondary without any subdivisions.)

A bibliography supplies all the information that footnotes do but in a slightly different style. An author's last name, for instance, is always written first in a bibliography, the first and middle names following it; the facts of publication are not enclosed in parentheses; and the use of commas and periods is different.

A bibliography lists works in alphabetical order[20] either (*a*) by author or (*b*) by editor, if there is one and no author is given, or (*c*) by title, if neither author nor editor is given. When, besides the author, there is given an editor or translator, his name is put between the title of the book and the facts of publication.

---

[20] Puzzling problems often crop up in putting bibliographical entries into alphabetical order. One of the best helps for solving these problems is the *A.L.A. Cataloging Rules for Author and Title Entries,* prepared for the Division of Cataloging and Classification of the American Library Association. 2nd ed. by Clara Beetle. Chicago: American Library Assoc., 1949. Pp. xxi + 265.

459

Ballou, Richard Boyd. *The Individual and the State. The Modern Challenge to Education.* Boston: Beacon Press, 1953. Pp. xxviii + 305.

Fremantle, Anne Jackson (ed.). *A Treasury of Early Christianity.* New York: Viking Press, 1953. Pp. 639.

Proceedings of the Littlemore Philatelic Society. Vol. III. University Park, Ark.: Meyers Printers, 1914. Pp. 420.

If an author's name appears only in the title of a work and nowhere else on the title page, put it in brackets.

[Wright, Chauncey.] *The Philosophical Writings of Chauncey Wright. Representative Selections.* Ed. Edward H. Madden. New York: Liberal Arts Press, 1958. Pp. xxii + 145.

If books and articles by the same author are listed one after another, the author's name is written for the first entry and, for the others, is represented by a line followed by a period. For an example of this, see the sample bibliography below.

The following sample bibliography could be attached to a theme about the thought of Kierkegaard. This particular bibliography is divided into primary sources (books by Kierkegaard) and secondary sources (books and articles about Kierkegaard). The number of pages in each book could have been given after the date of publication; the page numbers in the magazines had to be given.

PRIMARY SOURCES

Kierkegaard, Sören. *Christian Discourses.* Trans. W. Lowrie. New York: Oxford Univ. Press, 1939.

——. *Either/Or.* Trans. D. F. and L. M. Swenson. 2 vols. Princeton: Princeton Univ. Press, 1944.

——. *Fear and Trembling.* Trans. W. Lowrie. Princeton: Princeton Univ. Press, 1941.

——. *Training in Christianity.* Trans. W. Lowrie. Princeton, Princeton Univ. Press.

SECONDARY SOURCES

Brandt, Frithoof. "The Great Earthquake in Sören Kierkegaard's Life," *Theoria,* XV (1949), 38-53.

Chaning-Pearce, Melville. *The Terrible Crystal.* New York: Oxford Univ. Press, 1941.

Collins, James. "The Mind of Kierkegaard," *Modern Schoolman,* XXVI (1948-49), 1-22, 121-47, 219-51, 293-322.

Friedmann, Rudolph. *Kierkegaard. The Analysis of the Psychological Personality.* London: Peter Nevill, 1949.

Jaspers, Karl. "The Importance of Nietzsche, Marx and Kierkegaard in the History of Philosophy," *Hibbert Journal,* XLIX (April, 1951), 226-34.

Lowrie, Walter. *Kierkegaard.* Princeton: Princeton Univ. Press, 1938.

———. "Existence as Understood by Kierkegaard and/or Sartre," *Sewanee Review,* LVIII (July, 1950), 379-401.

Martin, H. V. *Kierkegaard. The Melancholic Dane.* New York: Philosophical Lib., 1950.

Patrick, D. *Pascal and Kierkegaard. A Study in the Strategy of Evangelism.* 2 vols. London: Butterworth, 1947.

STEP 7. THE FINAL COPY

N87 The following regulations will produce a neat, legible final copy that teachers will enjoy correcting and others will enjoy reading. The rules are for typewritten copy, but with obvious changes most of them apply to handwritten copy also.

N88 Write on only one side of each sheet.

N89 Leave a margin of at least an inch and a half at the top, bottom, and left of each page and a margin of at least one inch at the right.

N90 Double-space your typing.[21]

N91 Place your name, the course, the date, and other pertinent information in the upper right-hand corner, but in-

---

[21] This rule does not apply to a direct prose quotation that runs to two or more sentences and at the same time to four or more typewritten lines, to quotations of more than one line of poetry, to notes grouped together at the end of a theme, or to footnotes—all of which are to be single-spaced in order to set them off from the rest of the text.

side the margins, of the first page.[22] Put the name on its own line, the course on its own line, and so on.

N92   One-third down the first page, center the title of the paper between the side margins.

N93   Type the title all in capitals, with or without underlining, or in capitals and small letters, with underlining. Do not use quotation marks unless *part* of the title is a quotation from some other work. If the title contains within itself a second title, either (*a*) put the second title in roman type, or (*b*) italicize it and put it within single quotation marks.

N94   After the title skip two line-spaces and center your by-line under the title. (A by-line is the word *by* followed by the name of the author. It may ordinarily be omitted. It should be included if the article is to be published and the by-line is copy for the printer, especially if the author writes under a pen name different from the name in the upper right-hand corner of the first page.)

N95   After the by-line (or after the title if there is no by-line), skip three line-spaces and begin the first paragraph.

N96   The first lines of all paragraphs should be uniformly indented. Indent not less than three and not more than eight typewriter characters. In handwritten copy indent not less than half an inch and not more than an inch. Less is usually undiscernible; more is usually ugly.

N97   On the first page, midway between the last line of type and the bottom edge of the paper and midway between the left and right margins, center the arabic numeral *1*. Do not use the word *page*.

N98   Number pages 2, 3, 4, and so on, with an arabic numeral just inside the right-hand margin, midway between the

---

[22] "Other pertinent information" means whatever is necessary for the reader to identify the paper at a glance. If you are writing for publication, the editor will want to know the number of words; so put that in too. But do not clutter this corner with any unnecessary information.

top edge of the paper and the first line of text. Do not use the word *page.*[23]

N99 If you wish or are required to do so, use a running head from page 2 to the end of the theme. Starting just inside the left-hand margin, on the same line with the page number,[24] write your name in capitals and small letters; then a comma; and then the title all in capitals, with or without underlining, or in capitals and small letters with underlining. If the title is too long for the space, use a shortened form. The running head should stop at least five typewriter characters before the page number.

N100 Below are pages from a theme typed according to the rules above and to the rules for typing quotations and footnotes.

William Sands
Pl 185
Term paper for Mr. Welch
March 16, 1960

RESPONSE TO NICHOLAS KARALIS

William Sands

It has recently been argued, once more, that we have knowl-

edge of other minds. Nicholas Karalis states in the Review of Meta-

physics: "I shall try to prove that we can know an act of thought

which another mind is thinking, and that what we know or rethink is

the same act of thought which another mind is thinking rather than

---

[23] *Page,* though common enough, is unnecessary.
[24] See N98.

William Sands, Response to Nicholas Karalis   2

one merely similar to it."[1] It is good that Mr. Karalis has reagi-

tated this question.

. . . .

That numerical sameness must be distinguished from mere

similarity, then, I agree. Two men, for instance, are alike in hav-

ing the same nature, the same basic characteristics, realized in

each. Yet no one would take them to be one man; they are similar

but independent, specifically the same but numerically separate.

This is not, however, Mr. Karalis's view of the distinction:

> If an event A happens twice in time as numerically the same,
> then it is not, in its "two" occurrences, merely similar
> (and numerically different). That is, if what are supposed
> to be two different things are numerically the same, they
> are really one and not two.
>   It is my intention to prove that the act of belief "2 +
> 2 = 4" in Smith's mind is numerically the same as the act
> of belief "2 + 2 = 4" in Jones's mind. . . . I intend to
> show that "different" acts of thought can yet be numerically
> the same. This implies the rejection of the view that the
> only sense in which "different" acts of thought can be
> the same is the sense that they are similar instances of
> the same kind or class.[2]

. . . .

Refutation of Mr. Karalis's point of view is of no consequence

here, however. What I should like to do is to recall a different

analysis of our thought, perhaps best expressed by William

James. For James, taking into account the body-mind relation-

ship which affects our thinking, no two ideas are ever exactly the

---

[1]Nicholas Karalis, "Knowledge of Other Minds," Review of Metaphysics, IX (June 1956), No. 4, 565. "By an act of thought I mean a
mental happening in a mind rather than the object of an act of thought,
which is not itself a mental happening" (ibid.).

[2]Ibid.

William Sands, Response to Nicholas Karalis   3

same. A permanently existing idea which makes its appearance
before consciousness at periodic intervals is as imaginary an
entity as the Jack of Spades. Thoughts are something different
to all men and the same to no one twice. As James puts it:

> Every thought we have of a given fact is, strictly speaking,
> unique, and only bears a resemblance of kind with our other
> thoughts of the same fact. When the identical fact occurs,
> we must think of it in a fresh manner, see it under a some-
> what different angle, apprehend it in different relations
> from those in which it last appeared. And the thought by
> which we cognize it is the thought of it-in-these-rela-
> tions, a thought suffused with the consciousness of all
> that dim context. [3]

No individual thought can ever be identical with any thought which
has preceded or will succeed it. Not only are thoughts never the
same for two people but they are never the same for one man twice.

. . . .

My experience--in the sense of the dynamic activity which
constitutes my intellectual awareness of the things about me--is
simply private and personal. And, though my mind examines the
same evidence which another man examines, though it knows the
same fact as he, my knowledge is my own and his knowledge is
his own. It is only through communication with other men by speech
and writing that we find that they have internal experiences similar
to our own.

---

[3] William James, The Principles of Psychology (New York: Henry
Holt & Co., 1905), I, 233.

465

Definitions

IN GENERAL

N101 Definition is the explanation of the meaning of a word or phrase.

N102 A good definition explains a word in terms that are better understood by the reader than the word to be defined.

[Not a good definition for most readers:] Mallophaga are an order or suborder of ametabolous insects with mandibulate mouth, valvate labium, shovel-shaped head, and flat body.

[A better definition for most readers:] Mallophaga are bird lice.

N103 Two of the most common and useful forms of definition are synonym and the logical definition.

DEFINITION BY SYNONYM

N104 A synonym is a word that has the same or nearly the same meaning as another word in the same language.

N105 Define a word by giving a synonym that is better known to the reader.

An apothecary is a druggist.
He complained of vertigo; that is, dizziness.

N106 Find the most exact synonym you can.

[Not very good:] A condor is a bird.
[Better:] A condor is a vulture.

[Not very good:] A buccaneer is a robber.
[Better:] A buccaneer is a pirate.

[Not very good:] A dwelling is a building.
[Better:] A dwelling is a house.

N107 Keep parallelism between the word to be defined and its definition.

[Wrong:] *Chanting* [gerund] means "to sing" [infinitive].
[Right:] *Chanting* [gerund] means "singing" [gerund].

466

[Wrong:] *Oaf* [noun] means "stupid" [adjective].

[Right:] *Oaf* [noun] means "blockhead" [noun].

[Wrong:] *Rapture* [abstract noun] means "a mystic" [concrete noun].

[Right:] *Rapture* [abstract noun] means "ecstasy" [abstract noun].

N108 Verbal parallelism must sometimes yield to parallelism of thought. For example, if a noun, like *narration,* has an action sense, then it may be defined by a gerund: "*Narration* is 'telling.' " In a context where a participle has a descriptive rather than an action sense, it may be defined by an adjective: "*Enervated* means 'weak' " (instead of "*Enervated* means 'weakened.' ")

N109 Advantages of definition by synonym: (*a*) It is often the easiest method of definition for the writer—and often the easiest for the reader, since a synonym is brief, easy to remember, and does not clutter the mind with details. (*b*) It is often the more informal way of defining a term; it defines adequately without halting the easy flow of the composition.

He was an apothecary—one of those chemists who fill physicians' prescriptions and sell drugs, medicines, and allied chemical preparations—but he earned many a guinea on real-estate deals undertaken for the great lords of his day.	This is rather formal. The full definition between the dashes tends to halt the easy flow of the composition.
He was an apothecary—a druggist—but he earned many a guinea on real-estate deals undertaken for the great lords of his day.	This is informal. The synonym between the dashes slows the reader scarcely at all.

N110 Disadvantages of definition by synonym: (*a*) Definition by synonym is often very inexact. (*b*) Moreover, synonyms often do not supply very much information. If, therefore, you need greater exactness or more information

than can be supplied by a synonym, use a logical definition instead.[25]

For example, to define a chair as a seat does not say exactly what
a chair is; for a sofa or a bench is also a seat, and yet it is not a
chair. Again, to say that a condor is a vulture does not offer a
great deal of information. There are vultures that are not condors,
and condors have a number of interesting characteristics that such
a definition omits. If the reader did not know what a condor is and
if condors played a considerable part in the theme, he might have
reason to wish for a fuller definition.

THE LOGICAL DEFINITION

N111 Define a word by giving (*a*) its general class and (*b*) the
characteristics that make it different from the other things
of that class.

Word to be defined	Class	Distinguishing characteristics
chair[26]	seat	with a back, for one person
exposition	that form of writing or talking	that has for its purpose explaining or informing
boy	male human being	between the ages, roughly, of one and twenty-one
brittleness	quality of material substances	that renders them easily broken or snapped
creeps	moves along	with the body prone and close to the ground, or slowly or stealthily or timidly
spasmodically	in a manner	that is fitful, lacks continuity, or is intermittent
monotonous	occurring	without change or variety

---

[25] See N111-18.

[26] In a theme, logical definitions would not appear in the telegraphic style in
which they are given here. They would be phrased something like this: "A chair
is a seat that has a back and that is intended to hold one person."

N112   Do not give the widest, but the narrowest, general class the reader may be expected to know.

For example, in defining *man,* do not ordinarily say that man is a being. For, from God, who is a being, to electrons, which also are beings, man shares the word with too many things for this to be a useful class in most contexts. Say man is a rational animal.

N113   Do not use the pronoun *one* as the general class.

[Too vague:] A rifle is one that has grooves in the barrel to rotate the bullet.

[Better:] A rifle is a shoulder firearm that has grooves in the barrel to rotate the bullet.

[All right, since here *one* clearly means "a person" and is not vague:] An emperor is one who rules an empire. A renegade is one who deserts to the enemy.

N114   Keep parallelism in your definitions.

[Not parallel:] "Brittle": that quality of material substances that renders them easily broken or snapped.

[Parallel:] "Brittle": possessing that quality of material substances that renders them easily broken or snapped.

N115   Except for the cases in N116-17, do not repeat, in the definition, the word to be defined.

[Wrong:] An anthology is an anthology of poems or other literary compositions.

[Right:] An anthology is a collection of poems or other literary compositions.

[Wrong:] "Healthful": conducive to health.

[Right:] "Healthful": conducive to the well-being and vigor of the body.

N116   When the term to be defined is made up of two words, one of which is already well known to the reader, it is quite usual and correct to repeat the well-known word in the definition.

For example, readers may ordinarily be presumed to know what a rifle is; so this definition of an automatic rifle is in order: "An automatic rifle is a rifle whose recoil rejects the used shells, replaces them with new bullets, and fires the new bullets as long as the trigger is held in firing position."

N117 When the purpose of a definition is to show that the unknown word is merely a variation of a known word or a word built from a well-known root, repetition is quite all right.

Terrible: "inspiring terror."
Informal: "not formal."

N118 Over and above the general class and the necessary distinguishing characteristics, add other distinguishing characteristics and other information as you like or as the matter requires.

For example, you need not content yourself with this definition: "Mrs. Paul Durfee is a housewife and a mother." You may add, for example, that she is a widow, that she is thirty-seven years old, and that she has three children—as you like and as the matter requires. In this connection, note that a definition need not be confined to a single sentence. Moreover, it may be so interwoven with other matter that the writer defines only obliquely, while directly discussing something else; for example, see the examples under N109.

Business letters[27]

FORM[28]

N119 Make your letters clean—free of smudges, visible erasures, mistakes, crossouts, corrections, creases and tears, and strike-overs.

N120 Use white unruled paper, 8½ x 11 inches. Use only one side of each sheet.

---

[27] A good manual to consult for correct letter forms (and the forms of such things as announcements, resolutions, reports, and so on) is *The Secretary's Handbook,* by Sarah Augusta Taintor and Kate M. Monro (New York: Macmillan Co., 1949).

[28] For punctuation of the various parts of letters, see D24-26 and D84. For capitals see H13-15.

N121 Use a black typewriter ribbon or blue, black, or blue-black ink.

N122 Center your letter on the paper so that the margins are balanced all around it.

N123 Use block form—no indentions—for typewritten letters. Leave a line-space between the paragraphs.[29]

St. Thomas More College
Tower Hill, Massachusetts
February 24, 1960

The Holmes Advertising Agency
139 West 152 Street
New York 20, New York

Gentlemen:

At the advice of one of your copy writers, Mr. Harvey P. Morton, I am writing to inquire whether you will have an opening in your office next fall for a college graduate.

During my four years here at St. Thomas I made English my major subject. In my senior year I edited our literary magazine, the Utopian, and won the Chancellor Essay Award. I worked for three summers in the offices of a country newspaper.

If you want to make inquiries about me, let me suggest that you speak to Mr. Morton or write to the Reverend John Fisher, the president of St. Thomas More College.

Sincerely yours,

David Masterson

David Masterson

---

[29] It is still rather common to use indented form for the paragraphs within the body of a typewritten letter. One may do so, indenting the first line of each paragraph from five to ten characters. But do not use indented form for headings, addresses, signatures, and so on, in typewritten letters, even though you indent the paragraphs in the body.

David Masterson
St. Thomas More College
Tower Hill, Massachusetts

The Holmes Advertising Agency
139 West 152 Street
New York 20, New York

N124 Use single spaces for typewritten letters that run to more than four or five lines. Leave one line-space between single-spaced paragraphs, two between double-spaced paragraphs.[30]

N125 Leave three line-spaces between the date and the first line of the address.[30]

N126 Leave a line-space between the address and the salutation and between the salutation and the first paragraph of the letter.[30]

N127 Leave two line-spaces between the last paragraph and the complimentary close, and four line-spaces between the complimentary close and the typed signature.[30]

N128 When the first page of the letter carries a printed letterhead, then only the date is typed by the writer.

N129 The complimentary close may be placed laterally anywhere to the right of an imaginary line drawn down the center of the letter. It is good form to place the complimentary close so that it lines up, flush left, with the typewritten date at the top of the letter.[30] But always place the complimentary close far enough to the left so that the handwritten signature does not have to run into the right-hand margin.

---

[30] See the illustration under N123. Except for N130, these directions are somewhat arbitrary. Styles of spacing and placement differ. But the main objective of all of them is to present a pleasing picture and to separate clearly the various parts of a letter. The directions given here accomplish that end.

N130 Unless you have written several times to the same corre-
spondent and know he will have no difficulty deciphering
your signature, add a typewritten signature. Never use a
typewritten signature only.[31]

N131 You may type your position in the firm directly under the
typewritten signature and lined up with it, flush left.

N132 Use indented form for handwritten business letters.

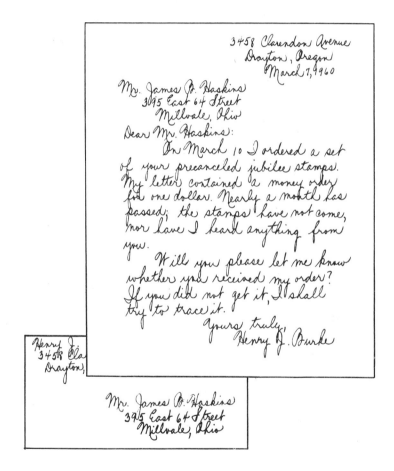

---

[31] Sometimes, usually in circulars, the name of the firm is typed after the complimentary close and followed by the written signature of the individual writer.

N133 Correct forms of address and salutation in business and formal letters are given below. (There are other, equally correct forms; but these will suffice.)[32]

Cardinal archbishop
His Eminence John Cardinal Hamilton
Archbishop of Hammondsport
135 Valley Drive
Hammondsport 3, Arizona
Your Eminence:

Cardinal
His Eminence Jules Cardinal Bourget
1492 West 63 Street
Kalmath Falls, New Hampshire
Your Eminence:

Archbishop
The Most Reverend Archbishop Henry McHarris, D.D.
16 Houston Avenue
Abilene 2, Texas
Your Excellency:

Bishop
The Most Reverend Nicholas Allen, D.D.
222 McKinley Place
Great Forks, Minnesota
Your Excellency:

Monsignor
The Right Reverend Monsignor Baffin Powell
221 North Main Boulevard
Portsmouth, Florida
Right Reverend Monsignor:

The Very Reverend Monsignor Herbert Holm
1459 Clement Street
Stillwater 7, Nevada
Very Reverend Monsignor:

---

[32] For punctuation of addresses and salutations, see D24-25 and D84. For capitals see H13-14.

Provincials of religious orders and congregations,
rectors of seminaries
The Very Reverend Herbert Neill, S.J.
4715 Central Avenue
Phoenix 6, Arizona
Very Reverend Father Neill:

Priest
The Reverend John Campbell[33]
2049 Parkside Boulevard
Toledo 7, Ohio
Dear Father Campbell:

Religious Brother
Brother Charles R. Skipwith, S.M.
Washington College
Washington Springs, Arkansas
Dear Brother Skipwith:

Nun
Reverend Mother M. George, S.H.C.J.
St. Mary's Convent
Albion, Kentucky
Dear Reverend Mother:

Sister M. Elizabeth, S.H.C.J.
Lady College
Trent 3, Iowa
Dear Sister Elizabeth:

Senator (national or state)
The Honorable John H. Madison[34]
The United States Senate
Washington, D.C.
Dear Sir:

Representative (national or state)
The Honorable Hugh A. Bradley[34]
The House of Representatives
Washington, D.C.
Dear Sir:

---

[33] The forms *Reverend Campbell, Dear Reverend Campbell,* or *Reverend* by itself are never to be used.

[34] The form *Honorable Madison* or *Bradley* is never to be used.

Governor
The Honorable Paul H. Bates[35]
Governor of Illinois
Springfield, Illinois
Dear Sir:

Mayor
The Honorable Ferris Payne[35]
Mayor of the City of Penceford
Penceford, Oregon
Dear Sir:

Judge (federal, state, and so on)
The Honorable Matthew Huntingdon[35]
United States District Judge
501 South Norton Street
Weaversville, Michigan
Dear Sir:

A senator, representative, and so on, and his wife
Honorable and Mrs. H. A. Bradley
Apartment 2B
12 Sheraton Square
New Bedford 17, Virginia
Dear Mr. and Mrs. Bradley:

Doctor
Dr. Colfax Twilliger
Medical Arts Building
4939 Maryland Avenue
New Orleans 12, Louisiana
Dear Dr. Twilliger:

A doctor and his wife
Dr. and Mrs. Colfax Twilliger[36]
The Cliff House
16 Bronson Road
William's Mills, Missouri
Dear Dr. and Mrs. Twilliger:

---

[35] The form *Honorable Bates, Payne,* or *Huntingdon* is never to be used.
[36] The form *Mrs. Dr. Twilliger* is never to be used.

476

Dean
Mr. Hobart Lane
Dean of the College of Arts and Sciences
St. James University
St. James, Idaho
Dear Dean Lane:

Business house
The American Soap Company
Stoddard Building
13-21 South 143 Street
Wrenton, North Carolina
Gentlemen:

Several men
Messrs. Mark and Cross
Roan and Seventh Avenues
Harpersburg 2, Wisconsin
Gentlemen:

One man
Mr. Lawrence Johnston
New Alton 6, Maine
Dear Mr. Johnston: (*or* Dear Sir:)

Several women
The Misses Templar
Templar Secretarial School
503 Iron Row
Norman 13, Illinois
Dear Ladies:

Mrs. Allen J. Crosby
Miss Ellen R. Scheinuk
16 Westpark Freeway
Clary, Minnesota
Dear Ladies:

One woman
Mrs. J. G. Barringer
3811 Cates Avenue
Chicago 25, Illinois
Dear Mrs. Barringer:

N134 There are a number of acceptable forms of complimentary close for business and formal letters. But those below are common and will suffice.[37]

Letters to clerics and members of religious orders
Respectfully yours,
Sincerely yours,

Letters to civil authorities
Very truly yours,
Sincerely yours,

Letters to all other persons
Sincerely yours,

CONTENT

N135 Be brief.

A Ordinarily keep your letter to one page or less in length.
B Do not become chatty.
C Confine yourself to one easily digested topic per letter. If there are several scarcely related topics, it is better to send several letters at once. This makes for brevity and easy reading, and permits the routing of different matters to different departments.
D Long compliments at the beginning or end of a business letter usually defeat their purpose by making the reader impatient. A short complimentary paragraph, provided you really have something to say, is in order. But avoid such bromides as *with every good wish* or *we hope that this finds you in good health.*

N136 Be plain.

A Do not use the peculiar jargon and wordy padding sometimes affected in business letters: *yours of the 7th inst. to hand; in reference to the matters that we have had under discussion, let me say that;* and so on.
B Avoid pomposity, ornament, gush, breeziness, long, involved sentence structures, and the passive voice.

---

[37] For punctuation of a complimentary close, see D26. For capitals see H15.

[Poor:] It is certainly hoped that our merchandise will meet with your complete satisfaction.

[Better:] I hope you will like the samples.

    c Use a straightforward *I* whenever you can (rather than *the writer,* a passive form, or *we*). *We,* however, is in order whenever you are expressing notions that clearly pertain to the organization rather than to an individual; for example, *we do not publish comic books.*

    d Avoid technical terms unless you have good reason for using them and are certain that your reader will recognize them.

[Poor:] The young man in question had a standard secondary education with the usual curriculum.

[Better:] He had an ordinary high-school education.

N137 Be accurate.

    a Supply all the information you should.

    b State definite qualities, quantities, order numbers, catalogue numbers, catalogue descriptions, dates, academic grades, places, names, ages, addresses, and so on.

    c Ordinarily acknowledge a previous letter received from your correspondent and give its date accurately. He will want to look up the carbon in his file and check what he said to you.

N138 Be prompt. Answer at the first reasonable opportunity.

Personal letters[38]

N139 Make your letters clean—free of smudges, visible erasures, mistakes, crossouts, corrections, and strike-overs.

N140 Write personal letters on white or light-colored stationery. The paper may be a single unfolded sheet varying in size from 5½ x 7 inches to 8½ x 11 inches; or the stationery may be in the form of a booklet.

---

[38] For punctuation of the various parts of letters, see D24-26 and D84. For capitals see H13-15.

N141 Use a black typewriter ribbon or blue, black, or blue-black ink.

N142 Use block form—no indentions—for typewritten letters. Leave a line-space between paragraphs of block-form letters. However, use an indented form for the paragraphs and headings of handwritten letters.[39]

N143 Center your letter on the paper so that the margins are balanced around it. The margins should never be less than half an inch wide; they may of course be wider if the message is short.

N144 Do not crowd the writing at the bottom of the page; start another page if it is necessary rather than destroy the appearance of your letter by cramped writing.

N145 If you use booklet paper, and the message is long enough to run to four pages, start at page 1 and go straight through to page 4. When the message is short, write on page 1; on pages 1 and 3; or on pages 1, 3, and 4.

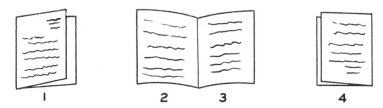

N146 It is customary to begin the letter with a heading in the upper right-hand corner. Write your street address on the first line; the city, zone number, and state on the second; and the date on the last. The rest of the heading may be omitted and only the date given if the recipient is certain to know your address or if the address is printed on the stationery.

---

[39] It is still rather common to use indented form for the paragraphs within the body of a typewritten letter. One may do so, indenting the first line of each paragraph from five to ten characters. But do not use indented form for headings, addresses, signatures, and so on, of typewritten letters or envelopes.

See N123 and N147 for examples of block-form and indented letters.

N147 Do not give the address of the recipient on the first page.

> Ozark Park
> Blue River, Missouri
> June 21, 1945

Dear Bob,

The directions you gave us for getting to the Park were helpful, all right. If we hadn't had them, we might find ourselves in Arkansas now — and still going. The detours we had to make were many, as you said, and rough, but we got along without trouble and arrived on time.

Will you do me a favor, Bob? Phone Mother and tell her we're all well. I should have written a letter to her yesterday but was too late for the mail. If she asks whether there's anything we want, tell her there is: some candy. Not chocolates, though; the weather is too warm.

Be sure to let us know when you're coming. We'll meet you at the train.

> Yours sincerely,
> Tom

O
P
Q

481

N148 These are correct forms of salutation in personal letters:

Dear Archbishop McHarris,	Dear Mayor Payne,
Dear Monsignor Powell,	Dear Dr. Twilliger,
Dear Father Campbell,	Dear Mr. Macklin,
Dear Brother Basil,	Dear Mrs. Barringer,
Dear Reverend Mother,	Dear Miss Templar,
Dear Sister Francis Regis,	Dear Tom,
Dear Senator Madison,	Dear Mother,

N149 The salutation beginning *My,* though somewhat more formal than the ones in N148, may be used in personal letters: *My dear Archbishop McHarris.*

N150 Never use *Sir* or *Madam* in a personal letter.

N151 *Dear Friend* and *Dear Miss* are not good form.

N152 The complimentary close should be in harmony with the salutation and tone of the letter.

    A *Sincerely yours* and *Yours sincerely* are the most formal.

    B *Cordially yours, Affectionately yours, Your loving son,* and similar expressions, suggest various degrees of affection and intimacy.

N153 A thank-you note may close with *Gratefully yours.*

O Description

In general

O1 Description is that form of writing or talking whose purpose is the creating of pictures, sounds, smells, and touch sensations in the imagination of the reader.[1]

O2 Pure description is description for its own sake and is nowadays seldom found except in books analyzing works of art, travelogues, and so on.

O
P
Q

---

[1] For matters not treated in this section but involving description, see R26-64 and P30-38.

O3 Running description is description used more or less incidentally to dress, enliven, or enrich narration, exposition, or argument. The description may be long (several paragraphs) or very short (just a word or two).

The viewpoint

O4 A viewpoint is the actual or imaginary position from which a writer or speaker sees what he is describing.

O5 Select a viewpoint and describe only what can be seen from it.

O6 Follow O5 with regard to the mental viewpoint or attitude of mind.

> For example, the appearance and character of a man are likely to seem very different to one who loves him, to one who hates him, to his valet, to his employer, to his dog, to a newsboy, to a man he has injured, and to a man to whom he has loaned money.

O7 When there is need, change the viewpoint.

O8 When you think that your reader might otherwise be confused, indicate that the viewpoint is changing.

From where we stood at the edge of the woods in front of it, we saw that the house was set in a clearing in the firs, halfway up the hillside, and that this gave it an air of privacy and rest. It was a large three-story frame building, whose weatherboarding had achieved by exposure to the

From where we stood at the edge of the woods in front of it states explicitly what the first viewpoint is; the two expressions *inside* and *at the rear of the house* give unmistakable notification of a change in the writer's viewpoint.

elements that shade known in Dallas as Lambert green, which makes houses look old, cool, and substantial. The front supported twin gables, each with its dormer window, one at either end of the gray slate roof. Tall chimneys rose above the ridge of the roof. There was nothing in the ensemble that an architect would care to sign his name to; but the house presented an agreeable, quiet welcome when first we came upon it in the clearing.

483

Inside, we were to discover, it was a pleasant-enough house if one intended to stay only the summer. The rooms were large and cool, the furniture plain but comfortable. The kitchen, a large, old-fashioned affair, was full of shining copperware hung on a rack above the table and on hooks about the walls. We liked it particularly.

At the rear of the house was a kind of patio with a little pool in the center, a place that invited me to set up my typewriter and table at once and get to work.

O9 Unless there is very good reason for not doing so,[2] finish with one viewpoint before going on to the next. Do not flit back and forth from one viewpoint to another.

O10 There is occasionally—not often—good reason for flitting back and forth from one viewpoint to another.

[In this passage, the writer wants sharp contrast. He has taken care, however, that there is no confusion:] I can explain the discrepancy, Your Excellency. Hale was in the hollow. I was on the hill. Hale saw only the cloud of dust that hung above the desert; I saw the flash of the sun on red tunics and gold braid. Hale heard only the faint sounds of a wagon caravan; I heard the staccato mutter of Spanish orders and Spanish replies. Hale smelled only the still air of the hollow; my nose was offended by the reek of the corpses jolting along in the last wagon. When I add that Hale had strictest orders not to leave the hollow in any contingency, it must be clear that this court-martial is doing him the gravest injustice, especially now that he is dead and can offer no defense.

The basic image

O11 In descriptions of some length or complication, ordinarily begin with the basic image.[3]

O12 In visual description, the basic image usually consists of the general size, shape, and color of the object.

It was a large white house, modeled on Mount Vernon and set in a great sweep of lawn.

---

[2] See O10.
[3] See O12-18.

He was a great, dark brute of a man, with a huge torso balanced on absurdly inadequate-looking legs.

O13 Often enough, the size, the shape, or the color is omitted from the basic image when one or another of them is of no significance to the description.

He was a great brute of a man, with a huge torso balanced on absurdly inadequate-looking legs.

O14 In auditory description, the basic image usually consists of a general classification of the sound that is heard.

As we turned the corner, our ears were assailed by a loud roar compounded of many noises, all fierce and frightening.

I noticed at first that it was a kind of light tapping, a sound I had never heard before, but similar to something I had heard.

O15 In tactile description, the basic image usually consists of a general classification of the touch sensation.

I felt something wet and viscous, and wondered for a moment whether I had put my hand into one of the still-warm pots on the stove.

Steve felt the dry, ropelike thing stir and writhe in his grip.

O16 In olfactory description, the basic image usually consists of a general classification of the smell as strong or faint, pleasant or disagreeable, and so on.

It was a pungent, disagreeable odor that seemed to envelop the whole quarter of town where the stockyards lay.

O17 In the description of things that are not experienced by the external senses (for instance, a mood or a person's character), the basic "image" is usually a general classification of the thing as good, bad, timid, dull, weary, hopeless, uneasy, cheerful, or something of the kind.

Von Tolen wasn't at all what you would expect a Prussian general to be. He was a nervous little mouse of a man, quite afraid of the world.

I can describe the feeling only as a special sort of uneasiness, a pleasantly unpleasant expectation that something exciting was going to happen.

485

O18 Occasionally it is quite reasonable to begin even a long or complicated description with something other than the fundamental image of the object.

What I noticed first was an eyebrow—a most imperious eyebrow, raised above a cold blue eye. When finally I was able to detach my attention from the eyebrow, I found that the eye was contemplating me steadily over a frond of one of those potted plants that some hotel managers still use to underscore the general ugliness of lobbies.

In this passage the writer has decided to make capital of one feature of his character—an eyebrow. He intends to harp on that eyebrow from time to time in the course of his story and so begins his description with it.

Filling in the picture

O19 Once you have the basic image, set down the most striking features of the object and then fill in a few minor details, if they are necessary to the description or will enrich it.

[Basic image:] One's first impression of Mr. Starrett was of a tall, dark, very slender man—with teeth. [Most striking features:] These teeth were not crooked, did not protrude, lacked none of their lawful number. Those above meshed nicely with those below. All of them were Mr. Starrett's own. Indeed, they were such unexceptionable teeth that it is a wonder that they were the first thing about him that one noticed. One noticed them because they were always, always visible, gleaming and resplendent, between lips fixed in a perpetual, mocking smile—a smile quite without common mirth but full of relish for some secret joke that Mr. Starrett found in everything he looked upon. The smile disappeared only when he gazed into a mirror. He seemed to find no joke there, and so the teeth retreated for the nonce to well-earned privacy and concealment.

[Minor details:] The rest of Mr. Starrett was good to look at. There were no unseemly bulges to betray his forty years. His handsome head was set with becoming features: intelligent-seeming eyes; a nose not too thin, not too gross; a manly chin. His hands were as slender as he and as graceful. He wore his comfortable clothes comfortably and looked like neither a movie star nor a stuffy bourgeois nor an eccentric. If it had not been for his smile, one would have found him pleasant to behold and would have been mildly interested in making his acquaintance.

O20 Occasionally, especially for reasons of emphasis, it is best to save your most striking detail till the last.

The mother superior was an energetic, intelligent woman, rather small in size and small in feature, movement, and gesture. She was more than approachable and genuinely interested in nearly everyone she met. She inspired respect and confidence; no one was ever known to treat her casually. This agreeable composition of qualities and appearance became remarkable when one finally noticed that she was blind—more so when one was told that she had been blind for thirty years.

The town was just as I had remembered it: the one dusty-yellow street with a line of stores on each side, gat-toothed with vacant lots; the church and the courthouse facing each other near the middle of town; and the water trough, dry for years, in front of the post office. There was one difference. The place was deserted.

BRIEF SKETCHES

O21 Often the full technique—basic image, striking details, and minor details—cannot be used without halting the theme objectionably. When this happens, do a brief sketch, selecting one or two striking or fundamental features of the object and letting them suggest the rest.

Brown entered a room that was *all glitter and gleam, from the chandeliers to the men's shirt fronts and the women's jewelry.* He hurried in the wake of his *frenzied* hostess from group to group, murmuring in response to introductions and moving on before he could make sure of a single name or face. Finally he was deposited near the refreshments with a trio that Mrs. Daggers seemed to think he might complement: *an empty-headed blonde occupied in saying nothing and sweeping the room with a selective eye; a handsome man who looked like an executive* and who turned out to be an executive's secretary; and Miss Dutreil. He would hardly have noted Miss Dutreil, *fortyish, mousy, and dowdy,* if she had not said a remarkable thing.

She said, "Mr. Brown, you were not in Mexico City last November, as you said you were."

That startled Brown into rudeness. "Just what are you talking about?" he asked.

P Narration

In general

P1 Narration is that form of talking or writing that has for its purpose the relating of a series of events.[1]

The narrative theme

P2 A narrative theme is a theme whose purpose is the relating of a series of events.

CHOOSING A SUBJECT

P3 Not the subject, but the treatment must be new.

P4 When the subject of a narrative theme has not been assigned or has not suggested itself naturally, jotting down the answers to these questions may stimulate your imagination a bit:

A What happened to me during the first eight years of my life that impressed me or others as interesting, strange, humorous, puzzling, difficult, or splendid? What happened during the second eight years?

B What problem, interest, amusing thing, hope, fear, fascination has occupied my mind a good deal lately?

---

[1] Almost always, the four forms of discourse (exposition, narration, description, and argument) are mingled in a composition of any length at all. Thus it happens that a narration may contain exposition, and so on.

c What have I read, heard, or seen that stirred, delighted, or amused me or that made me think?

d What do I dislike heartily?

e What do I like particularly?

f What have I discovered about living that is different from what people have told me it is or should be?

g What is there worth remarking about my dog or cat, my enemy, my friend, my father, my mother, or someone or something else that plays a large part in my life?

h What would I like to do with my life?

i What would I care to change in the world at large or in my world?

j What is that unusual life, so different from my own, that attracts me, even though the possibility of my living it is remote or nonexistent?

P5 Once you have a central idea for a narrative, start thinking around the subject that has occurred to you. Start doodling; that is, start writing down the fragmentary ideas that occur to you.

[Central idea:] Pirates

[Doodling:] I like pirates. I like pirates?

Why? Costumes? Life they lead? I wouldn't want to be a pirate in real life. Stinking ships. Why do I like pirates? Ah, because they did brave deeds gracefully.

I'll bet they seldom did. Or very few of them. My whole idea is based on Francis Drake, Rafael Sabatini, Hornblower stories, and Hollywood pirates.

I could *play* a pirate in Hollywood. Fun. Well, I could be an extra, anyway. Wear a cutlass and swing it. Imagine playing a pirate-extra in Hollywood and then having to come home each day to ordinary life.

Could do that. Have character play pirate-extra, then come home to drab, lonely life. Decides he will live like pirate. Turns home into ship. Builds crow's-nest atop chimney. Makes dog walk plank. Gets into trouble with neighbors for running up Jolly Roger on television aerial and striding up and down on front porch with patch over one eye, hailing passing pedestrians with "Ship ahoy!" County-asylum people arrive.

489

THE THEME TOPIC[2]

P6 When you have a subject and some ideas about it, select a theme topic.

P7 Upon the selection of your theme topic will depend to some extent the kind of treatment your narrative is to get: humorous, acid, sympathetic, and so on. On it will depend what you are going to stress: action, character, atmosphere, and so on.

Five ridiculous things happened when John Curlew tried to play pirate.[3]	This theme topic stresses events. In the development character will probably turn out to be secondary.
John Curlew was born out of time, as he discovered when he tried to play pirate.	This stresses character. In the development events will probably turn out to be secondary, though not unimportant.
There is no room for fools like Mr. J. Curlew, pirate, in this modern world.	This is unsympathetic—even acid. The emphasis will probably be on character.
Playing pirate, Mr. Curlew found himself beset by a world hostile to simple delight.	This is sympathetic to the main character—even sentimental. The treatment may be rather whimsical.
Against the drabness of a suburban neighborhood, John Curlew flashed madly for a moment, then was abruptly extinguished.	This stresses atmosphere, impressions, emotional reactions, and that sort of thing.

P8 Write out the theme topic. Writing it out often exposes weaknesses in it. A written theme topic, moreover, lying on your desk before your eyes, is a constant reminder of what the theme is about and keeps you from straying off into useless digressions.

---

[2] For the notion of theme topic, see M9-11.

[3] The theme topics given here are all based on the doodling that illustrates P5.

P9 If it is at all possible to do so—and it almost always is—state your theme topic in a single, uncomplicated, declarative sentence:

A A single, uncomplicated sentence—because the briefer and less complicated the theme topic, the easier it is to develop it coherently.

B A declarative sentence—because questions do not indicate and limit development. There are innumerable developments possible if the theme topic is "How did Denton beat Plainville?" But the two chief parts of the theme are already plain if the theme topic is "Denton beat Plainville by using a modified T and concentrating on Joe Jacoby."

C A complete sentence—because half-sentences and very elliptical sentences cause the same trouble that questions do.

P10 Limit the range of your ideas sharply when stating the theme topic, or you will find yourself writing an endless narrative.

P11 Make the theme topic as definite as you reasonably can.

[Vague, leading to uncertain planning and development:] It required several things to bring Dan McKay to terms.

[Definite, leading to clear-cut planning and development:] It required four attacks to force Dan McKay to resign.

THE PLAN OR PLOT

P12 Once you have written down your theme topic, write a plan or plot:[4]

A List and number the main events of your narrative in the order in which you wish to present them.

B Under each of these main events, list circumstances that contribute notably to it.

C Do not go into detail.

---

[4] The outline of a narrative is called a plan when it is the skeleton of a straight narrative (P42) and a plot when it is the skeleton of a plot narrative (P43).

ᴅ To avoid complications use the vivid present whenever you can. (In developing the plot or plan into a full narrative, ordinarily use the past.)

Plan of a narrative letter

Theme topic.—I am quite all right after being lost for a night.

1. I meet Eileen and make a date with her.
   In front of the church, on Sunday.
   As I am bringing boys from my camp to church.
2. I set out Monday evening in a canoe for Eileen's camp.
   It is two miles away directly across the lake.
   From there we are to use her car to drive to town for a movie.
3. I am taken from my course by a bonfire.
   I think it is directly in front of Camp Moony.
   It is either to the east or to the west of Moony.
   It is deserted.
4. Lost now, I paddle in one direction for a while.
   There is nothing by which to take a bearing.
5. I enter an inlet.
   The night is so dark that I cannot see anything but the shore that I am keeping on my right.
   As a result, I enter inlet after inlet, without knowing that I am doing so.
6. I discover that I am hopelessly lost.
7. I decide to tie up for the night.
   The night is long, but I have cigarettes; the night is cold, but I have a jacket.
8. At dawn, I find my way to Eileen's camp.
   She has aroused both camps.
   A search for me is on.
9. There are no bad aftereffects to the misadventure.

Letter developed from the plan above

> Camp Woogwooly
> Oskwog, Maine
> July 6, 1954

Dear Mom,

Now that you are hearing from me in person, you will have to believe that I am quite all right. I am glad that Mr. Twiller's telegram reached you in time to keep you from making a useless trip up here. It was silly of Joe to alarm you with his telephone call. Of

492

course, I'd like to see you; but I know that you would hardly welcome the expense of an unnecessary trip, especially now that things are not going well with Dad.

Here is the correct version of what happened, Joe's hysterical account notwithstanding. (Joe loves drama; you should know that.)

On Sundays I round up the boys in the camp and take them to church. Last Sunday—that was July 3—I met Eileen Kirsch just as we were going into the church. I had had no idea that she was up in this neck of the woods; and, as you can imagine, I was quite surprised and delighted to see her. It turns out that she is a counselor at a girls' camp near here, a much ritzier place than ours, situated just across the lake from us. Well, we made a date for the following night. Both of us welcomed the prospect of one evening away from the brats. (I like the kids in my cabin: they're fun and as interesting as ants under glass. They can teach me at least as much as I can teach them. On the whole they're well behaved, too; so I really can't complain. But once in a while I want to get away from their treble squeak. They sound like mice on a hot griddle.)

On Monday, then, I set out in one of our canoes for Eileen's camp, Moonetonkwonk. (These pseudoaboriginal names!) Eileen has a car up here with her, and we intended to use it to drive into town for a show. The movie and a drugstore are all that Oskwog has to offer in the way of night life—which is monotonous but convenient for my wallet. Now, the camp lies just across the lake, not more than two miles from us. I should have been able to hit it swimming blindfold under water. And I *would* have hit it, had I not been seduced from my course by the flickering of a bonfire.

Moony, I thought, is the only place hereabout that would build a bonfire; so that must be Moony.

I steered for the fire and was right upon it before I realized that it must be a good distance either to the east or to the west of Moony, since there was no sign of the camp. There wasn't so much as a star overhead; and, looking back across the lake, I found I couldn't see even the glimmer of a lamp at Woogwooly from which to take a bearing. I realize now that a little hill to the west of us must have come between me and the lights in the boys' cabins.

For a minute or so I sat staring across the bow at the bonfire. It was utterly deserted. The girls must have set it earlier and gone off and left it—bad woodcraft, even for a girls' camp. (To be quite

493

frank, they're usually much more careful about that sort of thing than we are.)

Well, I thought, there's nothing to do but to try the east or the west; and, since I don't know where the camp is, I'll go on in the direction in which the canoe is drifting. So, not alarmed but merely anxious not to be very late for my date, I struck out into the darkness ahead, keeping the shore on my right.

The night was really very dark; otherwise I would have noticed that I was leaving the lake and entering an inlet. As I know now, the inlet opened into other inlets and sloughs. By keeping a shoreline always on my right, I found my way—without realizing what was happening—from one pass to another, until I was trapped in a labyrinth of small waterways. It was not until, after some time, I had decided that I had gone east far enough, and had reversed my course, that I discovered what had happened to me. Almost immediately I was confronted by a shoreline that should not have been lying across my bow. For a moment I was confused, then I understood the situation. I paddled a bit longer to see if I could find a way out; but every five minutes or so brought me up against banks or shore that were unfamiliar, until it was painfully clear that I no longer knew north from nougat. It seemed foolish to spend the night threshing about in a maze; so I tied the canoe to a willow, put on my jacket and pulled the collar up about my ears, and spent the night smoking cigarettes and sleeping. To be quite candid, I did a good deal more sleeping than smoking. The bottom of the canoe was not altogether uncomfortable; there was plenty of room to stretch out; there was a cushion for my head.

At dawn I found my way, without much difficulty now that I could see, to Moonetonkwonk to let Eileen know what had happened. It was then that I found out that she had become alarmed, had phoned our camp, alarmed Joe, and started that torchlight boat-search on the lake that he told you about. I'm afraid the brats very much enjoyed looking for my body.

So there's the whole thing. You will want to know if I was cold. Not very. The nights up here, even in July, are not warm; but I had my jacket. Was I frightened? Yes, but not very much. Were there any aftereffects? Well, I was hungry from doing a lot of paddling I had not expected to do.

All my love to you,

PETER

TWO SERIES OF EVENTS

P13 Whenever you can do so without injury to the content or the reader's interest, write a separate narrative for each series of events. But it sometimes happens that two series of events that come together at one or two points must be kept going in the same narrative.

P14 Draw a two-column plan or plot, one column for each series of events. Encircle and connect those events in which the two series converge.

Wyck series	*Alfredo series*
1. General Wyck and General Alfredo plan to converge on Templi. Alfredo from east, Wyck from southwest. Rendezvous set for 8:00 A.M. the next day.	1. General Wyck and General Alfredo plan to converge on Templi. Alfredo from east, Wyck from southwest. Rendezvous set for 8:00 A.M. the next day.
2. Wyck makes better time than he had expected. Roads in better shape than reported. No mechanical trouble in motorized units.	2. A bridge halts Alfredo for four hours. Patrols had mistakenly reported it safe. It must be shored up.
3. At 3:00 P.M. of first day, Wyck meets and overcomes resistance. Ambush by small party causes delay of one hour.	3. Unmapped Fascist mine field delays Alfredo another three hours. Several casualties.
4. Nonetheless Wyck manages to arrive at rendezvous on time.	4. Alfredo arrives at Templi at 3:00 P.M. of second day, seven hours late for rendezvous. Hears no firing. No sound of Wyck.
5. At 8:00 A.M. sharp, Wyck attacks Templi. Meets full resistance. No diversion from the east.	5. Decides not to attack but to make contact with Wyck. Circles wide to southwest.

495

6. After five hours he retires. Four fifths of his troops are casualties.
7. At safe distance he sits down to wait for word of Alfredo.

> 8. Alfredo meets Wyck.
> 9. They decide to combine forces and attack again from southwest.
> 10. They are routed.

11. Wyck is killed.

> 6. Alfredo meets Wyck.
> 7. They decide to combine forces and attack again from southwest.
> 8. They are routed.

9. Alfredo leads remnant of forces back to Alva. Two thirds casualties.
10. Alfredo thinks it would have been better to halve forces after making contact and follow original plan.

Narrative developed from the plan above

The loss of Templi did not receive much publicity during the war, presumably for reasons of security. After the war, as far as I have been able to discover, it received no attention whatever. Yet it is a rather interesting episode in the fierce battle for the Micarno region.

Two identical forces—each a mixture of Italian and American infantry complemented by American tanks and other motorized units, one under the command of Brigadier General Maurice L. Wyck of the United States Army, the other under General Almiral Alfredo of the friendly Italian forces fighting with the Americans in Italy—planned to converge on the little but strategic town of Templi for a concerted attack at eight the following morning.

Wyck was to attack from the southwest, Alfredo from the east—the only other approach offering good cover.

Their divergent routes were about equal in length; so the two forces set out for Templi at the same time.

From the time that he left Alva, Wyck's progress was much more rapid than he had expected it to be. For once, reconnaissance had been wrong in the right way; the roads turned out to be in much better condition than reports had indicated. Moreover, the motorized units proceeded without the mechanical breakdowns so usual that commanding officers come to consider them inevitable—breakdowns that can snarl traffic for hours on narrow byways.

At 3:00 P.M., however, Wyck did run into trouble. A small party of Fascists fighting for the Germans—less than fifty—held up the advance for a little less than an hour with four machine guns, two of which swept the road where it passed through a narrow defile. They were finally cleared out without the loss of one American or allied soldier; and Wyck proceeded on his way, still well ahead of schedule.

The roads continued good; and so Wyck arrived at the southwestern approach to Templi well before his time, deployed his forces, and entered battle at precisely 8:00 A.M.

Within an hour it was apparent that he was meeting the full resistance of Templi. No one was creating a diversion at the eastern end of the little town. Hard pressed for a decision, Wyck fanned his men out in a quarter circle in the southwest and did what he could with what he had.

Where was Alfredo? Shortly after setting out from Alva, he had run into a serious annoyance. A bridge, the only crossing of the Laruna within miles, lay in his path. Whether through mistake or carelessness, patrols had reported the bridge to be in good shape. Alfredo discovered that it practically required rebuilding before it could sustain his vehicular traffic. Quite understandably loath to abandon his motor units, he spent four precious hours shoring up the supports with timbers and laying steel mats across its rotted, sagging floor.

Hardly had he crossed the bridge and once more achieved a good forward pace, when the head of his column tripped the first of the mines that Fascists had laid both across the road and a good distance to either side of it. Progress was agonizingly slow as his men cautiously picked their way, not without casualties, through the mine fields. To hurry the men would have been to murder a good number of them. His tension and irritation mounting as the precious moments fled by, Alfredo finally had to resign himself to arriving at least seven hours late for his rendezvous.

Meanwhile, at Templi, Wyck's unsupported troops were getting a very bad worst of it. By one o'clock four fifths of his men were casualties. He then made a decision that he would have made hours before had he not momently expected the arrival of Alfredo in the east. He withdrew to a safe distance and sat down to wait for word of Alfredo.

Some two hours after Wyck's withdrawal, Alfredo arrived at the eastern approach to Templi. There was, of course, no sight or sound of Wyck, since firing had ceased a good deal earlier. At this juncture, Alfredo proceeded more wisely than had Wyck. He determined to make contact with the latter before attacking the town.

497

Consequently, he circled widely to the southwest until he came upon Wyck with the remaining fifth of his forces.

At the conference that ensued, three possible plans lay before the generals: to give up Templi as lost; to combine forces and attack at one point; to divide their combined forces in two and proceed on the original plan of simultaneous attacks from the east and southwest.

It is a credit to their valor—though perhaps not to their military acumen—that they never seriously considered their first plan. They chose the second. But now, with the element of surprise gone and their total troops reduced almost by half, the attempt ended in a complete rout of the Americans and their allies and in the death of Wyck, who was killed in his command car. Alfredo limped back to Alva with only one third of the men who had set out from there two days or so before.

Assessing the defeat afterward, Alfredo said that he was now convinced that he and Wyck had made the wrong decision, that it would have been better to halve forces and follow the original plan of simultaneous attacks from two approaches.

Be that as it may, it is clear even to the layman that the battle of Templi was fought with a shocking disregard for elementary communications between separated groups. Had Alfredo been able to warn Wyck that he would be seven hours late in reaching the town, Wyck would have been able to hold his attack. Military men whom I quizzed about the affair were inclined, almost to a man, to shrug their shoulders and remark that not even in World War II were communications always what they should have been. In the case of Templi, that fact spelled disaster.

P15 When treating two separate series of events in the same narrative—[5]

   A Change from one series to the other no oftener than is necessary.

   B But do not let one series go unmentioned so long that the reader may forget about it.

   C Announce the changes from one series to another by bridge expressions like *meanwhile, on the other side of the river*, and so on.[6]

---

[5] See the example of a theme under P14.
[6] For a treatment of bridge expressions, see M25-31.

INTRODUCING AND CONCLUDING A NARRATIVE

P16 Ordinarily introduce a narrative in which initial suspense is not a major factor in one of these ways:

A By stating the theme topic in palatable fashion.

> [Theme topic:] I have found a friend.
>
> [Introduction containing theme topic:] We use a lot of words carelessly, and one of them is loneliness. Until I came to live alone for five years under the cold eyes of the Tarrana Indians, I had no idea what it meant. And that is why the next sentence has enormous significance for me. Today I have found a friend.

B By answering the questions *who, what, when, where, how,* and *why*—or as many of them as you find useful.

> After trailing Saulter High School for three quarters, the Bishop High School Marauders managed to salvage a 7-6 victory in the last three minutes of play this afternoon at Barry Stadium. Ten thousand prep-football fans watched the thrilling close of the game, as the Marauders uncorked everything they had in a desperate but successful effort to keep the state-championship trophy for another year.

P17 When your story is such that it would gain by being lively from the first word on, start it in one of the following ways and *only then* use one of the introductions of P16.[8]

A Start the story with an incident.

> Petrie had been watching for an hour, but nothing had happened in the tall gray house across the street. No matter; he had at his disposal all the hours that he would need, and he was determined to spend them in patience. He had come to the end of a long quest, and his quarry was in the gray house across the street. It would be silly, he thought, to let himself become impatient now after having been patient for so very many years. But he had to own to a certain excitement now that the end had come. He could not afford that excitement. His finger must be steady on the trigger. No slips.

---

[7] For general notions about introductions and conclusions, see M2-7 and M36.
[8] See P18-19.

Quite suddenly, without warning, the blank face of the gray house took on expression. The front door was opening. It did not open wide. Someone, standing in the shadow of the hall beyond the door, was looking out carefully before venturing on to the porch. "But he can't see me," thought Petrie, and the corners of his mouth rose in the faintest parody of a smile.

Now the person, apparently having discovered nothing to suggest retreat, stepped out on the porch. When the morning sunlight fell full across his face, Petrie gazed at it in unbelief and dismay. The wrong man! And yet he knew for certain that there had been only one man in the house. Then his eyes narrowed. No. Of course. The fellow had simply shaved off the beard. This was his man.

The man took a packet of cigarettes from his pocket, fished in it for a moment very deliberately, turning his head meanwhile to take in the whole length of the street, and finally put a cigarette into his mouth. His hand went back to his pocket for a match.

Petrie fired. The man crumpled to the floor of the porch, kicked grotesquely for a moment, and then lay still.

[The methods of P16 start here:] It was a long road that had led Petrie to the window across the street from the tall gray house where a man now lay dead on the porch. It began in Harley, Connecticut, where Petrie—Hale Petrie, quite respectable then before things had begun to happen to him, and a man who had never thought of killing—had worked behind the soda fountain of the only drugstore in the village and dreamed of marrying Cally Ralls [and so on].

B Start the story with a conversation.

"It is too bad, isn't it," sighed Letitia, "that whenever a really eligible man finds his way by accident to Bancroft, he is bagged by the Daltons before he can get to know any of the rest of us charming people."

"Eligible?" inquired Alice Train, as sharp and angular a woman as Letitia was round and placid.

"Eligible for Helen and Esther, of course." Letitia's candor was by turns amusing or disconcerting. "You do know, my dear—let's not pretend that you don't; we've known and liked each other too long for that—that I have two daughters who are of no earthly use to me and whom I should like to marry off to two pleasant, guileless, unsuspecting, well-to-do men."

"Why guileless and unsuspecting, Mamma?" asked Esther, stepping inopportunely from the house to the terrace where Letitia and Alice were sitting in the sun.

"You weren't supposed to hear that, my love," sighed Letitia.

"But I did hear it. So you might as well tell me. Why guileless and unsuspecting?"

"Well, then, my sweet—because someone not guileless and unsuspecting might discover, before he married you, that you, my dove, are a shrew; and that your sister, for all her appearance of cheerful vigor, has the backbone of an oyster and the same colorful personality."

[The methods of P16 start here:] Meanwhile, at the other end of town, the eligible young man most recently bagged by the Daltons was just waking from a prolonged rest in the comfortable bed in the best Dalton guest room. He was Herbert Q. Waterman—and looked it, right down to the Q. He understood very well that in Bancroft he was a catch, and he intended to do nothing to dispel that notion. The fact that his total wealth [and so on].

P18 Not every story should begin briskly, and so an incident or a conversation is not to be used in every case. Gauge the mood of your narrative.

P19 You must not keep the reader waiting too long before you use one or both of the introductions of P16. So keep the opening incident or conversation short. How short depends on the length of the story. A reader does not mind waiting as much as a chapter or two in a long novel; but in a rather short story—say, five hundred words—he ordinarily does not care to wait beyond a few paragraphs.

P20 Ordinarily conclude a straight narrative[9] in one of the following ways or by a combination of two or more of them:

A By giving a variation of the introduction.

[Introduction:] We use a lot of words carelessly, and one of them is loneliness. Until I came to live alone for five years under the cold eyes of the Tarrana Indians, I had no idea what it meant. And that is why the next sentence has enormous significance for me. Today I have found a friend.

---

[9] See P42.

[Conclusion:] And so I have a friend. Xuatl has all the filthy customs and manners of his people. When he grins at me with his filed teeth, he looks more like hunger than benevolence. But he has offered me a precious gift. He is sincere; he is good. I need his friendship; and he, poor man, has need of what I can give him.

B By pointing a moral, a lesson, or a conclusion, from the events related in the theme.

His had been what many an unthinking man would call a full life. Yet, when he came to die, he could not look back on a single act that would bring him comfort in his last conscious moment, ease his passage into eternity, or give him something to say to his judge. In the next world he must stand mute before God—he mute, who had so many frivolous things to say as he wasted away his precious years entertaining his pathetic little coterie.

C By recapitulating the main events of the narrative.

That is my story. It differs strikingly from the wild tales circulated by my adversaries. I was in France working on the *Herald* at the time that they claim I was in Moscow. From France I went to China to cover the fall of Nanking. From China I returned to California, where I have lived in retirement and silence until this moment, when the FBI has permitted me to speak and set the record straight.

D By speculating about subsequent events.

There you have the situation at the present time. No one would care to risk his reputation on a flat statement of what tomorrow will bring. But I am willing to hazard a guess, if it will be accepted as a guess and nothing more: Within thirty-six hours Paneast-Falton will sit down with union officials to write a new contract that will involve considerable compromise on both sides.

E By an observation not closely, yet not too remotely connected with the events of the narrative.

As the roar of that holocaust died and the gruesome work of separating bodies from the debris began, a boy who could hardly have been more than seventeen years old looked at me and said, "Golly, what a show!" He seemed pleased. I can only hope that he was hysterical.

502

PARAGRAPHING NARRATIVES[10]

P21 Many a narrative paragraph cannot be said in any strict sense to have a topic thought.[11] You will therefore need the following rules and suggestions.

P22 In general: when you are not dealing with topic thoughts, group in paragraphs those events and thoughts that. go together naturally.

P23 Start a new paragraph when the focus shifts to another character or set of characters.

> By half past ten, though Elise had left, it seemed that the bickering would go on all night. Groot, as usual, spoke right on without listening to anyone else. Aunt Tib made querulous little side remarks that sounded like the piping of a frightened bird above the storm. Peleas and Melisande added to the din by barking through the windows at the sort of thing that dogs see and bark at in the night.
>
> [Focus shifts; so a new paragraph:] William, in the meantime, had said nothing. It is not my quarrel, he thought, and any attempt to get into it will be resented as an intrusion.

P24 Start a new paragraph when there is a shift in mood or atmosphere.

> The little girl's face was, to be sure, a picture of woe. If she had been the sort to cry, she would have been crying; and somehow it pierced the heart of the bystanders the more deeply that she was not crying. The whole thing was the more poignant because we did not know her language and could not help her at all.
>
> [Mood shifts; so a new paragraph:] Quite without prelude to prepare us for the change, all shadows fled from her face and were replaced by a smile so warm and a glance so bright that one felt as one does when a fire is lighted in a cold and lonely cabin in the wilderness.

P25 Start a new paragraph when events take a turn from the line that they have been pursuing.

---

[10] For the punctuating and paragraphing of dialogue, see D119.
[11] See L8-13 and L15.

It was an ordeal for which they were not prepared, that trek through the desert. For days without end, it seemed, they made their way through all but intolerable heat and then at night sat or lay half frozen as close as they could get to the fire.

[Events take a turn; so a new paragraph:] About the seventh day Stebbins made a proposal that was to render life easier for a time but was eventually to lead them into disaster. He suggested that they sleep by day inside and underneath the wagons and travel by night.

P26 Start a new paragraph when there is a lapse of time.

He bade farewell several times to Miss Lindsey, started out the wrong door, found the right one, hooked his sleeve on its knob, disentangled himself, tripped over his own feet, and finally took his departure.

[Lapse of time; so a new paragraph:] Fifteen minutes later he was back again to retrieve his hat, which Miss Lindsey handed him without a word. She was quite afraid to speak.

P27 Start a new paragraph when there is a break in the action.

Hurtling down the slope, it crashed from boulder to boulder with harsh rending and pounding noises, and finally disappeared over the brink. After several moments there came from below the faint sound of a splash. Then all was still.

[Break in the action; so a new paragraph:] We looked at one another stunned.

P28 Start a new paragraph when there is a change of setting.

Altogether it was an unlovely forest whose great trees lifted their arms above us not so much, it seemed, in benediction as in a gesture of menace and oppression.

[Change of setting; so a new paragraph:] At length we emerged from the woods onto the plain. Here an immense prospect lay before us, apparently bounded only by the horizon and rolling away in gentle swells to the west.

P29 Start a new paragraph when there is a change from one series of events to another.

Hard pressed for a decision, Wyck fanned his men out in a quarter circle in the southwest and did what he could with what he had.

[Change from one series of events to another; so a new paragraph:] Where was Alfredo? Shortly after setting out from Alva, he had run into a serious annoyance. A bridge [and so on].

DESCRIPTION IN NARRATIVES

P30 Narratives that neglect the help of description are bare, colorless, dead. They are suitable only for reports in which dryness is at a premium. Ordinarily it is not enough to relate what people do, say, or think; you must often tell how they do, say, or think it.

P31 To make a narrative vivid, give dramatic details of bodily action.[12]

[Without details:] Jack gave an utterly inadequate answer.

[With details:] Jack flushed to the roots of his hair. He dropped his gaze to the floor, ran his finger around the edge of his collar, coughed once or twice, and finally stammered out an utterly inadequate answer.

P32 To make a narrative vivid, give dramatic details of sense perception. In other words, tell what your character sees, hears, feels with his sense of touch, and—if it will help—what he smells and tastes. Do not exhaust one sense and then go on to the next. Mingle the sensations in the same way in which one experiences them in real life. Combine this method with P31.[12]

[Without details:] With a great effort Hawkins jumped, caught the top of the wall, and pulled himself up.

[With details:] Hawkins leaped mightily for the top of the wall. His upflung right hand slapped smartly on the ledge and found a grip. The gulp of air that had been burning his lungs rushed through his lips in a tearing gasp. Dangling from a wrist already aching and beginning to swell, he cautiously brought his other hand up and rubbed in the loose cement at the top of the wall for a grip. He stayed there a moment, his head hanging back and his face turned upward, the sweat running into his eyes and turning

---

[12] See P36.

greasy and chill on his cheeks, where the fitful and ironically play-
ful breeze kissed them for a moment. He clawed at the wall with
his bare feet and heard the disgusting scrape of his nails against
the bricks. Finally his toes found a crevice. Summoning his strength
in a second effort that ran like fire down his arms and cut like a
knife through his toes, he pulled himself to where he could get one
leg over the wall, and then the rest of his body to the ledge. For
a moment he lay there, his face in the dusty, crumbling cement
still warm from the sun that had gone down hours before. The salt
sweat ran into his mouth, mitigating the dryness but not the thirst.

P33 To make a narrative vivid, give dramatic details of emotional reactions. In other words, tell in some detail what
your character feels.[13]

I was no sooner certain of my opponent's death than I began to
feel sick, faint, and *terrified*. The hot blood was running over my
back and chest. The dirk, where it had pinned my shoulder to the
mast, seemed to burn like a hot iron; *yet it was not so much these
real sufferings that distressed me, for these, it seemed to me, I
could bear without a murmur; it was the horror I had upon my
mind of falling down from the crosstrees into that still green water
beside the body of the coxswain.*

I clung with both hands till my nails ached, and I shut my eyes
as if to cover up the peril. Gradually my mind came back again, my
pulses quieted down to a more natural time, and I was once more
in possession of myself.[14]

P34 To make a narrative vivid, give dramatic details of thinking and speaking. In other words, you can often improve
a passage by telling not only what your character does,
senses, and feels, but also what he thinks or says, or
both—quoting his thought and speech either directly or
indirectly.[15]

[Without details:] The boys went down to the junk yard and
sold the car.

[With details:] The boys went down to the junk yard and sold
the car. Gol-lee! thought George; fifteen dollars. That will pay the

[13] See P36.

[14] Robert Louis Stevenson, *Treasure Island* (New York: Heritage Press, 1941),
pp. 156-57. The italics are the editor's.

[15] See P35-36.

whole debt and leave two dollars to spend after the dance. But since he knew how Tracy felt about giving up the jalopy, he kept the elation out of his face and merely muttered, "Well, that's that. Let's get out of here."

P35 Direct quotation (the speaker's own words) is usually more vivid than indirect quotation *(he said that, they asked whether)* and therefore better in climaxes. But either sort becomes obvious and monotonous if it is used almost exclusively.

P36 How much detail[16] you should use depends upon the importance to the story of what you are describing. Do not detain your reader with a detailed treatment of unimportant matters.

SUGGESTION IN NARRATIVES

P37 Occasionally, when you are certain that your reader will not miss your meaning, suggest character, mood, atmosphere, or incident rather than state it plainly.

[Plain statement:] It was on Tuesday of that week that I first met Mr. Helmuth. He turned out to be a mean old man. If that were all, it would be enough. But he turned out to be dangerous as well.

[Suggestion:] It was on the Tuesday of that week that I first met Mr. Helmuth. I had strayed through a breach in the wall where a freshet had dislodged some of the loosely laid stones and effected a rough gate. I found the estate on the other side very beautiful but in pitiful disrepair. The grass needed cutting; the flower beds were choked with weeds and dotted with blooms dead on their stalks; and the house that I could glimpse through the elms and evergreens could have done with a coat of paint. I came upon Mr. Helmuth very suddenly, as I turned the corner of an untrimmed hedge much higher than a man. He had obviously seen me before I caught sight of him, for he showed no surprise.

"You're trespassin'," he said.

"I know it." I managed a laugh, but it was embarrassed and apologetic. "I hoped you wouldn't mind. You're Mr. Helmuth,

---

[16] See P30-34.

aren't you? It was time to pay you a call anyway, since we're going to be neighbors."

"I'm Helmuth. I take it you're Fax. Well, Mr. Fax, I ain't much given to payin' or receivin' calls. You're trespassin'." His pale watery eyes looked resolutely over my shoulder. The weathered, loose skin of his face was crisscrossed with cracks like a piece of old leather. Some twenty years before, when he had been fifty, he must have been a great hulking man. But now he was stooped; all muscle tissue and fat seemed to have melted from his frame; for, wherever skin was visible—at his face, his neck, his forearms and hands—it hung loose, mottled, and heavy-veined, with scarcely anything between it and the bones to give it contour.

"I apologize, sir," I said, since he was technically in the right, "for trespassing. But now that I'm here, perhaps you'll let me look around your beautiful place. I especially envy you your elms."

He drew a revolver from the pocket of his trousers, flicked open the breech and turned it toward me. "What do you see?" he asked, his lip lifting slightly over one yellow fang.

"Why," I stammered, looking at the six brassy heads in the chambers, "why, a revolver, a loaded revolver."

He flipped the breech closed with his finger and pointed the gun at me. "Get goin'."

"What?"

He shot at the ground near my feet. "Get goin'."

P38 Suggestion is useful for putting the reader in the mood for what is going to happen and for intensifying his feeling of suspense.

Ta-ra-*rah*. The drumbeat is followed by an interval of silence in which is heard only the shuffle of feet. Ta-ra-*rah*—then the shuffle of feet. Ta-ra-*rah*—then the shuffle of feet. It is a dead march, or at least a march of the dead. Over the heads of the long column slowly streaming through the dusk, the angry heavens thrust out long menacing fingers of cloud, their edges smeared with blood by the dying sun. Round about them in the valley, the breeze sighs, rouses itself to a sobbing wail, to a scream, and dies. Along the narrow clay road, the poplars stand at attention, somber and inscrutable, as the doomed march forward to the beat of the dead march. The faces of the men are white and drawn. They know what awaits them. They feel that it is inevitable, and they march like a hypnotized battalion to meet what they cannot escape.

CLIMAX

P39 In narratives in which the order of events is under your control and particularly in plot narratives,[17] place your most interesting or most important event at, or very near, the end.

P40 Perhaps the easiest way to make sure that your plot narrative[17] will have climax is to plan it backwards from the most interesting or important event.

P41 As far as the circumstances of your composition permit, keep M38-41.

STRAIGHT NARRATIVE AND PLOT NARRATIVE

P42 Straight narrative records a series of events without introducing complications and solutions. It is the form of narrative found in most news accounts in newspapers, in most history books, and so on. It may be lively or quiet, factual or fictional.

P43 Plot narrative deliberately introduces complications and obstacles that the characters in the story must overcome if they are to meet success, happiness, and so on. Plot narrative is usually fictional—though not always. It always makes use of suspense and climax.[18] It usually stresses cause and effect in human beings.

---

[17] See P43.
[18] See P39-41.

In general

Q1 Argument is that form of talking or writing whose purpose is to convince another of the truth of some statement.[1]

Q2 Argument makes use of exposition, description, and narration, but for its own purpose.

Planning the argument

THE THESIS

Q3 The theme topic[2] of an argument is called a thesis or proposition.

Q4 A truth thesis states that a thing is or is not so.

God exists.
Americans do not love money.
Felicity Frisbie was a victim of circumstances.

Q5 An action thesis states that something should or should not be done.

Congress should not adjourn before passing the Lytton Bill.
You should vote for Ed Roberts for secretary of the association.

Q6 Write out your thesis.[3]

Q7 If it is at all possible to do so—and it almost always is—state your thesis in a single, uncomplicated, declarative sentence.[3]

---

[1] Persuasion is that form of talking or writing whose purpose is to make another feel or do what you want him to. Argument addresses itself to the intellect; persuasion, to the feelings or to the will. Ordinarily you must persuade your hearer as well as convince him; and hence, except in philosophy and mathematics classes, pure argument—an appeal to the intellect only—is seldom used. A mixture of argument and persuasion is the usual thing. For this reason the two are treated together in this book.

[2] For the notion of theme topic, see M9-11.

[3] For further treatment see N27-28 and N30-31. The rules and examples given there for theme topics apply to theses as well.

Q8 Avoid extravagant and superlative terms when stating your thesis.[4]

Q9 Make your thesis as definite as you reasonably can.[4]

Q10 Make sure that your thesis states only certain truths as certain.

For example, unless the thing is certain, say, "It is probable that fifty per cent of all Americans suffer from self-induced ailments." If the thing is not even probable, but merely possible, say so.

Q11 Make sure that your thesis does not commit you to prove more than you have to prove, more than you should, or more than you can.

For example, if your purpose were simply to clear a friend of charges of incompetence in office, you would do badly to state this thesis, "Jack White has performed the duties of treasurer in a competent manner and is, in fact, the most able member of this organization." If you fail to prove that he is the most able man, that failure may reflect on your proof of his competence, when you might with ease have carried the point of his competence alone.

Q12 Make your thesis as clear and concise as you can. If either you or your audience is vague about what is to be proved or what is to be done, you will probably lose their support. If your thesis rambles, it will be difficult for you or them to keep it in mind.

THE BRIEF

Q13 Write an outline of your argument.

Q14 The outline of an argument is called a brief. Since it has a different purpose from that of the outline of an exposition or the plan or plot of a narrative, it also has a different form.[5]

Q15 Always write a brief in complete sentences only.

---

[4] For further treatment see N27-28 and N30-31. The rules and examples given there for the theme topics apply to theses as well.
[5] See the example under Q20.

Q16 A brief has three principal parts: the introduction, the proof, and the conclusion.

Q17 The introduction—[6]

A States the thesis.

B Defines any terms that have more than one meaning or that might not be understood.

C Gives any explanation or background necessary to the understanding of the argument.

D States the issues.

Q18 The issues are the major points on which the truth or falsity of the thesis hangs. It is of the greatest importance that both the writer and his audience understand what the issues are. Confusion often conquers truth when the issues are not stated clearly and when the opposition is permitted to evade them.

Q19 The proof once again states each issue, following it with the word *for* and reasons.[6]

Q20 The conclusion recapitulates the issues as briefly as possible and restates the thesis.

    I. Introduction

        A. *Thesis.*—H. B. Stenson is guilty of plagiarism.

        B. *Definition.*—"Plagiarism" is the passing off as one's own the stolen writing of another.

        C. *Explanation.*—The victim of the plagiarism is Talbot Sparks.

        D. *Issues.*—I will prove my case by establishing the following issues:

            1. The two stories are identical.

            2. Sparks's story was written three months before Stenson's.

            3. Stenson had access to Sparks's story.

            4. Stenson made use of Sparks's story.

    II. Proof

        A. The two stories are identical, *for*—

            1. Mr. Judson, authorized by this court, has pronounced them so.

            2. Your own eyes will prove them so.

---

[6] See the example under Q20.

    B. Sparks's story was written three months before Stenson's, *for—*
        1. Three reliable witnesses testify that Sparks's story was written by July 3, 1949.
        2. Stenson's own admission and the testimony of a reliable witness show that his story was not written before October 7, 1949.
    C. Stenson had access to Sparks's story, *for* Sparks had given it to him for two days to criticize.
    D. Stenson made use of Sparks's story, *for—*
        1. There is no other reasonable explanation of the fact that the stories are identical.
        2. Stenson admitted to a reliable witness that he had copied the story and published it as his own.
  III. Conclusion
    Since the stories are identical, since Sparks's story was written before Stenson's, since Stenson had access to Sparks's story, and since Stenson made use of Sparks's story, therefore H. B. Stenson is guilty of plagiarism.

Q21 If you are going to use the brief as the outline for a written speech, you need not write out the conclusion as shown in Q20, since the matter it contains is already stated in the issues. But if you are going to use it for making an extempore talk, then you should write out the conclusion; for there will be no time to leaf back through pages looking for the issues and the thesis.

SOURCES OF PROOF

Q22 Argue from the statements of a reliable witness. Man is not a natural liar; hence his statement that a thing is so (his testimony) is excellent proof.

Q23 Your audience must grant you, or you must prove, these four things:
    A That there is nothing to show that your witness is given to lying. (If possible, show that your witness has a reputation for telling the truth or, better, is a man of outstanding integrity.)

513

B That your witness has no reason for lying in this particular case (that is, that it would be of no advantage to him to lie).

C That your witness has enough understanding to repeat accurately what he saw and what he heard.

D That your witness was careful and attentive in watching or listening.

Q24 Immediate (eyewitness) testimony is the more readily convincing; but mediate testimony, coming through several witnesses in turn, is quite good, provided it fulfills the four conditions of Q23.

Q25 Argue from accepted or established general truths or principles.

> I believe, gentlemen, that all of us hold the principle that one may not do evil even in order to accomplish good. It is true that Nevvers is slowly strangling decency and freedom in the city and the county. It is true, too, that it has proved impossible to pry him loose with any legitimate wedge. It is temptingly true that he has now been delivered into our hands and that, if I tell only one little lie on the witness stand tomorrow morning, I can send him to rot in jail where he belongs and assure the election of an honest man. But if I did so, I would forsake one of the precious principles that should separate men like us from men like Nevvers. I will not fight evil with evil. I will not become what I hate. And you will not ask me to.

Q26 The argument in Q25 can be reduced to this: It has been proved (or will be proved, or is accepted by all of you) that General Principle A is true (or good). But Particular Instance B is merely a form of General Principle A. Therefore Particular Instance B is true (or good).

Q27 Appeal to an accepted authority. An authority is a person whose views on a subject are generally acceptable because of his known and proved knowledge of the matter and because of his integrity.

> You may call upon the authority of a doctor to prove a point in surgery or internal medicine; you may call on the views of Planck

514

to prove a point in physics; you may call upon the authority of an engineer to prove a point in bridge building; you may call on the authority of a coach to prove a statement about the athletic ability of a member of his team or about changes that should be made in the rules of a game; and so on.

Q28 When appealing to an accepted authority, remember—

A A man who is an authority in one field is not automatically an authority in another. For example, the fact that Einstein is an authority in physics does not make him an authority in art.

B When the declarations of authorities conflict, the argument from authority must be dropped or must be bolstered by other arguments to prove the superiority of the authority you have selected. Authority is not a matter of majority rule, and so sometimes a single authority may outweigh a host of others.

c Whatever your audience may think, the value of an authority's statement is conditioned by his fallibility.

D When all the authorities agree, the strength and effectiveness of your argument is, naturally, increased and reinforced immeasurably.

Q29 Argue from a cause to an effect. Causes produce effects; so, if you can show that the cause of a thing exists, you will prove that the effect exists or will exist. However, if such an argument is to give a certain conclusion, there must be a necessary connection between the cause and effect; that is, the cause must be such that only this effect can flow from it. If there is not a necessary connection between the cause and the effect, the conclusion will vary in value from mere possibility to high probability.

For three and a half years, as you gentlemen well know from your study of the weather reports, no rain has fallen in this region, which was once covered with rich farms.

[Certain conclusion because of necessary connections:] This means, as you gentlemen can well understand, that no crops have been grown on this land, that cattle have died of thirst, and that human beings cannot support life here any longer.

515

Q30 Argue from effect to cause.

For example, if you came upon a skyscraper in the wilderness, you would at once conclude that either human beings or some higher agency had been at work; that is, from the effect you would correctly and with certitude conclude to the cause.

Q31 Argue from the evidence of circumstances. Circumstantial evidence, more often than not, affords only probability of high or low degree.

For example, if a man were seen to enter a bar and, two hours later, to stagger away from it, bawling a song at the top of his voice in the public street, one might conclude with some justice that these circumstances—the bar, the staggering, the loud singing—point to a bout of drinking.

Q32 Argue from specific instances.

A This argument must be founded on the examination of a great number of particular cases under a wide range of circumstances.

B Such an examination, however, can rarely be related to an audience in detail. It usually has to be summarized in a sentence or so.

In scientifically controlled and tabulated interviews with several thousand applicants for jobs in every region of the country, it was discovered that only 40 per cent of all American men have anything, or can formulate anything, but a materialistic purpose in applying for work. The other 60 per cent were unable to name anything but money and what money can buy as the object of work. For further details of the survey on which this figure is based, see [and so on].

C With some audiences it often suffices for conviction to supply only one appealing example.

I strongly urge you not to buy Rigomort theater seats for your auditoriums. I sat in, or rather thrust myself into, one of them the other day and found myself embraced with

The audience takes it for granted that the speaker, a man of integrity, would not condemn all Rigomort seating facilities unless he had made a prudent sampling of them all

516

alarming and acutely uncom-   or knew in some other way
fortable pressure by the arms   that they were all defective.
of the thing. When I tried to
stand up to let a patron of the
theater pass in front of me, one of the arm brackets tore away the
pocket of my coat; and the hat gadget on the bottom of the seat
clawed a vicious rip in my trousers. Yet I am of average size.

Q33 Argue from common experience.

We all know that during our waking hours our minds are never
entirely vacant, empty of thought. We are aware of things about
us and we are accepting and rejecting them. It is absurd, therefore,
to talk about keeping a child's mind empty and letting him grow
up to the age of thirteen or so before he chooses his own religion.
He will have been choosing all along; and, if we have not been
supplying his mind with the warm, rich truth during that time, he
will have been choosing cold, bare, pale reflections of it. You might
as soon speak of not feeding a child until he can decide for himself what he wants for dinner. Your child is like you, and you know
no one could have kept your mind blank for thirteen years.

Q34 Argue from analogy. The argument from analogy means
that, if two things are alike in some particulars, then they
will be alike in others.

To me, at least, it is almost inconceivable that a boy so very like
his great-souled father could have done the crime with which you
charge him. No one would have dared to accuse his father of such
a thing, for the world would have laughed the accuser to scorn.
Well, this boy and his father were cut on the same pattern. Every
presumption is against his having done or said an ignoble thing.

Q35 Use the argument from analogy charily, for it can readily
lead to false conclusions. It is best used as a merely persuasive proof; and, of course, it should not be proposed
to an audience as conclusive by itself.

Writing the argument

Q36 In general, argument will make use of everything that you
have learned about the other three forms of writing. An

argument fleshes the skinny bones of its brief with exposition, description, and narration. The points in the following rules, however, are worth mention.

Q37 Occasionally circumstances will be such that you can confine the introduction of your argument to the items listed in the introduction of its brief.

Q38 Most of the time you should use the opening paragraphs of your argument to catch your audience's interest and make them like you. (After this is done, take up the items listed in the introduction of the brief.)

A Concede something that they hold and that they do not expect you to grant.

There was a time, a long time, when I was immoveably certain that I was right in giving the order to send men into certain danger, into a situation that would be harmful to many of them. Not only was I sure I was right; I was stubborn in my belief, proud of my judgment, and would not listen to criticism from another. I went even further. I refused to admit any self-doubt; I would not let myself question what I had done and so closed off the possibility of self-criticism. This mistake, this fault, I now admit freely and fully. I have been much to blame. While granting it honestly, at the same time I nevertheless am convinced that I was right in giving the order that I did.

B Amuse them.

C Compliment them. Be sincere and specific. Insincerity, whether detected or not, degrades the speaker; and it is often detected. General compliments do not impress.

D Use a humble, straightforward, manly tone where they expect sarcasm, reproach, or invective.

Q39 Except when you have good reason to be impersonal—as, for instance, when you are trying to give the impression that you are merely presenting truth, not attempting to persuade anyone to anything—

A Use direct address (the second person), but judiciously.

B Use direct questions, but sparingly.

518

Q40 In writing an argument, consider the brief to be the outline of the proof, of the evidence, rather than an outline of the presentation. In the presentation, use all that is of advantage in exposition, description, and narration.

Q41 In a closely reasoned argument that is rather complicated, it is usually good, near the end, to recapitulate the issues and the thesis so as to leave with the audience as clear a notion as possible of what you have accomplished. The treatment, however, need not be dry.

> There, then, you have the case against H. B. Stenson. It has brought me no pleasure to make this charge against the man, to prove it so conclusively, to shock the many people who hold his name in esteem, to brand him with the stigma of meanness, of pettiness, of selfishness. I feel as did the old man who worked for my father when I was a boy. "Don't fight with little people, boy," he told me. "Little people are sufficiently punished by what they are." However, the rights, the name, and the property of another man were at stake in this case; and so I am glad that the truth against H. B. Stenson stands so firm and clear that you can come to judgment against him without hesitation. For, as I have shown, the two stories are identical; Sparks's story was written three months before Stenson's; Stenson had access to Sparks's work; and, by Stenson's own admission, repeated under oath by a reliable witness, Stenson made use of Sparks's work. The conclusion, of course, is clear: H. B. Stenson is guilty of plagiarism. May you find your certain duty of bringing judgment against him less unpleasant than was my task of bringing proof. Pleasant or not, it is a duty you must perform as good men and good citizens. Your distaste, I trust, will not outweigh your convictions.

Fallacies

Q42 A reasoning process that is not logical is called a fallacy. Sometimes fallacies are used deliberately, but more often they are the result of faulty reasoning. You should know the common fallacies so that you may avoid them in your own work and detect them when you are refuting the arguments of others.

IGNORATIO ELENCHI

Q43 Mistaking the question is arguing for or against something other than the thesis, motion, or resolution actually proposed for discussion.

[This speaker, supposed to be arguing the question "Military service is good character training," has mistaken the question and is arguing against drafting boys under eighteen:] To draft a boy under eighteen years of age is a crime against human nature! Until the time that he is at least eighteen a boy has need of the atmosphere, the guidance, the will training, the example that only a home can afford. After he is eighteen, perhaps the time has come to throw him from the nest and let him try his wings; but before that the risk of endangering his character is too great. I am against this iniquitous proposal.

Q44 To refute an argument that mistakes the question, call the attention of your opponent and the audience to the mistake and restate the actual question.

Mr. Clay has argued eloquently and at some length against drafting young men before they are eighteen. I find no difficulty in agreeing with him. But let me remind him that his eloquence was scarcely related to what is before the house this evening—the proposition that "Military service is good character training." I wish that Mr. Clay had brought his mind to bear on that topic, since that—and not the draft age—is what we came here to discuss. Let us reserve the draft age for another evening. Tonight let us talk about the question this meeting was called to consider: the effect of military service on a man's character.

PETITIO PRINCIPII

Q45 Begging the question is taking for granted what you ought to be proving.

I want to propose Helen Murchison as the best-dressed girl on the campus. She wears smarter clothes than anyone else here at Sarat and is therefore fully entitled to the distinction "best-dressed." Now that I have proved her the one most worthy of the honor, I am sure that you will all give her your votes.

Q46 The common refutation of an argument that begs the question is to show your opponent and the audience that he has not proved, but merely stated, the question.

I hope that neither Miss Murchison nor Miss Peters will take offense when I point out that the latter has offered no evidence, but has merely stated, that Miss Murchison is the best-dressed girl at Sarat. In a momentous matter of this sort we must have a better guide to a decision than mere statement. Now *my* candidate, as I shall *prove* [and so on].

VICIOUS CIRCLE

Q47 A vicious circle is proving *A* by *B* and *B* by *A*.

It is easy to see that *cow* is a noun in this sentence. Look, it is modified by an adjective, *sprightly*. Adjectives, you know, modify only nouns or noun substitutes; and, of course, there is no question of a noun substitute here. *Sprightly*, I'll admit, looks like an adverb, since it ends in *ly*. But it is clearly an adjective here, for it modifies the noun *cow*.

Q48 An effective way of refuting a vicious circle is to strip it of verbiage and present it in all its naked illogic.

Joe, you have proved that *cow* is a noun because it is modified by the adjective *sprightly* and that *sprightly* is an adjective because it modifies the noun *cow*. No, Joe. You could prove Gromyko to be papal secretary of state in that fashion.

POST HOC, ERGO PROPTER HOC

Q49 False causality is assuming that, since one thing happens after another, it is therefore caused by that other.

I will never drink milk again. Last night, just before I went to bed, I drank a glass of milk. Then this morning, when I tried to get up, I found that I had a bursting head and that my stomach was one great ache.

Q50 A simple question will often refute false causality.

Could nothing else have made you feel ill? Do you think that you should conclude that milk was the culprit without looking for a more likely suspect?

FALSE ASSUMPTION

Q51 False assumption is taking something to be true that is not true and building an argument on it.

> The presence of Jacob O'Neill in this hall tonight gives some notion of the unbridled boldness, of the shamelessness, of the arrogance of the man; of his utter disregard for what decent people like yourselves think of him. You see with what sort of person you have to deal, my friends. He defies you to your face! What will be your answer?—Excuse me. What's that? You say Mr. O'Neill is not in the hall tonight!

Q52 False assumption is such a bad blunder that the best refutation, ordinarily, is to call attention to it without gloating. Occasionally, however, it is necessary to be severe about it, lest the audience be misled.

FALSE APPEAL TO COMMON KNOWLEDGE

Q53 False appeal to common knowledge or consent is using a phrase like *as everybody knows* or *only a fool would deny that,* when the point in question is not a matter of common knowledge or consent and may even be untrue.

> I don't have to take time out to prove to people as enlightened as you that American-style democracy is the only good form of government. Only power-mad rulers and benighted Europeans, long accustomed to the surrender of their freedom of thought, would dare to offer any rebuttal.

Q54 False appeal to common knowledge or consent is one of the more vicious fallacies when used deliberately. For it plays upon that snobbishness in people which makes them reluctant to admit that they do not know something or that they are peculiar enough to think differently from their neighbors.

Q55 The refutation of false appeal to common knowledge or consent is (*a*) to point out that you, at least, do not know or do not consent to the statement of your opponent, and (*b*) to cite men of excellent knowledge and authority who disagree with it or deny it.

ARGUMENT BY UNFAIR IMPLICATION

Q56 Argument by unfair implication is the stating of a fact or a truth but using it to imply something that does not follow from it.

The other day I was talking to a medical student, and a rather bright one. I asked him whether he knew what St. Anthony's fire was and what its cause was. He said he didn't know; he couldn't answer my question at all. A fine medical school he goes to! What kind of doctor is this country turning out?

The implication in this argument is that if a presumably bright medical student cannot answer a question, then the training given in our medical schools is poor.

Q57 The refutation of argument by unfair implication is to examine your opponent's statement and the conclusion he draws from it, and to show that the connection he implied between the two does not exist.

Mr. Glenn seems to feel that if a medical student does not know the answer to a question his education is defective. I think Mr. Glenn is being quite unfair to the student and the medical school. (I am acquainted with both.) First of all, the term "St. Anthony's fire" is one not commonly encountered as a synonym for erysipelas or ergotism. And neither of those things can our medical student be expected to know much about at this stage of his training.

AMBIGUITY OF TERMS

Q58 Ambiguity of terms is an illogical shifting of the meaning of words.

Please, dear Lilian, don't get the idea that you're impeccable. You aren't. You often make mistakes, as you and I both know very well. Just last week you used mineral oil in your potato salad instead of salad oil. And just yesterday you gave your husband the wrong address when he was going to the cleaner's. Oh, no, Lilian; you aren't impeccable. You can make mistakes like anybody else.

Q59 The refutation of an argument based on ambiguous terms is to redefine the terms.

DEFECTIVE INDUCTION

Q60 Defective induction is an argument based on too few instances or on an examination made unscientifically, without sufficient variation of circumstances or controls.

Sheep, my friends, are all white. I know. I have two sheep, and they are both white.

Q61 The refutation of defective induction is either to show that too few instances have been examined or that the examination was unscientific, or else to bring up a fact that refutes the induction, according to the old dictum, "An argument cannot batter down a fact" *(contra factum non valet illatio).*

The gentleman who spoke just before me proved, or seemed to prove, that all sheep are white. I should hesitate to attack his conclusion were it not that I happen to have a sheep with me—a sheep that is black. Bill, will you please bring in that sheep?

FALSE ANALOGY

Q62 False analogy is arguing that, because two things are alike in some particulars, they will therefore certainly be alike in others.

For example, in a widely current television commercial, the salesman dips two sponges in water, one coated with a water-resistant material. The uncoated sponge becomes soft. Then he says that the same thing happens to whiskers that have been cleared of water-resistant film by his product. He often concludes with remarks implying that he has *proved* that his product softens whiskers.

Q63 The refutation of false analogy is to point out the differences between the two things that are compared and to show how these must be taken into consideration no less than the similarities.

R Interest and force

In general

R1 Interest is that quality of writing which attracts and holds a reader to what the writer is saying.

R2 Force is that quality of writing which moves a reader to feel, judge, will, or act as the writer wants him to.

R3 Interest and force are not merely a matter of the rules that follow. They are also a matter of unity, coherence, emphasis, and variety. (See these headings in the index.)

Selecting words and expressions

THE RIGHT WORD

R4 Use the right word or expression. This general rule is made practical in the following particular rules.

R5 Use words and expressions clear to the audience for which the theme is intended.

It is my pleasant privilege to announce that on the imminent anniversary of the signing of that document by which our great nation threw off the yoke of a tyrannical mother country there will be a great pyrotechnical display in the

This speech, bad writing in itself, is hopelessly worded if it is intended for pupils in the fifth grade. But they could understand the version below without any difficulty.

vicinity of Moore's Wharf on Back Bay about eight-thirty in the evening. Billets admitting you to this extravaganza go at the ridiculously low tariff of ten cents each. But before I enter into commerce with you for the sale of these admissions to volcanic won-

525

ders, I must have the solemn pledge of this assembly of splendid little potential citizens of our commonwealth that not one of you will attempt to break through the cordon surrounding the men who will activate the instruments of the display, but that you will all content yourselves with the role of spectator. Ladies and gentlemen, will you gage me your honor for that?

I'm happy to tell you that on the Fourth of July there will be a big fireworks display near Moore's Wharf on Back Bay about 8:30 P.M. Tickets to see the fireworks cost only ten cents. But before I sell you any tickets, all of you must promise that you will not try to go beyond the lines and get close to the men who will be shooting off the fireworks, but will stand and watch where you are supposed to. Do you promise?

R6 When you cannot tell, except in a very general way, who your audience will be, keep R7-18.

R7 Ordinarily use current words—words in common use. (This requires a good deal of reading; otherwise you will not know what words are in common use.)

[Doubtful:] It is a parlous journey to cross this sea.
[Better:] It is a perilous journey to cross this sea.

R8 Ordinarily, when you use an uncommon word, make sure that other words around it can carry the main sense without it.

You will learn to add color and life to your themes, sparkle and verve.	Even if *verve* is not understood, the other words make the main meaning of the sentence clear.

R9 Unless you have good reason for using them, avoid foreign words and phrases and those words that good dictionaries mark "archaic," "obsolete," "rare," "especially British," "dialect," and so on.[1]

R10 You would have good reason to use the words and phrases discussed in R9 if you could not express the thought adequately or accurately without them. You would not have

R

---

[1] See R10. For the use of slang, see R16-17.

good reason, you would merely be silly, if you used them to show off.

R11 Use words or expressions suitable to the kind of theme you are writing: words which convey the mood and atmosphere you wish to create, and which are proper to your particular purpose and for your particular readers.[2]

R12 In formal themes[3] ordinarily avoid colloquial words and expressions; that is, words marked "colloquial" in the dictionary or expressions characteristic only of rather informal conversation.

We the people of the United States, in order to fix up the rather sloppy union we have had up to now, to make sure that everybody gets what's coming to him, that nobody gets funny at home, and that we won't be a pushover for a foreign enemy, that people get their big needs taken care of, and that we and our kids have a generous slice of freedom, do here set up this Constitution of the United States.

Section 1. When it comes to making laws, well, we'll just let Congress handle that.

The style of the paragraphs at left would be ill suited to the Constitution of the United States, of which they are a parody.

R13 It would not be contrary to the principle of R12 to include direct quotations which contain colloquialisms in a formal theme, provided, of course, that the quotation furthered your purpose.

R14 In informal themes, use colloquial words and expressions where they best achieve your purpose—best carry the meaning, best establish the right mood and atmosphere,

---

[2] See R12-18.

[3] Formal themes are themes that, by reason of the subject matter, the occasion, the audience, or something of the kind, should be somewhat impersonal and rather dignified. Such are term papers; constitutions of an organization; speeches on formal occasions (valedictories, for example); impersonal reports, essays, and so on; ordinary business letters; letters to officials; letters of congratulations, acceptance, or condolence written to other than intimate friends.

characterize a person or express an idea economically and vividly.[4]

The fact is, Jack was making a general nuisance of himself. So much so that Sheriff Bannock Burns, an advocate of stern and, always, singular justice, began picking vigilantes. Sheriff Burns had been around quite a while. He was observant and pretty tolerant

This quotation from a high-school student's composition uses colloquialisms to advantage, for it indirectly produces the atmosphere proper to a western by means of typically informal language.

for a lawman. He had to be. But he knew the countryside well. He knew when somebody's yearlings got into the wrong corral, or why a local rancher was suddenly—and unexplainedly—well to do.

R15 Great care is needed in the selection of colloquialisms. They must not clash with the rest of the theme, with the mood, with the occasion, and so on. For example, the colloquial *ain't* might mar a good newspaper account of a basketball game, whereas the colloquial *youngster* would be quite in order.

R16 Even in informal themes use slang only sparingly and judiciously; when, that is, nothing else would accomplish your purpose so well.[5]

R17 Most new slang gets old quickly, and much of it dies altogether in a rather short time. It is therefore a good idea, generally, to avoid new slang fads even when they

---

[4] See R15. "Good English varies according to the occasion just as our dress varies according to the occasion. Evening dress would be out of place in playing a football game. Loose colloquial English . . . is frequently as appropriate as a loose-fitting garment in moments of relaxation. The lesser grammarians, who so generally present only one form of English, not only show their bad taste, but do a great deal of harm in that they impart erroneous ideas of language. . . . Those who always think of our popular speech as ungrammatical should recall that our present literary grammar was originally the grammar of the common people of England" (George O. Curme, *Syntax* [Boston: D. C. Heath & Co., 1931], III, vi). By permission.

[5] Slang is not easy to define. Webster's New Collegiate Dictionary (1956) offers this definition: "Slang . . . 2. The jargon of a particular calling or class of society. 3. Language comprising certain widely current terms having a forced, fantastic, or grotesque meaning, or exhibiting eccentric humor or fancy."

seem to serve your purpose. There are, moreover, degrees of respectability in slang.

R18 Ordinarily do not use a big word or a sonorous, high-sounding expression where a little word or unpretentious expression will say the same thing as clearly, movingly, and economically.

[Ordinarily poor:] Decapitate the miscreant.
[Ordinarily better:] Cut the scoundrel's head off.

R19 Use the accurate word or expression.[6]

For example, do not say "The scene was gorgeous," if there was nothing magnificent or resplendently beautiful about it. Content yourself with something like "The countryside was very pretty." Do not say "Then a marvelous thing happened," if the reader is going to discover that you really should have said "Then a surprising thing happened."

R20 The accuracy required by R19 is literary, not scientific. Scientific accuracy is ordinarily out of place except in scientific themes.

[Poor:] Tomlin was of average size, weighing about 160 pounds, standing 5 feet 10, and having a waistline of 29 or 30 inches.
[Better:] Tomlin was of average size, agreeably tall and slender but not remarkably so.

THE CONCRETE AND THE PARTICULAR WORD

R21 A concrete word or expression presents persons and things as they really are. An abstract word or expression presents persons and things stripped down to a bare idea.

Abstract	*Concrete*
God created *man*.	God created *you*.
Age complains.	*An old man* complains.
Paul wanted *wealth*.	Paul wanted *a big bank balance, an estate, a fleet of Cadillacs, and a yacht.*

---

[6] See R20.

Justice must prevail.

Ward Riley must get back his stolen money.

Improvement results from constant effort.

With a lot of practice, you can correct that slice.

R22 A particular word or expression calls to mind only one idea—or, at least, fewer ideas than a more general word or expression would. A general word or expression is one that could call to mind a number of ideas.

General	*Particular*
The man brought home a dog.	*Uncle Henry* brought home a dog.
People are waiting for you down in the drawing room.	*Janet and the electrician* are waiting for you down in the drawing room.
Stalin was *ruthless*.	To get his way, Stalin *starved two million people*.
A *dog* makes a good and faithful companion.	An *Airedale* makes a good and faithful companion.
The *noise* frightened him.	The *gunshot* frightened him.

R23 Make liberal use of concrete and particular words and expressions.[7]

R24 Concrete and particular expressions are not better than abstract or general ones for every purpose. The latter, while less vivid, have their important uses. Use abstract or general terms—

A To save words.

B For precise statements of principle or definition.

C To phrase brief, clear topic statements that will be made more concrete or particular in the development.

D In summaries of matter that has been or will be treated concretely and particularly.

---

[7] See R24. Some words, while they are not actually abstract, have what has been called "the smell of abstraction." Technically, the italicized words in these sentences are both concrete: "*God* has been good to me"; "*The Deity* has been good to me." But *the Deity* brings with it a faint air of the abstract word *deity* (without the article) and hence lacks the vividness of the word *God*.

E To avoid loading a paragraph with too much detail.

F To relieve too much concreteness and particularity.

The manner of telling

IN GENERAL

R25 The ordinary way to tell a thing is to say it straight out. Most of your writing should be like that. To go in for too many intricate expressions is to weaken your style and rob it of sincerity. On the other hand, although people admire what is solid and plain, they do not like too much of it. It is therefore necessary to vary plain talk with the little turns that bring pleasure if they are not used awkwardly or too often.

FIGURES OF SPEECH

R26 A figure of speech is a change from the ordinary manner of expression, a change used for effect.

R27 A simile is a comparison between things that are in general unlike, a comparison made with the use of *like, as,* or other comparative words. More briefly, a simile is an express comparison between unlike things.[8]

Thérèse has large, dark eyes.	This is a plain statement.
Thérèse's eyes are like the night itself, large and dark and full of soft mystery.	This is a simile. Eyes are compared to night in some points in which they are alike. Eyes on the whole are very unlike night (in fact the two differ entirely in nature, which is usually the case with the terms of a simile). The comparison is made with a comparative word—*like*.

---

[8] The comparison must be made between things that are in general unlike, or there is no figure of speech. For example, "Mary is as tall as Katherine" is not a figure of speech but an ordinary comparison.

531

R28 A simile may be short or long.

For example, many of Christ's parables are long similes: some, for instance, that begin, "The kingdom of heaven is like . . ."

R29 A simile may be negative.

Tracy could no more have written this note than a snake can cross its legs.

To put the matter gently and to avoid bruising your feelings—in my opinion this daub of yours resembles a painting about as much as a ten-watt bulb resembles a sunset.

R30 The comparison in a simile should be better known to the reader, easier to see, or more appealing to the imagination than a plain statement of the thought.

He was as timid as a rabbit during the hunting season.	This is a good simile. It is probably more vivid and less vague than the plain statement of the fact that "He was timid."
His eyes were like chrysolite.	Too few people know what chrysolite looks like. Unless written for mineralogists, this simile is of little value.

R31 Similes are often awkward or too obvious. In such cases, use a metaphor.

[Awkward simile:] We could not hear above the wind, which was like a wild orchestra.

[Better:] We could not hear above the wild symphony of the wind.

R32 A metaphor is a comparison between things that are in general unlike, a comparison made without the use of *as*, *like*, or other comparative words. More briefly, a metaphor is an implied comparison between unlike things.[9]

The night is in Thérèse's eyes, large and dark and full of soft mystery.[10]

---

[9] What is said about the simile in R27, footnote 8, and R28-30 applies to metaphors as well.

[10] Compare this with the example of a simile under R27.

You see, Michael's trouble is that he is a turtle. Whenever he sees the shadow of something that might be unpleasant, he quickly withdraws into his shell and holds himself close in nervous tension until pretty certain that the danger is past. In that way, it is true, he escapes a lot of the annoyances that plague other people; but he has more fears. Worst of all, he misses so much of the life he might enjoy if only he stuck his neck out a little more frequently. And it is ironic that, despite all his efforts to protect himself from harsh realities, he is almost fated to share the doom of turtles: to be stepped on, crushed, or tossed into the soup. For even turtles cannot protect themselves from big things. They can only take what is in store for them—take it like turtles. It's a pity that Michael is not less of a turtle and more of a man.

R33 Although similes and metaphors are at bottom the same, not every simile can readily be turned into a metaphor.

R34 Personification is a particular kind of metaphor. It is a figure of speech that gives the qualities or actions of persons to abstractions and other things that are not persons.

History is not kind to conservative men.	History is treated as a person, since only persons can be kind in the strict sense.

Fear lived with us in that house. It stared at us from the mirror in the morning. It gripped our throats when we tried to eat. It sat by our beds and caressed us with icy fingers when we tried to sleep.

R35 Balance or parallelism can be considered a figure of speech, though not in the sense that it is to be used only occasionally. Ordinarily use like structures for like thoughts.[11]

R36 When parallel structure becomes lengthy, it is often advisable to break it in order to avoid monotony. The break is usually, though not always, most effective if placed near the end.

Cissie was upstairs on the sleeping porch, and she heard nothing. David was drying dishes with Kathy in the kitchen, and they heard

---

[11] See K12-18.

nothing. Mother was ironing in the basement, and she heard nothing. Aunt Sylvia was listening to a television show; and [break] whatever she heard, it was certainly not the howl of a jaguar.

R37 Antithesis is a particular form of balance or parallelism. It is a figure of speech in which opposed ideas are balanced and placed next to each other or in parallel positions.

That isn't the truth; it's a lie.

You seem so wise, and yet how foolish you are.

Brake inspection costs you one dollar; an accident may cost you one life.

We thought him honest; he is deceitful. We thought him wise; he is only shrewd. We thought his own people esteemed him; they despise him. We thought he loved us; he hates us.

R38 Antithesis is usually a very forceful, very striking figure. Do not use too much of it.

R39 Climax is a figure of speech in which thoughts are arranged in ascending order of importance, interest, or effectiveness for a particular audience.[12]

R40 Anticlimax is a figure of speech in which, for purposes of humor or scorn, climax is observed up to the end of a series of thoughts which appear to be building to something important and then some unimportant idea is mentioned in the last, most important position.

If you want to understand Daglesby's influence in the school, you must remember that he is no ordinary man made up, like you and me, of a soul, two arms, two legs, and so forth. You must realize that he belongs to a race apart, to the golden boys who represent the best that America can produce. You must weigh the fact that he is one of the demigods, a little larger than life and the dream come true of every man in the country. You must learn to accept this tremendous truth—he is a successful football player.

Here thou, great Anna, whom three realms obey,
Dost sometimes counsel take—and sometimes tea.[13]

---

[12] See K28, L28-29, and M40.

[13] Alexander Pope, "The Rape of the Lock," iii, 8. "Anna" is Queen Anne of England, reigning when this poem was written. *Tea* is pronounced *tay*.

R41 Irony is a figure of speech in which one thing is said while obviously the opposite is meant.

[Said to a man riding an ancient, spiritless hack, incapable of more than a painful walk:] Think you'll be able to bust that bronc?

R42 Irony may be gentle or cutting. When it is cutting, it is called sarcasm.

[Said to a bouncy partner at a dance:] I like to dance with you; but then, when I was a little girl, I liked to seesaw, too.

[Said of England's most bloody executioner:] Gentle Topcliff!

R43 Apostrophe is a figure of speech in which an absent or dead person or a personified thing is directly addressed by the speaker.

What, Washington, would you say now of "foreign entanglements" if you could see the world as it is today?

Ambition, you have been a cruel mistress to me. I will serve you no longer.

R44 Substitution[14] is a figure of speech in which, because they suggest each other in some way or are otherwise closely associated—

A The maker or source is used for the thing made.

Along with many another illustrious, godly author, *Thomas Aquinas* was burned when Elstra made a bonfire of "subversive" books.	Thomas Aquinas, the writer or maker of the books, is substituted for the books.

B The thing made is used for the maker or source.

Capital has learned to sit down and talk with *labor*.	Capital, the thing, is substituted for the people who possess it. Labor, the thing, is substituted for the people who perform it.

---

[14] "Substitution" is a name used in this book to replace *metonymy* and *synecdoche*. Metonymy is a figure of speech in which a word is used for another which it suggests or which is closely associated with it. Synecdoche is a figure of speech in which the part is put for the whole or the whole for the part.

c The sign is used for the thing signified.

I'm afraid we will have to punish those *sullen looks*.	Unless he is unreasonable, the speaker does not wish to punish the looks, which are only a sign, but the person who wears them or the attitude that they signify.

D The container is used for the thing contained.

Who steals my *purse* steals trash.	Iago does not mean the container—the purse itself—but the thing in the purse—money.

E A part is used for the whole.

We sailed for Barcelona in a good *bottom*.	Part of the ship, bottom, is used for the whole ship.
Drought gripped the land. Not a *green ear* stood on any *stalk* in all that country.	The species, ears of corn, is used for the general classification, vegetation.

F The whole is used for a part.

The *nation* went to the polls that day to vote for life or death.	The whole nation is used for those that actually voted.
This *animal* builds great cities like London.	The general classification, animal, is used for the particular species, man.

R45 Hyperbole is a figure of speech in which the writer exaggerates, not in order to deceive, but to emphasize a point, create humor, or achieve some similar effect.

An *endless* stream of wharf rats poured over the side the moment the ship docked at Suez.

R46 Paradox is a figure of speech in which, to jolt the reader into a new realization, the writer states a seeming contradiction that will later be explained or that will yield sense on second thought.

He who loses his life for My sake will save it.

R47 Onomatopoeia is a figure of speech in which words are used whose sound suggests their sense.

There broke on our ears the *clang* of *cymbals* and the *strident, brassy blasts* of *haughty trumpets.*

R48 Do not strive for onomatopoeia unless you have good reason to think your audience or reader will be in the mood for it. It falls very flat when the context or the reader is not ready for it.

R49 Alliteration is a figure of speech in which the same sound is repeated noticeably at the beginning of words placed close together.

*F*ull *f*athom *f*ive thy *f*ather lies.

R50 Of all the figures of speech, alliteration should be used the most sparingly. Only reading aloud can teach a writer to use it well.

R51 Make sure that every figure of speech is consistent with itself and consistent with the thoughts around it.

[Badly mixed figures:] Gentlemen, I smell a rat; I see it in the air; and I will nip it in the bud!

R52 To avoid hackneyed, worn-out writing—

A Work out your own original figures to express your own thoughts.
B When unable to produce an adequate original figure or when the context deserves only a trite, dull figure, do not call attention to the one you have borrowed or emphasize it in any way.[15]

R53 A great many figures of speech have become so common that they have passed beyond triteness into the very idiom of the language; for example, *best in the long run, right-hand man, as the crow flies.* There is no prohibition against these common figures, unless you use a great number of them too close together.

---

[15] See R53.

R54 If you use figures of speech merely as ornaments, something added to a theme to "pretty up" your work, you will fall into what is called, without compliment, "fine writing." Follow R55-58.

R55 Rethink every thought that you write down. Make sure that it is now your own.

R56 It often helps to write the first draft of a theme in the form of a letter to someone you know or at least to someone real, and then afterwards to remove the paraphernalia of the letter.

R57 When writing the second draft of a theme, ask yourself constantly of each sentence, each figure—
  A Does this directly or indirectly help the meaning of the main thought of the theme?
  B Does it help the central mood or atmosphere?
  C Does it fit the audience for which I intend the theme?
  D Does it fit the real or pretended writer?

R58 Probe your mind and feelings until you find out why you like or dislike this or that passage in your own or in others' work and until you know whether your reasons are good or bad.

COLOR IN WRITING

R59 Open your eyes to the colorful glory of the world, to its variety and shading.

[Good, but wanting in color:] When she had been warped away from the dock, she flung out her great sails before the following gale, heeled a little under the impact, and then stood smartly down the bay. I tell you it made my heart stand still to look at her.

[With color:] When she had been warped away from the dock, she flung out her great crimson sails, quartered with gold crosses, before the following gale. Her black hull heeled a little under the impact, and then she stood smartly down the bay in the filtered-yellow afterrain. I tell you it made my heart stand still to look at her.

R60 It is often good to determine color for a reader by appealing to something he is certain to know well.[16]

[Good:] His hair was brownish-red.
[Probably clearer:] His name, like his hair, was "Rusty."

[Good:] They used an ugly rough-finish brown tile in the shower room.

[Probably clearer:] They used an ugly rough-finish milk-chocolate tile in the shower room.

[Good:] Over her white shirt and dark slacks she wore a bright red jacket.

[Probably clearer:] Over her white shirt and dark slacks she wore a gay, ñeon-red jacket.

R61 Often it is not important that a reader get a definite notion of the color of an object. Do not slow your writing and bore your reader by going in for precision where precision is not necessary.

SUGGESTION

R62 Do not always make things so plain for your reader that there is nothing for him to do but passively nod his head. Use suggestion now and then.

R63 Suggestion is supplying the reader with sufficient, and only sufficient, information for him to make out the thought correctly and easily by himself.

[Plain statement:] Thompson is a coward.
[Suggestion:] Oh, Thompson talks a good fight.

[Plain statement:] The prisoner died at three o'clock.
[Suggestion:] By three o'clock the prisoner's soul, at least, had escaped its cell.

[Plain statement:] It looks as though the senator has been accumulating wealth unethically.
[Suggestion:] I'm afraid there's jam on the senator's fingers.

---

[16] See R61.

[Plain statement:] Hazel was a mediocre writer.

[Suggestion:] Hazel made the columns of the *New Yorker* once, when a critic recommended her novel to insomniacs.

[Plain statement:] Pearson sobbed out his plea. The judge was not impressed. He merely smiled thinly.

[Suggestion:] Pearson sobbed out his plea. The judge smiled thinly.

RHYTHM

R64 Read your writing aloud to yourself. Then revise your sentences according to the verdict of your ears.[17]

Examples of good prose rhythm

When all is done, human life is, at its greatest and its best, but like a froward child that must be played with and humored a little to keep it quiet till it falls asleep, and then the care is over.

But little do men perceive what solitude is: for a crowd is not company, and faces are but a gallery of pictures, and talk but a tinkling symbol where there is no love.

Far away rang the cry of Judith to the watchmen on the city walls, Open the gates! God is on our side. Open the gates! His power yet lives in Israel.

In the common experience of misery, in the common sorrow of great catastrophes, in humiliation and distress, under the blows of the executioner or the bombs of total war, in concentration camps, in the hovels of starving people in great cities, in any common *necessity,* the doors of solitude open and man recognizes man.

---

[17] Balance and antithesis (R35-38), climax (R39), anticlimax (R40), onomatopoeia (R47-48), and alliteration (R49-50) are involved in rhythm.

Index

for emphasis, H153, H160
foundations, H117, H120
freshman, H119
geographical names, H105-6
God, H35-48
    adjectives accompanying names
        of, or referring to, H38-39,
        H45, H47
    adverbs in names of, H39
    body and blood, H42-43
    divinity, providence, deity, H40
    false deity, H48
    heart and *Sacred Heart,* H43
    humanity and *hypostatic union,*
        H44
    name, holy name, fatherhood,
        sonship, H41
    names used as descriptive predi-
        cates or appositives, H37
    pronouns and adjectives referring
        to, H45-47
    proper names, H35
    substitutes for proper names,
        H36
gospel, H25-26
government, H113
governmental assemblies, bureaus,
    commissions, courts, depart-
    ments, offices, and so on, H113,
    H116, H120
gulfs, H105-6
heaven, H62
heavenly bodies, H155
hell, H62
historical events and eras, H132-33
holidays, H142-43
Holy Eucharist, H72-74
Holy Family, H55
Holy Mother (the) Church, H67
holy name, H41
Holy See, Apostolic See, Chair of
    Peter, H82
holy souls, H60
holydays, H142-43
host, sacred host, sacred species,
    H74
House of Representatives, H116,
    H120
humanity (of Christ), H44
hypostatic union, H44
I (personal pronoun), H150
indexes, H131
indirect quotations, H7
islands, H105-6

junior
    school term, H119
    title following a name, H97
kingdoms, H101, H105-6
kinship names, H98-100
lakes, H105-6
language and languages, H137, H139
letter, H147
letters (correspondence), H13-15
    addresses, H13, H158
    complimentary close, H15
    headings, H13, H158
    salutations, H14, H88
libraries, H109-10
line, H147
line and sentence, H1-16
magazines and periodicals, H125-30
Mass and its parts, H69-70
military groups, H121-24
Missal and its parts, H33
monk, priest, nun, and similar words,
    H81
month and months, H141, H143
monuments, H109-10
moon, H155
mother
    Blessed Virgin, H54
    kinship name, H98-100
motion pictures, H125-27, H129-30
mountains, H105-6
musical works, H125-27, H129-30
mysteries of the rosary, H77
mystical body and *mystical union,*
    H44
name (of God), H41
navy, H121-22
newspapers, H125-26
nicknames, H93
non-, H19
north, south, east, west, H107-8
note, H147
Notes, heading in expository theme,
    N68
nun, monk, priest, and similar words,
    H81
O (exclamatory word), A124, H150
oceans, H105-6
offices, H116
oh, H151
operas, H125-27, H129-30
orders, religious, H79-80
organization and organizations, H117
outlines, N40
page, H147

ships, H149
short forms of titles, H145
societies, H117, H120
sonship (of Christ), H41
sophomore, H119
stanza, H147
states and sections of states, H101,
    H103, H105-6
streets, H104, H106
sun, H155
Supreme Court, H116, H120
television stations, H117, H120
territories, H101, H105-6
the, H125-26, H156-60
titles, H16, H125-29, H135-36
    articles *(a, an, the)* in, H125-26,
        H156-57, H159-60
    conjunctions in, H125, H156-57
    for themes, N93, N99
    personal. *See* Capitals, personal
        titles.
    prepositions in, H125, H156-57
    short forms, H145
    word following hyphen in, H96,
        H129-30
    See also Capitals, books; Capitals,
        essays; Capitals, paintings; *and
        so on.*
    *See also classification of particular
        name you are concerned with.
        For instance, if you wish to
        know whether "Elks Club"
        should be capitalized, see*
        Clubs, capitals.
towns and sections of towns, H101,
    H103, H106
trade names, H148
trains, H149
transubstantiation, H74
tribe and tribes, H137-39
un-, H19
unspoken thoughts, D114, H4
verse, H8-10, H125, H129-30, H147
week, H143
Whereas (in resolutions) and the
    first word following it, H152
word following hyphen in title, H96,
    H129-30
word following *Whereas* and *Re-
    solved,* H152
words directed by a person to him-
    self, D114, H4
words followed by numeral or letter,
    H146-47

year, H143
*yes, no, oh, good-by, good morning,
    amen,* and so on, H151
zones, H101, H103, H105-6·
Cardinal and cardinal archbishop
    form of address, salutation, and com-
        plimentary close in business and
        formal letters, N133-34
    form of salutation and complimentary
        close in personal letters, N148-
        49, N152
Cardinal numeral adjectives, A97
Cards, library catalogue, N17-20
Case, C178-81
    after *it is* in informal speech and
        writing, C161
    after *than* or *as,* C219, C288
    appositives, C196-97
    changes in form of nouns, C180,
        D154-64
    changes in form of pronouns,
        C181
        indefinite, D165
        interrogative, A50, D166
        personal, A28, D166
        possessive, A29
        reciprocal, D165
        relative, A43, D166
        self-pronouns, A37
    complicated by expressions like *I be-
        lieve* and *do you suppose,*
        C153, C216, C250
    definition, C178
    direct objects, C152-53, C215-16
    in general, C178-81
    indirect objects, C156, C217
    nominative, C178-81
        after *than* or *as,* C219, C288
        form, A28-29, A37, A43, A50,
            C180-81
        of predicate verbs, C160-61,
            C213-14
        self-pronouns, A42
        with infinitives, C214
        with nominative absolutes, C192,
            C210
        with participles, C192, C210
    not affected by parenthetical clauses,
        C153, C216, C250-51, C392
    nouns. *See* Case, possessive.
    object of predicate verb or verbal
        direct, C152-53, C215-16
        indirect, C156, C217
    object of preposition, A142, C218

551

Could, substitute for subjunctive, C115
Could and *can,* A72, C36, C89-93
Counties, capitals, H101, H103, H106
Countries, capitals, H101, H105-6
Courses, academic, capitals, H137, H139-40
Courts, capitals, H116, H120
Cousin, capitals, H98-100
Cover over, start in, and so on, C340
Creeds
  capitals, H34
  no italic or quotation marks, D131, H34
Cross, capitals, H44
Current words, for interest and force, R7-10

Dangling modifiers, C308-10, C397, K10-11
Dash, D20, D86-98
  after headings in outlines, N37
  before items indented like paragraphs, D81, D97
  before summarizing expressions, D87
  interrupted sentences, D81, D86
  nonrestrictive appositives, D91-94
  nonrestrictive modifiers, D96
  parenthetical expressions, D88-89
  sparing use, D98
  sudden changes in structure, D86
  unfinished sentences, D86
  with figures only (error), D95
  with question marks and exclamation points, D89
Dates
  abbreviation, F2, F7
  commas, D39
  figures, G12
  hyphening, G20-22; N78, footnote 13
Day, capitals, H133, H142-43
Days of the week
  abbreviation, F7
  capitals, H141
Dead, incomparable adjective, C280
Dean
  form of address, salutation, and complimentary close in business and formal letters, N133-34
  form of salutation and complimentary close in personal letters, N148-49, N152

Decades, numbers, G7
Declarative sentences, B7
  in outlines, N51
  in theme topics, N28, P9
  in thesis or proposition of argument, Q7
  period, D2
Deduction, source of proof in argument, Q25-26
Deem, taking both direct object and objective complement, C150
Defective induction (fallacy), Q60-61
Definite article, A99
Definitions, N101-18
  definition by synonym, N104-10
    advantages, N109
    disadvantages, N110
    parallelism, N107-8
  in general, N101-3
  logical, N103, N111-18
    distinguishing characteristics, N111, N118
    general class, N111-13, N118
    parallelism, N114
    repetition of word to be defined, N115-17
Degrees, academic
  abbreviation, F5
  capitals, H97
Degrees (Fahrenheit, and so on), numbers, G10
Degrees of comparison, C272-73. *See also* Comparison of adjectives and adverbs.
Deity, capitals, H40
Deity, false, capitals, H48
Democrat, republican, and so on, capitals, H114-15
Demonstrative adjectives, A83-88
  in bridge (transitional) phrases, M30
  that and *those* for what is remote, and so on, A85
  them (error), A86
  this and *these* for what is near, and so on, A85
  this here and *that there* (error), A87
  with singular and plural nouns, A83, A88
Demonstrative pronouns, A31-36
  agreement with antecedents. *See* Agreement, pronouns.
  in bridge (transitional) expressions, M29-30

561

Events, capitals, H132-34
Every
    affecting agreement of predicate
        verb, C15, C35
    affecting agreement of pronouns and
        possessive adjectives, C236,
        C238
    See also Indefinite adjectives.
Everybody, everyone, followed by
        they and *their,* C236, C238
Evidence of circumstances, source of
        proof in argument, Q31
Examples, for variety in developing
        main ideas
    in the paragraph, L37
    in the sentence, K64
    in the theme, M59
Except for *unless* (error), C352
Exclamation point, D15-19
    after exclamatory expressions, D15,
        D17, D53, D89
    after literary titles, D27
    at end of literary title set off on a
        line by itself, D27
    end punctuation, D1, D15-
        19
    with dashes, D89
    with marks of parenthesis, D106-7
    with quotation marks, D124
Exclamatory sentences, B10
    exclamation point, D15
Exclamatory words, A2, A122-
        24
    diagraming, J30
    punctuation, D15, D53, D89
Expectation, expressions of
    be, C47
    go, progressive past, C45
    ought, C63
    shall and *will,* C66
    should, C77
Experience, common, source of proof
        in argument, Q33
Expletives, A2, A125
    diagraming, J5
    it
        as object, A125, footnote 38
        frequently used before noun
            clauses, C386
        requiring singular predicate verb,
            C12
    there, verb agreement after, C8, C18,
            C34
    used for variety, K48

Exposition, N1-153
    accuracy in, N2
    business letters, N119-38. *See also*
        Letters (correspondence).
    clarity in, N2
    definitions as kind of, N101-18
        by synonym, N104-10
        logical, N103, N111-18
        See also Definitions.
    economy in, N2
    in argument, Q2, Q36, Q40
    outlining, N32-56. *See also* Outlines.
    personal letters, N139-53
    theme (term paper, research paper),
        N3-100. *See also* Expository
        theme (term paper, research
        paper).
Expositions and fairs, capitals, H134
Expository theme (term paper, research
        paper), N3-100
    bibliography, N86
    choosing a general subject, N4-9
    jotting preliminary notes, N11-12
    model theme, N100
    outlining, N32-56. *See also* Outlines.
    preparing final copy, N87-100
        by-line, N94-95
        direct quotations, N60-63
        double-spacing, N90
        first page, N91-95
        footnotes, N69-85
        identification (writer, date, and
            so on), N91
        margins, N89
        notes at end of theme, N64-68
        page numbers, N97-98
        paragraph placement and inden-
            tion, N61, N95-96
        running heads, N99
        title, N92-93
        use of one side of sheet, N88
    putting preliminary notes in order,
        N13
    reading, N14-25
        list of reference works, N16
        taking notes, N22-25
    rough draft, N57-59
    steps in writing the theme, N10
    theme topic, N11, N26-31
        should be definite, N31
        should be free of extravagant and
            superlative terms, N30
        should be stated in a declarative
            sentence, N28

should be written out, N26-27
should limit the general subject, N29
Express statement that something is important, for emphasis
in the sentence, K30, K34
in the theme, M48-51
Expressions on different language level from rest of composition, quotation marks, D135
Eyewitness (immediate) and mediate testimony, source of proof in argument, Q22-24

Fact, expressions of
indicative mood, C105
shall and *will*, C66
Fairs and expositions, capitals, H134
Fall, capitals, H144
Fallacies in argument, Q42-63. *See also* Argument, fallacies.
False analogy (fallacy), Q62-63
False appeal to common knowledge (fallacy), Q53-55
False assumption (fallacy), Q51-52
False causality (*post hoc, ergo propter hoc*, fallacy), Q49-50
Family names (relationship), capitals, H98-100
Father
kinship name, capitals, H98-100
priest
abbreviation (error), F9
capitals, H91
See also Priest, capitals.
Fatherhood (of God), capitals, H41
Fathers of the Church, capitals, H78
Feast days, capitals, H141-43
Federal government, capitals, H113
Festivals, capitals, H134, H141-42
Fewer and *less*, C253, C279
Figures (numbers), G1-22. *See also* Numbers.
Figures of speech, R26-58
alliteration, R49-50
anticlimax, R40
antithesis, R37-38
apostrophe, R43
balance, R35-38
climax, R39
common, R53
correct use, R51-58
definition, R26
"fine writing" (error), R54

hyperbole, R45
irony, R41-42
metaphor, R31-34
metonymy, R44, footnote 14
mixed figures (error), R51
onomatopoeia, R47-48
paradox, R46
parallelism, R35-38
personification, R34
sarcasm, R42
simile, R27-31, R33
substitution, R44
synecdoche, R44, footnote 14
Final copy of expository theme, N87-100. *See also* Expository theme (term paper, research paper), preparing final copy.
Finally, bridge (transitional) word, M26
Find, taking both direct object and objective complement, C150
"Fine writing" (error), R54
First, bridge (transitional) word, M26
Footnote, capitals, H147
Footnotes, N69-85
abbreviated references, N84
abbreviations, N83
biblical and classical references, N81-82
books, N72
essays, articles, and unpublished material, N80
ibid., N84
idem, N84, footnote 18
loc. cit., N83, footnote 17
methods of writing, N70
nonbibliographical footnotes, N85
op. cit., N83, footnote 17
second references, N84
For example
semicolon before, D76
use of *e.g.*, F1
For instance, semicolon before, D76
Forbid to and *prohibit from*, C337
Force, R1-64. *See also* Interest and force.
Foreign words and phrases
abbreviation, F1
italic, D150
use in composition, R9-10
Formal letters, N119-38. *See also* Letters (correspondence).
Formal themes, colloquialisms in, R12-13

563

prayers, no italic or quotation marks, D131, H30

pronouns, apostrophe with, D165-66. *See also* Pronouns.

proper names, commas with appositives and adjectives that are part of (error), D49

question marks, D7-14. *See also* Question marks.

questions, indirect, D5, D69

questions, requests and orders phrased as, periods, D4

quotation marks, D112-37. *See also* Quotation marks.

quotations. *See* Quotation marks *and* Quotations.

radio programs, italic preferred to quotation marks, D139

reference cards for research, N24

reference works, no italic or quotation marks, D142, H131

remarks inserted into quotations, brackets, D109

restrictive and nonrestrictive appositives, D47-49, D77, D91-93, D100

restrictive and nonrestrictive modifiers, D50-52, D96

running heads in themes, N99

runovers corrected by, B5

sacred writings, no italic or quotation marks, D144, H21, H23-25

salutation of letters, D25, D84

Scripture references, colon, D85

semicolon, D72-76. *See also* Semicolon.

sentence quoted within another sentence, comma before, D68

sentences, broken up, D20-21, D23

series of books, quotation marks, D128

series of words, phrases, or dependent clauses, D9, D28-40, D75, D82

short stories, quotation marks, D127

statues, italic preferred to quotation marks, D147

stories, quotation marks and italic, D127, D139

summarizing expressions, D80, D87

suspended expressions, commas, D67

technical words or terms, quotation marks, D134

television programs, italic preferred to quotation marks, D139

that clause at beginning of sentence, comma, D45

time of day, colon, D83

titles in the possessive, D160, D162

titles of themes, N93

two nouns possessing something separately, apostrophe, D164

two or more adjectives, D30

unfinished sentences, D20-21, D23

unspoken thoughts, no quotation marks, D114

words followed by their definition or explanation, italic and quotation marks, D133

words that need setting off for clearness, quotation marks, D132

words used ironically, quotation marks, D136

words used only as words, D151, D169

Pure description, O2

Purgatory, capitals, H62

Purpose, expressions of

go, progressive past, C45

may and *might*, C88

shall and *will*, C67

so that preferred to *so*, C360

Question, argument, Q3-13, Q43-46

Question marks

after headings in topic outlines, N41

at end of direct question, D7-13

at end of literary title set off on line by itself, D27

with dashes, D89

with marks of parenthesis, D106-7

with quotation marks, D124

Questions

direct

definition, B8, footnote 2; D7, footnote 2

do in, C51

in argument, Q39

in outlines (error), N51

interrogative sentences, B8

question marks with, D7-13, D27, D89, D106-7, D124, N41

requests and orders phrased as, periods, D4

within a sentence but unquoted, capitals, H3

words, phrases, clauses in series, question marks, D9

in narrative themes, P34-35
quotation marks with, D112. *See also* Quotation marks.
indirect
  capitals, H7
  comma before (error), D69
  in narrative themes, P35
  with quotation marks, D115

Race and races, capitals, H137-39
Radio programs
  capitals, H125, H129-30
  italic preferred to quotation marks, D139
Radio stations
  abbreviation, F10
  capitals, H117, H120
Railroads
  abbreviation, F8
  capitals, H117, H120
  no italic, D149
Raise and *rise*, C168
Re-, hyphen, D177
Reading, Step 3 in writing expository theme, N10, N14-21
Real for *really* or *very* (error), C265
Real presence, capitals, H74
Recall of (error), C330
Recapitulation in argument, Q20, Q41
Reciprocal pronouns, A60-61, D165
  number, A61
  possessive, D165
Recollect of (error), C330
Redemption, events of, capitals, H55-57
Reference, clear. *See* Clear reference.
Reference cards for expository themes, N22-25
Reference works
  capitals, H131
  list, N16
  no italic or quotation marks, D142, H131
References
  biblical, colon, D85
  notes and footnotes, N69-85
Reflexive pronouns, A39-40
Regions, capitals, H105-8
Relationship (kinship) names, capitals, H98-100
Relative adjectives, A89-91
  apostrophe with (error), D166
  in dependent (adjective) clauses, A90, C381, C389
  which, A91, C393

Relative adverbs, A121, C391
  in dependent (adjective) clauses, C381, C389, C391
Relative clauses, C388-93. *See also* Clauses, adjective (dependent, relative).
Relative pronouns, A43-49
  agreement of predicate verb with, C11
  agreement with antecedents, A45-48, C11, C227, C234
  apostrophe with (error), D166
  case, A43, D166
    complicated by parenthetical expressions, C153, C216, C250-51
    not affected by antecedent, C226, C249
    See also Case.
  gender, A45-47
  person, A48
  requiring antecedent in another clause, A49, C247
  singular and plural, A43, A48
  test of, A49, C247
  that preferred to *which* in restrictive clauses, C248
  used only in dependent (adjective) clauses, A44, C246, C381, C389. *See also* Clauses, adjective (dependent, relative).
Reliable witness, source of proof in argument, Q22-24
Religions and their members, capitals, H65-68
Religious (Brothers, Sisters, and so on)
  capitals, H79, H81, H84, H91
  form of address, salutation, and complimentary close in business and formal letters, N133-34
  form of salutation and complimentary close in personal letters, N148-49, N152
Religious orders and congregations
  abbreviation, F5
  capitals, H79-80
Religious services and devotions
  capitals, H75-77
  no italic or quotation marks, D131
Religious terms, capitals, H21-83. *See also the particular term; for example,* Capitals, dioceses.
Religious titles, capitals, H79, H81, H84, H91-92
Remember of (error), C330

About this book

William Nicoll of EDIT, INC., designed *for writing English*. It was set in the composing room of LOYOLA UNIVERSITY PRESS. The text is 11 on 13 Caledonia; the reduced matter, 9 on 12. The text display type is Spartan Heavy; the title is in Alternate Gothic 2.

The book was printed by SLEEPECK PRINTING COMPANY, the endsheets by ARGUS PRESS. It was printed on WARREN's 50-pound Silkote Offset paper and bound by A. C. ENGDAHL AND COMPANY, INC., in JOANNA WESTERN Parchment Impreglin.